TRANSHUMAN AND SUBHUMAN

ESSAYS ON SCIENCE FICTION AND AWFUL
TRUTH

JOHN C. WRIGHT

Wisecraft

PRAISE FOR JOHN C. WRIGHT

"One of the most eloquent, articulate, intelligent voices in genre fiction. I don't say this lightly but I really do believe he is our modern C.S. Lewis."

—LARRY CORREIA, author of *Monster Hunter International* and *The Grimnoir Chronicles*

"Wright may be this fledgling century's most important new SF talent."

—*PUBLISHER'S WEEKLY*

"Every now and then someone comes along who not only can say things nicely, but can say *important* things nicely. That somebody, in the modern age, is John C. Wright.
"

—TOM KRATMAN, author of *Caliphate* and *A Desert Called Peace*

"An elegant stylist and a true visionary."

—*LIBRARY JOURNAL*

To all the readers and friends who came to my aid in my hour of need: Robert James Wigard, Mark Ping, Dave Stumpf, Pierce Oka, Brian Niemeier, Brian Love, Joel C. Salomon, Ben Zwycky, Ryan McGrath, Jean M. Balconi, Nathan McClellan, Michael F. Flynn.

FOREWORD

A cloud was on the mind of men, and wailing
    went the weather,
Yea, a sick cloud upon the soul when we were
    boys together.
Science announced nonentity and art
    admired decay;
The world was old and ended: but you and I
    were gay;
Round us in antic order their crippled vices
    came—
Lust that had lost its laughter, fear that had
    lost its shame.
Like the white lock of Whistler, that lit our
    aimless gloom,
Men showed their own white feather as
    proudly as a plume.
Life was a fly that faded, and death a drone
    that stung;
The world was very old indeed when you and
    I were young.

They twisted even decent sin to shapes not to
    be named:
Men were ashamed of honour; but we were
    not ashamed.
—*G.K. Chesterton (1908)*

THE WRIGHT STUFF

BY MICHAEL F. FLYNN

Some of you, upon spying this collection, perhaps upon a remainder table in a cobwebbed bookstore or on a radhi-pile in the back alleys of Royapuram in Old Madras, may rightly wonder to yourself, "John Wright? Who he, hah?"

If you have been already enjoying his rants and essays on-line, no introduction is needed; so why are you reading this? But some have perhaps read what Publisher's Weekly called his "ornate and conceptually dense prose" in the *Golden Age* or *Orphans of Chaos* trilogies or, more recently in his *Count to the Eschaton* sequence (It's too late to call it a trilogy), and have picked up this volume out of curiosity.

Still others have wondered whether there is somewhere a non-medicinal remedy for low blood pressure.

Wonder no more. Some of these essays are guaranteed to raise your blood pressure sufficiently that blood will squirt from your eyes like soda from a shaken can. So read them carefully. And wear safety goggles.

If you agree with Mr. Wright, you will be taken for an entertaining ride. If you do not agree, I ask you to keep in mind Robert A. Heinlein's dictum: "I never learned anything from a man who agreed with me."

"Ornate and conceptually dense prose" will often carry multiple meanings. Mr. Wright launched into life as a lawyer and has the Way Cool mind power of laying out an ordered and orderly argument, something to which the Late Modern is so unaccustomed that he might dash his foot upon an unexpected syllogism and hop about in excruciating pain. But Mr. Wright is also quite able to rabble-rouse a jury and some of his polemics are pure entertainment, on the order of John Belushi writhing on the floor on the old SNL.

In "The Hobbit, or, the Desolation of Tolkien", Mr. Wright is assaulted again and again by the Hammer of Stupidity, and recalls a poster for the movie:

> "Upon seeing that odd poster, a spasm like biting with a tooth whose filling has worked loose onto a chip of ice wrapped in tinfoil and hot mustard jolted through my unwarned brain."

He is more serious when marking the milestones on the road to perdition in "Transhuman and Subhuman" and discusses the path toward:

> "...the four stages of a decay toward the nihilist abyss: the worldly man, the cultist, the occultist, the anarchist. ...The Worldly Man is content to mind his own business and seek his own pleasures after his own fashion, and demands his neighbors do the same. The business he minds is to maintain the public peace (as in STARSHIP TROOPERS) and to get laid (as in STRANGER IN A STRANGE LAND).

When Mr. Wright talks about "Saving Science Fiction

from Strong Female Characters" it will be well to pause and wonder what he's getting at rather than succumb to a knee-jerk reaction to the literalist meaning of the title. Such reactions typically owe more to the make-up of the knee than to the substance of the mallet. (A hint: if a female character is relentlessly praised as "kickass," what victory is it exactly that has been won over the masculinist values of the Patriarchy?)

Mr. Wright has been known to write namby-pamby fantasy with no anchor in reality, in contrast to my own firmly grounded, scientific tales of galactic empires, tunnels through space-time, immortal Danish madmen, and similar accounts. But whether fantasy or science fiction, Wright shows a broad grasp of our genre. You will find here appreciations or critiques of Gene Wolfe, A.E. van Vogt, Keith Laumer, Ted Chiang, Arthur C. Clarke, Philip Pullman, and others. In each case, he takes one or more of their stories and analyzes what works or fails to work, why it resonates with us or not. Contemplating Snow White and her little woodland helpers, he writes:

> *If, like me, you have too much free time on your hands, you have probably wondered why Snow White, at least as Walt Disney portrays her tale, has small woodland animals to help her with her household chores, with bunnies and chipmunks scrubbing dishes, songbirds helping to sew and fawns dusting the furniture with their white tails. If, like me, you have too much education on your hands, you probably have used Aristotelian categories to analyze the question.*

Few are the authors who could create an Aristotelian discourse out of Snow White. But in "Whistle While You Work", Wright leads us to an intriguing thesis regarding the very different ways in which a) Snow White and b) Tarzan of the Apes interact with their animal buddies.

Regarding Laumer's *The Glory Game*, he looks at how noir sensibilities inform a certain subset of science fiction and where they lie on the hedonist-to-nihilist scale.

> *Noir stories are not nihilist stories, albeit they are cantilevered over the abyss of nihilism and dangle their toes.*

He criticizes Pullman's *His Dark Materials* in "The Golden Compass Points in No Direction", less on Pullman's atheism than on the failure of his art, where he sacrificed story in order to preach a sermon. Authorial promises are made, but not delivered. Character arcs veer off course. "Chekhov's gun" remains unfired.

> *Mr. Pullman started with a story, a Paradise Lost version where Lucifer was the good guy facing impossible odds by defying an unconquerable god; but he ended with a message, where there are no odds because there is no god, merely a drooling idiot. So all plot logic flies out the window....*

We cannot close this introduction without some comment on Mr. Wright's well-known stance on the shortfalls of the Late Modern Age. That he's agin' 'em should elicit no calls for the smelling salts. He is an unapologetic devotee of logic and reason and Western Civilization, and in fact was so even years ago when he was an atheist. To some measure, this makes him a conservative as Late Moderns dice and slice the political psyche. But by other measures, he is a liberal of the old, romantic sort. (Recall Chesterton's aphorism that while he still believes in liberalism, he no longer believes in liberals.) And by still other measures, he cuts crosswise to Late Modern categories entirely, being a refugee from an earlier age. The fault may lie in the wrong measures rather than in the Wright author.

So you will find here too faint echoes of the distant horns of Elfland, sometimes in the most unlikely places such as "Science Fiction: What's it Good for?". He actually believes in art and beauty and that even the hardest of hard SF is all about magic and myth.

> *"So a movement started to expunge the gold and purple, the glory and the nobility, the gaiety and wonder, and most of all the miracles from art and literature."*

Neither does he make a secret where he locates the well-springs of Truth and Beauty. His logic and reason dragged him by the neocortex toward the bosom of Mother Church. Reason wasn't the only factor—there was another impetus as well—but he has often said that if Vulcans had a religion they would be Catholics. The Church too found much to admire in the old pagan Stoics. She just didn't think it was enough.

The connection of reason and faith is so iron-bound that Mr. Wright can wonder whence comes the "Faith in the Fictional War between Science Fiction and Faith"? Science Fiction is, after all, full of the images and tropes of faith, and all stories that resonate with readers derive in one way or another from the "greatest story ever told." Wandering too far from this core is not merely theologically unsound, it is bad art.

> *"Pullman was as blasphemous as Heinlein in STRANGER IN A STRANGE LAND, but not as funny...."*

On a personal note, I first met Mr. Wright at a Philcon several years ago, when we were booked to do autographing in the same time slot. He is a fellow of impressive stature, gentle and good-natured unless aroused, widely educated in the great books of Western Civilization—funny how often that leads to the Tiber—and an entertaining conversationalist.

The autographing session was scheduled around lunchtime and just before it was to start, the lovely and talented Mrs. Wright—L. Jagi Lamplighter—brought him his lunch, which she had secured elsewhere at the con. And then Mr. Wright did two remarkable things.

First, he divided his lunch in half and offered one half to me. Second, he bowed over his lunch, crossed himself, and said Grace.

You don't often see both grace and Grace together at an SF con.

TRANSHUMAN AND SUBHUMAN

I am intensely skeptical of Transhumanist ambitions. Much as I admire their intermediate goals of increasing human lifespan or human comfort through medical technology, their long term goals cause me reservations, or even revulsion. Allow me to explain using the most indirect means possible: by discussing fantasy stories.

Anyone who does not sense or suspect that modernity is missing something, something important that once we had and now is lost, has no heart for High Fantasy and no taste for it.

I don't regard this statement as controversial. To me it seems not worth discussing that the present age differs from the past. The only question worth discussing is the nature of the differences, and, by extension, the nature of the future the present trends will tend to create.

What is wrong with the world? Where are we heading?

Are we heading toward the higher peak of the superhuman, or to a subhuman abyss? If I may be permitted a drollery, let me phrase it this way: shall our children be the Slans of A.E. van Vogt, or the Morlocks of H.G. Wells?

A philosophical discussion would use different terminology and would bore to tears readers not philosophically
inclined. So instead of discussing the nature and extent of
the influence of Locke and Marx and Shaw and Nietzsche,
let me discuss instead more popular manifestations more
fun to read, that is, science fiction writings, and discuss the
nature of the influence of J.R.R. Tolkien, and Robert E.
Howard, Michael Moorcock, of Robert Heinlein, Ayn Rand,
Ursula K. Le Guin, and Peter Watts.

This may seem an odd way to proceed, to discuss a
philosophical problem in terms of science fiction yarns. It is
not odd at all. Art, including popular art like genre fiction, is
an attempt to put one's view of the world into a succinct and
concrete example or image: And the drama of art issues
from the innate drama of the world, its wonders and
horrors.

Readers of science fiction have an advantage of perspective over readers who limit themselves to mainstream books,
namely, that any works taking place in a year as yet unborn,
or in a world as yet unknown, must concentrate their attention on those things we take for granted; because in worlds
to come they may indeed no longer be taken for granted,
nor exist at all.

The science fiction reader, as if from the vantage point of
some shining skyscraper of the future, can look back
through time to this our present, and see what we here
might not.

Fantasy likewise occupies a different vantage. A reader
of fantasy stands outside of time altogether, as if atop the
haunted mountain of far and unvisited Kadath topped by
the onyx citadel of the dream gods, or the scarred and
smoking slopes of sinister Mount Doom where evil was
forged, and he looks from a dreamland or a Middle Earth –

where magic lives in all its horror and wonder – into a world, our world, a grayer world, where magic does not.

The main difference between fantasy fiction and realistic fiction is the presence of magic. The main difference between Tolkien-style fantasy and Robert E. Howard-style fantasy is the attitude toward magic.

In High Fantasy, magic is usually not magic at all, but miracle: a wondrous good beyond hope reaching from without the edges of the world. When Gandalf the Gray returns from the dead as Gandalf the White, that is not a Raise Dead spell. There is also, like its shadow, black magic, which has a satanic character and tone. The practitioners are necromancers and witches, and not friendly witches like Glinda or Sabrina or Samantha or Hermione, but cruel witches like Achren or Jadis.

High Fantasy occupies the mental universe where (1) truth is true, (2) goodness is good, and (3) life is beautiful unless marred by sin and malice, and when marred life may yet, not without terrible price, be saved.

That this is an honest, virtuous, and sublime picture of the universe is a high matter for debate beyond the scope of this essay: for now, let us accept for the sake of argument that it is a healthy view of the universe, one suitable for the psychology of human life, and joy.

In Sword-and-Sorcery, by contrast, the magic is malign: Conan kills evil sorcerers with the edge of the sword. There is magic afoot in the world, but it is cruel, and to study it leads one along the paths of madness. Any benevolent magic tends to be the aid of wise men or the caprice of unseen powers as unexpected as a dolphin helping a drowning sailor stay afloat. This is the view of magic the pagans of old had: something that disgusted and terrified even those who indulged in it.

There is not a separate name for the genre that follows Gary Gygax or Michael Moorcock or Jack Vance, but we should note many a story where the magic power is nothing more than an alternate technology, to be used for good or ill as the practitioner sees fit. There is no spiritual element to such depictions at all. Let us call it Sword-and-Magic-User fiction.

In the mental universe depicted by Sword-and-Sorcery or Sword-and-Magic-User, the noticeable thing lacking is a figure like Aslan in Narnia or Elbereth in Middle-Earth. There is no Christ; no Virgin Mary. Men like Conan and (ironically) Solomon Kane are on their own. Elric, Corum, and the like are also on their own: a universe torn between forces of inhuman law and inhuman chaos lacks the sense of hierarchy implied by High Fantasy, where Prince Caspian serves Aslan who in turn serves the Emperor-Beyond-the-Sea.

High fantasy has a Roman Catholic flavor to it, whereas Sword-and-Sorcery is somewhat Protestant. Conan in particular represents the rebellion of a healthy barbarian against a corrupt and over-civilized decadence. Truth might still be true, but you are on your own to find it: no authority speaks with authority. Gandalf may come from the Blessed Lands, but not Ningauble of the Seven Eyes.

Again, Sword-and-Magic-User tales are syncretic, polytheistic, disinterested in things of the spirit. Call it Unitarian.

Science fiction is about the magic of the future. It differs from other magical stories because the magic is metaphorical: it concerns the miracles of modern science rather than the miracles of God; the magic of technology rather than the magic of hobgoblins. It differs from other genres because we or our children may one day see scientific miracles come to pass, even as readers of Jules Verne and their children saw in their day such fantastic things as the submarine, the flying machine, the moonshot.

But then again, even among Hard SF writers, we find their most famous works steeped in magic as much as any tale of King Arthur or Achilles; it is merely called by other names. The powers of Paul Muad'Dib or Michael Valentine Smith or the prophecies of Hari Seldon or the luck of Teela Brown are not called magic, but they are. These characters hail from Hard SF classics of the genre. Nor does this differ for softer science fiction: Darth Vader from *Star Wars* can read minds as easily as can Mr. Spock, and can levitate objects as easily as Bill Bixby's uncle from *My Favorite Martian*.

In Science Fiction the role of magic is ambiguous, and this reflects the ambiguous attitude of the modern age toward all things supernatural.

To be sure, we all tell ourselves that no modern enlightened man believes in magic, and many an enlightened modern treats science as a useful tool by which means he can make for himself what sort of life he pleases: but then again, an unusual number of we modern men substitute an attitude toward science which is indistinguishable from a cult belief, as if science will discover laws of history or psychiatry and tell us the truth about human nature that will set us free; or else it is indistinguishable from an occult belief, as if new discoveries will harness parapsychological or psionic powers, and a New Age will dawn of mystic revelation, or an expression of some life-force or evolutionary end-purpose moving us down the channels of time toward Utopia; or else it is indistinguishable from devil worship, as if science justified or required the extermination of the unfit, the unborn, the unwanted, or the genocide of lesser races in the name of dry-eyed and ice-hearted Darwinism, or looks upon mankind as an expendable raw material out of which to build the superman.

These four types represent the four stages of a path of decay toward the nihilist abyss: the Worldly Man, the Cultist, the Occultist, the Anarchist.

In sum, science fiction precisely reflects both the exhilaration and also the discontent of man in his modern world, particularly his attitude toward the magical and supernatural.

The exhilaration comes from one source: the greater liberty, knowledge, technology, and wealth we enjoy than our medieval and ancient forefathers. The discontent comes from the same source as the discontent of our forefathers, which our greater liberty, knowledge, technology, and wealth cannot assuage, and indeed quite aggravates, namely, the depraved, corrupt and self-destructive nature of human nature.

The writings of Robert Heinlein serve as a perfect example of the Worldly Man, that is, the man who rejects Revelation, and seeks truths nowhere but in practical morals and empirical facts. The attitude portrayed in his writings toward religion is ecumenical neglect and contempt. Christianity is a source of a threat to liberty, as personified by Nehemiah Scudder (who is overdue, since he was predicted to be elected in 2012) but never depicted as a source of any goodness, charity, or beneficial reform.

Other religions, particularly esoteric or even Martian, are worthy of respectful disbelief. The attitude tolerates religion provided it is castrated and kept as a private pastime for lesser beings. One day we will outgrow it.

The Worldly Man is content to mind his own business and seek his own pleasures after his own fashion, and demands his neighbors do the same. The business he minds is to maintain the public peace (as in *Starship Troopers*) and to get laid (as in *Stranger in a Strange Land*).

The virtues needed to accomplish this can be lauded — no one waxes more poetic in his praise of the sacrifices of servicemen than Mr. Heinlein — but those virtues have no metaphysical or theological foundation. For the Worldly Man, "absolute truth" is a question for folk with too much time on their hands.

Ayn Rand does not display this avuncular tolerance for Christianity: the religion is condemned as an unambiguous evil, and its practitioners as hatred-eaten mystics. (Other religions, one assumes, find no more favor in her eyes, but there is only one she condemns.) This is not the impatience of a Worldly Man for the mirage called absolute truth; this is the odium of one who defends an absolute truth against its rivals, or, to be precise, the hatred of a heresiarch for orthodoxy.

Rand is an example of a Cultist amid the science fiction community (and do not tell me Ayn Rand is not a science fiction writer: an inventor discovers the secret of a self-generating power source from atmospheric electricity, and combines in a secret society with other inventors of super-metals and voice-activated locks and mirage-casting ray-screens and with masters of pirate battleships to overthrow the evil world masters who control a sound-wave disintegration ray? John Galt is cut from the same pattern as Doc Savage or the Gray Lensman).

The Cultist takes the science and industry which affords the Worldly Man his pleasures, and scorns his pursuit of mere pleasure: truth, hard truth, absolute truth is the object of the Cultist's search. Nothing exists but matter and hard facts, and the question of how to organize human life on earth is a deduction from facts. Any opposition or lack of enthusiasm is seen as treason.

Don't be misled by my example to think I am singling out libertarian writers for scorn. Socialists like H.G. Wells and atheists like Philip Pullman would serve just as well. What gives the Cultist his particular flavor is the humorlessness, the intolerance, and the zeal of his pursuit. I call it Cultic because the poor fool is trying to place a simplistic or mechanistic understanding of the universe in the place of divine revelation: he serves an idol.

The Cultist believes he has discovered the secret to a life of happiness on Earth, and the discoveries always retain an eerie simplicity. I remember hearing one science fiction writer once saying how everything in life would be better if only religion were abolished. Really? Everything? Religion is the source of *all* evils? Cultists of other breeds select a different one, a simple scapegoat whose abolition will usher in the Utopia: for Ayn Rand, eliminating altruism is the panacea; for H.G. Wells, eliminating private property. I can think of at least one feminist SF writer who thinks the abolition of men would do it, or, at least, of all masculinity.

The Cultist, whether he wishes it or not, is always an enemy of virtue. This is because the nature of virtue is a matter of the careful balancing of extremes between two relative evils, and the extreme repudiation of absolute evils. The Cultist is an absolutist, and admits of no balance, no median. The Cultist is bedeviled by the alluring simplicity of his panacea, his one idea, and so compromises with absolute evils as if they were matters of taste. It is no accident that both Heinlein and Rand praise keeping one's oaths in their writings, and both portray favorably the violation of matrimonial oaths by fornications and adulteries.

In the same way the Cultist rebels against the worldliness of the Worldly Man, the Occultist rebels against the Cultist, and insists that there is more than just a material world and one brief and stoical life lived within it.

Ursula K. Le Guin seems to me to be the most famous and most articulate representative of this stance within the science fiction community: while her books have favorably portrayed an anarchist utopia (as in *The Dispossessed*), she lacks the grinding dogmatism of an Ayn Rand. Note the gentle parable of *Lathe of Heaven*, that no direct solution to problems actually solves them, or the explicit teaching of the relativity of all truth in *Four Ways to Forgiveness*.

I don't mean the word Occultist here to mean a palmist armed with Tarot cards. I am using the word in its original sense. I mean it is one who believes in a hidden reality, a hidden truth, a truth that cannot be made clear.

In the modern world, the Occultist is more likely to select Evolution or the Life-Force as this occult object of reverence, rather than the Tao. Occultists, in the sense I am using the word, explicitly denounce no religion nor way of life except the religion of Abraham, whose God is jealous and does not permit the belief in many gods, nor the belief in many views of the world each no better than the next.

Postmodernism, which rejects the concept of one overarching explanation for reality, is explicitly Occultic: the truth is hidden and never can be known.

Occultists tend to be more wary of the progress of science and technology than Cultists or Worldlies. They see the drawbacks, the danger to the environment, and the psychological danger of treating the world as a mere resource to be exploited, rather than as living thing, or a sacred thing.

The Occultists believe in undemanding virtues, such as tolerance and a certain civic duty, but even these are relative and partial. There is beauty in his world, indeed, the beauty of nature is often his only approach to the supernal, but that beauty is in the eye of the beholder, and there is no absolute truth and very little goodness aside from good manners and political correctness.

Of the final stage, the pure nihilism I here call Anarchy, I can think of only one representative in science fiction, Peter Watts, and at that only one of his books, *Blindsight*. As with Heinlein, I am not speaking of the author himself, whose opinions I do not know and refuse to guess. I am merely speaking of the worldview as portrayed in his fiction.

(The nihilist viewpoint is more often seen in fantasy or horror, as in H.P. Lovecraft, where the universe has literally nothing but roaring madness at its core, with crawling chaos serving it).

The Anarchist rebels against the soft mysticism of the Occultist and against the zealous dogmatism of the Cultist, but he also despises the Worldly as weak and inconsequential, if not an enemy.

For the Anarchist, the only truth is that there is no truth, no absolute truth, and even the few virtues maintained by the Worldly as necessary to maintain the social order are despised. Contrast the soldier Amanda Bates in *Blindsight* with Juan Rico in Heinlein's *Starship Troopers*. The virtue of loyalty which forms the core of Rico's character is utterly lacking in Bates.

There is no discussion of morality in *Blindsight*: all decisions are at first merely a matter of expedience, and then, after the universe eliminates the uselessness of human consciousness as an evolutionary excrescence, no decisions whatever are made. The meat machines merely carry out their inbuilt programming.

The aliens turn out to be unintelligent in the sense of

being non-self-aware, but more intelligent than man in terms of being more highly organized. They are the 'Chinese Rooms' of Searle's famous thought experiment brought to life, and, in this tale, the Chinese Room is better organized than the human brain and can outthink it. The entire Earth at the end of *Blindsight* is overrun with vampires the human race created itself, (a bizarrely meaningless and self-destructive act), and society fails when too many humans enter the artificial paradise of electronic nirvana, uploaded into worlds of their own dream-stuff, so that the remaining real life population cannot maintain the machinery, (a bizarrely selfish and self-destructive act).

This is pure quill nihilism. For the Anarchist, life is meaningless, and destruction is the only creative act. The destruction of human life on Earth is part of the necessary evolutionary process to eliminate the ineffectiveness called the soul. Only the vampires are left, sleek and efficient and not human in any sense of the word, not even self-aware.

In the Anarchist world, (1) the only truth is that there is no truth, (2) vice and virtue are interchangeable, equally meaningless, and human action is an epiphenomenon of biological motions, (3) beauty is ugly and ugliness is beautiful. Here we have reached the mere opposite of the world of High Fantasy.

Here we have reached the abyss. In the anarchist world, no act is meaningful except to throw a bomb, and blow up the innocent. Man is lost in a despair so huge that it does not even seem like despair any longer.

If you wish to see a visual metaphor of this state of mind, stroll through any modern art museum, and look at the distortions and aberrations of the human form displayed there. All of modern art is nothing but propaganda for one Anarchist principle, namely, that beauty does not exist, and that ugliness can be made beauty merely by all of us agreeing it is so. The proposition is false, and cannot be made true, no more than modern art can be made free of technical defects, much less aesthetic ones.

Now we can see what the modern world is missing, aided by the admirable clarity of the blindsight of *Blindsight*. The Anarchist is rightfully devoted to destroying everything in the world, including himself; for if in fact there were no truth, goodness, nor beauty in the world, or no way to achieve them, then destruction is desirable. If we were all just programmed meat machines, suicide is the noblest option.

But if there is beauty, even it is ineffable, something never to be captured in words, a mystic feeling elusive as a ghost, then the Occultist is right to eschew all talk of truth and virtue, and is right to tolerate any man's approach to the inapproachable thing called beauty.

But if there is truth, even if it is hard and cold and tinged with bronze, the Cultist is right to impose it on the world, no matter the cost in human suffering, and let all competing truths and claims of other virtues be damned. The only beauty is what serves the Cause.

But if there is virtue, then men must get along with each other, and also go along with each other just enough to maintain the public weal. The talk of truth can be tolerated as long as no violence is done in its name, and beauty is in the eye of the beholder.

But if there is magic, then there is a force in the world which sets the standard of truth and beauty and goodness, and bright magic is both more fair than dark magic, and merits our loyalty. Each man must find that light for himself, because no authority is to be trusted.

But if there are miracles, and I mean miracles from God,

then there is an authority, a divine and loving Father who has both the natural authority of a parent and of a creator and of a king. If one of those miracles is the Resurrection, then to all these other claims of authority, the divine can also claim the most romantic authority of all: the authority earned by merit. Christ has authority because he earned it by suffering the quest to the bitter end, and rescuing the fair bride from the red dragon. The crown of thorns is his reward.

If there are miracles, there is at once truth and beauty and goodness, for all these flow from the same source.

The question, finally, is one of philosophy, and, all drollery aside, it cannot be reduced to an analogy to science fiction. The philosophical question is whether Revelation is Truth? Unfortunately, without going into a long discussion of how Descartes and Hume and Kant attempted to ground philosophy on an epistemology of rationalism or empiricism, and failed to produce a coherent account of life, that last question cannot be answered.

That question must wait for another day. We asked what is wrong with the world. What is wrong is that modern thought is caught in the disease of nihilism, the idea that there is no revelation.

That disease causes the worldliness of sophisticates who wish religion would not bother them. They say that whatever truth there is or is not, it is not central to the business of life.

That disease causes the stiff ferocity of zealots in any number of political movements with semi-religious or cultic overtones, from libertarianism to totalitarianism. They say truth is what the Cause says it is.

That disease causes the tiresome vagueness and severe intellectual disorganization of moral relativism and postmodernism. They say truth is private, partial, relative, ineffable.

That disease causes the madness of nihilism. They say truth is not truth.

The rise of science and technology did not cause this disease, but the prestige of science aggravated it, because theology and philosophy cannot be reduced to algorithms, nor can skeptics willing to bow to the results of an experiment be persuaded to bow to virtues, powers and principalities they cannot see. There is a scientific method and a Socratic method, but there is no method for making revealed truths a living part of your soul.

Transhumanism, beyond its near-term goals of improving human life through medicine and expanded human life span, has a long-term goal of abolishing human mortality. This is a worldly doctrine carried to an extreme.

Immortal humans would be devils, since we would decay in our sins over the centuries, becoming ever more selfish and arrogant. Ah, but another long-term goal of transhumanism is to eliminate human sin and selfishness through technological manipulations of whatever bodies or housings our thought happen to occupy in the days after the Singularity. The Transhumanists, with childlike faith, merely assume the technology to redact, edit, program and condition human thoughts and personalities one day will exist, and we can turn our leaden souls to gold.

The problem of who would program whom, and who conditions the conditioners, can only be solved by reversion to the Cultic frame of mind. Simplistic absolutes are the only things the Thought Police can impose on the human cattle. Sinners themselves, their ability to envision, much less create sinless epigones, is no greater than the ability of men and women now, here in this era, to raise perfect children. We cannot even picture what such Perfect People would be like, unless we picture a simplistic caricature: the John Galt of the Libertarians, or the New Man of the Marxists.

The Perfect People would, of course, assuming anyone survived the perfection operations and the surrounding wars and genocides, still retain the mind-conditioning technology. Now there are only two possible options: first, they would retain enough of their human nature to be discontent with life. Seeking contentment, and not finding it in perfection, they must of course turn to what I call Occultism, the search for hidden things that cannot be put into words. By the mere process of trial and error, some other form of being will eventually be created, perhaps intelligent, perhaps self-aware, but not human in any sense that we mean the word.

The second option is that the Perfect People would not retain their human nature. Creatures without souls but with intellects capable of free will are devils. The only thing they can do is destroy. At that point, eventually, the great anarchy will reign, and the only thing these heirs to the once-great human race will find to occupy their immortal and endless and meaningless time is discovering ways to destroy themselves and each other.

That is why I am skeptical of the Transhumanist ambitions.

2

THE HOBBIT

OR, THE DESOLATION OF TOLKIEN

I loved the first Hobbit movie and hated, hated, hated the second. It was stupid on every level of stupidity. It should rightly be called *The Desolation of Tolkien*.

Before swan-diving into the sewer of total stupidity that is the *Desolation* movie, my intractable Southern courtesy requires that I say something good about this movie. Well, as it happens, there was not just one thing good about this movie, there were three: Ian McKellen, Martin Freeman, and Richard Armitage. They played their parts so well that I feel I have met the real Gandalf, Bilbo and Thorin.

Sylvester McCoy did his best with what he was given, but the movie maker put bird poop in his hair. Which is not, come to think of it, so very different from what the movie maker did to us, his audience. This was to make Radagast the Brown, one of the divine and august Istari who journeyed from the Blessed Lands beyond the Uttermost West to aid Middle Earth in its dark hour, to be as silly-looking a human whoopee cushion as possible.

On to what I hated with a nerdrageous passion that knows no sense of proportion: let us start at the beginning.

No, let us start before the beginning. While still in the lobby, I saw a poster for the movie which had handsome pictures in full Middle Earth make-up of Gandalf the Gray, Thorin Oakenshield, Radagast the Brown, Legolas Greenleaf, and Tauriel the Who the Hell is She. Quick quiz: what person after whom this movie is named does not appear on his poster? Hint: Not the dragon. Second question: how many of these characters are not in this story at all?

Upon seeing that odd poster, a spasm like biting with a tooth whose filing has worked loose onto a chip of ice wrapped in tinfoil and hot mustard jolted through my unwarned brain. Had I only taken it as an omen and fled shrieking into the night at that moment, I would have been spared much woeful nerdgrief.

One of my favorite scenes in *The Hobbit* is the meeting between Gandalf and Beorn. Gandalf, being a wise old man, does not bring in thirteen dwarves and a hobbit all at once and beg hospitality from the fearsome and proud freeholder whose homestead dares the eaves of Mirkwood itself, nor does he use any charm other than his charming demeanor. Instead he toys with Beorn's curiosity as he tells the story of their adventures so far, introducing each pair of additional dwarves, as if by a slip of the tongue, so that the fierce freeholder is won over. Had this scene been in the film, it would also have brought the audience up to speed.

You see, the scene is charming because it is a children's story, and in children's stories, tricks like this work, and they do not need to be magic tricks. Gandalf comes over as a wise man, a counselor, not a magic-powered superhero.

The drama here is that the dwarves are stranded without any gear or provision or provender, and if the lonely and stubborn Beorn, a man distrustful of travelers and beggars who has no love for dwarves, does not help them, they starve and the quest fails.

Gandalf also drops a hint that Beorn is not as he appears. Some dark secret, redolent of the supernatural, clings to this figure somehow able to survive in the eave-shadows of a cursed and haunted wood.

No, instead Beorn's dark secret is revealed from the get-go, and he complains about having been enslaved and his people exterminated, and it is as about as hamfisted and heavy-handed a characterization as can be crammed into a five minute clip of film. Nothing comes of it and it comes from nowhere, since the dramatic tension of having to win his alliance lest the quest fail does not exist in this version.

His makeup is stupid, as if he is the Middle Earth version of Samson, who, instead of having his power hidden in his hair, has it hidden in his eyebrows. He looked like Freddie Jones in his Mentat get-up in the 1984 film version of *Dune*. I was expecting him at any moment to chant: "It is by will alone I set my mind in motion. It is by the juice of Sapho that thoughts acquire speed, the lips acquire *stains*, the *stains* become a warning...."

There is a scene where the dwarves want to keep the ponies loaned by Beorn but their overlooked last member, Bilbo, reminds them to keep their promises—at which moment the looming shadow of a bear-like shape is seen on a ridge nearby, watching them, silent as an angel of vengeance. Or at least that scene is in the book.

I do not remember that scene, which is the first step of Bilbo's character arc to becoming the hero of the company, as being in the film. Maybe I had to get up to get popcorn. I do remember the eerie hints of Beorn's true nature not being present in the film, but instead a garish special effect, maybe tossed in for a pointless reason.

Wow. I am already weary under the heavy load of stupid things, and we have not even reached Mirkwood yet. How about a mini-vacation, dear reader? There were two other thing that were not just done right, they were done brilliantly: the gateway to Mirkwood looked like a gate should look if long lost elves had carved it; and there is a scene, taken straight from the book, where Bilbo climbs a tree and for a moment sees the winds of the world above the leaf-gloom, and beholds the black butterflies of Mirkwood in the sunlight. Peter Jackson did that scene, and did it perfectly.

Now let us descend back down into the abyss of poor filmsmanship, like Bilbo reluctantly shimmying down the tree away from the sunlight, smiling clouds, and fluttering butterflies. Farewell, one good moment! Hail, boring inanity!

The quest enters Mirkwood, and Gandalf leaves them with the warning that they are not to depart from the path. Leaving the path is bad.

In the book, as in any number of old myths, fairy tales or medieval legends, they are indeed lured off the path due to weakness of character. In the book, the dwarves see what seems to be the campfires of a gay company dancing and feasting with music and rich ale and savory meats, and when they blunder off the path toward the vision, it turns out not to be men but rather forest elves, who vanish in a twinkling, as by magic, and the dwarves are left dazed and asleep amid the mossy forest roots.

In the movie, they try not to leave the path, but then they get stoned at Woodstock, because maybe they dropped some bad acid, man. The vibes turn bad, man, it's a bad trip! And Bilbo turns and sees himself. WHOA, this is so heavy, dude!

Okay. Does anyone who has ever told a story to a child

actually need lessons in how it is done? The rule is very simple. Adults will allow you to cheat the story. Children won't. If the story says that only Love's First Kiss will wake the sleeping princess, an adult might allow you to pull an ironic trick such as having the prince be the villain and the sister's love save the princess. But no kid will allow it. It is cheating. There is an unspoken contract, as binding as any enforced by an unsmiling and clear-eyed king who rules with a rod of iron, between the teller of the tale and those who enter the tale. The rule in children's stories is that you don't say things you don't mean.

Gandalf tells them not to leave the path. He does not mean it. If he meant it, the dwarves would be tempted to leave the path due to a weakness of character, or fear, or hunger, and the hobbit would remind them to stay on the straight and narrow. Get it? It is the first rule of storytelling. Maybe it is the only rule. Storytelling is serious and telling a children's story is even more serious, because children are more severe critics than adults, and their sense of justice is more finely honed.

Other complaints? I have a Cotillion, which is a number larger than Vermilion.

There was not enough Mirkwood in the film. It was supposed to be murky, and seem endless, and gloomy and forbidding, and you were supposed to feel lost. Instead the dwarves zipped through the endless miles of gloom in, what, like an afternoon? Did they even camp overnight?

Time for another vacation from Stupidityland. There was something that was not in the book but that was so damned cool that it almost makes up for the disappointment of Beorn.

When Bilbo puts on the ring which he got from Gollum,

he can hear the spiders talking and understand their evil speech, for he is partway into the shadow realm.

Ah, I loved that idea.

Then there was a fight scene where the filmmaker threw gallons of glop in 3D toward my eyes. Vacation over.

In the book, Bilbo lures the spiders away from their prey, the helpless dwarves, by calling them names, such as Lazy Lob, Crazy Cob, and Old Tomnoddy and, of course, Attercop. It is a classic Jack-taunting-the-Giant fairy tale gimmick, as fresh and ancient as Eastertide, where the little guy lures the big guy with eight legs, clustered eyes, and a pincer mouth away from the prisoners.

Vocabulary trivia time! *Attercop* –n. 1. a spider. 2. an ill-natured person. [Old English attorcoppa, from ātor poison and cop head]

In the movie, no such luck. No such attercop. Instead we get a *World of Warcraft*-style CGI fight with giant spiders. Now with extra glop.

This film was like being hit in the head over and over with a hammer, and with each blow, the IQ of the audience dropped another few digits. At this point a particularly fierce blow of the Stupidity Hammer struck home. Yes, fans, it was time for Legolas to come onstage!

I do not know if you have ever played *Dungeons & Dragons* or any of the various role-playing games that occupied my youth, but if you had, you would be familiar with the phenomenon called 'the moderator's pet NPC.' This is when a moderator introduces a character into the adventure who does everything better than any player character, and the entire universe (the moderator's invented universe, that is) showers him with blessings and love. You might see a similar phenomenon among writers of fan fiction, when they intrude themselves into their favorite scene as 'Mary Sue' the ensign who saves the Enterprise.

Well, watching Legolas, a character not in this book in any way, shape, or form, I felt I was watching the moderator's pet NPC in action.

It was like seeing Legosue, not Legolas.

And then came another blow of the Stupidity Hammer: the interspecies romance between the cute elf-girl and Kili, who for some reason did not look at all like a dwarf.

Look here, I am a married man, so I have been forced by the wife under the threat of domestic displeasure to go see my fair share of romances. Cowering and uxorious, I went. These included *The Bridges of Madison County* not to mention the remake of *Pride and Prejudice*, which I simply adored. Romance, like children's fables, has a simple rule. The couple needs two things: (1) some strong reason for them to be together and (2) some strong obstacle which keeps them apart. The drama of romance consists of item (1) against all odds and beyond all hope overcoming item (2).

But in the movie now and hereafter to be called *The Desolation of Two Hours of My Life That I Will Never Get Back Again*, there was item (2), namely that the two creatures were not of the same order of being, not to mention the Son of Earth was in the dungeon of the elf-king; but there was no item (1). What did they have in common, again, exactly? What did she see in him? What was the basis of their mutual attraction?

Time for another mini-vacation from the endless blows of the Stupidity Hammer! We get to see a scene set in the underground halls of Thranduil the Elf-king. Whatever else Jackson does wrong, he does his set direction right, does his art direction right, and every prop and weapon and artifact and smallest thing looks simply perfect. I loved the set of the throne room.

AN-NNN-ND then, for a small but very painful smack of the Stupidity Hammer, we get to see Thranduil's face melt for a second, as if he is hiding by enchantment (an enchantment that slips when he is angry) some old scar from where the dragon burned a huge hole in his cheek so that all the teeth of his skull are visible. Or maybe his face was burned by acid only on one side, and he hates the Batman so much that he will flip a coin to see whether he will spare his captives or kill them. And he only steals things related to the number Two. Yes, that is it: Thranduil is Two-Face. But whatever he was, he was not like a Tolkien character.

Ergo the scene where Thranduil kills an orc after the helpless prisoner cooperates is not because the director forgot that no Tolkien elf would ever break his word of honor in such a sadistic and low and nasty way, not even to an enemy; no, the orc just lost the coin toss! (That noise you just heard was the sound of my brain sloshing against the scuppers of my skull under the impact of the Stupidity Hammer.)

Of course nothing comes of Two-Thranduil's melted face, except to show that he hates dragons. Because otherwise there is no reason to hate a dragon, because we all love them, right?

Then the Stupidity Hammer lashes out again, this time as a blow to the groin of every man in the audience, because, SURPRISE! The lovely and eternally young elf-maiden, instead of doing elf-maidenly things like dancing in the moonlight on the surface of enchanted lakes or singing magical songs to beguile the watchful terrors of Thangorodrim, turns out to be Xena the Warrior Elf Princess. Yes, she is the roughest, toughest, most kick-ass Spartan Marine

Navy SEAL Special Forces Ninja Battlebabe in the entire warrior-harem of the elf-lord's politically correct gender-neutral and gender-accommodating fashion-model army. She makes as much sense as a platoon of bathing beauty Cataphracts or the dread and dreaded Playboy Bunny Brute Squad.

All medieval and classic cultures of the ancient world, including those on which Tolkien modeled his elves, routinely exposed their young and marriageable women to the fortunes of war, because bearing and raising the next generation of warriors is not needed for equality-loving elves.

Equality-loving elves. Who are monarchists. With a class system. Of ranks.

Battles are more fun when attractive young women are dismembered and desecrated by goblins! I believe that this is one point where C.S. Lewis, J.R.R. Tolkien, and all Christian fantasy writers from before World War Two were completely agreed upon, and it is a point necessary in order correctly to capture the mood and tone and nuance of the medieval romances or Norse sagas such writers were straining their every artistic nerve and sinew to create.

So, wait, we have an ancient and ageless society of elves where the virgin maidens go off to war, but these same virgin maidens must abide by the decision of their father or liege lord for permission to marry?

At that point, another blow of the Stupidity Hammer descended, when we see Gandalf, all by his lonesome self, wandering into the stronghold of Dol Guldur.

In the book the stronghold of Dol Guldur was, you know, a *stronghold*. Hence the name. That means it was a fortress, filled with soldiers of the dread sorcerer known only as the Necromancer. In the book, while the scene is not onstage, the hints dropped imply that Gandalf and his brother wizards of the White Council put forth their strength and assailed Dol Guldur and drove Sauron forth. "Assailed" means they besieged the place, which means they parked an army in a circle around the tower, battered the walls, used catapults and trebuchets and battering rams to crack the gates: you get the picture.

Instead, in the movie, Gandalf waltzes in, tells Radagast not to waltz in, gets mugged by orcs, and then Sauron shows up as a huge black special effect and telekinetically pins the old man up against a wall — and does not kill him.

Okay. Time for another lesson in storytelling: This is a lesson, which, unlike the others, only modern fantasy writers know, and which not all children or all women fans of romance know. This is because in the old days wizards were never the main characters; they were either wise councilors and prophets like Merlin, or they were antagonists whose curse or enchantment was the main obstacle to be overcome.

But when the wizard is onstage as the main character, you have to adopt what I call the Jack Vance Rule. I call it this because Jack Vance is the first author successfully and adroitly to have applied this rule in his *The Dying Earth*. The Jack Vance Rule is: (1) The wizard has to be able to do something unusual, or else he is not a wizard, (2) he cannot do everything, or else there is no drama; therefore (3) the story teller has to communicate to the reader whatever the dividing line is that separates what the wizard can do from what he cannot do, so that the reader can have a reasonable expectation of knowing what the wizard can and cannot do.

In *The Dying Earth*, the rule established that wizards could only force into their three-dimensional brains the ultradimensional and reality-warping syllables of at most three to seven spells a day, which, once they were spoken, evaporated from the wizard's brain like a dream at waking, their force expended, unable to be spoken again. Sound familiar? It is such a simple and clear and elegant rule for how to limit magic that Gary Gygax used it in his Dungeons and Dragons game, which then outstripped Vance in fame, so that modern readers often find Vance disappointingly similar to a D&D game.

Any rule will do. In *Green Lantern* comics, the magic ring can do anything as long as it is green, and it is helpless against the color yellow.

In the book, Gandalf does not need his rules defined because he is not a main character. He is a wise councilor and a wonder worker in the fashion of Merlin. He never does anything more magical than throw a pinecone full of napalm at a warg, lock a door, break a bridge, or hold up his staff to forbid an unclean spirit entrance into a gateway. He is roughly as magical as your average Army chaplain who carries a flamethrower.

In the movie, however, the wizard is a main character who faces another main character, also a wizard, in a duel of magic. The results are lame and stupid because the audience sees a bunch of meaningless lightshow effects, with no idea of what allows either side to win or lose. I felt like astronaut Bowman entering the spacewarp of the monolith in Kubrick's *2001 A Space Oddysey*. Wow. Pretty lights.

My only consolation is that this lame duel of magic was nowhere near as lameriffic as the wizard duel between Gandalf and Saruman in *Fellowship*, which consisted of old men flying about on wires slamming each other into walls with their Green Lantern-style telekinesis.

This also was the main drawback of the *Harry Potter* movies, by the way. In the final duel between Harry and his

Dark Lord, (same job, different guy), they point their wands at each other. Then they grimace. Then they point their wands at each other even harder.

Bilbo is not onstage during all this. Where is the Hobbit in this film, allegedly called *The Hobbit*, again?

Ah, but then we see Bilbo. After his friends are captured by wood elves, using his ring of invisibility, he sneaks into the buried palace of the elf lord. Unseen, his wily eyes spy out that the elves drink wine imported from Laketown, and float the empty barrels downstream as part of their trade and traffic with the human settlement.

He waits until the jailor is drunk, steals the keys, frees the dwarves, and, instead of attempting to sneak them past the heavily guarded upper gates, takes the dwarves to the loading dock beneath the wine cellar, seals them in the barrels, and clings, still unseen, to a barrel himself as the unsuspecting elf prentices pole the empty barrels downstream to Laketown. It is simple and brilliant. Unfortunately, he gets a wetting, and takes a headcold: a little bit of realism, if not comedy relief.

Oh, no, wait. That is not what happens.

Just then, just when I thought I would be free from the repeated blows to my tender head of the Stupidity Hammer, the Stupidity Hammer rose up from the shining screen, drew back, whirled hugely, and with great force and might and main slammed me right between the eyes so my brain squirted out my ears a yard past my shoulders in both directions.

Bilbo does not seal the barrels.

I will wait for you to recover in case you just got the sensation of a Stupidity Hammer clonking you from the page. Then I will repeat myself, because it is so dumb you might not believe me:

Bilbo does not seal the barrels. He leaves the tops open.

So the dwarves are perfectly visible, by which I mean visible to the eye, by which I mean not hidden. By which I mean people with eyeballs can see them, such as the elf-people from whom they are allegedly trying to escape.

Bilbo leaves the barrel tops open when he is dumping the barrels into the water, which is a substance, so I am given to believe, that enters openings and makes things wet inside, and sometimes even sinks things.

Now the Thirteen Stupid Dwarves and One Stupid Hobbit are floating away on the smooth and placid river. Ah, but with another and fiercer blow of the Stupidity Hammer, I now see that the river is a rock-filled rushing rapids of white water which no one would ever float barrels down as part of their trade and commerce, and which is guarded by a water-gate that stupidly cannot be lowered in time, and which is prone to sudden attacks for no reason by hordes of stupid goblins, so that an endless, endless three-way battle erupts between the barrel-dwarves, the dancing and skip-ping acrobat elf archers (including their young women!) and the roaring and ever-missing goblin horde ensues. It is like a ride in a fun carnival! Except stupid!

As I was in the theater, gripping the popcorn-stained carpet in my teeth because I was dazed from the last blow of the Stupidity Hammer, and I started to stagger weakly to my feet, when, lo and behold! I was treated to the sight of a roaring dwarf sticking his arms and legs out through the wood of a barrel, bashing enemies left and right.

This was the only moment in the whole sucktastic movie when any dwarf warrior actually does anything effec-tive against his hereditary foes, the orcs. Roaring dwarf wears barrel. Arms, legs, stick out. The wood acts as armor, and he rolls on people and stuff.

And therefore a giant hammer of pure stupidity lashed out of the screen and felled me again. I lay mewling, clutching my head with my sweaty hands, whimpering for my Mommy to make it stop. MAKE IT STOP!

But it did not stop. It. Did. Not. Stop.

For awesome Legosue, in his awesome flying-trapeze artistic awesomeness, had to flip across the screen and shoot goblins full of arrows. I wish he had had a boxing glove arrow, or one that shot out poisonous smoke, or one that had a lit stick of dynamite lashed to it. That would have been EVEN COOLER!!!! And then Legolas could have joined the Enterprise as the newest midshipman recruit, yet saved them all from the Klingons, and Lt. Uhura would have fallen in love with him.

Well, the Legolas Movie went on for a few more hours, and we got to Laketown. Every fan of Tolkien was eager to see the George R.R. Martin-like intricacy of the political by-play between the various Machiavellian factions of Lake-town. We all remember the dashing smuggler, known only as the Scarecrow of Romney Marsh, who was trying to sneak past the secret police and the border guards to free French Aristocrats from the guillotine of Laketown, right?

Eh? What is that you are saying? There is nothing like all this crap I just made up in anything written by Tolkien? That it would only have bogged down and sullied the rather clear message about greed and ambition versus the virtues of a simple life, which *The Hobbit* represents? Oh. Well, yeah. You know that and I know that but Peter Jackson does not.

Excuse me, I must take a moment to consult my inner orc:

Peter u bagronk sha pushdug Jackson-glob búbhosh skai!

So, what happens next that could possibly be even stupider and make even less sense than what I have said so far? OF COURSE! Kili comes down with a headcold or a war wound or something, and since dwarves are wimps who give up as soon as convenient, he has to be left behind, so that Agog the Disrespectful, that orc who has been hunting Thorin with the menacing intensity of Tommy Lee Jones hunting Harrison Ford in the remake of *The Fugitive*, could show up in Laketown for another endless, endless scene of elf wonderboy Legolas shooting orcs with his elf wonder bowmanship! YEAH!

Oh, yes, you recall all those Dwarf warriors and warlords who go to war, and cut things into bits with axes and are as doughty and terrible as all getout because they do not retreat and they never get tired and they are ferocious and tough as the rocks they cleave? And strong enough to slay orcs in secret wars hidden in dank tunnels far beneath the earth?

Remember those dwarves? Those dwarves are not in this movie.

No, in this movie, the wife and the little children of the smuggler do more damage to the attacking orcs than the dwarves. The dwarves are here for comedy relief.

Oh, and instead of goblins, who, you know, act like a horde of barbaric and vicious fighters, and do things like cover the battlefield and use scimitars and recurved bows to shoot enemies, in THIS movie there were ultrasupersneaky ninja-goblins! Looks like the Stupidity Hammer landed a solid blow on my medulla oblongata!

We have a scene where ninja-goblins are wafting across rooftops, using their ninja-karate-magic to hide from the guards. I am sure I saw a scene where they used suction cups to climb a skyscraper or special radioactive insect clinging powers, but maybe I am confusing them with The Shadow, or with the Spider-Man. Or maybe Peter Jackson was.

Okay so then there was another fight, this time between ninja-orcs and the awesome flying acrobat ninjette-bowgirl elf. I think her name is Arrowette or Artemis or something.

Just kidding. To be quite honest, the actress Evangeline Lilly is not only quite attractive, she handles both the demands of the acting and a physical stunts very well. Indeed, I am afraid I have a bit of a crush on her, with her long lustrous hair, her finely chiseled cheekbones, her kissing-soft feminine lips, her soft curves aching with the promise of luscious loveplay.... Oh, wait a minute. I think I am looking at Orlando Bloom. Er, never mind. Sorry, Miss Lilly.

Just when I picked myself again off the sticky floor of the theater, blearily wondering where the Hobbit character after whom this movie was apparently named might be hiding, BAM! The familiar Hammer came down again. This time, it was a scene where Orlando Bloom is standing a zillion feet away from the evil orc bounty hunter Slopgog the Unmentionable or whatever his name is, and he does not shoot him with an elf arrow.

I sat there, rocking back and forth with my eyes crossed, and through the stream of drool and vitreous humor leaking down my chin I muttered again and again, "Shoot him with an elf arrow. *Shoot. Him. With. An. Elf. Arrow.* SHOOT HIM WITH AN ELF ARROW!"

But no. No elf arrow was forthcoming.

Blogsnog the Debunker, or whatever his name was, strolled in a leisurely fashion down the narrow walkway of Laketown, not ducking for cover, and meanwhile no one was calling for the town guard, and the elf guy continued not to shoot him with an elf arrow.

You see, the film slimer, er, maker, wanted this scene to be like a gunfight in an iconic Western, with Clint Eastwood and John Wayne staring at each other with narrowed eyes as each strides menacingly ever closer, spurs jangling with each step. Of course, in a Western, both are armed with revolvers, and both are wary of making the first move lest the other man prove fast enough to draw and shoot first, but then both shooters want to close the distance to improve their aim. That is what makes such scenes tense.

Here is what makes a scene spectacularly NOT tense. One guy has a gun and the other has a knife, or a club, or maybe strangling wire or even a stick of butter, because no one gives a rat's fart for what the other guy has because you can shoot him first.

If you have the weapon that, you know, shoots, you can shoot the guy who has no weapon that shoots, and so there is no downside to letting him see you go for your gun, or, for that matter, use a winch to load your crossbow in a leisurely manner, because you can raise it and turn him into a pincushion before he can attack you with his club or strangling wire. Or stick of butter.

In such a case, he will be running toward you at full speed, because if he walks a menacing walk, well, that gives you time to roll a cigarette, light it, put your foot in the stirrup thingie on the crossbow, clamp it to your belt winch, and crank the string back, yawn, read a magazine, drop a bolt in the slot, check the grease on the bolt, aim, make vacation plans, check the wind speed, and fire a bolt through this heart and left lung and out his back in a 3D spray of unnamed orcish life fluids.

Unless you are a superspeed acrobat wonder-elf, in

which case you can shoot him nine times a second and spell out your monogram in his vital organs.

Well, who cares? Neither character was in the book anyway. I think I lost consciousness at that moment, overcome by the fumes of the butter-substitute substance coating the theater floor between the seats. I woke a little later, and elfboy still had not shot Urgslug the Irkisonic, or whatever his name is. My wife had to stuff a wide handful of popcorn-flavored food substitute into my face, in order to smother the broken, wretched burbling—*shoot him ... with ... an elf arrow.*

Of course, the wife was shouting SHOOT HIM at the screen during this event, so the point of her behavior was not clear. Maybe she remembered that I invited her to this turkey, and we paid for many children and my mother-in-law.

I was semi-conscious for a long and dreary and utterly pointless scene where the Scarecrow of Romney Marsh was looking for the one last remaining black harpoon thing was the only McGuffin that could kill the dragon, and then only when fired from a standing catapult that looked like it had been designed by the Professor on Gilligan's Island. Why there were not a hundred of these, and scores of giant harpoon shooters, I do not know. But I am glad that Ishmael and Queequeg will appear in the sequel.

As it turns out, it did not matter that I, or for that matter the script writer, were only semi-conscious because, as with everything else in this movie, nothing comes from the scene and nothing led up to it.

Please, let no purists tell me that Bard and his Black Arrow were indeed in the book. You are mistaken. You are confusing them with Kirk Douglas's character Ned Land in Disney's *Twenty Thousand Leagues Under the Sea.* He is the one who harpoons the evil dragon with his dragon harpoon. In Tolkien, Bard the Archer shoots an arrow. Got it? Arrow. Pointy thing. Flies. Like what the superelves use.

The next time I regained consciousness, it was in time to view one of my most favorite scenes not merely from Tolkien's *The Hobbit*, but indeed from all literature whatsoever. You know what scene I mean!

Bilbo, donning his ring of invisibility, is pressured by the justifiably frightened dwarves to sneak into the lair of the loathsome wereworm, Smaug the Great, who is found asleep on the heaps of hoarded gold.

Bilbo steals a single cup, the smallest trifle, and this wakes the dragon to wrath, who emerges from the mountain on wings of flame, and finds and destroys the dwarvish camp, and eats their ponies. The dwarves flee into a secret door, hiding in an upper corridor, unwilling to go down and see what Smaug is about when he returns, shivering with rage, to his unclean burrow.

Those of you who are keen on literary references will see the parallel. In *Beowulf* we recall the nameless escaped slave, who, happening upon the grave of dead kings, enters it seeking shelter, and instead finds the wereworm aslumber on the heaped hoard.

He steals a cup to bribe his lord to receive him again and forgive his escape attempt. But the sequel is horrific:

When the dragon awoke, new woe was kindled.
    .... The guardian waited
    ill-enduring till evening came;
    boiling with wrath was the barrow's keeper,
    and fain with flame the foe to pay
    for the dear cup's loss.—Now day was fled
    as the worm had wished. By its wall no more

was it glad to bide, but burning flew
folded in flame....

The whole point of the scene is the difference between a good and kindly lord, one who open-handedly rewards his brave earls for their faithful service in battle, and the insane greed of the dragon, who cannot bear to part even with the smallest trifle, and who knows every article and implement and coin to the smallest detail.

As in *Beowulf*, so here. This second time Bilbo enters the stifling lair, the canny dragon wakes, and sweeps the dark around with his hypnotic, penetrating eyes, but Bilbo is invisible. Bilbo is clever enough to amuse the dragon with flattery and riddles, putting the noisome monster off his guard.

I am pleased to say that my favorite line—or at least part of it—appeared in the midst of this mockery and wreckage of one of my favorite books.

"The King under the Mountain is dead and where are his kin that dare seek revenge? Girion Lord of Dale is dead, and I have eaten his people like a wolf among sheep, and where are his sons' sons that dare approach me? I kill where I wish and none dare resist. I laid low the warriors of old and their like is not in the world today. Then I was but young and tender. Now I am old and strong, strong, strong. Thief in the Shadows!" he gloated. "My armour is like tenfold shields, my teeth are swords, my claws spears, the shock of my tail a thunderbolt, my wings a hurricane, and my breath death!"

And then, as by now we should have suspected, the steam-powered Stupidity Hammer caved into the front of my skull with the force of a pile driver. Because Bilbo took the ring off.

Okay, I get it. I get the idea. This movie is a sequel to the successful *Fellowship*, and the audience knows the ring is actually the One Ring, and therefore major mojo and bad news and so on. It is supposed to simply scream EE-VIL-LL whenever it appears on screen, and ergo again Bilbo has to yank it off his finger as often as possible so as not to become a shadow beneath the vaster shadow of the Dark Lord. I got it. I got the concept.

But the execution of the concept was a big, fat skull-whack from the now all-too-familiar Stupidity Hammer.

Smaug can defy armies of men and elves, but when a three-foot tall burglar materializes right in front of his nose, he can suddenly neither bite nor strike nor breathe fire. Or, rather he does all these things, but is suddenly affected by some odd nerve disease that makes it impossible for him to control his limbs, so the bane of the Lonely Mountain, the destroyer of kingdoms, the scourge of Esgaroth, he flails and spits flame and hits to the left and right of his targets.

Just so we are clear on this point: Smaug suddenly and for no reason finds he cannot kill a perfectly visible hobbit, because Bilbo suddenly and for no reason thought it was a good idea to doff his magic ring while standing before the dragon so as to make himself perfectly visible.

Well, things go from bad—no, excuse me, they were already WAY past bad. This dial had been cranked up to eleven when the meter only goes to ten—things go from inexcusably stupid to indescribably stupid.

I should not attempt to describe it. The pain... the pain....

And yet I must! It is my penance for having spent real money on this turkey and inadvertently aided the forces of brain-gag by rewarding them for this craptastic jerktrocious smegbladder of a film. My money crossed their palms! Peter Jackson went out and bought himself a Starbucks cup of coffee with the four bucks he got from the forty dollars I spent on tickets! Forgive me, O Muses! I MUST SUFFER! (And you shall suffer with me, dear reader).

The next scene is almost too stupidcallafragilisticexpeallidumbass for words to describe it. In fact, in the last sentence, was something that was not a word and did not describe it, proving my point. But what happened next is this:

When the dwarves heard the ruckus of Smaug unable to kill Bilbo, they decided Smaug must be the biggest pussywillow in Middle Earth, and unable to hit the broad side of a lonely mountain, because the twelve (or is it ten?) short men scrambled down into the lair and stronghold of the diabolical monster who killed WHOLE FINGOLFIN ARMIES and KINGDOMS and CRUD LIKE THAT because he is MORE OF A BADASS THAN FINGON GODZILLA!

Where was I? Oh, yeah, on the floor, in the fetal position, weeping blood from my eyes and brain goop from my ears, calling on mommy to make it stop. But. It. Won't. Stop.

The comedy relief pantomime dwarves, who could not manage to fight a group of shrimpy, non-fire-breathing goblins except with elf acrobat-ninja help while wearing comedy relief barrels, now attack Godzilla. The rockets of the jets and the gunfire of the tanks of the Japanese Self Defense Forces can do nothing against the monster, and wading through the high tension power lines only enrages him, so he ignites a petroleum refinery.

But the dwarves come to attack him, and their plan is to dance on his nose.

They ignite the furnaces, thinking perhaps that hot

things will hurt the demon-serpent whose inward parts are filled with fire hotter than any furnace in Middle Earth can achieve. Good thinking. If that works, you and Thor head out to find the water-breathing sea-serpent coiled around the world and drown it. In water.

Now, no doubt you are asking — well, if the dwarves are so hardcore balls-o'-brass brave in this scene, why were they so cautious about the army-eating dragon earlier? I mean, this is a monster that eats armies. He deep-fat-fries and eats whole armies.

I dimly recall that there were some scenes of short people swinging on long lines, unless I am confusing this with a similar scene where Frankenstein's monster with a glowing skull window, while trying to escape from Dracula, was spider-manning across a deep chasm in the movie *Van Helsing*. Or maybe that was Spider-Man trying to escape from Doctor Octopus atop a speeding train. Or maybe it was the last board in the famous video game *Dragon's Lair* made by that guy who animated *Rats Of Nimh*. I dunno. It is all a popcorn-oil-flavored blur now.

With the infinite weariness of one who wishes only to die and be reborn due to bad karma as a stinging centipede, I pried open one gummy, tear-crusted eye and focused it dimly at the great shining screen of neverending movie dumbness.

I saw a giant statue of a dwarf king made of molten gold fall over on the dragon. It hit the dragon and he shook it off, sending expensive droplets, worth a thousand dollars an ounce, off in every direction. He was not hurt in any way.

That was the plan.

It was a two step plan: Step (1) dance on the dragon's nose and then Step (2) construct or find a conveniently placed

Lady Liberty-sized master mold of a cast statue of Durin the Great or someone, fill it with the molten gold conveniently stacked and prepared in the furnaces, which conveniently all heat up to the proper temperature and need no crew to work any of their moving parts, and wait until the flying version of Godzilla, the guy who EATS WHOLE FUNDIN ARMIES is hovering on his vast batlike wings right in the exact right spot, and drop the entire molten statue on his head, because he will be too surprised and stupefied to use his vast batlike wings to move eight meters to the left or two meters up and ergo avoid the falling Lady Liberty-sized but still hissingly molten statue of Durin the Great or someone.

Ah, but not to worry, because the third part of the plan, right after the dragon shakes off the molten gold because it cannot hurt him in any way, is better than the first two parts! In the third part of the plan, the dragon shakes off the molten gold and opens his mouth and breathes out fire which kills every living thing in the chamber where he is and all the corridors and chambers to each side of him, as he destroys everything in his vast, inhuman, unstoppable rage.

The dragon then uses his nose like a bloodhound, and scents his foes, if any survived, and follows them one by screaming one, slithering his snaky body into narrow spaces if need be, or if the prey attempts to hide in holes too small for him, he vomits fire on them, burns up all the oxygen in the room, and laughs while they die.

Failing that, he topples titanic pillars and statues to block any escape exits he discovers, and then goes to the main gate and takes up a position and waits for them to starve to death, all the while shouting out mocking riddles to them, or perhaps catching the king's deer and, with puffs of his fiery breath, cooking the venison so they can smell the savory fumes.

Whoops, I am sorry, that is not the third part of the plan. The third part of the plan is that the dragon loves the idea of people breaking into his lair and taking his stuff, and he does not really want to disturb them, and so he flies away to go attack Laketown, perhaps because he is miffed at the customs agents who are stopping the Scarecrow of Romney Marsh and mad about the treatment of French aristocrats.

The end. To be continued in our next episode. Perhaps there will be even less of Bilbo in Part Three.

Let us be clear on that last, dumb, super dumb, stupidly dumb scene of dumbfounding dumbness. Let us review, one more time, the steps of this awesome, awesome plan:

1. Send down Bilbo.
2. Have him take off his magic ring while standing directly in front of the dragon's nose.
3. Listen for the sound of the dragon inexplicably not killing the hobbit in one-eighth of one second.
4. Rush into the dragon's lair.
5. Hope he misses you while trying to swat you.
6. Dance on nose.
7. Swing on things, run in circles.
8. Hit him with a zillion cubic feet of molten metal. Watch to make sure he is not wounded or inconvenienced in any way as he shakes it off.
9. Watch as he flies off for no reason whatsoever, during the one moment when nothing in Middle Earth or Upper Heaven or Lower Hell could possibly have forced him to depart, namely, the

very moment when someone is trespassing on
his horde.

Since that was the plan anyway, I wonder why the plan
was not to forget about the stupid map and key and Durin's
Day and all that rigmarole, march into the front gate, hope
the dragon misses, et cetera, and watch him fly off to go
burn Laketown, and then gather up as much loot as your
donkeys can carry. Repeat every week for 151 weeks or until
you have all the hoard.

The paramedics had to haul my broken and bleeding
body and wet, soggy brain out from the theater after the riot
police, mistaking my hysterical leaping and gargling caused
by post-traumatic movie disorder for a threatening gesture,
had been forced to club me down, and as I was dragged
away, leaving a long slimy snail trail of popcorn butter-
flavored oil behind, my last words could be heard, as weak
as twitching ants blinded by exposure to fumigation fumes
who crawl out into the sunlight to die:

"Shoot... him. with... an... elf... arrow...."

3

WHISTLE WHILE YOU WORK

I f, like me, you have too much free time on your hands, you have probably wondered why Snow White, at least as Walt Disney portrays her tale, has small woodland animals to help her with her household chores, with bunnies and chipmunks scrubbing dishes, songbirds helping to sew, and fawns dusting the furniture with their white tails.

If, like me, you have too much education on your hands, you have probably used Aristotelian categories to analyze the question.

If, as a child, you ever asked the question, "But WHY must I go to bed?—I am not sleepy!", and heard the answer, "Because Daddy says so!", and you found the answer unsatisfying, you experienced the frustration of hearing the wrong kind of answer to the right kind of question.

The sleepy child is asking for a justification, asking what fair purpose lights out for unsleepy children serves, and the impatient parent is explaining a formality, that a command from a lawful authority must be obeyed independent of its fairness. It answers a different "why" than the "why" that was asked.

Aristotle answers that there are four kinds of answers to the question "why".

1. Final cause is motive, or, in other words, it is the answer in terms of that for the sake of which the thing is done to explain the thing.
2. Formal cause is structure, or, in other words, it is the answer in terms of how the thing is put together, the relation of parts one to another.
3. Material cause is substance, or, in other words, it is the answer in terms of the content, what stuff the thing is.
4. Efficient cause is the past, or in other words, it is the answer in terms of the history of cause and effect leading up to the event being described.

In this case, we can discard the answer that, "Snow White has maidservant bunnies because Uncle Walt put them in the story"—this tells us the efficient cause, and we don't care about that.

Likewise, we can dismiss the answer that, "Snow White has maidservant bunnies because it is a fairy tale and therefore made of make-believe: in real life, when I tried to get my bunny to clean the rug, he left poop pellets over everything, and ate the leather slip covers on my couch"—this tells us that you never want to ask me for advice on housekeeping or animal-training.

Likewise again, to answer that, "Snow White has maidservant bunnies because they are a convenient, labor-saving pets for her," gives the story-world final cause, that is, it tells us Snow White's motive inside the story, but it does not tell us the real-world final cause, that is, it does not tell us Walt Disney's motive outside the story.

Presumably the motive of Uncle Walt is to tell a good and memorable and charming story to entertain both young and young-at-heart. That we can presume, but it does not answer the question asked. In this case, the answer we are asking is one of formal cause, that is, what makes this particular conceit entertaining, that is, charming and memorable and good?

We want to know what about having shy and wild deer befriend and love a virginal maiden appeals to any audience whose hearts are fit for fairy tales. We want to know what about furry animals doing human chores appeals to those young children and any graybeard philosophers innocent or wise enough to delight in fairy stories.

The alert reader will note that I introduce a thought into this question slyly, but, if I may be allowed, crucially. I propose that we cannot answer what makes a story element fit for being told in a fairy story without answering what makes a heart fit for hearing a fairy story.

Let us answer the smaller half of the question first, as it is easier. I assume nearly everyone who likes fairy stories, and who likes seeing wild animals befriend the virgin princess in the story, sees immediately what the appeal is. Any reader who cannot see it is asked merely to imagine the same conceit in other types of tales, so as to see how wrong or comical it would be there.

Imagine the detective story where the hard-boiled gumshoe, having just survived a beating from Lash Canino, the thug of Eddie Mars the gambler, and only now realizing that his old pal, Sean Reagan, whom everyone thinks ran off with Eddie's wife to Mexico, is actually dead, stumbles into his ratty apartment lit only by slanting strips of light from the Venetian blinds. A cigarette is dangling from his bleeding lip, and hatred glinting from his swollen black eyes. He stumbles over to his gun cabinet, and his pet groundhog, Mr. Flunbuffly, hands him a tumbler of scotch. Dwinky the Fawn reloads his shooting iron for him.

Such a scene could be done for comical effect, or absurd, or as a wild hallucination after a svelte dame slips someone a Mickey, but it is foreign to the mood of Film Noir whodunits and utterly outside the conceptual frame of what a detective story universe allows.

To use a less absurd example, imagine a similar scene either in a Sword-and-Sorcery story, or a myth, or a work of science fiction or High Fantasy.

Conan the Barbarian we can imagine strangling a vulture with his teeth while being crucified, because he is the baddest of badasses ever to tread the bloodstained pages of pulp magazines. We cannot imagine Blinknose the Beaver sharpening the sword of his fathers before sending him with a few words of sage advice to face the snake-god of Stygia in the windowless and primordial temple from which the smokes of incense and the screams of victims on moonlit midnights arise.

If the veil between man and nature is ever parted for Conan, and this applies to all the Sword-and-Sorcery I have read, what comes through the parted veil is a monster, an abomination stirred up by the aforementioned sorcery, something to be slain with the aforementioned sword. Conan dwells in a Lovecraftian universe, where the things beyond mortal ken are hostile, unearthly, indifferent, and they do not want to talk to you.

Cthulhu does not want to be your friend.

The Great Old Ones in this respect are more horrible than the Mephistopheles of Faust. They do not want to tempt you, and will make no bargain, signed in blood or no, for your soul.

Now, I am not saying all Sword-and-Sorcery is Lovecraftian, but I am saying the sorcery is more often Eldritch than it is Disney. I don't think I ever read a single tale of this kind where Elric of Melnibone or Solomon Kane had his fairy godmother turn a comedy relief mouse into a steed for him to ride to war. It is not the kind of thing Arioch, Lord of Chaos, does for you.

But note that Siegfried from the Wagner opera seems to have as many animal friends as Snow White. He plays with a bear that terrifies his foster father, Mim the Dwarf, and he understands the speech of the songbird that warns him Mim means to murder him. A myth has some element that Sword-and-Sorcery is lacking. The common thread here is that Siegfried is like Tarzan or like Romulus and Remus, a man both closer to nature than any civilized man, but also possessed of a glamor or a power due to this innocence.

But note that the opposite of Snow White is seen in these Noble Savages: Siegfried is stronger than the bear, and can play with him as if with a puppy, in rough friendship, but in no way does he domesticate the bear, or set him to cooking or cleaning or sweeping, or even helping him to forge a sword.

Science fiction differs from fantasy and fairy tales in one special conceit: the magic and the wonder in science fiction is confined to those which can be fit into a naturalistic universe, one where only those mysteries of the universe that can be discovered by science are real.

Now, this might not seem like a deep difference. After all, we might ask, what is the difference between a dragon from planet Pern or Velantia and a dragon from the Lonely Mountain or from Neidhöle? What is the difference between a Slan or Lensman or Vulcan who reads minds and an Elf-Queen who reads hearts? What is the difference between the Time Traveler, who visits the Morlocks of AD 807901, and Ebenezer Scrooge, who visits the graveyard in a Christmas of some future year closer at hand?

To travel in time or read minds or deal with dragons are alike in that they are wonders and mysteries, things we cannot do in real life. But the difference is clear and deep: the flying lizard creatures of Pern are extraterrestrials. Fafnir of Neidhöle is supernatural. What Slans or Lensmen or Vulcans do, according to the rules of their own make-believe universe, is a natural effect, either a skill that can be learned, or a native talent no more supernatural than an electric eel's ability to discharge a shock. The Time Traveler built a time traveling machine, which any competent workman with the Time Traveler's blueprints and materials could duplicate. The conceit of the story is that Time Machine is just as impossible as a radio would have been in the Bronze Age: something that does not exist but could. The Ghost of Christmas Yet to Come is a ghost, a spirit, something science cannot explain nor science worshipers admit possible.

If the Gray Lensman came back to his barracks from a hard campaign of blasting Boskonian space-pirates out of the ether, he could not find a fuzzy animal mopping the floor or polishing his raygun. He could find an underperson or uplifted animal, of course, something from the island of Dr. Moreau changed by science to be intelligent; or he could find any number of fuzzy extraterrestrials. Indeed, a suspiciously large number of extraterrestrials are our all-too-terrestrial fellow earthcritters merely propped up on their hind legs. Kzinti are cats, for example, and Selenites are termites.

Green Martians are Red Indians, and Green Osnomians are Red Martians (who are nudists), and Romulans are Romans, and Klingons are Russians (unless, later, they are Samurai), and Vulcans are Houyhnhnms (who are horses).

But in each case, if the story is science fiction and not fantasy, the reason why the talking animal talks is that some undiscovered but quite natural property of natural science allows for it, such as the natural evolutionary development of intelligence on extraterrestrial worlds.

A second difference is one of familiarity. A talking fox or a talking tree we can easily imagine to be like the trickster from *Pinocchio* or Treebeard from Tolkien. But a Martian is either a monster, something strange and dangerous, or an alien, someone strange whether dangerous or not. Possibly the Martian is a space princess named Dejah Thoris, who happily is both gorgeous and naked, but even she must be alien in the sense of exotic and alluring, if she is to be a convincing Martian.

There is a veil between the human world and the Otherworld in fairy tales which the tale penetrates, and we imagine what life is on the other side. In science fiction the veil is between the human world and other places in time and space and other dimensions, between the natural world we know and unknown worlds equally as natural as our own. They can be extraterrestrial and even extra-dimensional, but they cannot be literally uncanny, nor, in sense that Elfland or the Inferno is, can they be unearthly.

But now we are far afield, so let us quickly return to the point of the appeal of seeing a maiden befriending animals to do human tasks. I hope we are all agreed from the examples above, and many others we can imagine, that the appeal is a longing to be at peace with nature, to cross the gap which even those men who do not believe in the literal Garden of Eden will admit exists. There is something in the human soul that longs for Arcadia, for the Golden Age of Saturn, for the time which modern science says never existed, but all myths report once did exist, when man and nature were one, and beasts were our brothers.

To be sure, there is many a modern myth, spun by Rousseau or Marx and seen in stories like *Dances With Wolves*, about the Edenic times when we were all noble savages. Some of these myths pretend to be scientific, but real science, studying the skull wounds of Neolithic corpses, can tell the murder rate back in the Stone Age was higher than anywhere in the modern world, and that includes inner cities during riots and provinces at war. It should rightly be called not the 'Stone Age' but the 'Homicide by Stone Axe Age'.

Whatever science or pseudoscience says, anyone whose heart is fit to hear fairy tales knows a sense of loneliness and loss which is soothed, but only in part, by the sublime beauties of nature. There is something out there we all want to embrace, and to have it talk to us.

That, by the way, is the point of the appeal of having the fuzzy woodland friends do chores. If Snow White were seen keeping house for the dwarves, but what she did was get a cat to keep the rats out of the grain store, go duck hunting with her faithful hound Greatheart, and hitch up a horse or ox to plough the field, or keep bees for their honey or chickens for their eggs or keep lambs for their veal, then the gap between man and nature is still in place, and the virgin has not lured the wild things over the gap to our side.

No doubt by now some readers are puzzled at my repeated use of the words virgin and maiden, and, if those

readers went to public school instead of getting an education, they are not only puzzled but offended. This brings up
a second and larger point about woodland creatures
working at human tasks, which is, namely, what power does
the fairy tale virgin possess which enables her to overcome
or ignore the gap between man and nature which afflicts the
rest of the Sons of Adam?

It is, of course, her innocence. Much as it appalls the
brain-dead zombies indoctrinated by public schools, innocence is better than the cynicism or shared guilt or victi-
mology taught by modern thought, and, if we place faith in
the account Moses told the Children of Israel about Eden, it
was lack of innocence that drove the parents of mankind out
of paradise.

Even more appalling to the zombies, the perfect symbol
and image of innocence is virginity. That is a word that is
not much in use these days, except perhaps as a badge of
shame, for reasons too uncouth to mention in this article.

The odd thing is that even the modern cynics—provided
they do not notice or do not admit to themselves what these
symbols mean or which longings of sad human nature fairytales satisfy—even they can have hearts fit to hear fairytales.
What they cannot do is reconcile this with their heads. They
must compartmentalize and separate with thought-tight
cells their love of fairytales with the empty and empty-
headed cynicism that passes for wisdom in this modern
world.

In this regard, let us briefly touch on the masculine side
of the question. Why is it that Siegfried and Mowgli and
Tarzan have this same Disney Princess oneness with nature,
but it has no domestic flavor to it, no sweetness and charm?
To ask the question is to answer it: boys are different from
girls, and it is only the modern mind, and the perversions

encouraged by the modern mind both intellectual and sexual, which have the effrontery to say otherwise.

Where the innocent virgin princess lures nature across the gap of Eden to our side, and heals the primordial loneliness by making companions of the wild beasts, the noble savage prince rips off his shabby cloak of civilization, dons his leopard-skin loincloth, takes his knife between his teeth, and leaps across the gap to the savage side, clawing his way up via dangling vines and man-eating plants to the brink on that far side, there to wrestle apes and strangle lions. If you don't get the difference, then you don't understand what makes girls girlish and boys boyish.

Now, let me not be accused of saying that in imaginative tales the girls are cooperative with nature and boys are competitive. That is not what I am saying at all. Both sexes, merely because we all are human, are prone to that sorrow and loneliness which the contemplation of the beauty of nature soothes, in the same way that looking at the photo of a distant loved one is soothing; but it also, like adoring a photo of a loved one, tempts and exasperates the same mood that it soothes. We still feel apart from nature.

The loneliness is not a desire for companionship alone. Dog owners and cat owners have an emotional rapport with their pets. The loneliness is a desire for camaraderie, that is, for speech and communion with other intelligences beside man.

I call it communion because there is more involved in this longing than merely interaction with nonhuman intelligences. In the earliest science fiction story I've read that stars nonhumans, *The War Of The Worlds* by H.G. Wells, the Martians are simply monsters. They do not speak and make no bargains with mankind any more than Cthulhu does.

Their intelligence involves no community or common ground with man.

And, again, because Science Fiction is a naturalistic genre, one where supernatural events are foreign to the suppositions of the tale, often what is emphasized in a tale starring alien beings is precisely that they are alien. As John W. Campbell, Jr. famously challenged his writers, a truly alien alien would be as smart as a man but not think like a man. For me, the best example of nonhuman intelligence in a story was in *A Martian Odyssey* by Stanley Weinbaum. Tweel the Martian has only limited communication with the human with whom he travels, and the major appeal of the character is both his obvious high intelligence and his sheer incomprehensibility.

The first story, (and best example), I can recall where an alien with a speaking role spoke in a truly alien fashion was *The Moon Era* by Jack Williamson, where an alien called 'Mother' was portrayed sympathetically, albeit clearly not human. She was an alien and not a monster.

Oddly enough, the second best example comes from *Heroic Age*, a Japanese anime, where the Silver Tribe were portrayed as both elfin and highly intellectual, whose concerns were understandable, but were not human concerns.

However, the most common use of aliens who are aliens and not monsters derives from *Galactic Patrol* by E.E. Doc Smith. In that background, creatures of different psychology and different morality from man—such as the plutonian Palainians who are as cowardly as Nivens' Puppeteers, or the placid Rigelians who are morally perfect but too placid and inert to commit heroic acts, or the berserk and bipolar Velantians — all are faced with a common threat, and all are loyal to the ideas of reason and the ideals of civilization and democracy.

Everything from *Star Trek* to the composition of your average party of adventurers in an *Advanced Dungeons & Dragons* game reflects this "melting pot" idea of the Galactic Patrol. I cannot bring to mind an example where the underlying tale is not a war story, or an expedition or adventure involving physical danger, because that is the kind of thing where team spirit is both necessary and expected.

In such stories, if the story is done right, the elements or quirks that make each race different from the others are present, but are overcome by their common camaraderie, their team spirit. When it is badly done, the aliens are just humans in stage makeup, and all their differences are on the surface, so there is nothing for the team spirit to overcome.

I should mention that many of the most famous science fiction authors have some of the least convincing aliens. This may be due to the editorial influence of John W. Campbell, Jr., who did not like stories where aliens were superior to humans in any way.

But, for example, in Robert Heinlein's *Have Space Suit—Will Travel*, the Wormfaces are just monsters. There is no pity spared for any of them, none have names, none express any regret or differences of opinion about their role as world conquerors and eaters of man. And the Mother Thing, one of Heinlein's best aliens, is suspiciously similar to the Mother from Williamson's *The Moon Era*, which I mentioned above. The Mother Thing has one personality trait: she is loving. Heinlein does a better job with his Martians from *Stranger In A Strange Land*, by making them, in their adult stage, sexless, and therefore, according to Heinlein's theory of psychology, utterly lacking in drive and ambition.

Again, the aliens in Arthur C. Clarke, such as his Overlords in *Childhood's End* or his monolith-builders in *2001: A Space Odyssey,* are not really alien as much as transcendent and incomprehensible: Tweel with godlike powers.

The prize for the best aliens, in my judgment, should go to Poul Anderson. I hope I will be forgiven if I praise this lesser known author too much, but he actually took the time to invent plausible social and psychological differences between his invented creatures and mankind and base them on plausible differences of biology, sexual strategy, diet and evolution.

I will point out that fantasy and fairytale rarely if ever portray the nonhuman intelligences, talking dragons or singing elves, encountered in the tale as unlike man, except that the supernatural or infernal creatures are greater in age or dignity or power.

Elves usually have kings and queens as we do, and rarely —Tolkien is the great exception—do they have histories and kingdoms and wars. In this regard, Tolkien's elves are almost indistinguishable from Man. They seem to be long lived men, the main difference being that they are not under the curse of Adam, in that they do not seem to plough fields and grow crops and send out fisher-folk for food. If they hunt, it is for sport. The point of Tolkienian elves is that they are unlike Shakespearean elves in *A Midsummer Night's Dream,* who were diminutive tricksters and sly spirits. But note again both the elves of Tolkien and Shakespeare are closer to nature than Man, or are at one with nature, or are its guardians and tenders.

Now, some say the elves and dwarves of myth and legend are the lesser spirits or fallen gods toppled from Olympus by the triumph of the God of Abraham and the growth past polytheism into a more sophisticated world-view, that is, they are a memory of the Old Gods which echoes in the nursery tale. I have my doubts: such explanations strike me as "just so" stories invented after the fact to explain stories without explaining them: giving the efficient cause rather than the formal cause. I am more inclined to believe the simpler story that elves are spirits of the woods, like dryads, and mermaids are sirens and sea fairies, and dwarves are earth spirits or svartalfar, personifications of the powers and beauties and terrors of nature, or memories of angelic powers, fallen or unfallen, our ancestors dimly sensed moving behind the stage scenery of the world.

You see, no one by definition can desire a communion or community with a beast, or a tree, or a mountain, a sunset or a storm or a sea wide beyond awe's own power to measure. What we all yearn for, those of us who are not unfit in our hearts, is communion and speech with the intelligence behind these things, the spirit of nature, or, if you will permit me, the author of nature. Those with fit hearts can tell instinctively from the beauty and order of nature that a great and potent Creator made all these wonders.

If Mother Nature were the blind machine the moderns blaspheme her to be, none of her products would make us catch our breath in fearful admiration, neither nebulae nor novae nor rearing stallions nor rushing rivers nor gentle rains nor the smile of the rainbow. If there is no Designer, there is no grand design to admire, except perhaps for that which the pattern-seeking frailty of the human mind, staring at a Rorschach inkblot, decides to deceive us into imagining we see.

At this point, we can answer the two parts of the question that was asked at the beginning.

Snow White can cajole the beasts of the wild to aid her housekeeping because she is an image of sweetness and innocence; and one of the most powerful images of innocence, the innocence of Eden, is the image of Nature herself blessing and loving and aiding the unfallen innocent. A clear and charming symbol of this blessing is the aid of natural animals bestowing their friendship, and a clear and charming symbol of the supernatural nature of the aid is to have the animals cross the gap severing the sad children of man from Eden, to act, for an afternoon, for a brief and magical hour of music, as man's true friends, able to aid us in our work.

We are all exiles here. Christians believe this literally, but nearly all of mankind no matter of what belief feels at times the same way.

(Perhaps John Galt from Ayn Rand's *Atlas Shrugged* is an exception: but then again, by his own bold estimation, he is a prelapsarian man, since he boasts of being untouched by original sin.)

We yearn for the blessing of Nature and communion with her, and this yearning, for reasons only Christians can explain, is a nostalgic one.

As I say, to tell stories about unfallen virgins in fairy tales or savage princes able to tame bears and wrestle lions, which is fairy tale; and to tell stories about the talking animals of other planets, which is science fiction; or the talking animals of earth, or elfin spirits of wood and mountain, which is fantasy — all such tales are like looking at a picture of an absent loved one.

And, despite what other science fiction authors will tell you, the evidence for life on other planets is and continues to be zip, zilch, nada, nothing, and the evidence for intelligent life is even less, and even if they were there, no electronic signal of ours will ever reach them nor any of their signals reach us—space is just too big and life is just too short and the speed of light is just too slow. From a purely scientific point of view, there is more evidence of Elves than there is evidence of Martians. We have at least some eyewitness reports of elves seen by people in Iceland.

So why is the intelligent alien one of the most common ideas in science fiction?

Why do we tell imaginative tales like this? A detective story, even an unlikely one, could be true, and could happen, as could a story about cowboys or pirates or knights or braves or samurai, and love stories could happen and do. But no muskrat is ever going to clean your sink, and I sincerely doubt a boy raised by wolves is going to defeat a tiger in combat. And you will never talk to a Martian.

Why? The first reason I already said. We are lonely for the nonhuman intelligences which science fiction fans speculate may be in the heavens, and which Christians firmly believe compose the stellar hosts of heaven.

The second is a far more powerful reason. If Man were merely an intelligent animal, something derived by blind natural selection, and bred only for our ability to continue breeding, then we would not tell stories. It is a useless habit, one that neither secures food nor wards off predators nor aids in the seduction and rape of she-humans nor increases the number of her spawn.

Some might say that it is a side effect of language using ability, a defect of the brain, so that we humans misuse that faculty of imagination nature evolved in us solely for planning military campaigns against rival tribes of mastodon hunters, and the linguistic skills to coordinate hunting and fishing and slaying rivals. Some might say language was evolved to be precise and scientific, merely a tool for remembering facts of the past we have seen and constructing speculations of the future we shall see, and that this tool of language is misused if we play make-believe about things not of the past or future, and attempt to peer into the unseen realm. I say those who say storytelling is an abuse of the faculty of language are abusing their own faculty of language, and telling us a story, and a bad one.

I propose we want to give tongues to animals and woods and waves, and we want to command the mountains and the clouds to speak to us, because we yearn to be creators ourselves. What greater gift can any father give his child than to teach him the gift of speech? If we had the power to grant this gift to our pets and livestock, surely we would, and indeed, to exchange defiance and threats and terrifying boasts with the lions and wolves who are the enemies of man would also be a delight. Beyond this, to speak to the river and ask it why it runs, or to the sunshine and inquire of its cheer, or to command the raging storm be silent, this is a delight that saints and angels know which man, exiled from Eden, has lost. We are dumb and deaf in a world given to our dominion.

I propose that there is something of the creator in the poet, and that this is because we are created by a Creator in His own likeness and image, and so naturally must reflect the nature of creation in us. We want to bring things to life, to create worlds, to grant speech to animals and to command nature, because that is the joy of creation.

We cannot, in this life, create worlds, except in fiction. We cannot possibly have this desire from anything in nature. It is supernatural in origin.

It is like a young man in love daydreaming about the words and sighs and kisses he means to exchange with his beloved. The daydream raptures him, and draws his thoughts away from the dirt and toil of his daily life, and for an hour, in his heart, he dwells in the bliss of the honeymoon cottage. But there is an element of sorrow and longing and sadness in his daydream, or in him, because it is not real. It does not truly satisfy him.

Let me end, as befits a writer of speculative fiction, with a final speculation. Should we ever find a world like Perelandra, whose happy natives resisted the temptations that toppled the Adam and Eve of Earth, or should we ever reach in a next life the cosmic realms inhabited by archangels and dominions and potentates and powers, it is possible that they might not tell stories of the imaginative kind discussed here. Psalms and hymns, to be sure, or epics of praise for glorious deeds, or love songs, or all the other kinds of tales the other muses inspire, all might be present in the unfallen world.

But stories of fairytale and fantasy and science fiction I speculate may indeed be absent in those happier and higher realms. The saints in heaven will have realized the immense longing we here in exile on Earth cannot fulfill on Earth. They will do as their Father does and sing the songs of creation.

Imagine instead of imagining the talking cats of Kzin or dragons of Pern, using the gift of speech as we all secretly know it is meant to be used, and speaking the worlds and stars into being.

Why should they daydream, and not do? No youth sighs over his beloved's picture when she is in the bridal bower and demurely shedding her veil.

4

SCIENCE FICTION, WHAT IS IT
GOOD FOR?

One thing no science fiction writer inventing any future predicted was the future where science fiction replaced the mainstream literature.

It was foreseeable—mainstream fiction, after all, was never mainstream. So-called mainstream literature is a modern and recent invention, and was meant to appeal only to a limited audience of limited taste, an audience with an artificially cramped and narrow view of reality. In the same way time casts down tall towers and crumbles empires to dust, so too it throws down artifices.

One of the artificial things that happened was that the literary mainstream decreed, as a matter of dogma, that matters fantastic and wonderful, the doings of saints and demigods and their wars with demons and dragons, and anything that smelled like Elfland, or even like adventure-land, would be banished.

There would be no more flights to the moon on hippogriff-back, nor faces that launched a thousand ships, nor witches who turn sailors to swine, nor voyages to the land of the dead, nor wrestling matches with man-eating

Grendel, nor swords upheld from the bosom of the lake by arms clad in shimmering samite, nor three weird sisters prophesying the doom of kings.

And the matter of science fiction, Martian invasions and time machines and invisible men, was exiled from highbrow literature. It is telling to note that this degree of exile fell during the years when the most daring prophecies of Jules Verne and his fantastic machines that swam beneath the sea or thundered through the air were just beginning to come true.

Human nature, for better or worse, always eventually comes to the fore again. And human nature likes and needs stories that are stories.

The artifice of exiling the fantastic in literature cuts against the nature both of story-teller and story-lover, since stories by their nature are nursery tales, concerned with simple moral truths and talking animals. Only as they develop do tales take on other tasks, such as to glorify heroes, and keep alive the memories of our forefathers and their deeds, and to celebrate the blessings bestowed on one's people, tribe, and nation, and express wonder and gratitude for the gift of living in this gorgeous and dangerous world.

Does it strike you as odd, perhaps even insane, to hear the duty of a teller of tales described in this fashion? When is the last time you heard a story that told a simple moral truth, or even that took place in a universe where moral truths were true? When is the last time you heard a fiction that glorified Washington, or Jefferson, or Adams, rather than deconstructed them? When is the last time the wonder of the universe was the subject of a passage in a story or poem you read?

It is almost as if the tellers of tales think their duty is not to these things, but to undermine, question, satirize, mock and subvert these things. It is as if the tellers of modern tales think their duty is to unnerve the audience, unsettle tradition, and overthrow the American way of life, Christian faith, and Western love of reason.

I will not dwell on this particular point further; you have perhaps yourself heard tellers of tales expressly say that their purpose is subversion. They cast themselves in the role of playing the Socratic gadfly, to sting the complaisant into questioning their values. But Socrates questioned things to learn the truth of things, that he might live the examined life, that he might know himself. And men who hold all truth to be relative, or to be a fable meant to uphold an unjust social order, have no purpose to their questions, except to erode the world.

Let us turn to the question of when and why this wrong turn happened. Others have written on this topic more fully than can I. I will mention only in brief that it became the fashion—and it was only the fashion of a season, not an irrevocable evolution as claimed—to write and read stories about quotidian things, about drunks and adulterers and ordinary people suffering ordinary problems.

From the pages of glossy magazines were banished all pirate gold and secret passageways and secret societies run by masterminds called the Napoleon of Crime. The evil instead was quotidian, the treachery of philandering husbands or crooked businessmen, not the plundering of drug-maddened Voodoo cultists or berserk Vikings or the hordes of Tamerlane. The good was quotidian as well, the bravery of farmers or housewives or clerks facing poverty or social injustice, and not the bold and chivalrous acts of a Paladin of Charlemagne or a lone Texas Ranger facing paynims or outlaws or painted savages.

Unromance was the order of the day: ordinary events

happening to ordinary people, usually without much plot. You need drama to have plot, and drama requires the bold clash of starkest black and brightest white, heroes and villains both larger than life. When the emphasis is on realism, or what is called realism, the three-act structure of a plot, the setup and climax and resolution, begins to seem artificial. And in a world where there is no good and evil, and nothing worth fighting for, there is insufficient tension to have a satisfactory plot.

With no other occupation for their genius, the teller of the storyless story then concentrates merely on technique, on wit, on the telling of ordinary events, the tedium and small betrayals of ordinary life, with as much verbal pyrotechnics as possible, layers of allusion, riddles of words and unexpected contrasts of metaphor, or experimental techniques, such as writing without punctuation marks. And so, step by step, we descend into the plotless purgatory of works like *Ulysses* by James Joyce.

Obviously no one of sound taste enjoys reading such a book. Its appeal is to those rare and sick minds that vomit up wholesome fare, who hate fairy tales and police dramas and romances and Westerns and historical pageants. The sickness is a rejection, through ennui, of all that is romantic and splendid and heavenly and hellish and dramatic and grandiose and sublime both in this world and the next.

The mind that says the quotidian is all that there is or all that is worthwhile shies back from greater worlds. He is not seeking grandeur in everyday things, (for that grandeur indeed is there, if you know how to seek it). He is seeking a darkness to destroy the grandeur. He seeks to strangle laughter with a sneer. Can anyone recall a single joke, simple and good-natured, not an irony and not a witticism, appearing in *Ulysses*?

Such was the mainstream. But notice, please, the earliest limit on what is rightly called mainstream. *Das Rheingold* by Wagner, if written these days, with its fables of pagan gods and giants, abominable gnomes and mercurial mermaids, would be accepted only by the science fiction and fantasy publishers, not by the prestigious mainstream printing houses.

The romances of Jane Austen and Margaret Mitchell may perhaps, if we stretch a point, be considered mainstream, but by their emphasis on the follies of love or the manners of the rich, or the tumult of war and its aftermath, the mood and tone is certainly antithetical to the realism beloved of this narrow school of writing I decry as mainstream. Romances belong in the popular mainstream, which is a different (albeit connected) stream from the literary mainstream.

I propose that the earliest writer properly called mainstream in both the popular and literary sense was Charles Dickens: and yet his earliest book, and the best remembered title, is his *A Christmas Carol*, which is a ghost story as much as is *Hamlet*, and a time travel story as much as anything by H.G. Wells. So even at this late date in history, the realistic and the fantastic were still Siamese Twins, two parts of the same body.

Notice that everything before that time, the work of Shakespeare and Dante and Milton and Aristophanes and Euripides and Homer and everything in between was not mainstream, or, rather, there was nothing outside the mainstream. Shakespeare would write about magicians like Prospero as easily as about kings like Richard or braggarts like Toby Belch. Aeschylus could write about Prometheus the titan as easily as about Cassandra the slave-girl. There simply was no division or demarcation between so called realistic and fantastic stories. All stories were realistic; all stories were fantastic.

What, then, was it that formed what we now call the mainstream? I say it was the Great War. The First World War crippled something in the consciousness of Europe, and in the intellect of the European Intellectuals, and our envious intellectuals in America, seeking for some reason approval from the genius of Europe which we fled here to avoid, followed along like dogs chasing a parade wagon.

I suggest that the mainstream was not a philosophy, but a feeling or a fashion, that is, an emotional stance that was never put into words. It was a deliberate rejection at first of only the openly fantastic things, dragons and invaders from Mars; then next it was a rejection of the things that are fantastic but which some people take as real, such as ghosts or the sunken continent of Atlantis; and finally a rejection of those things which are fantastic and wonderful in real life, the heroism of ordinary men, the saintliness of ordinary women, not one of whom is truly ordinary.

Not just men died in the Great War, but an entire social and political system, and, more importantly, a spirit of the nations, a vision and view of life which was their animating principle. Before the Great War, they believed in ideals like nobility and tradition, in the private ownership of property and the duty to serve the public weal. They believed in virgin maidens and faithful wives. They believed in private modesty as well as public pomp, kings and queens arrayed in gold and purple. They believed in the captains of industry and the captains of war, the silk hats and the tin hats.

Now, if you are a child of the modern age, you are already hearing a voice in your ear, whispering: that the Victorians did not actually believe in chastity, since they had

more whores per square mile of London than any era before
or since. That nobility is merely the rich grinding the faces
of the poor. That pomp is vanity. That industry is plutocracy.
That war is hell, and Colonels are devils in hell. And on
and on.

Did you hear it? I would be surprised if you did not. It is
in the air we breathe, it is part of our unspoken cultural
assumptions. It is the effluvium that rises like a mist from
the words and ideas of the mainstream literature, movies
and songs and media in which we are immersed and
drenched. It is the voice of accusation. It is the voice of division. It is the sneer of scorn.

The fundamental idea that died in the Great War was
the idea of Christianity. That was when God actually died in
the soul of European history. By the end of the Second
World War, which was actually the second round of the
same war, God and His law no longer had the majority influence in shaping the laws and institutions of the Europeans.
They thought about other considerations first.

Let me be clear: these ideas were decades older than the
Great War. That war was only the final point of no return,
the point at which the ever steeper drop of the slope into
darkness became a brink.

The attacks against the concept of the divine were as old
as Lucretius, as old as Eden. But in the Eighteenth and Nineteenth Century these crackpot notions gained respectability,
slowly won over the intellectuals, who lured the rest of
society toward their simplistically elegant and simply wrong
notions.

So, the artistic world is nothing but the concrete images
that make real and solid the emotional and spiritual
atmosphere of the age. The artistic world lost faith in

romance and grandeur and adventure during and after the Great War because it lost faith in God.

The barren and roaring chaos of the universe presented to the imagination of him who regards God as myth is void and sad, filled with mindless violence and meaningless pain, and the Great War was as sad and meaningless, as truly horrible as any event in history.

This world view is not even tragic. Tragedy is cathartic. The empty events, the impact of dinosaur-killing asteroids, the broken legs of monuments of Ozymandias found in antique lands, the sheer emptiness of the blind star-gulfs overhead where our ancestors thought the angels danced— all life in such a world is merely meaningless, a grain of dust lost in a desiccated desert.

So a movement started to expunge the gold and purple, the glory and the nobility, the gaiety and wonder, and most of all the miracles from art and literature.

No more paintings of the Creation on the Sistine Chapel; instead we have paintings of cans, of Campbell's soup cans. No more dragons nor knights, no more Pre-Raphaelites. Instead, we have Picasso, and scrawls a baboon could make by ingesting paint, and splashing out colors by flinging his poop.

Ghosts and supernatural evils were, naturally, harder to expunge, since they are more in line with the emotional makeup of the empty and godless universe. Supernatural horrors are in keeping with the horrors of discovering life to be meaningless and love to be a sour joke: writers like Edgar Allan Poe, despite his connection to popular genres of detective and horror tales, retained his respectable place among in the eyes of the self-appointed guardians of literature.

The mainstream maintained itself artificially. Whenever a book that started as a mainstream novel, such as, let us say,

Gone With The Wind or *Casino Royale*, which had the fire of romance or intrigue, adventures in times long gone or in exotic locales across the sea, if its more fantastic and romantic elements caught the public imagination and other writers began writing in the same background, the novels were thereafter considered "genre" novels, love-stories or spy thrillers, and no longer of interest to the literati.

Science fiction preserved the exiled creatures of the fantastic through these dry years. Science fiction rather cleverly exploits a loophole in the whole worldview that rejects the supernatural. The loophole is that wonder still persists in the unknown, which includes other planets and future advancements. And where there is wonder, and where there is the unknown, the gods and giants and abominable dwarves can make their appearance again, disguised perhaps as Morlocks or Martians or Monolith-builders, higher powers and lower monsters. And even, thanks to Anne McCaffrey and E.E. Doc Smith, dragons can return once more, disguised as extraterrestrials from Pern or from the haunted planet Velantia.

Fantasy made a slower comeback, and at first even science fiction readers were wary of it. There were a number of fantasy worlds with all the tropes and props of medievalism and the supernatural, but set in space with the magic called psionics to give it the glamor of scientific respectability.

After Tolkien, fantasy slowly but steadily re-conquered the territory that the mainstream had usurped. Look at the top ten best-selling movies of recent years, and odds are that eight or nine of them out of ten will be movies with some fantastic or supernatural element, from *The Wizard Of Oz* to *It's A Wonderful Life* to *Star Wars* to *Superman* to *Avatar*.

When persons known for their allegiance to the self-anointed elite, pundits and pedants and the President of the United States, can make casual references to Jedi mind-powers or the One Ring from Mordor, then space opera and fantasy epic have sunk into the marrow bones of the popular imagination. When books that, in my day, a schoolboy would be chastised for bringing to class are now required textbook reading, and when South American writers can write science fiction and fantasy and have it be smuggled into the literary establishment by being called 'magical realism'—well, at that point, it is not premature to read the eulogy of the narrow literate fashion of the mainstream.

The term of exile is over.

Mainstream writers can write once again about fantastic things: love affairs with vampires, let us say, or science fiction dystopias who slay the children of the rural under-class in annual gladiatorial games.

Star Wars, more than any one single cause, brought science fiction out of its ghetto and into the public eye. Now note this irony: since before the days of Michael Moorcock's 'New Wave' of science fiction, writers of sciffy yearned for the aura of respectability surrounding the European literati and their New York epigones, the subversive and experimental writers who concentrated on style and ignored story-telling.

In order to play their guitars of seduction before the moonlit windows of the proud fair maidens of the elite, the envious science fictioneers attempted to play the songs that found favor in their ears. The attempt was doomed from the start, because the thing the elite disliked in the science fiction field was the field itself, that is, the sense of wonder, the belief in the future, the love of the fantastic, the glory of utopia and the horror of dystopia.

We did not win the favor of the mainstream by adopting the tropes and formulae of high literary style into our humble craft of telling stories about space princesses being rescued by loveable space rogues and poor but honest space farmboys who grow into space knights with way cool mind-powers. It was a film, deliberately made to echo and glorify the most lowbrow and popular elements of that least literate branch of sci-fi, namely, the Buck Rogers style space opera, which enamored the public. It was a simple tale about a space princess being rescued by a loveable space rogue and a poor but honest space farmboy who grows into a space knight with way cool mind-powers. The mountain, so to speak, came to us.

There were other factors, to be sure. With the flop of the Soviet Union, the elite's dream about heaven on earth lost most of its magnetic and mesmeric force. There was also an inherent logical contradiction built into the nasty and narrow fashion of unfantastic fiction, because the same worldview which subverted all authority from God in Heaven to the cop on the street corner, subverted the cause of virtue by enabling and magnifying the Cult of Youth. Impulsive action, provided it was "authentic" or heartfelt, was glorified above self-discipline, and the energy of youth was glorified above the justice and prudence and courage and temperance of age. Unfortunately for the cause of the unfantastic in fiction, youth is as naturally allured to the fantastic as they are to the idealistic.

They grew up continuing to like childish things, super-heroes and space opera, and did not put their childish things away as the elite, with sneers, demanded. They continued to feast on tales of heroes: the childish things were also the noble things.

Young men want noble things, to slay dragons and

rescue damsels in distress, to help widows and orphans and win glory. Young women want even nobler things, to be rescued by a handsome prince on a white charger with a heart of fearless gold and a sword of peerless fire. And they want to win the kind of men who win glory.

Many a young man these days, poisoned by the venom of envy called feminism, will deny this, and even more young women. Then the men will go out and read paperbacks about spies or special forces officers who do what knights do, and the women go out and read paperbacks about heiresses kept as wards by scheming guardians who need to be rescued by brooding yet stalwart young barons.

It may be inconvenient to the pretenses on which the modern unfantastical literary fashion is based to say that people like things that they have always liked in stories. But human nature will out. For good or ill, for fair or foul, human nature will out.

And the young men (it was more men than women) found the principalities and the principles they sought in science fiction. And the young women (it was more women than men) found the princesses they sought in the field of fantasy.

The literary are still aghast at the popularity of authors like Robert Heinlein and Anne McCaffrey. But he fed the imagination of the young, and told them how to be good rebels and statesmen in the American Revolution on the Moon, or how to be good citizens and soldiers and good starship troopers, or how to be naughty little messiahs from Mars and get all the girls. And she fed the imagination with the simple and simply satisfying formula of retelling the Cinderella fable over and over again, about the overlooked and ignored young heroine who grows into her greatness.

Heinlein and McCaffrey appealed to the reader's human nature.

Anyone who is unimpressed with sneering atheism will be unimpressed by the famous science fiction works by Margaret Atwood or the fantasy of Phillip Pullman and those of their ilk. Pullman was as blasphemous as Heinlein was in *Stranger In A Strange Land*, but not as funny, and the ending of his *His Dark Materials* was dark indeed and unsatisfying. (Pullman's hero and heroine end up parted by a law of nature invented at the last minute by a lazy author, which decrees that persons of different earths in the multiverse sicken and die if they immigrate).

It is the kind of thing one reads when a surfeit of happy endings leaves a bad taste in the mouth, and you need a swish of pagan vinegar to wash out all that Christian saccharine endemic to Western civilization. Everyone likes a vacation from happiness occasionally, I suppose.

The miserable and empty universe of the pagans after the Gotterdammerung has slain the cruel but noble gods is a nice place to visit, but no place to set up a household and raise your kids.

The artistic images of the emotional world of the unfantastic fashion are like the melancholic world of the pagans, where fate is deadly and there is no escape, where not even swift Achilles can outrun his doom: Like the pagan world, but lacking the bravery of a Conan who gaily curses great Crom, his god, even while praying to him, and without the dignity of a Horatio who proclaims the sweetness and decorum of dying for the ashes of one's fathers and the altars of one's gods.

Gods are as despised as fathers in the one-dimensional world of unfantasy, and nothing is worse than death, simply because the mindless biological process known as life is the only life that there is.

To live in a universe-sized concentration camp ruled by rough tyrants like Zeus and Crom is bad enough. To live in a universe-sized coffin without even a tyrant god as a tormentor is unimaginable.

And, to be sure, those who live in such universes do their best to banish the imagination from their stories, and to write make-believe only about beliefs that require no making: fictional versions of newspapers and diaries.

The majority of human history and the three dimensions of human nature, spiritual as well as mental and physical, are lost on writers who are one-dimensional.

Lest I be misunderstood, or accused of overweening pride, let me hasten to say that Atwood and Pullman are admittedly skilled and worthy of the awards and plaudits they have won. This does not mean they are broad in their choice of subject and approaches. An artist can draw a picture of the rotting skull of a dead dog on a dungheap with maggots and blind worms crawling on its exposed brains with perfect perspective, shading, composition, and balance of light and dark, and yet it is still a picture of a dead dog.

Writers like Pullman and Atwood are like Mr. A Square of Flatland. The spiritual and philosophical dimensions of reality are closed to them.

(Yes, I say these allegedly philosophically deep authors lack philosophy if they lack knowledge of the spirit. Philosophy without theology is a word game for bored schoolboys like Wittgenstein and for dull-eyed egomaniacs like Nietzsche, not a method to tell men how to live and how to die; the modern attempts to draw out the implications of such philosophies have ended in paradox and pettifoggery, and have drawn modern philosophy into well-merited contempt.)

Very well: let us now take it as given that science fiction is in the mainstream again, and fantasy writers like Tolkien occupy the high position once held by Wagner and Shakespeare and other writers who touch on fantastic things, or who put gods or ghosts, Alberich or Caliban, without a blush into their tales.

What now? Whither goes the future of science fiction and fantasy? What is it for? What purpose does it serve?

We know what purpose removing imaginative and fantastic elements from literature served: it was for the admitted purpose of subversion, to denigrate Western Civilization, which is another name for that energetic, frantic, and progress-loving and reason-loving civilization issuing from Europe, North Africa, Asia Minor and the Middle East which is animated by the spirit of the Christian Church, and which dies without it.

Are you surprised, O reader, to hear me call Christianity the spirit and soul of reason and progress? The words have been successfully subverted to refer to their mere opposites. Contrast, if you will, the gaiety and boldness of a civilization that eliminated the slave trade worldwide, despite the economic loss involved, with the grinding passivity of civilizations like those of Imperial China or caste-based India or the tyrannies of the Aztecs and Mayans, where the soul is scraped clean of hope, faith, and charity by a view of the world which promises an endless wheel of eternal reincarnations, without a creation, without a cessation.

Now imagine that same hopelessness without even the inhuman justice of Karma, without the promise of a next life, and you have the image of what a Post-Christian civilization would be like: rule by a caste of Mandarins without the honesty of admitting it to be a caste system, with as many human sacrifices as the Aztecs—without the candor of calling the many victims aborted in the womb or slain by the slow torture of dehydration in the sickbed of the terminal ward "human". Call that nightmare world what you will, but you cannot call it a fruit of progress or a scion of right reason without telling such lies as makes men lose their souls.

If to usher in the dystopia of a Post-Christian world was the point of removing imagination from literature, of removing the making from the make-believe, what is the purpose of restoring the imagination?

Ah, one might as well wonder what is the purpose of wonder? What is the purpose of art?

The question has confounded and preoccupied wiser heads than mine, and yet the answer, or part of it, seems clear enough even to a humble inquiry. For if we imagine a world without imagination, we will see what it serves.

Picture if you will some inhuman race of Lunar insects or Martian mollusks or posthuman Morlocks as envisioned by H.G. Wells who are as rational as man, who can plan for the future and perform abstract intellectual operations as mathematics and science might require. They have all the virtues proper to beings of their condition, let us say, and let us grant that they are more admirable than mankind in this area, being more peaceful, perhaps, or showing more compassion for the poor.

But they tell no stories.

Let us say the Morlocks have news reports, and have also a faculty for distinguishing central elements to be left in the report with peripheral elements to be discarded. They can tell stories of things that really happened. But they have no imagination, no ability to mix and match elements from their history and environment and invent a realistic unreality. The Morlocks have no ability (as we Houyhnhnms call it) to "say the thing that is not."

What would be lacking from their lives? Obviously the question can only be answered poetically, not literally. They would lack that oasis, and fountainhead, and wellspring where we mortal men seek waking dreams to refresh us. They would lack the waters of the Hippocrene that restore the soul or the wine of Bragi that elevates the spirit. They would lack for nothing but nectar and ambrosia.

All stories that are proper stories take place in the mental universe where the supernatural is possible. Even a perfectly worldly story like *War And Peace* or *The Brothers Karamazov* occurs in a mental landscape where the miracles of saints or the visions of the dead might happen, even if they, during the events described, happen not to be encountered; but the wonders and horror of wars that shake the world are encountered, or crimes that question the justice of God do happen.

Stories serve several quotidian purposes. I listed them above: they are fables to instruct the young and epics to preserve the memory of the great, and ghost stories to tell about campfires to give us all a sense of proportion and remind us, (like the charioteers of Caesars during their triumphs and ovations), that all men are mortal. But there is something more that they serve, a purpose which is utterly unworldly, and utterly inexplicable to the Morlocks, who have no imagination, and need none.

We sons of Adam are exiles here on this world. It does not suit us. We are not comfortable here, and those who say they are comfortable in this world of injustice and disease and death are not more sane and more well adapted to the environment than we who dream; they are merely inert in their souls, too dull to hear the horns of Elfland softly blowing.

We tell stories because we are homesick for heaven and afraid of hell. We make stuff up because we don't know or remember what it might be like on the other side, the unspoiled side, of life.

Here in this world, justice loses, and beauty is weak, and truth is shouted down, and everything goes wrong. But we know, in our souls if not in our hearts, that we deserve better. We deserve and yearn for a world where justice triumphs, and beauty is all powerful and truth cannot be quenched by lies any more than insubstantial shadows can fly from earth to the center of the solar system and strangle the sun. So, to remind ourselves of what we have forgotten, we talk about times in real life when justice triumphed, or the beauty was not marred, or truth could not be hidden. And for the same reason we tell tragedies when the truth destroys men like Oedipus or justice carries out a fearful vengeance on man like Agamemnon; and yes, again, we tell ironic stories, stories that grin like skulls, where all these things go wrong, and innocent men are buried alive or children die in their prayers and leering evil triumphs, and this reminds us that we do not belong in the world where these things happen. As I said above, these bitter stories of horror and despair are a vacation meant to clear the palate, a sour lime and bitter salt after the tequila.

Even those of us who do not believe, in our heads, in other worlds beyond this world, and other lives after this life, show by the types of stories we take for our myths and legends and epics and nursery tales that, in our souls, our dreams are better than our lives. If these dreams come from nowhere and for no purpose, then all dreams are vain, or are opiates, and the unfantasists are right to condemn and

eschew them as escapism. They are as right to banish
wishful fantasies of Arthurian knights and giant-slaying
Jacks and Homeric heroes and shining samurai as they are
to scoff at fantastic nightmares of blood-drinking ghosts and
haunted cities beneath the sea, monsters in the dark or in
the cracks between the ulterior dimensions of timespace.

If the unfantasists are right, there is nothing before the
blood of childbirth and after the mud of the grave, and what
lies in between is the stingy happiness which the pursuit of
meaningless pleasure can find, or vain ambition, or love
which is like a drowning couple clinging to each other's
warm bodies in a maelstrom, eager for one last kiss before
the storms eat them, and no memory is left.

But if the dreams are echoes of the real primordial
disaster that is still reverberating through the cosmos with
the fall of Lucifer or the fall of Adam, or if the dreams are
whispers through the crack in the prison wall of mortal life
from immortal lips outside, then escape is not only our joy,
but our duty.

Science fiction looks to the future, or to the extraterrestrial wonders of the present, or to anything odd and above
the merely quotidian to inspire and fire our dreams. It
requires less faith in the unseen or supernatural than wilder
stories told by Shakespeare or Milton or Virgil, because the
skeptical imagination cannot be skeptical toward the idea
that skeptical inquiry into the roots of nature yields technical and scientific advancements which, by definition, we
cannot now, trapped in the present, know. Nor can the scientific curiosity be incurious about the curious things which
curiosity might uncover. The very core of science fiction is
the certainty that the future is uncertain, that things change,
either in progress or regress or both at once, and even the
most unimaginative imagination must admit that the future

world and extraterrestrial worlds are unimaginable. It offers an escape from the everyday, which even those who hate escapism cannot call escapist.

What is science fiction for? One might as well ask what a window in a jail cell is for, or what a magic mirror in a wizard's cell is for.

5

JOHN C. WRIGHT'S PATENTED ONE-SESSION LESSON IN THE MECHANICS OF FICTION

Here is the John C. Wright patented one-session lesson in the mechanics of how to write fiction.

A word of explanation:

I wrote the following to a friend of mine who is a nonfiction writer of some fame and accomplishment, who was toying with the idea of writing fiction. We batted around some ideas and I have been encouraging (read: pestering) him to take up the project seriously.

He wrote back and said that while putting the logical format to a work of nonfiction was clear enough, he was not big on this artistic and poetical stuff. I took it upon myself to show him the logic behind the stuff that dreams are made of.

So here is what I wrote to provoke him to write, and I share it with any and all comers who wish alike to be writers.

For my part, I am eager to share my trade secrets. I do not fear competition. Unlike every other field, my value as a writer goes up, not down, the more competition I have, because more science fiction writers means more science fiction readers, a larger field, and more money in the field.

So I think everyone should try his hand at writing. I cannot read my own work for pleasure, after all.

~

LET me try to encourage you. First, get that book I recommended, *Writing The Breakout Novel* by Donald Maass. Second, actually set aside time to write your novel, time when you are not allowed to do anything else or find any other distractions. Sit and stare at the blank page for four hours. The tedium will either break your brain or break open any writer's block.

I am so totally not kidding: if you want to learn kung fu, you must learn to break bricks with your head. If you want to be a fiction writer, you must learn to stare at a blank page with nothing but your name on the top without flinching, without weeping, without getting up to get a beer to fortify your faltering courage.

How it is done? How does one fill in the horrid pallid blankness of the blank paper, as monstrous as the whiteness of the White Whale sought by Ahab? Good question. There is a craft to it, a certain mechanic.

Let us take an example of a hypothetical first chapter of a hypothetical book. Let us pretend the book is called *Old Men Shall Dream Dreams*.

Chapter 1: The Nightmare on Notting Hill

At first, I thought he was carrying the corpse of a child.
My professor of Applied Military Theology, Colonel

MacNab, came walking slowly into my little room in southeast London, the little oblong box on his back, and a cold and grim look on his features. I stood up and pulled off my cap, and MacNab scowled. "Not to worry. 'Tis not human. We think. Clear a space and give us hand, there's a good lad."

It was dark except for the moon, and the streets below had been cleared of traffic. The only noise from outside was the clatter of an anti-aircraft gun being pulled by a team of horses up the lane toward the churchyard, and the swearing of the teamster.

I pushed the papers I was grading to one side, and the pint of bitter to another. This unfortunately put it within the Professor's reach, and while I was hauling the small coffin off his shoulders to the table, he helped himself to a long swig at my drink, which I thought most unsanitary of him. "You have terrible taste in ale, lad!" he exclaimed, wiping his mustache on his sleeve and raising my mug for a second long pull. "When are you going to stop drinking this penny-shop swill? Did you make it in your bathtub?"

I drew the blackout curtains and lit a lamp from the fireplace. He bent to open the casket lid.

Whatever I was expecting, it was not this. I crept slowly closer, raising the lamp, and the yellow light spilled over the little body. It was no bigger than three feet, dressed in a bright green jacket, complete with folded cuffs with brass buttons, a waistcoat with knee breeches. It looked like a gentrified yeoman or squire from the last century.

The hair on its head was dark and curly, as was the thick hair on its bare feet. There was some stubble on its cheeks, enough to prove this was no child. The eyes had not been sewn shut, and one of them was open, showing a milky white slit behind, watching me sardonically. The body had been packed in little fragrant leaves, so there was no smell. The *decomposition was not advanced: the skin was colorless and dark, and pulled back slightly from the lips.*

"Was this what the German agents were trying to smuggle out of Notting Hill?" I asked MacNab. "A circus clown? Why did they bury him in costume?"

MacNab snorted, "Clown! The Oldfoots of Southfarthing are not a large clan, but their roots go back to the origins of the Shire. He is Odro son of Otho. Or so the letter we recovered in his vest pocket says. The fairytale languages department translated it."

"Who is he?"

"An imaginary being. And not one the author had in the forefront of his mind. It comes from some background material he toyed with and never wrote down. At first I thought it was another Oompa-Loompa, but Dahl over at the Home Office says it comes from a world even more divorced from Mundane Earth than his. Look at how solid, even after death! This is the third complete manifestation. You recall how much trouble the second manifestation gave the Department."

"Are you sure this is a manifestation? It looks so... normal. Not dangerous a bit. Are you sure this is not a midget?"

"A midget who can vanish through a hedgerow without stirring a leaf, who can throw a dirk across a crowded street and through the mailslot of a door to hit a brownshirt in the leg, and who can talk to birds and cab horses and get them to do what he says? Oh, he led us and Jerry a merry chase indeed. He was talking to someone or something in the river before the German agent did him in."

"German agent?"

"Or the agent of a darker power. We did not recover any bodies, and there were at least three on the team. The motor launch the villains meant to make their escape upon was pulled underwater by some powerful creature, a giant squid or *something, and was lost with all hands. The police are dragging the river now."*

"A giant what? There is nothing like that in the Thames!"

"And nothing like Mister Otho Oldfoot of Southfarthing. We think he comes from a completed universe, not a fragment. I asked doctor Smithwork to come by and do an autopsy, but I will wager a whole evening of drinks that Smithwork will find no cause of death. There is no bullethole, no stab wound."

"Poison?"

"Spiritual poison. He was slain by the Great Fear."

"But—then why ask Dr. Smithwork to come here? Surely the campus laboratory..."

"I see you still have your little statues and trinkets hanging up all over your flat. Virgin Mary. Saint George. Saint—who the hell is that with the dog?—and I'm sure you said your beads. We might have need of all that superstitious fa-de-la before the night is through. You have a crucifix? Put it on. You have any holy water, holy oil, sanctified communion cookies? We may need something to throw at the shadow when it materializes here."

"Laymen are not allowed to carry around the blessed Host to throw at people."

"Who said anything about people?" Professor MacNab grunted and took another swig from my mug, scowling. "Ach! You drink swill. Can't you afford to buy something better?"

I took my crucifix from a drawer, crossed myself, and donned it.

"Do you have anything—a cross, a bible?" I asked him.

"Course not! I'm a man of science."

"And if the shadow that wields the Great Fear manifests here?"

"I'll hide behind you and cry like a girl, as befits a man of science."

There came a knock at the door.

If you notice what I did in this short scene, you can learn to do the same

The first thing to make up when writing is a conceit, a pretend thing, a false to facts idea that the reader will accept for the sake of the story. It has to be pretend, because if it is real, you are writing nonfiction.

The conceit it is actually the easiest part of the writing process: everyone has ideas for good stories. Every professional writer I have ever met carries a notebook in his back pocket (or her purse) to jot down story ideas as they come to him. Conceits for stories occur to most bookish people between once a week and once a day, but only pros write them down and remember them. That is why we are called "conceited." That is also why pros react with snorts of scorn when amateurs ask us where we get our ideas. In the first place, no one knows where ideas come from, and in the second, they are commonplace, and in the third, ideas are insignificant. The significant thing is the execution of the craftsmanship in carrying out the idea.

The conceit for the hypothetical novel *Old Men Shall Dream Dreams* is that the Inklings (J.R.R. Tolkien, C.S. Lewis, Charles Williams) were secretly involved in a British project to investigate Nazi interest in the occult, and that some of the material in their famous books was, of course, a reflection of some real things their work for the government ran into, but which they were not allowed to reveal due to the Official Secrets Act.

Now every book has a beginning. The same story can start in one of two places: in *medias res*, like *Paradise Lost* by Milton, which starts in the middle of the action, rather than from the beginning, like *The Book Of Genesis* by Moses.

The second thing is the basic technique for revealing the plot. If you have ever performed a striptease act in stiletto heels atop a sleazy bar and gotten drink-besotted yet lustful customers to thrust large denomination bills through the g-string barely covering your swaying shapely hips to brush against the luscious tickling smoothness of your warm yet naked velvety skin, you already know the technique. But (ahem) since I am a grossly overweight middle aged man, and the visual image involved here requires we wash out our brains with Listerine, you might need the technique explained in a more step by step fashion.

It has to do with showing just enough onstage to create in the mind of the audience that something more, some-thing interesting, is next to come. The writer lures the reader into turning the page.

The first line is the "hook." By mentioning an arresting image, the corpse of a child, but saying that something, whatever it is, is not the corpse of a child, the paragraph automatically provokes the reader to wonder what it is. What is not a child's corpse but would be mistaken for one?

Curiosity is the most powerful and simplest of the lures to trick the reader into turning the page. Whole books and whole genres, called Mystery stories, entertain a large segment of the reading world just with the lure of curiosity and nothing else.

The exact same number of words could indeed put across the exact same information, but if the answer is given the reader before the reader has time to wonder about the question, the paragraph provokes no curiosity, and will seem oddly flat. Consider the same story opening with, "A dead Hobbit from Tolkein's universe was brought by MacNab to my flat in London during the Blitz."

The second sentence contains a second hook: the phrase

"Professor of Applied Military Theology" is comical, but interesting, and it tells the reader what kind of story this is. The reader now knows he is not in our real world, and he wonders what kind of world he is in. A science fiction reader, in particular, will automatically start to wonder what the laws of nature and unreal conditions of that unreal world might be, that there would be such a class as Applied Military Theology.

The line "Don't worry. It is not human." is another pure negative lure. The reader automatically wonders, if it is not human, what is it?

The "Don't worry" is there partly for ironic effect, since most people would find the presence of a dead nonhuman humanoid more disturbing rather than less. Humor, particularly dry humor, acts as a lubricant to make it easier for the reader to slip further into the story. You as a writer are trying to cast a spell like a hypnotist, trying to make the reader forget the real world for an hour and believe in the make-believe world as if it were as real. Everything that lubricates and makes the process easier is a plus.

The "Don't worry" is also partly for character development. MacNab sounds unsympathetic about the death of the nonhuman he is carrying, or perhaps he is merely so hardened by war as to be unsympathetic to any death.

The second paragraph establishes the time and place, not by saying "Dateline: London, during the Blitz" but by including details specific to that period. There are many periods in history where teamsters drive horses, and many where there are anti-aircraft guns, and blackouts, but none where there are all three together. The reader makes an unconscious act of imagination, and fills in details of scene and setting.

It is especially important in a science fiction setting,

where the reader assumes that the setting is not our world, to establish immediately that the setting is very much like our world. By the second paragraph, the reader knows this story takes place not far from real history, but that it differs from our world by the introduction of one abnormality: a small corpse that looks like a child "but it is not human."

The third paragraph is character development. A first person viewpoint character needs very little; the reader will automatically assume the viewpoint character is like him unless told otherwise. The other character in the scene is given a single personality quirk—he both steals a drink and complains about it, and he does not have particularly drawing-room manners. This is meant to be funny and endearing rather than annoying, and to portray in one stroke a brusque or absent-minded fellow.

Since we have by now established a setting and given him a name, the reader can be trusted to fill in the details of some sort of stereotypical Oxfordian professor, perhaps a blustery, bossy or jolly type. It is important to trust the reader (because you have no choice not to) to fill in lifelike details. The bit of business of stealing a drink establishes that the two characters are friends. The use of the word "lad" and other clues show that the professor is either the older or the superior of the viewpoint character.

Please note that the technique for establishing character is the same as the technique used for establishing setting.

The paragraph does NOT say, "MacNab and I are old friends, despite that he is my mentor, and we were at ease with each other, even during desperate and dangerous situations. He helped himself to my drink without asking while my hands were full, which I thought was annoying, but forgivable. We share things like friends, but sometimes he shares more of my things than I do of his."

What the paragraph does instead is put on clues that are unique to relationships of that kind, so that the reader deduces, rather than is told, that the relationship is one of that kind, a close but unequal one.

Again, having MacNab steal the drink but then complain about it, is meant to be funny, or at least ironic. Since MacNab makes several comments about drinking, the reader fills in the blank that he is a hard drinking man, who has (or who imagines he has) a discriminating taste in alcohol.

Notice the difference a small change in one of these clues can have. Had MacNab taken the drink, but instead of calling it bathtub swill, sighed and said, "Sorry to nick your drink, Old Man, but running is thirsty work! I've seen things this night—well, never mind what I have seen. Fear can dry your mouth out, that's all. And too much fear—damn, I am parched, that's all."

This would have been of a different tone, but still setting out hooks and lures. The speaker interrupts himself, and does not say of what he is afraid, or from whom he was running, and this provokes reader curiosity again. It also would set a slightly more serious and menacing tone than the tone I selected. Selecting tone is a matter of judgment. The only general rule is that the tone should reinforce the general tone of the story. Don't start a horror story with a joke; don't start a joking story with a horror.

There is a certain delicate judgment involved in character development, since the selfsame words which strike one reader as funny will strike another as repellent. The only solution there is to be careful about first impressions, and to keep a certain consistency to re-enforce the impression you want to persuade the reader to create in his imagination.

This, by the way, is why writers use stereotypes. Far from being the evil thing all the rest of the world regards them as being, writers cannot write without stereotypes of people, places and things, and this is because our entire art consists of creating the illusion of a complete picture or a complete world out of a splinter or fragment of description, with the reader's imagination filling in the majority of the details. One cannot do this without knowing what pictures the reader is likely to have in his imagination beforehand.

What the reader wants not to do is to find himself being asked to use the stereotype in his head in a tired, trite, shopworn, or expected way, because then the reader notices, and is rightly put off by the trick being pulled on him.

The defining characteristic of stereotypes is that they are unadmitted, unthinking, unconscious and unselfconscious, and using a stereotype in an expected way brings to the reader's attention that he has these stereotypical sets of assumptions floating around in the back of his mind — and many a reader (especially a reader who thinks of himself as thoughtful) is a little miffed to discover that these unthinking assumptions are there, or are being played upon.

A reader whose stereotype assumptions differ from your own is even more aware. I recall reading a short story where, for example, nothing was described of the character aside from that he was a CIA agent. The writer expected me to fill in the details, so I (who come from a military background) filled in the details of a stalwart and patriotic member of the intelligence community. The writer (who must have come from a different background) told the story as if the character's sinister and malign nature had been established— because, to him, the stereotype of the CIA agent is sinister and malign. And for me the spell was broken.

One way to avoid that error is to make sure that you use at least two stereotypes, preferably two stereotypes that contradict each other when describing any one character. In Tolkien, for example, Bilbo Baggins of Bag End is both a dragon-hunting adventurer friendly to elves and wizards and also an overweight avuncular old bachelor who complains about guests hanging on the doorbell all day. Kal-El of Krypton is both a heroic Herculean strongman and also a mild-mannered reporter. Fu Manchu of the Si Fan is both a criminal conspirator and also a dignified Mandarin too proud to break his word, and a scientific genius. Note that each of these qualities could be described (or, better yet, adumbrated) in a sentence or two, but that the character also possesses an opposite quality.

While Bilbo, Superman, and Fu Manchu at one time or another, have been denounced as being stereotypes, note their enduring popularity; and compare them to the relatively flat and uninteresting versions of their less famous imitators, Curzad Ohmsford of Shady Vale, Marvelman, and the Mysterious Wu Fang. If you said "Who?" at these names, my point is made.

What makes Bilbo different from every other knight errant is that he is a short little stay-at-home squire. What makes Superman different from other vigilante supermen is that he is a hick farmboy trying to make good in the Big City. What makes Fu Manchu different from other crime lords is his code of impeccable honor. The first two are heroes you can feel sorry for; and the last is a villain you can admire.

The next paragraph is the first satisfaction of the curiosity provoked in the first paragraph. The thing that is not the corpse of a child and not a human being is described. The details are meant to fit in to some sort of picture the reader is forming in his mind, but not fit nicely or precisely, so that the reader can sort of tell what is going on (we do not want the reader totally lost at sea, lest he put the book down) but not allowing the reader to see all that is going on.

The reason for this is allure: it is like the striptease mentioned above. When the nubile young doxy pushes the loop of fabric off her shoulder, and turns away, and looks back over her shoulder with half-lidded eyes, it is meant to allure the filthy old voyeurs in the audience into seeing the beginning of the curvaceous delight of the bosom exposed, but not all, not quite, not yet. A young woman taking off her bra when no one is looking does so in a more businesslike way, and the allure is minimal.

The paragraphs after each serve two purposes at once. Each one is supposed to answer, or partly answer, the readers' question about what is going on, but then also to raise a new question or new twist on an old question. Pacing is the art of placing the questions and answers not too close together and not too far apart to keep the reader turning pages.

You tell the reader the corpse is not a human being. This raises the question of what it is. Then you mention German agents to make the reader raise the question of what the Germans are up to. Then you tell the reader what the corpse is: a short humanoid dressed in green and yellow. You mention what slew the corpse, something called the Great Fear. This raises the question of who or what is the Great Fear. Then you tell the reader what the German agents were up to, trying to smuggle the hobbit down the Thames. Then you mention Darker Powers. This raises the question of what are the Darker Powers and what kind of dread and hellish thing do you use a crucifix rather than a Tommygun to face? Then mention that they may be coming here. Then say there is a knock at the door.

It is a simple pattern with many variations: question, distraction, second question, first answer, second distraction, third question, second answer, and repeat. The longer the pause between question and answer, the longer the reader is kept lost at sea.

The biggest question, *will the hero slay the villain and get the girl?* has to be introduced in the first chapter and kept until the last chapter to answer. So you either have to introduce the villain, or the clue leading to the henchmen leading to the villain, in the first chapter, or you have to introduce the girl and make her seem lovely to the reader. If your hero is a Hobbit rather than a Frenchman, you are allowed to introduce a lovely bit of home and hearth and beloved countryside rather than a lovely girl.

The villain can be anything (animal, vegetable or mineral) that the hero hates or fears or needs to overcome.

The clue that starts the thread that leads to the villain can be a very small thread indeed. Consider the following opening of two paragraphs, eight lines in total:

> "*When Mr. Bilbo Baggins of Bag End announced that he would shortly be celebrating his eleventy-first birthday with a party of special magnificence, there was much talk and excitement in Hobbiton.*
>
> "*Bilbo was very rich and very peculiar, and had been the wonder of the Shire for sixty years, ever since his remarkable disappearance and unexpected return. The riches he had brought back from his travels had now become a local legend, and it was popularly believed, whatever the old folk might say, that the Hill at Bag End was full of tunnels stuffed with treasure. And if that was not enough for fame, there was also*

his prolonged vigour to marvel at. Time wore on, but it seemed to have little effect on Mr. Baggins. At ninety he was much the same as at fifty. At ninety-nine they began to call him well-preserved; but unchanged would have been nearer the mark. There were some that shook their heads and thought this was too much of a good thing; it seemed unfair that anyone should possess (apparently) perpetual youth as well as (reputedly) inexhaustible wealth."

The thin thread here is that, of course, it is too much of a good thing that anyone should possess perpetual youth and inexhaustible wealth. That thread leads step by darker step to a magic ring, which turns out to be a cursed magic ring, and the curse is from the darkest of Dark Lands itself. Mr. Bilbo's perpetual youth is not just unnatural, it is a gift from the pit of Hell, and the Witch King on a black steed is already being drawn and lured toward peaceful Hobbiton by the dread ring, the Ruling Ring, the One. The Witch King is but a lesser shadow of the Great Shadow. And the gold band on the stubby hand of the silly little hobbit man is the power that can enslave the will, darken minds, corrupt souls, and ruin the world. The thread leads all the way to the Cracks of Doom.

Tolkien knew what he was doing; for he actually introduces his villain in the second paragraph of page one. The reader wonders at the long life of the harmless country squire, and may perk up his ears, but he is not yet to suspect the chain leading back link by link to the Dark Tower. The question of "Why is Bilbo so lucky?" leads, question by question, to the question, "Now that Frodo is broken by the Ring, and put it on his finger while standing in the very Cracks of Doom in the center of the Dark Land, how can the world be saved when destruction seems certain? And where did that wretched Gollum go?"

Just as the villain does not need to be a villain, so too the girl does not need to be a girl, or even a human being, or even a physical thing, she only needs to be something, anything, precious to the hero that he seeks and follows and vows to win. She can also be at the end of a very long thread with many twists and turns, but the beginning of the thread has to be in chapter one.

All the little questions follow smaller arcs within the chapters.

Please note the difference between a science fiction reader and a normal reader or "muggle" at this point. A muggle has a very low tolerance to no tolerance for being lost at sea when it comes to matters of unearthly or extraterrestrial props, setting, events. If the scene is too strange to him, he will not make the imaginative leap to fill in the details, his mind will be blank of images, and the strangeness will repel rather than allure. He will say, "but that is not real!" and the hypnotic spell will break, and he will close the book.

Science fiction readers are the opposite. They like the sensation of being lost at sea and not knowing what is going on, and will wait with the patience of Job to be allowed to figure out the unreal reality, provided, of course, that you play fair with them, and actually have a real unreal reality to figure out.

Let me emphasize two points:

Point one: first, this willingness to be lost tends not to work across genre boundaries. The reason why a collective groan of disbelief rose up to heaven from the massed fans of *Star Wars* was because of one line in one scene in *The Phantom Menace*, when the Jedi says Jedi powers are based, not on a mystical energy field binding the galaxy together, but due to microscopic bodies in the bloodstream. The groan was because the genre boundary had been crossed.

A mystic energy field is something everyone sort of recognizes from New Age ideas, or Theosophy, or Oriental humbug. It is a simple and clear idea, and it is a mythic idea, from a fantasy story or a fairy tale, including fairy tales taking place "Once upon a time long, long ago, in a galaxy far, far away." The mystic energy field fits the mood and fits the tone because it fits the genre of the fairy tale.

Microscopic psionic organisms are a "nuts-and-bolts SF" sort of idea, not from fairy tales but from "hard" SF, the sort of thing Larry Niven might invent to explain the esper powers of Gil Hammond or of the Thrint Slavers, but not the sort of thing found in the Narnia books of C.S. Lewis. It was tin-eared on the part of George Lucas, it broke the mood and thus broke the hypnotic spell of the story, and that is why every fan groaned. It violated the boundary between fairy tale conventions and Hard SF conventions.

Imagine the difference if, in the first *Star Wars* movie, in the first scene where Luke meets Obi-Wan, Obi-Wan is called "a student of mind science" rather than "that crazy old wizard" and, instead of handing Luke a magic sword of his father, Obi-Wan pulled out a hypodermic needle and announced, "Your father was biologically programmed to be a Telek. You have the genetic ability too! I will inject you with psycho-mitochondria cells. These will enter your blood stream and allow your body to produce and generate the psychic energy forces that the Telek can produce. It will be painful, but your body can adapt. Are you willing?"— that would have been in the same mood and tone as the stupid scene in *The Phantom Menace* where a Jedi Knight does a blood test to discover whether a moppet is a Jedi, but it would have established a very different, and very unfairy-tale-like, story universe.

The science fiction reader, unlike the muggle reader, will "grant" you at least one unreality on which the rest of your reality is based. The reader knows darn well that Time Machines do not exist, but if you want to tell the story of the Morlocks munching on Eloi of AD 802701, the reader will grant the Time Machine as a courtesy to you, the teller of the tale, to get your hapless hero to the time and place of your setting that you may tell your tale.

Science fiction readers are more generous with their imagination than other readers, and science fiction writers should be grateful for the latitude they allow to us, or get the heck out of the business of science fiction writing; so say I.

Science fiction readers do demand that we writers play fair. Once we make an implied promise, we must carry through on the promise, or else the readers feel not merely disappointed, but cheated, as if we lied to them. One implied promise made in the scene given above is that there is a realistic world behind all these dropped hints.

If you write a paragraph where someone makes refer-ences to the Department in charge of manifestations from other universes and fairytale languages and so on, you are promising that you, the writer, have already thought through all the logical implications and the background of such a conceit, and that the details will be present in the story each in its proper place at the proper time, and that the ending of the tale will follow from the beginning in an unexpected but logical way, given the unreal conceit.

The writer promises that he has thought through the implications of a version of World War Two where the Allies and Axis Powers have secretly made contact with creatures from nearby imaginary universes. Having Hitler become a Ringwraith when he brings through Sauron to Berlin in Chapter Six keeps the promise, since this is a logical outgrowth of the conceit. Even having MacNab discover that his own world is imaginary to yet a third world, where he with trembling fingers turns the pages of a book called *Old Men Shall Dream Dreams* by John C. Wright keeps the promise, because it is a logical outgrowth of the conceit. You, the author, have to make up whether the Inklings are inventing the universes they write about, or are merely sensing or discovering them. You have to know, before it happens, what would happen if Aslan the Lion, summoned by the Allies, joins a last ditch night mission over Berlin, accompanies the inventor Caractacus Potts in his flying car and the good witch Eglantine Price on her flying four-poster bed, to confront Sauron the Great in the nave of Saint Hedwig's Cathedral at midnight while the city burns.

This is true both for science fiction and for fantasy. You have to know how the system works, or the reader will sense that you are just guessing. As above, when Lucas had the Jedi power operate by microscopic blood cells, he betrayed that he did not know how his system worked.

Mystery writers, by the bye, are under the same constraint. They make the implied promise to the reader that the murder in Chapter One will be solved before the end of the tale, and solved by some reasonable means, not by a miracle (miracles are not allowed, not even if the detective is Father Brown) and that the murderer will not be the person everyone first suspects. If that promise is not kept, the readers are not just bored, they are outraged, just as if they had been defrauded of their book-buying dollar and their book-reading time.

Point Two: Second, and much more significant is the

point that the writer never tells the reader anything unless there is absolutely no other choice.

Instead the writer *lets* the reader figure out things from hints.

If you can help it, you never say, "It was London during the Blitz." You say, "Out the window a horse-drawn cart was hauling an anti-aircraft gun." If you can help it, you never say, "He and I are old friends and don't stand on ceremony." You say, "He stole my drink and wiped his mouth on his sleeve."

You show the readers clues and trust them to figure out the details. This rule is so significant that it has its own name: "Show, don't tell."

The next few paragraphs establish the plot. Plots are about conflict. Conflict means (1) someone we like wants something VERY BADLY and (2) someone or something else whom we like less is standing in the way and (3) someone we like is going to take a reasonable step to get the something he wants VERY BADLY and (4) the reasonable step will go badly wrong in an unexpected way, but in a way that in hindsight seems logical or reasonable.

Then you repeat. The thing that goes badly wrong means that the someone we like has to take another step to get around the bad wrongness and back toward the something he wants VERY BADLY. He takes the next step, and everything goes even more badly wrong.

Then he loses his map. Then his flashlight falls into a storm drain and he has an asthma attack and his seeing eye dog dies. Then the cop who pulls him over for speeding while driving drunk in the nude turns out to be the short-tempered father of the bride he is marrying tomorrow.

Then it goes more badly wrong for the someone we like, much more badly. Then the party is attacked and scattered by a band of goblins, and then the Gollum is on his trail, and the lure of the Ring is slowly destroying his mind. Then he finds the blasted corpses of his foster parents killed by Imperial Storm Troopers, and his house burnt to the ground. Then Lex Luthor chains a lump of Kryptonite around his neck and pushes him into a swimming pool and fires twin stealth atomic rockets at the San Andreas Fault in California and at Hackensack, New Jersey.

And the spunky but beautiful girl reporter falls into a crack in the earth and dies. Then he is stung by Shelob and dies. Then he is maimed by Darth Vader and discovers his arch foe is his very own father, and he loses his grip and falls. Then he steps out unarmed to confront Lord Voldemort and dies. Then Judas Iscariot kisses him, Peter denounces him, he is humiliated, spat upon, whipped, betrayed by the crowd, tortured, sees his weeping mother, and dies a painful, horrible death and dies. Then he is thrown overboard and swallowed by a whale and dies.

Then he gets help, gets better, arises from his swoon, is raised from the dead, the stone rolls back, the lucky shot hits the thermal exhaust port, and the Death Star blows up, the Dark Tower falls, the spunky but beautiful girl reporter is alive again due to a time paradox, and he is given all power under heaven and earth and either rides off into the sunset, or goes back to the bat-cave, or ascends into heaven, and we roll the credits.

That is how a plot is done. The someone we like is the protagonist. We have to like him. He does not have to be pleasant, he can even be a repellent in many ways, but we nonetheless have to get caught up in his life and adventures.

The something in his way is the antagonist, and it can be nature or a person. We do not have to hate the antagonist, and, indeed, some of the more memorable antagonists are men who might have been friends under other circumstances.

The thing he wants VERY BADLY is the McGuffin, the whatsits that drives the plot.

The reason why he wants it is his motivation, and you have to invent a deep and tear-jerking motivation, something that gets a hook in the reader, or otherwise the reader will put the book down and go watch a rerun of Gilligan's Island on TV.

The McGuffin is usually important in order to make it clear why the someone we like wants it so VERY BADLY. No one ever wrote a gripping story about an election to the local school board, unless (under the hands of a crafty writer) the someone we like has some reason why he absolutely, positively must win the election and get on the school board or else something he (and we) greatly fear will come upon us.

The cleverest writers give the someone we like not one but two things he wants VERY BADLY, and then puts them at odds with each other.

I love Romeo but hate his Montague family. I love the Shire but want to travel like Uncle Bilbo and see elves and dragons. I love Lois Lane but I have to act like a mild mannered dweeb to hide my powerful secret lest my effectiveness as a crimefighter be compromised, so the girl I have a crush on has a crush on my alter ego and won't give me a date. I love Jerusalem and would gather her people to me like a hen gathering chicks beneath her wings, and yet her people kill the prophets sent to heal and save her. I love Oz but I want to go home. I think I will miss you most of all, Scarecrow.

You see, none of these conflicts are about things people only sort of like. It is always about love. You may think me blasphemous to use the Passion of the Christ as an example of drama, but not so: this is the one true story, the greatest story ever told, the tale of tales even as Christ is the King of Kings, and all truly inspired fairy tales and fiction have to contain some echo or reflection of the One True Tale, or else it is no tale of any power at all, merely a pastime.

The most powerful and potent tales, even when they are told awkwardly and without grace or poetry or craft, are stories of paradise lost and paradise regained; sacrifice, self-less love, forgiveness and salvation; stories of a man who learns better.

This is why, even in the rather brainless fairy tale setting of *Star Wars*, Darth Vader has his soul saved when he sacri-fices himself to slay the Emperor and save his son. I thought it was awkwardly handled, even stupidly, in that final scene (my gripe is that it was supposed to be a scene of powerful temptation, but the Emperor had nothing to tempt Luke with); but the power of selfless love, sacrifice, and redemp-tion nonetheless brought a tear to my eye.

This is why in the second *Star Trek* movie, *The Wrath Of Khan*, the powerful scene is the selfless sacrifice of Spock as he steps into a radiation-flooded engineering chamber to make a final and desperate repair, laying down his life for his friends. Greater love hath no Vulcan.

This is why Superman, instead of putting on a crown and declaring himself World Ruler, has to live as a mild-mannered and painfully shy reporter who cannot get a date, and why he must fight crime in secret, with no one knowing about his double life: it is a sacrifice. He sacrifices the praise and love and companionship he craves in order to save mankind.

This is why Frodo cannot retire to the Shire with a breastpocket full of medals and ribbons and awards and a pot belly, sitting at the local pub and regaling wide-eyed hobbit-lads with tales of his exploits in the Great War. He is sacrificed, and must depart across the sundering seas, having served without reward.

That is conflict. That is motivation. Together they make plot.

You read a book from front to back, but you write it from back to front, either knowing the ending (if you write by plot) or knowing the mature version of the hero (if you write by character arc) or know the mood you want to create (if you write by theme). Once you have the end result you want firmly in mind, you work backward step by step.

Do you write by plot? To have your hero saved by the malice of Gollum, you must introduce Gollum in an earlier chapter.

Do you write by character arc? You cannot have Mattie Ross be a loving and mature young woman at the end unless she is an unlovable and immature arrogant young pushy judgmental know-it-all at the beginning, and you cannot have Rooster Cogburn be a lovable crusty old one-eyed Marshall at the end, unless he is an unlovable arrogant crusty old one-eyed hard-drinking curmudgeon at the beginning.

Do you write by theme? To establish a mood of radiant glory when Aslan rises from the dead, you must have the four children recoil with wonder at the mere mention of his name when Mr. Beaver speaks it, even though they do not know the name, because the mood of wonder leads to the mood of glory.

The patented John C. Wright one-session lesson in how to write is not your last lesson. A good second lesson is to read a book you like and reverse engineer all of its tricks, figure out exactly how the writer does his sleight of hand, by what craft he crafts his spell, and put yourself mentally in the shoes of the stage magician, not the audience, and look at everything backward, from the reverse side.

And that second lesson is not the last lesson. To be a writer, you have to teach and train yourself how to write until it becomes second nature. I mistrust all "how to" books and articles (including this one) and suggest instead the best method to learn is to try and fail and try and fail again.

Now comes the hard part. To be a writer, you must write. To be a professional writer, you must sell what you write.

Go to it.

6

SWORDPLAY IN SPACE

Why is the preferred weapon of the Galactic Empire the sword? It is to answer that question and perhaps one or two other questions of deeper import that this essay attempts.

Science fiction is now old enough that a perspective of its changes over time is possible, to contrast the dreams of past futures with the present futures.

A particularly telling survey should look at future war stories. Of all the institutions of man, war is the one that is the closest mortal men ever reach to hell. In war, good men do bad things, law and order breaks down, but also becomes tyrannical as military exigencies force civilian rights to one side, and continual fear, danger, desperation, and stench of death renders life brutal and miserable and hopeless. There is one small ray of heaven in this hell, tiny as a thread of sunlight that steals through the lock of a prison door, which is that the emergency can from time to time bring out acts of selfless and un-self-regarding fortitude, patriotism, honor, sacrifice, and heroism.

War is fundamental. A man's views on war tell you the

basic axioms of his view on life. Because of this, a popular war story will tell you in an abbreviated form much about the storyteller's most fundamental ideals and fears, and that of his audience.

I have long maintained that science fiction is the mythology of the scientific age.

A mythology is an exploration by means of concrete images of the abstractions and passions of the age; myth speaks in a vocabulary of anthropomorphized figures.

The scientific age was one in which the empirical method explained the natural world to man with shocking clarity, gave him an unprecedented degree of dominion over it, made technological change a part of human experience, and, for better or worse, banished belief in magic, banished the world where woods were haunted by elves and villages by witches, to the remote fringes.

Hence while science fiction is often defined as stories about future technology or future attitudes toward technology, I submit that a more useful definition would look at the themes, not at the props, of the stories. Science Fiction themes cluster around the factors crucial to the scientific revolution: the shock of clarity when the system of the world is revolutionized: the thrill or terror which accompanies dominion; the wonder or the horror of technological change and its social ramifications; the grim romance of naturalism, when man finds himself alone in a universe of astronomical grandeur and appalling, unending emptiness.

I made the bold statement above that a man's views on war tell you his views on life. This is because his views on war should tell you what he thinks worth killing for and dying for, what he thinks death is, or virtue, and whether there is more to life than this world; and from this you can assess his character, distinguishing the shallow from the profound, the romantic from the realist, the craven from the noble.

In the ultimate analysis, there are only five basic attitudes toward life: the Hopeful, the Noble, the Ruthless, the Idealistic, and the Despairing.

The Hopeful believe in life after death and in supernatural justice in that next life, which will mete out the rewards and punishments men elude on earth; and therefore this ideal can encompass both the extravagant pacifism of a Saint Francis or the extravagant bravery of Saint George. They have no illusions about the horrors of war, but they fight with a joyful abandon and a scrupulous chivalry, because the war, to them, is both physical and spiritual, and a small part of a larger cosmic reality.

The Noble are skeptical about such cosmic justice, but dedicate themselves with stoic melancholy honor to work such justice as their frail human hands can work; this view also has no illusions about the horrors of war, but also recognizes the glory of self-sacrifice in a noble cause.

The Ruthless are skeptical about cosmic and human justice, and see the conflicts in life as inevitable and irreconcilable. They believe that the ends justify the means, and they believe in total war, fought to extermination. For the Ruthless, any trick, any lie, any act or torture or terror is permitted, so long as it is efficient in its service to the cause. Ironically and absurdly, they also believe human nature is malleable, and can evolve to a point when all war shall cease. Note that the utopia is envisioned to be without flaw, therefore to be so desirable that any ruthlessness is justified to achieve it. Gallons, nay, oceans of innocent blood are justified if this permits we can sail to paradise on the red flood.

The Idealistic believe the ends never justify the means,

and that no evil is ever necessary, no violence ever practical. This is a utopian belief in pacifism, a notion we might call "total peace", which is as foolish as the theory of total war. It is a theory which blames the existence of the instruments of war for the existence of war. It is a belief that disarmament in the face of an enemy will enlighten him, soothe his fears and allay his ambitions, and render him a lover of peace. In other words, the Idealistic believe that the utopia envisioned by the ruthless has already somehow been achieved, and human nature already been perfected. Idealism is the stark opposite of the ruthless belief in an endless Darwinian war between irreconcilable enemies: it is the idea that there are no real foes, merely unmet friends, no real conflicts, merely misunderstandings.

The Despairing hold with none of this. They are as skeptical of the utopianism of the idealists as they are of the craven treasons of the ruthless; they regard nobility as a deception, and hope as a madness. They believe in nothing, fight for nothing, value nothing aside from their own selfish appetites. They are willing that other men fight and die for them, that they might mock their benefactors and sneer at heroes.

Now, these are not five pigeonholes with neatly limited edges where any one story or any one man can be neatly stowed. Think of them instead as five directions or dimensions toward which a man can move, closer to one and farther from another.

With this in mind, let us take a semi-random sample of some well-known science fiction books, and make a guess about the view of life betrayed.

I say 'semi-random' because for the purposes of this very unscientific and rough overview, I compare more than one list I found here and there of the hundred greatest science fiction stories of all time.

These tales are all so famous that I include no spoiler warnings nor summations of them. I assume you've read them, dear reader. If not, why are you wasting time reading this?

The list is also heavily skewed toward older novels. No Military SF properly so called is included at all. This is because in order to get a hundred people at random to compile a list of a hundred favorite SF books, the older the book is, the more people have had more chances to read and recommend it. Military SF is too young a subgenre to be gathered into a list compiled this way.

Of these several lists of one hundred bests, most had no battles in them, and contained no speculation about future combat, but of those that did, one immediate fact was obvious: the writers of scientific romances are lousy predictors of the real future. Which is as God and Nature intended, no doubt.

Writers are lousy predictors of the future because making an accurate prediction, despite that an occasional Jules Verne yarn or Analog story might contain one, is not the point of telling a scientific romance. The point is to tell a myth using the setting and theme and moral concerns inherent in the scientific worldview. The science fiction writer is caught in a tension between two apparently opposite goals: the first goal is to use mythic archetypes and images that will appeal to the reader's imagination, or more, which will come to life in the reader's imagination and shed bright light on all his other ideas and ideals, as inspiration and insight. The second goal is to create an illusion of realism, a verisimilitude, by extrapolating from known technology to the tools and weapons of the unknown future or unknown other worlds, to make the unreal seem realistic.

Tales that seek the first more strongly than the second are called Soft Science Fiction, and they include Space Opera, which seeks to wow the audience with astronomical magnitudes and epic action, but also Sword-and-Planet stories as well as Sword-and-Spaceship stories, which seek to charm the audience with archaic-flavored adventures in a futuristic or extraterrestrial setting.

Tales that seek the second are called Hard Science Fiction, or Nuts-and-Bolts stories, and the less wild the extrapolation, the harder the science and the more persuasive the verisimilitude.

Of these two, only the second will make a serious attempt to think realistically about future war, but even they are obligated by the nature of their craft to emphasize those things that will be different, new, and strange about the way our children will conduct war in years to come. Hence, even of the 'Hard' SF war stories culled from the list of hundred greatest, few or no soldiers fire bullets from rifles that use gunpowder. That is too quotidian, too much like the current time of the reader, not exotic enough.

Some of the hardest science fiction is the earliest. While TWENTY THOUSAND LEAGUES UNDER THE SEA by Jules Verne was not a war story, the ironclad submersible vessel, the Nautilus, was a warship. Anachronistically, she was armed with the same arm as a Hellenic trireme: a ramming prow. The military applications of the invention were clear: submersion was the same as invisibility, and gave Captain Nemo mastery of seven-tenths of the world.

THE WAR OF THE WORLDS by H.G. Wells established the best known of science fiction tropes, namely, that of extraterrestrial invasion by scientifically superior Martians.

To this day, someone unfamiliar with science fiction regards it as a field filled with little green men shooting heat-rays. The war here is as shocking to the Englishmen as, in real life, the English invasion was to the aborigines of Australia or the Americas. The combatants are too unequal for it to be considered a war properly so called: it is merely slaughter and devastation, and the humans are gassed like rats. The invaders are eventually destroyed without any human intervention by a remorseless Darwinian principle: they are not suited by natural selection for our germ-ridden planet, germs which, by killing our ancestors, created as if by process of elimination our various resistances and immunities. The high civilization of Mars millions of years ago eliminated from their world all microbes that cause illness and morbidity, which they would no more keep around than we would keep man-eating tigers in our city streets.

A PRINCESS OF MARS by Edgar Rice Burroughs is the first of the Sword-and-Planet stories. The science fiction is much softer than that seen in Wells or Verne, but some sober scientific speculation does underpin at least some of the concepts in this yarn, such as the effect of raising children communally on the family structure. Other parts are pure flights of fancy. Here is the best example of what we might call "the rule of no gunpowder"—the Martians fight with radium-powered atomic bullets loaded in rifles with a range of over a hundred miles, but also fight with longswords, and wear no armor.

Much as I love this tale, it is admittedly juvenile. The hero, under the lighter gravity of Mars, has superhuman strength, and he is also the best swordsman of the world, who fights his way from pole to pole of a world filled with barbarians and beasts to win the heart of the fairest of women, and a princess. He saves the entire planet from asphyxiation at the end of the first volume, overthrows the gods in the second volume, and becomes the warlord and leader of the entire globe in the third.

This tale depicts battles in the most romanticized fashion imaginable: it is like the heroic combat of Homeric heroes, but without the unblinking honesty of Homer, who described death wounds with the precision of a battlefield surgeon. I do not recall hearing a single wound described, or a funeral, or an act of mourning, in all this Martian ILIAD. Even more romanticized is the universal eagerness of the Martians for war: there is not a single monk, or even an unarmed man, on the whole planet.

THE SKYLARK OF SPACE by E.E. Doc Smith is akin to PRINCESS OF MARS in more ways than one. The combat is again utterly romanticized without the slightest reference to the pain and horror of combat. When the interplanetary ship Skylark reaches the world of Osnome in the multiple star system at the core of our galaxy, we find the same social elements as were present on Burroughs' Mars, namely, a warrior race of nudists who have no concept of, nor appetite for, peace.

GALACTIC PATROL and its many sequels in the Lensman series by E.E. Doc Smith shares this attitude of romanticized heroism, albeit there enter for the first time some hints of the ruthlessness of an unromantic nature: the Patrolman and Boskonians kill each other without remorse and do not accept nor seek surrender, and the narrator emphasizes that in hand-to-hand combat the Gray Lensman fights with no holds barred, no 'Marquis of Queensbury rules' but instead it is as dirty a fight as any bar brawl.

In both SKYLARK and the Lensman series, the wars are genocidal wars of extermination, and whole worlds are snuffed out with (to a modern reader) an alarming insouciance. In the final Skylark book, SKYLARK DUQUESNE, an entire galaxy is destroyed as countless millions of suns are teleported through the fourth dimension to occupy the same three dimensional space as their target suns, igniting both into novae. The entire galaxy is a cloud of supernova energy from core to arms. E.E. Smith books portray a war of superhumans and super-scientists with superpowers.

Books like BRAVE NEW WORLD by Aldous Huxley and NINETEEN EIGHTY FOUR by George Orwell do not have any battle scenes in them, but the attitude of the books toward war is nonetheless defined: the wars between Oceania, Eurasia and Eastasia are utterly cynical, meant only to serve as an excuse to cow the subject populations of the various tyrant states, and consume goods and people, because, or so it is asserted, each of the three tyrannies is so powerful that the other two allied against it cannot possibly destroy or uproot it. (Absurdly, it is asserted that goods and resources must be consumed in war, or otherwise the socialist tyrant states would produce goods too over-abundantly.)

Likewise, the World State in the year After Ford 632 has no rebellions, no civil disturbances, no migrations, and nothing that would cause or permit any acts of violence.

Both these philosophies are in the 'Ruthless' category: the only difference being that Big Brother is from a time of perfect control of man before the Utopian perfection of man through science, and the world-state of Ford is from a time after. Both philosophies of war are naive to the point of nonsense. Any speculative fiction writer who does not predict wars and rumors of war to continue to Doomsday is writing very speculative fiction indeed.

STARSHIP TROOPERS by Robert Heinlein is as orig-inal a way to tell a war story as was GONE WITH THE

WIND, which told the story from the point of view of the Southern women left behind during the fighting. In this case, TROOPERS is told from the point of view not of a superhuman hero but of an infantryman, who neither knows the causes nor the outcome of the war. It is eerie that the cause or matter of the war is simply never mentioned, and there no hint in the book of the ultimate outcome. It is a book about patriotism, romantic only in the limited sense of praising the virtue and valor of the enlisted man, the grunt, the able seaman, the footslogger.

The 'hard' science fiction comes in such elements as extrapolating that technology will give a single future soldier the firepower of a modern platoon, or even a battalion; the use of armored exoskeletons to make each man a walking tank; or extrapolating how to perform a paratrooper drop from orbit.

Sociologically, the book postulates a social system something like that of ancient Rome, where men earned their citizenship by military service, which is perhaps the least wild of the speculations in the book, but is the one which engenders the most criticism.

And by 'criticism', I mean slander and hatred from the various craven and weak-minded critics who are stung too deeply by the book's unapologetic message about civic responsibility. I do not think it necessary either to repeat or to answer their unserious criticisms. The selfish brats do not like being told they are selfish. It wounds their precious self-esteem.

The war, once again, is portrayed as somewhat sanitary, albeit, unlike the purely romantic books, there is death and self-sacrifice throughout; indeed, it is the main point of the book. This book is the best SF example of what I call the noble attitude with all its melancholy.

THE MOON IS A HARSH MISTRESS, also by Robert A Heinlein, retains much of the same atmosphere, but in this case it is a retelling of the American Revolution in Space. The attitude is inching, however, toward the ruthlessness which finds that the ends justify the means. The hardest SF speculation in the book is the use of nonexplosive payloads, that is, merely rocks, dropped from orbit onto targets, landing with the force of meteors.

THE FOREVER WAR by Joe Haldeman is more clearly in the ruthless territory, since the main point of the book is that relativistic effects will act like the sleep of Rip Van Winkle whenever the soldiers return from cruise to an increasingly older and stranger Earth. The sacrifice of the men is something imposed by the exigencies of a war which ultimately turns out to be pointless. Mr. Haldeman displays something of the anti-war attitude that was fashionable during the Vietnam war, where, for some reason never clear to me, the American string of uninterrupted victories convinced the American public that the weak, cruel and vile communist enemy was undefeatable, or, at least, undefeatable at a reasonable loss of blood and treasure. So, depending on how much of that spirit the reader sees in FOREVER WAR, one might arguably put this in the idealist territory.

More clearly in the idealist territory is Mr. Haldeman's FOREVER PEACE, which contained perhaps the least believable resolution to a war tale I have ever read. The book itself is very well crafted—I mean no disrespect—but the philosophical speculation on which the final plot resolution hangs was poorly conceived. The speculative idea is that in the future soldiers will be linked nerve-to-wire into fighting groups that operate war machines by remote control, and that a side effect on the psychology of the soldiers is that, if exposed to this nerve-link for too long, they will develop so much empathy that war and violence will be impossible. As if all violence were merely caused by mere misunderstanding, and none by fear, greed, ambition, or honor. Obviously no one has performed the experiment and discovered this, but, seriously, most hatred between peoples in this world is between neighbors who understand each other very well indeed.

LORD OF LIGHT by Roger Zelazny and DUNE by Frank Herbert occupy the same territory as A PRINCESS OF MARS, except these authors come up with a reason why the soldiers of the future on far worlds do not use pistols and rifles, but instead have psychic powers, swords and knives, tridents, spears, lasguns and lightningbolts. The warfare here, despite the archaic or mythic flavor of the weapons, is an occasion of death and sorrow.

In case it is not clear, the reason why the sword is the preferred weapon of the Galactic Empire is that the easiest way for an author to summon up images of grandeur, either godlike or Oriental or barbaric, or images of chivalry, is to hearken to the past; and a sense of things both half-familiar and hauntingly romantic is most easily achieved by such archaisms.

That Paul Atreides is a prince as well as a Messiah, and that Sam is a god, give them a mythic stature that Juan Rico, Manuel Garcia O'Kelly-Davis, and William Mandella do not achieve. But the trade-off is that Rico and Mannie and Mandella are more human, more solid, and they bleed when you cut them.

ENDER'S GAME by Orson Scott Card is a tale which is only about the sorrows of war, where even the victors suffer from the sacrifices they make. It has spawned as many sequels as A PRINCESS OF MARS and GALACTIC

PATROL, but in theme is the opposite. The original short story retains a considerable power to move the heart. It is the only book on the list I can put in the 'Hopeful' category, because its realism about the horror of war is absolute, but its hope in salvation even of souls bent, broken, and ruined by war is also absolute. It is not a pessimistic nor despairing book. The only other book I can think of which has this attitude toward war is not a science fiction book at all, but a fantasy, indeed, the fantasy: I see the same attitude in J.R.R. Tolkien's trilogy.

As for books in the despairing category, stories that say that there is nothing worth fighting for, I tend not to read such things, but authors such as Kurt Vonnegut come to mind, and this category is more popular these days that it had been in times past.

7

THE GLORY GAME

OR, THE BITTERNESS OF BROKEN IDEALS

I s it better to be good or look good?

I have been rereading some of the novels of Keith Laumer, a sadly under-recognized master of the SF genre. As before, this is not a book review as much as a meditation prompted by revisiting a youthful pleasure. My bookshelf has all the same paperbacks I read when I was in school, in pristine condition, and placed in the same order. This bookshelf was first filled long ago enough that those authors were alive. None now are: Frederick Pohl, the last of the giants, passed away this month. Readers who wish to read reviews of modern books must patronize the journal of some man more prone to read modern novels.

In this case, the short novel involved is called *The Glory Game* by Keith Laumer, published in 1973. The novel is well crafted, concise, without a wasted scene or word, and therefore has the clearest and most trenchant point of any tale I have ever read that is actually a tale and not a tract. The novel is so concise that the twist ending would not exist were it not for the last line, nay, the last four words.

I regret that I must reveal those four words at the end to

discuss them, so I would ask any reader to go out, buy and read the novel, and only then return here.

The characters are rough sketches, painted in broad, energetic strokes, as befits an adventure yarn. However, this is not an adventure yarn but a morality play. The fight scenes consist of two scuffles and one shoot out. The war which serves as the backdrop to the events is never fought. The meat of the drama is in the simple but winning formula of having the hero told to violate his principles and refusing.

The writing style is masculine, muscular, brief, and copies that same staccato brevity that Noir writers like Hammett and Chandler perfected.

The tone is pitch-perfect Noir at its darkest. Noir stories are not nihilist stories, albeit they are cantilevered over the abyss of nihilism and dangle their toes. The point (if it can be called that) of a nihilist story is that nothing is worth doing because all ideals are foolish and dead. The point of a Noir story is that the world holds out nothing worth doing, but the tarnished knight, no longer unstained white, carries out the hard demands of his high ideals despite all this. In Noir tales, the ideals are dead but were not foolish, and a man lives up to them out of a sense of melancholy respect for their memory. It is like saluting the flag of a sunken Atlantis.

As for the plot, all plot elements serve the point efficiently. Writers wishing to master the technique of a crisp, fast-paced, tense, curt, driving plot could do worse than studying this short novel and noting the cleanness of the story structure.

The Glory Game is set in three acts:

In the prologue to the action, we meet Tancredi Dalton, Space Naval Commodore on the eve of what is perhaps a military exercise and perhaps something more. We meet his girlfriend Arianne the daughter of an influential Senator Kelvin on the Armed Services committee.

(I have no idea what prompted Laumer to select *Tancredi* as a name: It may refer to a leader of the First Crusade, the hero in tragic opera by Rossini, or to a main belt asteroid.)

During his last night of shore leave, the whole theme in miniature is played out. At a nightclub, Tancredi Dalton sees some servicemen being slighted by the waiters, who renege on a promise to give the men good seats for the floorshow after taking their bribe. Dalton stops a brewing brawl and intimidates the waiter into living up to his promise. The servicemen, not mollified, harass the waiters, trip the civilians and provoke a fight with the bouncers. Dalton again interferes, this time bringing his steely-eyed intimidation skills to bear on the servicemen, whom he orders back to barracks double-time.

Arianne is puzzled and appalled by Tan's colorblindness to the political ramifications of his actions, since he alienated both the civilians by siding with servicemen, and then alienated the servicemen by siding with the civilians. Dalton asks why it is so difficult to understand his creed: one is supposed to do what is right without having any unrealistic ideas about the cost.

Then comes the setup: An alien race called the Hukk have been prying into Terran space, attacking colonies and committing raids; these fierce warriors are weaker militarily than the Terrans, but more aggressive. The fleet has been called upon to perform exercises near Hukk space, as a show of force, in a place dubious electronic intel says the Hukk Armada is gathered. Dalton is approached by the Softliners, who want to answer Hukk aggression by supine concessions, waving the olive branch; and then Dalton is approached by the Hardliners, who want a preemptive military strike without a declaration of war, followed by general massacre of the Hukk worlds.

In Act One, Senator Kelvin the Hardliner reveals to Dalton that Admiral Starbird has secret, sealed orders not to engage the Hukk even if fired upon, which means the destruction of the Terran fleet, which must be halted at all cost; Undersecretary Treech the Softliner reveals that another Commodore named Borgman has secret, sealed orders to relieve Admiral Starbird of his command before he opens his secret, sealed orders, and then Borgman will carry out the general massacre, which means a genocide of the Hukk civilians, which must be halted at all costs. Dalton is given a third set of secret, sealed orders allowing him to relieve Admiral Starbird of command *before* Commodore Borgman relieves Starbird of command, so that Dalton can prevent the massacre.

The Hardliners demand Dalton work for them, because he is the man who will be in the crucial position when the fleet sails. He says only, "I'll think about it." The Softliners, after trying to abduct him, likewise make that demand for the same reason. He gives them the same answer. "I'll think about it."

Hence, both sides demand his loyalty, albeit he has agreed to nothing. He tells them both he is working for no one but the Constitution, to whom he gave his oath. Neither side understands him.

Dalton, figuring the situation from the Hukk point of view, realizes that they, like their human counterparts, are playing the Glory Game. That is, they want the maximum advantage military force can bring with minimal losses on their side. The Glory Game is a practical and non-idealistic approach to military policy, an attempt to maximize gain (including terrain, but also face, reputation, honor) while minimizing loss (shame and life and treasure). It is *Realpolitik.*

He realizes from several clues that the logical option for the Hukk is to send their Grand Armada to Luna while the Earth fleet is out of position performing their meaningless exercises, because the Earth intelligence has been deceived as to the Hukk fleet location. Defying, (without technically disobeying), his orders, Dalton pulls his tiny contingent of the fleet back toward Earth at full flank speed, and convinces the Hukk Grand Admiral, by sheer poker bluff and hardcore stare, that the Hukk fleet is outgunned and outflanked and outnumbered. The Hukk Grand Admiral, impressed, believes the bluff and surrenders. The alien warships strike their colors and dump their guns.

The Hardliner Commodore Borgman radios ahead and orders Dalton to open fire on the helpless Hukk ships, and proceed with the massacre. Dalton, who gave his word of honor to the Hukk Grand Admiral, refuses. Dalton shows Borgman his secret sealed orders overriding the second set of secret sealed orders overriding the first set of secret sealed orders, so he is technically not disobeying a lawful command. So he alienates the Hardliners.

In Act Two, Dalton is showered with rewards by Treech and his powerfully-placed Softliner party, and given a promotion to Admiral, because he saved the Hukk from genocide. Dalton is asked to help promote a controversial treaty which will give the Hukk aid and weapons and a lollypop and a pat on the head and dismantle the Terran Fleet, in an act of suicidal mass stupidity that seemed utterly unrealistic when I read it as a child but which, rereading it as an adult, seemed if anything a trifle mild and under-stated. (Real politicians bent on preemptive surrender would do much, much worse.)

As before, his girlfriend Arianne urges him to play along with the powers that be, to pick a side and stick with it. However, when called upon to testify before Congress, Dalton cannot bring himself to speak out-and-out lies, nor will he sign on to the falsified after-action report, nor go along with the huge deception the Softliners are attempting to pull on the people.

In one glaringly anachronistic scene, a newsman actually asks him for the truth, the whole truth, and nothing but the truth, and reports it. That scene would be laugh out loud funny if someone tried to write it about newsmen of this day and age. Can you imagine a *newsman* actually being interested in the truth? It is like a whore being interested in chaste romance.

The Softliners are now alienated; everyone hates Dalton; he is cashiered and sent off to oversee a junkyard of old Naval hulks on the dusty dry and dismal frontier planet of Grassroots.

Act Three is a reprise, the same theme in a minor key. The scene opens but three months later. Dalton quite by accident discovers strange signals from space, investigates, and gives chase to a one-man Hukk scoutship, which pancakes into the ground while attempting to evade him. Aboard is a dead spy and Hukk plans for invasion. (The Hukk, as Dalton predicted, interpreted the peace treaty rewarding their aggressive behavior as an invitation for further aggression.)

Dalton attempts to tell the local mayor of Grassport, but when His Honor discovers him to be none other than the disgraced Admiral Dalton, the Mayor dismisses Dalton as a lunatic, and recommends sitting tight, doing nothing, and letting the all-wise Terran bureaucracy handle everything.

With no further ado, Dalton breaks into the arsenal,

abducts the local recruitment officer, Sgt. Brunt, and heads out to the location where the Hukk are landing their assault boat. With the aid of some rifles set on autopilot, and some sniper skills, Dalton damages the boat, and kills half a dozen Hukk officers and crewmen before Brunt, betraying Dalton, wanders into the kill zone waving the white flag.

Dalton pretends to surrender, and then draws his holdout pistol, threatening to shoot through Brunt to kill the Hukk Captain cowering behind him. This Captain had been part of the Grand Fleet which surrendered to Dalton previously off Luna, and remembers him, therefore both fears him and trusts him, and agrees to terms.

The Hukk agree to withdraw if and only if they can save face: that is, Dalton must agree never to reveal that they actually set foot (in their case, set claw) on the frontier planet. Dalton agrees, even though that means he faces scorn from the mayor for ringing a false alarm, and possible criminal prosecution from the militia for breaking and entering and stealing their rifles.

At this point arrives the expected reward for virtue: Brunt turns out to be a Major in Naval Intelligence, specifically sent to the planet to keep an eye on Dalton. Now that it has been proved that Dalton was right about everything all along, was honest and being slandered all along, the Navy Intelligence Corps is willing to embrace him with open arms, let bygones be bygones, and give him his old career back.

Dalton says, "I'll think about it."

The four-word ending impressed me as a child and impresses me more as an adult, albeit now I see the melancholy, the painful sorrow, beneath that brief and stoic sentence. It means that the Naval Intelligence Corps is no more to be trusted to protect a man's conscience than is the

Senatorial staff, the bureaucrats, the State Department, or the Joint Chiefs who form the backdrop of corruption and compromise against which Dalton shines so brightly, and so alone.

It means there is no reward for virtue. None.

It means virtue is not its own reward, virtue means merely getting a boot in the teeth when a man is already beaten into the ground.

As a youth, I was too sunny and filled with the milk of human kindness to be able to comprehend such a bitter moral to the story. I just thought it meant Dalton did not need the approval of his peers, that he was a nonconformist (as was I, and all of my generation. We were nonconformists together, in perfect lockstep, each careful to be a nonconformist exactly like all the others). Like I said, I did not get it.

Dalton is a martyr. He is a witness to a higher moral code than any code found in this life. But, since this is a science fiction story, and since it was written in the seventies, no introduction of any religious theme would have been welcomed here. It would have been against the mood, which, as I said, is Noir in its purest and darkest form.

It is Noir, but is it science fiction?

The story of *The Glory Game* contained no science fictional speculations at all. It was in that sense a very conservative book, dwelling on what was the same in human nature in all ages past and present. It could have been set in any setting with the same impact.

But if we define science fiction to include only those tales that have scientific speculation as the center of their plot, we are defining science fiction to exclude my genre, Space Opera, which is defined as an adventure story in a vaguely Science Fiction-flavored setting.

The rule of thumb is a thought experiment: imagine the

same story set in the present, on Earth, or in the historical past. Eliminate the scientific speculation present. If the story can still be told, it is not SF. In SF the speculation is the heart of the story. If you can tell the same tale on the sailing ship *Enterprise* or from the viewpoint of plucky rebels fighting the Roman Empire or the Spanish Empire rather than the Galactic Empire, then the tale is not SF properly so called.

On the other hand, this is a crisp and clear definition, very serviceable to fans of Analog, and other 'Nuts and Bolts' types, so I dare utter no protest against it.

The definition clearly works for Hard SF. Let us take three examples from Heinlein, Asimov, and Clark, by common consensus, the hardest of Hard SF writers, or at least the most famous.

There is no story in *Stranger In A Strange Land* if Mike the Martian is not from Mars, does not have psychic powers, and was not raised by a more advanced species than man. The science fictional speculation about what a higher civilization would be like which stands to industrial, monogamous and monotheistic civilization as the civilization stands to primitive polytheist and polygamous savages is the core of the book.

The same story being told about, let us say, a castaway infant raised in the jungle wilderness returning to his family in London could not contrast the shortcomings of civilization with future splendors of the orgy-ridden nudist communism which Heinlein, (and apparently every heresy since the dawn of time), has seen as the futuristic or utopian superior of civilized virtue. Such a story can, however, contrast the shortcomings of civilization with the noble savagery of more primitive times — such is the point of

Tarzan and *A Princess Of Mars* and Conan stories and countless others.

The story is innately progressive, showing how the next
step in evolution, the superman, can throw aside his
clothing and his marriage vows as easily as he throws aside
the curse of Adam saying he must toil for his bread. The
superman lives without sin and without law. And without
clothing.

By contrast, *Starship Troopers*, (a book I myself far prefer),
could have taken place anywhere, anytime, since it is only a
story of boot camp and a series of lectures on civic responsibility. Nothing would have been lost by making Mr. Rico
into a grunt storming Normandy Beach, or a footslogger in
Caesar's Gallic campaign, or an Apache brave learning the
rough and manly discipline of the warband. Only the props
and backdrops would change, not the plot and theme.

Here we find an inherently conservative message in an
inherently conservative story, that is, the tools of war
change, but men don't.

Likewise, there is no story in *Foundation* without the
Seldon Plan, (and, to be blunt, precious little with it), that is,
without the science fictional speculation that human history
is subject to predictable laws just like the gas laws.

The story is a story about social engineering. A math-
ematician and a group of academic intellectuals decide to
save civilization by manipulating history, and their plan
leads to a Second Empire. The idea of giving votes to
plebeians simply never comes up.

By contrast, *The Stars Like Dust* could have been written
as a historical novel concerning the declining Roman
Empire facing the Golden Horde.

Likewise again, *Childhood's End* is a book I take to be the quintessential science fiction book. It is almost a myth, not a novel, since the main characters are all utterly forgettable. There is no story aside from the central conceit of a more advanced species aiding, (or forcing), mankind up the next step of the ladder of evolution to the realm of the superhuman. The concept of the ladder of evolution where supermen stand to men as men stand to apes is pure Science Fiction, indeed, is almost the definition of Science Fiction.

The Overlords fulfill all the Progressive dreams in one fell swoop. As the gigantic saucers hover over the cities of man, there is suddenly one world government, an end to war, and (oddly, considering the world is about to be destroyed) no more bullfighting nor cruelty to animals. And that silly mental disease called religion is brushed airily aside in a paragraph: man is too grown up for gods. Then in the climax of the book, the children of men become gods, man goes extinct, the world is obliterated, and the children of men fly off as pure spirits to merge with the Galactic Overmind also known as the Pleroma, the disembodied paradise of the Gnostics. The destruction of the material world and a life of pure and disembodied intellect was the central concept of Neoplatonism and every other heresy since the dawn of time. Think of it as taking nudism to the ultimate extreme.

By contrast, uh... I cannot think of a single novel or short story by Arthur Clarke which was not science fiction, that is, a story that could have been told in some other milieu without losing its point.

I warned the reader that this would not be a book review but an exploration of another chain of thought to which rereading this book led me. Here below is that chain of thought. And, for better or worse, it is a long one.

The theme of the book, as I said above, is abnormally

clear, because Laumer skillfully has left out anything which might detract or delay from emphasizing that theme. This story is as sharply pointed as a fable by Aesop. The point is the answer to the question famously asked by Socrates, but surely asked by all men in all ages when they reach a certain age, whether it is better to be seen as evil while truly being good, or to be seen as good while truly being evil?

The question divorces the reward of virtue from the reality of virtue, at least, in the view of the world where the only reward is the esteem and applause of men. Tan Dalton does what is right, come hellfire or floodwater, and does not flinch at paying the price in terms of esteem lost, prestige ruined, career savaged, character slandered—and he does not get the girl in the end.

The setup of the paradox of seeming rather than being good is simple enough: Dalton is presented with two political parties, a stupid party and an evil party, both of whom have a dumb and cowardly answer to a not-very-complex question, but a question that requires bravery and fortitude to answer. He cannot in good conscience join with either party, and so he is isolated, despised by both, and scorned by all. In other words, he is given for his goodness the exact same reward rightly given to evil men.

One thing that particularly delighted me both as a child and as a man about Dalton's answer is the pragmatic idealism of it. Pragmatically, it is unwise either to overreact or underreact to the aggression of an ambitious but weaker alien menace. But whether it is unwise or not, it is *unfair* on idealistic grounds not just to Mankind, but to the Hukk aggressor also, to meet aggression with a reward, because it confuses them into a false picture of the world, one where they can make many small piecemeal attacks with no fear of massive, overwhelming, or, (in this case), genocidal retaliation.

Now surely no one raised in a Christian nation, (even one that is culturally Christian if not officially), is unaware of the answer to the Socratic question. The non-Christians who, for whatever reason, accept Christian value judgments as valid can see in the example of Christ on the cross, or Socrates drinking hemlock, the reward of being good rather than looking good. Until very recently, the picture of a man willing to make any sacrifice to do the right thing, despite any slander or false accusation, was a paramount ideal of our civilization.

The self-aggrandizing hucksterism of a Cassius Clay was not a mainstream ideal, nor was success at any cost, nor did anyone listen to smirking cads who said that winning was not everything, but the only thing.

Even children were taught the ideal of seeking the reward of virtue not in the opinion of the fickle world: Superman is garbed as a drab and mild mannered reporter who cannot even get a date, no worldly reward comes to Clark Kent for his good deeds; Spider-Man is hated as a menace by the city he saves, so if anything, his reward is even less. These are the men upheld, and rightly so, as heroes to our children. Glory Hounds like Booster Gold or Gilderoy Lockheart are rightly portrayed as distasteful, comedic, or villainous.

We are a society that by tradition—Christian tradition—mistrusts those who seek the good opinion of society. How alien this is to the caste system of the Hindu or the Mandarin philosophy of Confucius cannot be overemphasized: in those systems, position in society was identical with virtue. The shame of losing face was the evil, of losing family honor, or getting caught.

On that level, the self-sacrifice of our clean-cut Naval hero in our short adventure novel is nothing extraordinary except perhaps, (as I said), the clean clarity of the point. It is what we Westerners expect. In a happy ending, the merit of the hero is finally rewarded with an overdue recognition, perhaps an apology and a reconciliation. In a tragic ending, the merit of the hero is undiscovered until after his death, if ever.

But, again, the ironic twist of the last four words—"I'll think about it,"—is that of a man who is not eager to accept the alleged reward his overlooked merit has finally earned.

I call it ironic because Dalton is not a Christian who believes in God, nor even a Socratic philosopher who believes in a transcendent ideal of truth worthy of such self-sacrifice. He is just a competent man trying to do a difficult job made more difficult by the evil and stupidity of his political superiors.

I call it ironic because there is a second note or overtone behind this main note of self-sacrifice, the note of Noir cynicism, of hardheaded pragmatism, of dry-eyed unsentimentality which would seem to undermine the idea of self-sacrifice in any form.

For the author goes out of his way in the opening pages of the book, practically the first scene, to permit Dalton to explain what is meant to be a philosophy so plain and clear that none of the craven shortsighted politicians in the book understand it, nor the politician's daughter either. Dalton has the following dialog with Arianne, his girl, which is worth reciting at length, because otherwise the point may be lost.

The humans have forced the moron-level natives of the planet Aldo Cerise onto reservations to make room for humanity, which she regrets, but he justifies with these words:

> "The human race has reached a point where it has to expand into space. Planet-bound, we'll choke on our own waste-products... we have to live, and living means growth, and growing means expansion. A single planet cannot hold us, Arianne. We have to go out, or die."

Heinlein has almost the same argument in almost the same words in his famous and ferociously maligned *Starship Troopers*. Also, I watched the first episode of *Lost In Space* with my kids today. I had forgotten that population pressures are expressly the reason that sends the space family, Robinson, to pioneer a new homestead on an inhabitable planet of Alpha Centauri. In these days of underpopulation, looking at the fears of overpopulation always evokes a weary headshake of wonder in me: what made our parents willing to be buffaloed by the likes of Paul Ehrlich?

Hearing this cold doctrine of population pressure leading to war, Arianne wonders:

> "Why couldn't we limit ourselves to totally uninhabited worlds? Why does our advantage have to mean some other race's disadvantage?"
>
> "You know as well as I that worlds where we can live without artificial environment are rare, and every such world has evolved its own life—is the product of life."
>
> "Of course. I just wish it were somehow different."
>
> "So do I—in a way. And in another way, I accept the laws of nature. The fox is a beautiful animal. Without rabbits to live on, it would soon die out. That's nature. Who are we to decide unilaterally that the order of nature is wrong?"

"So we just go on, perpetuating a dog-eat-dog—or fox-eat-bunny—existence?"

"No—but we have to remember to make the distinction between what's true and what we wish were true."

A paragraph later, the conversation resumes. Dalton remarks that the curious urge to take unwise risks is peculiarly human:

"The old primate trait: climbing down out of a nice safe tree to see what it's like out on the grassland among the lions."

"Don't talk about me as if I were an anthropological specimen," Arianne said.

"But you are, my dear," Dalton said, "And so am I. That is what we have to keep in mind every time we're tempted to play God."

Finally, looking over the colony town of this harsh new world, Arianne wonders at the desperate courage of the first settlers. Dalton comments:

"They did what they had to do. Now the Hukk are doing what they have to do. Our blunder was in not stopping them sooner...."

For a short novel which I have praised several times for being crisp and clear, this is remarkably convoluted and obscure. Dalton seems to be saying that men should avoid overweening pride. Certainly that is not a startling message, and appears in all good stories since Homer. But note what he is dismissing as an act of overweening pride: the act of regarding men as being somehow above nature and in a position to condemn it, namely, to condemn the Darwinian struggle of the fittest to survive.

For Dalton, war is not an evil, or, rather, not an unavoidable evil.

War is just a fact of the business of life, the side-effect of coming, as he puts it, out of the nice safe tree to see what it is like on the grassland. Life is a zero-sum game, so races, in order to survive, must expand and occupy the inhabitable terrain, displacing or exterminating the weaker races as they go, and meeting the expansion attempts of competing races of equal strength with all the terrible ferocity and glory of war: Which, for some reason too obvious to mention in this dialog quoted here, must be fought bravely and honorably, without tear or trembling to face defeat and death at enemy hands, and without buffoonery, chicanery or even treason at friendly hands.

Dalton accepts this grim business as the laws of nature. To rebuke or refuse these laws is yielding to the unsound or perhaps insane temptation to play God.

This unsentimental, plain, and practical doctrine comes across as brisk and cold as a slap of cold water in the face. Life is what it is, and the hero plays the best hand he can with the bad hand he's been dealt.

But why not cheat at cards? Without God, or some transcendent standard of behavior, why must one fight the dog-eat-dog dogfight of Darwin with honor and honesty and good sportsmanship? Why not fight like a dog? Absent God, then there is no referee nor umpire to the great game of life, and no one to chide the winners for cheating, or to cast down the proud from their seats, or to declare the meek blessed.

To be sure, there may be angry retaliation from someone you've cheated when it comes to a rematch, and had you treated him honestly, you might have befriended him (or at least made a temporary alliance of convenience before turning on him when the odds change). But this consideration only applies to enemies whose retaliation you fear, on onlookers whose opinion influences when and on what side they will fight you when their turn comes. And in the remorseless *realpolitik* world of Dalton, their turn will always come.

But behold the paradox. If life is a Darwinian struggle with no umpire, fear of retaliation is a reason not for honorable conduct, but for craven conformity and party-loyalty to whatever faction it is more prudent, from a survival standpoint, to join. Fear of retaliation at most is a motive for looking good but never for being good. What pragmatic reason is there for being idealistic?

There are a number of writers who believe in this odd combination of idealistic pragmatism, but none of them to my knowledge can answer this question. To answer would be too idealistic, I suspect.

If like me, Tancredi Dalton's philosophy reminds markedly you of things said by characters in Robert Heinlein books, or Gordon R. Dickson, or Poul Anderson, or half a dozen others I could name, you may be wondering about the similarity.

Do not wonder. Writers, and the readers who support them, have a large but finite number of philosophical stances, given the current situation of the intellectual and cultural history of the West, about which they can cluster.

Naturally writers less concerned with philosophical

coherence can range over a wide set of stances, since such men can contradict themselves more often, but those of average coherence gravitate to a very small number of positions.

The reasons, most importantly their view of man and man's place in the cosmos, such men give for their conclusions on one issue are more likely to inform their conclusions on other issues, because drawing a distinction or exception as to why their general logic or general worldview does not apply in this case is an extra effort, and introduces an ever greater possibility of self-contradiction. Something like a natural Occam's Razor operates in all human consciousness, rewarding simpler and clearer explanations over jury-rigs of *ad hoc*.

Now, you might say that only philosophers are interested in avoiding self-contradiction in their worldview; that everyone else follows the general trend of their times, or repeats the opinions of their parents or of the talking hairstyles on the television.

You would be partly right, but only partly. Philosophers are concerned with rational consistency, the kind of thing one can put into words. Layman are concerned with a consistency of mood or general outlook, a consistency of judgment, the kind of thing one cannot put into words, but by which one lives one's life.

There is a reason why those who favor high taxes and high minimum wage laws also by and large favor gun control: because both value judgments about the role of property and the role of self-defense are informed by a more fundamental judgment about the civility and independence of man versus the prudence of trusting Caesar, either with gold or with iron.

Not every man who favors high taxes is a gun-grabber: I

once met a man who was not. But he had to go to some elaborate explanation, one might say rationalization, to reconcile his view of man as weak and untrustworthy, ergo not to be allowed control of his own money, with his view of man as strong and trustworthy, ergo not to be disallowed control of his own means of self-defense.

Let us therefore map out, in far more detail than any patient reader would care to see, the whole landscape of thought as it exists from now until the end of the world.

Usually the books that have the profoundest effect on us are those encountered in the green youth of early adulthood, in the late teens or early twenties, which provide some schema or structural explanation of the complexities of life young adults so dearly need to orient themselves. In my case, however, there is at least one book I encountered later in life which provided a framework of pellucid clarity for understanding the relation of schools of thought one to another. There is many a student who regards the description in Plato's *Republic* of the degrees of the degeneration of the state as just such an epiphany. This was to me what the *Republic* was to them. It comes from a tract called *Nihilism* by a man who delights in the name Archmonk Brother Seraphim Rose, albeit he was born Eugene Rose.

Rose's scheme groups the schools of thought of Western man as he falls away from Christianity into four general categories.

The first school of thought is the classical liberal position of the pragmatic man, which says that religious opinion is a private matter that ought not to disturb the public weal by insisting on any special or central position in life. Instead of God as the source and center and summit of civilized life, or precise theologically defined dogmas addressed to the last nuance, we should have instead a rogue and vague dogma saying only that each man should mind his own business.

In this school, each man is free to seek his own pleasures in his own way, climb to the summit of his ambitions without necessarily stepping on those below him, (but not necessarily giving him a hand either). We all must agree only on general rules of civility and good sportsmanship needed for public order; we need to encourage and obey the civic virtues of teamwork and self-sacrifice where needed to keep the family, the city, and the market free from fraud, trespass, or invasion, and perhaps to curb such gross immorality or bad taste as pollutes the public weal. Each man must show respect for the religious opinions of others without showing uncomely zeal for his own.

In this school, ideals are impractical, because the world is imperfect and cannot be made perfect; but civic virtue and the prudent exercise of liberty and civilized tolerance of the dissent of others, which is their prudent exercise of their liberty, is crucial. A healthy respect for what are called 'Judeo-Christian Values' is crucial to the civil order. God is not crucial.

Ironically, this is the Liberal position as classically understood, characterized by Locke and other Enlightenment writers, what would now be called Conservative. That is the diametric opposite of what is now called the Liberal position is a source of confusion.

To avoid confusion, let us call this pragmatic and man-centric school of thought 'Worldliness.' The Worldly want to leave heaven alone and tend to business here on earth. They are hard-headed and hard-hearted men, idealistic only for ideals that work, impatient with theory, concerned with results.

The second school of thought is the sharp rebellion

against this. Where the Worldly position seeks worldly
wealth, civic peace, and the comfort of conformity in opinion, the Radical rebellion seeks Heaven on Earth, Utopian
visions made solid, and all pragmatism is rejected as treason
against the Great Dream of the Great Cause. Religion and
Worldliness are rejected with scorn in favor of Ideology.
Ideals are impractical, so this school holds, only because
men are weak vessels too selfish to practice them; all the
world could be made perfect if only sufficient force was
used on weak men by a sufficiently enlightened and
despotic Glorious Leader.

The only Ideology to afflict the modern era is Socialism
and its various mild epigones, Fabianism, Leftism, Feminism, Environmentalism, Political Correctness, and other
Marxist offshoots. Nowadays they are accustomed to deny
their Marxist roots, but gaily and liberally use simplistic
Marxist myths about oppressors and oppressed to analyze
human relations between man and workingman, man and
women, man and nature, man and ideas. The relation is one
of a ruthless Darwinian struggle for survival between man
and fill-in-the-blank, and even saying "he" rather than "he
and she" is defined as an act of oppression.

In this school, freedom is dismissed as selfishness and
sacrificed to the common good or the Great Dream of the
Utopian vision. Man lives for his neighbor, or, to be precise,
for the Utopian vision. The only rules demanded are those
of loyalty to the Great Dream. Civil order is not the paramount value, as disobedience, (either peaceful or violent or
ultraviolent), to established hence 'reactionary' civil
authority is not just allowed but required. All institutions of
the state and church and civil society are to be smashed, or,
in the less violent version of the Ideology, subverted,
suborned, and subordinated to the Utopian vision. Only the

Great Dream merits love, loyalty, respect, honesty, courtesy; only the Great Dream has rights; anyone disloyal to the Great Dream is an enemy. Life is Crusade.

Hatred of God and Man, hatred of Judeo-Christian and indeed all civilized values of any sort, is required in the long run, albeit a pretense of respecting ideals such as compassion for the poor or the equality of man is needed during the initial subversive period, to gain the aid of useful idiots.

Because this school of thought changes its name and its public rationale as frequently as the fashion industry changes the height of skirt hems, and because this school is fundamentally subversive, that is, fundamentally based on an inner circle deceiving the useful idiots of an outer circle who believe the opposite of the movement's true purpose, no unambiguous name can be assigned these ideologues.

They are Socialists in economic issues, feminists on family questions, Greens on questions of industrial policy, Race-baiters and Hatemongers on questions of race, absurdist in art and vulgarians in culture, totalitarians in politics but libertarians when it comes to questions of vice and victimless crimes. They are materialists on philosophical issues, secularists on religious issues, pacifists on military issues, (unless the question is civil war and the overthrow of their own institutions, whereupon they are bloodthirsty war hawks and apologists, nay, groupies and shrieking bobby-soxers of the world's filthiest dictators).

In sum, they are idolaters who substitute the worship of Caesar for the worship of Christ; they are Gnostics in the posture of eternal rebellion both against God in Heaven and civil society on Earth. They are chameleons who adopt any ideals or values or party lines needed for so long as needed to destroy them, including Pragmatism, including Worldliness. They are Politically Correct and factually incorrect.

They seek to destroy civilized institutions here on Earth and drag Utopia down from heaven to replace them, indifferent, or even glorying, in the bloodshed required.

To avoid confusion, let us call them Ideologues. They are utterly unworldly, rejecting the pragmatism of the Worldly Man as cold and loveless and unspiritual.

The Ideologues are as nearly a pure evil as mankind has ever produced or can imagine, but please note that their motives are the highest and noblest imaginable: they seek things of the spirit, peace on earth, food for the poor, dignity given to all men, and all such things which are the only things, the holy things, that can electrify dull mankind and stir him to take up the banner and trumpet and shining lance of high and holy crusade.

The pure putrefaction of their evil springs from their materialist philosophy, which says that man can create Eden on Earth; and overthrow the Curse on Adam, that he must labor for his bread; overthrow the Curse of Eve, that says she will be subject to her husband; and overthrow the curse on the snake, that says he will be bruised. Merely reaching out one's hand, breaking all the laws of reason and morality, will allow one's eyes to be opened, and to be God.

The materialist philosophy says that in a godless world all we need do to overthrow the laws of economics and the limits of human nature is shed enough blood and make enough sacrifices of other innocent people, and the mouths of endless cornucopias will be opened. You cannot make an omelet without a genocide of innocent eggs, and without Walter Duranty to get a Pulitzer for lying his ass off about it.

The Ideologue position is a revulsion and a rejection of the Worldly Man and his civilized pragmatism. The Worldly Man accepts necessary evils. The Worldly Man is willing to go to war for peace, and willing to tolerate his neighbor for peace. The Ideologue tolerates no one and nothing, not even an unspoken thought, if it is against the Party, against the Program, against the Great Leader, or against the Great Dream. The Ideologue is a heresy-hunter. But he is also a coward, since he is not willing to go to war; it revolts him that reality makes war necessary. He thinks peace comes from placating enemies with gifts, or enlightening them through education to the wonders of the Great Dream.

A third school of thought is in sharp rebellion against the first two. These are otherworldly types, Theosophists and Spiritualists and New Age gurus and believers in various Americanized forms of Buddhism or Witchcraft or Astrology who utterly reject both the materialistic worldliness of the Worldly Man, and the fanaticism and bloodlust of the Ideologue.

The otherworldly men seek peace through renunciation, and escape from the turmoil of life through the pursuit of inner tranquility, perhaps aided by mystic visions, meditations, or voices from the outer worlds, or hallucinogenic drugs.

Not for them the looming smokestacks of the scientifically planned socialist utopia of the Ideologues, nor the loud billboards and hungry strip malls of the Worldly. They want to live in Hobbiton, or Arcadia, or with the tribes that only exist in the imagination of Rousseau, noble savages in harmony with nature, or perhaps the movie *Dances With Wolves* or *Avatar* (not the real one).

This movement has never been numerous enough to merit its own name, and although they often combine with their enemies, the Ideologues against their mutual enemies the Worldly Men, these otherworldly men have no name. Call them Spiritualists.

The Spiritualists are utterly unpragmatic and irrational

about their religious sentiments. They are the type of men who believe in angels but not in God. They have no use for theology or reasoning about spiritual or moral issues, much less metaphysics. They are the dilettantes and aesthetes of the spirit world, seeking sensation rather than understanding, novelty rather than certainty, seeking a spiritual truth that will serve them and flatter them and provide for them, not a God whom they must serve.

They feel toward the things of the spirit what the Worldly Man feels towards worldly goods in the marketplace. The only thing the Spiritualist does not want is a final answer, an organized religion, a Church. He wants to hear gossip from the Ghost of Cleopatra but not words of power from the Prophet Jeremiah. The only thing the spiritual seeker does not want is for the Holy Spirit to come to seek him out.

The Spiritualists are as nearly worthless in peace or war as it is possible for any warm bodies occupying space and breathing in otherwise useful oxygen can be, but their motive is noble and high and pure. They suffer the same revulsion about worldliness and the same yearning for something better as does a hermit standing on a pillar in the desert.

Their drive is indeed purely spiritual, but it does not drive them toward the only reality worth seeking in the spirit world, namely, the Holy Spirit. Hence the effort is self-centered, reaches nowhere, inspires no social revolutions, builds no observatories, erects no universities, opens no charity hospitals, captures no Holy Lands, kills no Saracens, galvanizes no missionaries to spread the Good News of Fashionable Theosophist Blither to the unenlightened savages. Charity, the burning love of the Christian, is impossible in the Spiritualist framework because charity requires an objective standard of values, a living truth as terrible as unquenchable fire, and not merely a selfish seeking for truth.

Although much less violent and much, much, much less dishonest than the Ideologues, the Spiritualists are also, ironically, farther from God and farther from the truth. The Ideologue is at least willing to join a crusade, man a barricade, march in a protest, send money and mash notes to gangsters in Russia and sadists in Cuba, and falsify news reports about the murders and enormities of their fellow travelers.

The Ideologue has a perverted ideal of charity toward the poor and downtrodden in the same way that the homosexual has a perverted ideal of romantic love; and it is just as sterile and vile. But in the same way that the sodomite at least is a step above masturbation, in that his love at least turns outward toward another man, the Ideologue is at least concerned with destroying allegedly unjust social institutions such as church and state and marriage and sanity, whereas the Spiritualist wishes, like the shy cenobite, to withdraw from the shock and jar of the world and seek the ineffable in private. Spiritualism is the otherworldly version of the Sin of Onan.

The final school of thought is not a school of thought at all, but an exhausted rejection of thought. This is Nihilism, and it is the dominant philosophy of our age, and the unspoken assumption underlying nearly every major social policy debated or enacted today.

Nihilism is the metaphysical posture that no truth is actually true. If no truth is true, life is what you yourself have the strength of will to decree it to be, like God separating Light from Darkness at the dawn of time, by fiat. If no truth is true, no flag is truly worth dying for or fighting for or even arguing about, and no marriage is final and no contract is binding and your word of honor means nothing, and you owe your friends no loyalty.

If no truth is true, the only impermissible sin is to believe and preach and practice the truth.

Nihilism shares with Worldliness its patience for dissent. Since no truth is true, there is no point in disagreeing with another man, nor even having a deep conversation with him on any topic, not even to discover whether he disagrees or not.

Nihilism shares with Ideologues their contempt for worldly and material things, for ambition and self-made men. None of these things are worth seeking in and of themselves, but only if you, in your godlike self-sovereignty, deem or decree them to be worth seeking.

Nihilism shares with Spiritualism its distaste for theology or reason or organized religion.

The Nihilist lives in a formless void, and believes only in himself, his willpower, his self-image and his self-esteem. His motto is that life is what you make it.

He sees the long and tragic history of man, with all its kings and slaves and wars and empires and monarchs and democracies and despots and with all its philosophers and saints and sages, and sees that none of these things have brought peace.

And so he condemns all systems, all sagacity and all saintliness to oblivion, and promises that as soon as men realize that there is nothing in the universe, then nothing will be worth fighting for, and man will have peace.

The Nihilist does not mention that man will no longer be man in any recognizable sense of the word, merely a dull lump of meat seeking to beguile the hours with diversions both refined and profane until kindly death relieves him of the intolerable burden of a conscious existence he did not seek and does not use. Nihilism is the cult of death.

Unlike the Worldly Man, or the Ideologue, or the Spiritualist, the Nihilist seeks nothing but to bolster his self-esteem and entertain himself to death. Nihilism is an end-state. There is no room for a rebellion away from Nihilism because there is nothing away from which to rebel.

The reason why I say the scheme of Seraphim Rose maps out the mental landscape from now until the end of the world is that Nihilism is a dead end. There is no further point of degeneration beneath which to fall. Once your philosophy tells you all philosophy is vain, you cannot erect a new philosophical variation on that foundation. There will never be such a thing as Neo-Nihilism or Post-Nihilism.

The reason why I say the scheme is complete is that there are no other major variations possible, once Christianity is abandoned, for a worldview.

Christianity is the only religion that combines reason, ethics, spiritualism and individualism into one coherent theological picture of the cosmos and man's place in it. Christianity is the center of the map of possible worldviews. Everything that deviates from it abandons one of these or the other in order to emphasize its opposite.

Imagine the map with reason to the north, spiritualism to the south, individualism to the west, and ethics to the east.

The Worldly Man moves north toward great Reason, abandoning the mysticism of Spiritualism to the south. He keeps his ethics and his individualism, but in a distorted form; for he attempt to shift ethics and individualism onto a secular footing, and give practical rather than idealistic reasons to justify his ideals.

The Ideologue moves east, abandoning individualism

and self-centeredness in favor of the great collectivist daydream of a unified crusade to create a unified world. His effort, odd as it sounds considering the appalling evil of his means and goals, is toward ethics. He wants life to have an overall ethical meaning, a crusade, a moral structure worthy of his devotion. Absent God, of course, what he gets is a political party. His spiritualism becomes distorted and placed on a secular footing, so that instead of seeking the Utopia of the New Jerusalem in Heaven, he seeks the Utopia of the Socialist Commonwealth in Tomorrowland, and instead of worshiping God he worships science, (or, rather, SCIENCE!), which promises him an endless uplift to superhuman wealth and power. His reason is likewise distorted. Reason becomes 'freethinking' which means an idolatry of scientific materialism, and involving a loss of philosophy and free inquiry. Instead of debate, the freethinker merely accuses his opponents of bigotry and bias, or undermines the opponent's argument as being illegitimate for some other reason. And this he calls reason, and he is much inflated with his self-opinion on how reasonable and scientific he is.

The Spiritualist moves south, losing sight of reason, seeking intuition and mystic revelation. He is an individualist in that his quest is a lonely one, but whether it ends in the Buddhist desire to quench the self, or in the Christian desire for redemption and glorification via non-Christian means, cannot be known beforehand. His ethics continue but they are distorted in the opposite fashion as the Worldly Man's, for the Spiritualist seeks emotional and mystical and ineffable reasons for his ethical behavior. Moral rules have force not because they were revealed by God, but because they were revealed by personal visions.

The Nihilist moves toward individualism and abandons

ethics. He keeps a distorted view of spirituality and reason, just enough to justify his belief in himself and his own ability to create his own reality for himself.

Again, we may be able to assign certain meaning to the diagonals of this diagram, such as by placing Fabians, (peaceful Ideologues, socialists rather than communists), to the northeast, or Nazis with their mystical worship of Blood and Iron to the southeast, Libertarians and other arch-rational individualists to the northwest, and Satanists and Witches with their self-centered view of the spirit world, which they regard as no more than a source of power, to the southwest.

There is of course a pagan worldview possible before Christianity is introduced, and heretical or breakaway worldviews copying only some aspects of Christianity, such as Islam or Mormonism. But as a practical matter, classical paganism has been absorbed into the Christian worldview and baptized, so that one cannot be an Aristotelian or Neoplatonist or Stoic without gravitating toward Christianity. Neopaganism has nothing to do with paganism except its name: Neopagans are Spiritualists, men seeking an undemanding form of spirituality without the demands of a strict moral code. Pre-Christian schools of thought would tend to gravitate nearer the center, with Oriental religions such as Taoism toward the spiritual, Oriental systems like Confucianism toward the ethical, (away from the individual), and Greek philosophy toward the reason.

We can also assign the various Protestant sects positions nearer and farther from the center. Calvinists and Lutherans, for example, who have a deep mistrust both of Aristotelian philosophy and organized religion, might be placed either westward or southward of the very center, more spiritual or more individual, or, due to their greater keenness to avoid the evils of drink and concupiscence, the Puritans might be placed immediately to the east, closer to the ethical pole.

But this would involve needless complications, and give an appearance of particularity where none exists: this chart is good only as a very rude overview of what large numbers of smart people, taken as a group, have in common in their thinking, and the commonality is one of mood and world-view, not one of specific philosophical axioms.

We science fiction fans can, however, place any author famous for any strong opinions without much debate on this map. (We are only identifying how the way each portrays his characters betrays his view of man in the cosmos, not making any bold assumption about what the author himself might think on a given issue.)

Heinlein and the John W. Campbell, Jr. authors, whether conservative or liberal on any particular question, portrayed in their books a view of man as strong and independent, a creature evolved to explore, expand, and conquer: they are Worldly Men, ranging to the north. Ursula K. Le Guin portrayed a view of man as a creature best served by seeking a tranquil life, preferably in a bucolic setting. She is to the south, a Spiritualist, specifically a Taoist. China Mieville is an Ideologue; Michael Moorcock is a Nihilist.

Armed with this perhaps over complex and inefficient classification system, the stance of Tancredi Dalton, and perhaps of Keith Laumer, becomes more clear. Like a character in a Noir story, Tan is a tarnished knight, someone who does the right thing despite the jeers and brickbats of the world, not for the greater glory of God and recompense in heaven, but for no glory and without recompense. It is an absurdly bitter worldview, for it calls upon men to embrace the tribulations and torments of martyrdom, but denies them the martyr's palm in heaven. The most you can hope for is the quiet nod of fatherly approval from your own conscience.

Dalton's stance is that of a purely Worldly Man who has pulled away from the spiritual axis of the map so far that the question is not even raised once in the text, and the only mention of God is in the context of what not to pretend to be. But he is still near enough to the center to admire and promote Christian ideals of knightly behavior, such as mercy toward a fallen foe, or such as keeping one's word of honor, which have clear justification in the Christian worldview but only sentimental justification, or none, in a pagan worldview or a pragmatic one.

But Dalton is drifting, rudderless and unanchored, toward the drear and muddy waters of Nihilism. The only source of his moral code is a brusque Darwinian view of the inevitability of war, due, (of all stupid things), to population pressures and pollution increases. This view cannot logically justify honor toward a fallen foe nor self-sacrifice when faced by a dilemma, but it can justify those things in terms of mood and worldview, that is, man is presented as being both foolish and brave for climbing from the safe tree to the dangerous lion-haunted grasslands, and this foolhardiness will carry him one day to the stars, but will not banish the lion from the haunted darkness, nor make it lie down with the lamb.

This is the point of view of a Western man, raised in a culture seeped with Christian notions of chivalry and fair play and equality and nobility, but who has lost confidence in the center. It is the point of view of the knight errant who lacks faith in the crusade, and hides the red cross he wears.

We must also add a historical note to put this in perspective:

The 1970's, when this was written, at the height of the Cold War, was a low point, perhaps the lowest point, in the confidence of the West.

Christianity was slowly being shoved out of the public square as old-fashioned, unscientific, absurd and repressive, and being replaced by an incoherent mush of Darwinism, which said that man was a beast; Freudianism, which said that morals were unhealthy but uninhibited self-indulgence and selfishness was healthy because the mind of man was an irrational machine; Marxism, which said that all human society was a ruthless war between oppressor and oppressed; and Nietzscheanism, which said that God was dead. So man was no longer the apex of created life, no longer a rational animal, no longer a political animal, and no longer could turn to any higher power for help.

The Cold War was being fought during an era when we were continually being told by our intellectual class that we were in the wrong but that our mortal enemies, the vilest lying-ass butchers and mass murderers in history, were in the right.

But the decline and loss of confidence of the West has roots earlier than that: the disaster of World War One had far greater repercussions overseas than here, but our artists and novelists took their inspiration from the European intelligentsia, sitting among the graves and memorials of the Great War which did not end war after all, amid the toppled crowns and the crumbling cathedrals. The intellectuals told the world that the war had not been to stop barbaric German aggression, but instead had occurred for no reason and to no point. Christianity had failed to stop the horror. The intellectuals, seeking a more fashionable home than the discredited Church, fled to each quarter of the mental map given above, to silly spiritualism and barbaric nihilism or to cold and optimistic rationalism, but most of all, as a stampede, they fled toward the crusade of the Great Dream of socialism.

Americans reacted with disdain and a crusade of their own against the Red Menace. This is clear enough in the writings of the 1930's and 1940's that at least half of the popular authors were unimpressed with this utterly unchristian and starkly anti-American, (and anti-human), worldview that was proving so alluring to the shattered Europeans. The classical Noir story, the whole detective genre as defined by Hammett and Chandler and their many epigones, comes from that era. Each is a tale of a lonely individual using his brawn and brains to overcome corruption and the collapse.

Each is a tale of medieval knighthood, a tale of King Arthur, but not of Arthur finding the Holy Grail, no: Noir stories are each a tale of Arthur on the margin of the sea watching in grim yet dry eyed sorrow as the tired but gold eagles of Rome disappear over the horizon, leaving England forever, and watching behind him the lamps of civilization go out, with none to reignite them but him.

Keith Laumer was a fan and epigone of the hard-boiled school of writing, and all his serious characters are serious in the Chandler and Hammett motif. A Noir hero, even a Space Navy hero, cannot appeal to any higher power or higher authority for his moral standard, but only to an unspoken and hard-won hardheadedness which admits of no more compromises, no matter how weary the load continuing to bear him down.

That is what I now see rereading this simple morality play as an adult which I did not see as a youth: Tan Dalton has to speak those last four words and refuse, or, at least, express caution about, rushing toward any reward which will recompense him for his loss.

The Worldly Man can maintain his optimism about leaving God on the sidelines and concentrating on building up the strength of the city and the wealth of the market-place. Wars and famines come. The rains come and the flood.

When that happens, he has three basic choices: he can react with childish petulance, and demand the world and everything in it be revised to make war and poverty impossible. That is the reaction that is half a step toward the Ideologue. That is where you find Isaac Asimov or Arthur C. Clarke and all the other confident Worldly Men of science fiction when the future they predicted turns out darker than we hoped: they tell you not to lose hope because the experts in the government will fix it. Man is infinitely pliant and pliable, and any day now we can expect utopia to be discovered in a lab. This folly at least has the gleam of optimism.

Or he can react with stoicism and cynicism, and tell himself not to believe life's fairy-tales, and to make the needed sacrifices not for any particular reason, but only because of his own isolated but understated heroism. That is the reaction that is half a step toward the Nihilist. There is where you find Tan Dalton, and perhaps Keith Laumer and Bob Heinlein and all the other confident Worldly Men of science fiction when the future they predicted turns out darker than you hoped: they start talking about how each man is an island, and owes no other man anything. Man will never improve nor change, and the heroic man who sees what is right for himself and works for himself and triumphs for himself will never change, nor bend, nor yield. Man is not pliant. This folly at least has the dignity of pessimism.

Or, he can realize that worldliness by its very nature and inevitably leads to disappointment if it is not based on otherworldliness. Even as all math is based on principles not themselves open to mathematical proof or disproof, even as all physics is based on assumptions no physical experiment can prove or disprove, the Worldly Man, when he realizes the simple truth that all nature is based on the supernatural, only then can he restore God to the central place in his life and in his society. Only then can that man have a rational view of life that does not idolize rationality. Such idolatry is not rational at all, but is instead a reluctant cynicism, a yearning for the untarnished ideals of yore, and an irrational desire to be good even at the cost of a present evil for which the cynic sees no future recompense.

8

GENE WOLFE, GENRE WORK, AND
LITERARY DUTY

The Nebula Awards have just honored Gene Wolfe with a Grandmastership. The honor is overdue, and all lovers of literature should rejoice. Gene Wolfe is the Luis Borges of North America. He is the greatest living author writing in the English language today, and I do not confine that remark to genre authors. I mean he is better than any mainstream authors at their best, better in the very aspects of the craft in which they take most pride. The beauty, nuance, and manner of his prose, the depth and realism of his characterization, his ability to give each character a unique and memorable voice and speech-mannerism, the profundity of the themes he addresses, the dry and trenchant wit, the relevance to daily concerns, the ability to open the eyes of the readers to the horror and wonder of life —I defy anyone to name his superior in craft and execution either in the genre or out of it.

With no little satisfaction, I was contemplating this victory for one of my favorite authors, (not to mention a fellow member of the famous Secret Conspiracy of Catholic Science Fiction Authors), when I was reminded of the larger question: When we honor an author, if the honor is not just flattery but is honestly meant, then we are honoring him for his skill, inspiration, and pertinacity in accomplishing a goal we admire. What is the goal of science fiction?

The obvious answer is that we science fiction writers, like all entertainers, are paid to tell entertaining tales, and must not cheat the audience who pays us of what they have a right to expect in return. That answer is sound enough as far as it goes, but it begs the larger question of what constitutes honest entertainment. What is it? More importantly, what is it for?

And in this case, the question was not just about pay but honor, which is a payment more rare and precious than gold. One only honors those who accomplish their duty. What, if any, be our duties as authors to literature, to our audience in particular and society in general, and to the truth?

The answer may perhaps be most easily seen if we look at it negatively. We might see what the duty is if we ask what is the source of the disappointment, (or even outrage), seen when such an honor is denied.

You will frequently hear the complaint in science fiction circles that mainstream literature does not take science fiction seriously. This complaint is partly fair and partly unfair.

The complaint is fair to the degree that those who serve as watchdogs over the standards of good taste and moral edification in fine literature are not doing their duty justly and impartially. If, instead doing their duty justly, the watchdogs are excluding from public attention memorable works of art on arbitrary or elitist grounds, we have a right to complain. Or, (more to the point), if the watchdogs are adversaries rather than advocates of good taste and edification in fine literature, we not only have the right to complain, we have the right to riot, to storm their Bastille, and haul the snobs off to the guillotine of public scorn.

The complaint is unfair to the degree that we who write science fiction literature decide to write hackwork space-adventure stories or vampire romances instead of reaching as if with the quill of an angel of fire toward the highest ambition of literature.

It is also unfair to complain that science fiction is snubbed by the watchdogs of literature if we are talking about cases where it is not. By this, I mean, if we are talking about any book which becomes known to the general public either despite the watchdogs, (overleaping the fences whose narrow door they guard), or welcomed by the watchdogs.

Specifically, I mean books like *Nineteen Eighty-four* by George Orwell, *Brave New World* by Aldous Huxley, or even *Atlas Shrugged* by Ayn Rand. These books, whether praised or excoriated, are not now ignored by the watchdogs of literature nor by the general public. Indeed, the word "Orwellian" has passed into public use to describe the art of using impudent absurdities as propaganda weapons—and the word "Orwellian" did not become famous due to a reference to *Down And Out In Paris And London* or any other book written under the name Orwell, but only because of his Science Fiction novel.

For that matter, the complaint is unfair if it is anachronistic. When I was young, science fiction was written for boys, published in paperback, meant as cheap mass-market entertainment to be read once and forgotten, and spoke to such deep and lasting question of the human condition as were addressed by the average episode of *The Twilight Zone* or the average superhero comic book—by which I do not mean they lacked all depth, merely that they touched on deep issues only in a glancing way, meant to produce a startled or jarring moment of awe or irony or wonder, not to provoke lingering meditation on sublime truths.

This has changed in my lifetime. Science fiction is now so much part of the mainstream that opinion-makers, pundits, political leaders and others who speak on serious topics make references to *Star Wars* or *The Lord Of The Rings* without hesitation or blush or, (more significantly), without any fear of being misunderstood.

Part of this is demographics: the youth in the 1950's did not surrender their comic books and paperback space operas upon reaching old age in the 2000's. Pundits make passing reference to popular stories, not because they are great stories, (they may or may not be), but because they are popular.

Part of this is the result of the evolution, (whether unintentional or as a byproduct of editorial crusades), within the genre itself: science fiction stories routinely tackle deeper issues in a deeper way than were seen in the early days. In other words, the watchdogs are less likely to scorn science fiction, first, because they grew up with it, and, second, because science fiction in the main is no longer as crude and juvenile as once it was.

I am assuming that any reader who is in sympathy with modern ideas, or, rather, postmodern anti-ideas reads the opening dozen paragraphs above with a growing sense of vague discomfort, or a stalking suspicion that he has strayed into a moral atmosphere alien to his particular mental outlook. 'Who in the world...' (our hypothetical postmodernist may well ask) '...dares talk about good taste these days, or truth, or beauty, or believes that art has an innate and natural role determined by objective rules of moral reasoning which impose an obligation on the artist to serve some greater good? Truth? What is truth?'

Good question, Pontius! Well, for one, I talk about truth because that is what honest men talk about. What good is served in talking lies?

To believe that truth is true is not due to daring, but due to humility: the honest man does not think he gets a veto over reality. A humble man says you don't vote on laws of nature, you cannot create reality, and you did not father yourself out of nothing.

A postmodern man says truth is fluid and subjective. This both makes man less than an animal, for it says his brain is not suited for survival in reality because his brain does not give him true information about reality; and more than a god, for it says that, like a god, each man creates his own universe; and more than god, for not even a god can create himself of himself from himself. Pagan gods, who are not eternal, like Zeus, have to be born from Saturn or Uranus or Chaos, and so cannot be his own maker. The God of Abraham, who is eternal, cannot from his position of primal perfection evolve into something more perfect, because to perfect perfection is a paradox. But the self-made reality-creating modern man somehow does what both pagan and Christian divinities cannot.

That this stance involves intolerable logical self-contradiction does not shame the postmodernist into rethinking the bumper sticker slogans of his position. As befits creatures both above gods and below beasts, they have no shame. Shame is a human characteristic, befitting humble men.

But let us return from this digression to the question at hand: what is entertainment? What is it for? (And, let us not forget to return to the larger question of why we honor those who successfully entertain us, rather than just pay them.)

The humble man of whom I just spoke will be shocked to learn that entertainment, at least as far as fiction is concerned, is untrue. Even from the beginning it was so. The events in *The Iliad* did not happen literally as described, and even if there was such a war, Ares and Aphrodite were not wounded in it, nor did the heroes of Achaia utter their oratories, vaunts, and defiance in such perfect dactylic hexameters. Fiction by definition is untrue, but none save the most literal fool is fooled by this untruth, for it is not meant to fool.

What is it meant for? That answer is known to everyone who asks: Fiction is untruth that serves truth. Or, in other words, art is the magic by which the muses express truths that cannot be expressed as truthfully by mere literal words, nor as memorably, adroitly, or trenchantly.

In all this there is a divine irony, a heavenly cunning, for the muses use lies, which are the instruments of hell, against the hellish goal of magnifying ugliness and deadening our lives, instead use those lies to tell truths larger than literal words can carry, granting us richer life and deeper.

At this point, both any hypothetical honest man and the postmodern man reading these words must be blinking in puzzlement at that last sentence.

Perhaps their eyes drift from this essay to their nearby bookshelf, where they see a science fiction book about, for example, an immortal amnesiac with a double-brain using his superhuman mind-powers to teleport galaxies into collision or destroy and recreate timespace; or another book starring a half-clad yet fully buxom princess from the fourth dimension who is abducted by a lascivious sea-monster; or a book about a giant spaceship made of gold; or a book about a Texas gunslinger trying to fight off an invasion of space monsters.

Whereupon the honest man and the postmodern man no doubt, (when done laughing), must say in unison: "No, sir, you go too far! Entertainment is not about some profound and cosmic truth of human nature. It is about beguiling an idle afternoon with adventure stories. Entertainment is the amusement of the imagination. Entertainment is diversion, divertissement, and distraction."

Well said. But, O hypothetical honest man and dishonest postmodern man, from what do the readers of such tales seek diversion? From what must they be distracted?

I am not sure how a postmodern man would answer. A modern man from the previous generation might say that the artist and the audience were slightly at odds, for the audience wanted to be diverted from the boredom which comes from a bourgeoisie existence of oppressive racist wife-beating hypocrisy (or whatever), and the artist, as a loyal servant of the cause of ushering in socialist femmtopia (or whatever) had the task of subverting the tastes and hence the loyalties and political sentiments of the audience, and winning their hearts over to the revolution. Other modernists were rebels without so clear cut a cause, or none at all, but wanted to express dissatisfaction with the world as it was, and draw attention to social problems that needed fixing; but their approach and basic psychology was the same as the revolutionaries, they were merely not so consistent and fixed in purpose.

But postmodernists are famed for their lack of belief in any socialist or Christian or spiritualist or utopian "narrative" which they regard, one and all, as malign attempts to seduce or subvert the natural loyalties of man. (And in their criticism of what I have here called the modernist man, they are exactly right: what writers of the modernist school wrote was propaganda, not true art). Logically, this means the postmodernist is estopped from seducing or subverting the reader's loyalties to a new scheme of life, (if I may use a useful but obscure legal term—I mean they have lost the right to do that which they condemn in others).

Now, I am not going to disagree with the modernists, but will say instead they are not bold enough to tell the whole truth. Writing stories about beggars and orphans so as to raise public indignation as part of a program of social reform is diversion from the dangerous self-satisfaction that arises from living a too-comfortable life, but there is clearly something here beyond mere diversion. The artist is attempting to call forward the better angels of their nature in the readers.

But I draw your attention to the fact, which you may look into your own heart and confirm for yourself, that even allegedly shallow adventure stories, or romances, are more than mere diversion. I know a man who, as a boy, read *A Princess Of Mars*—of which a less realistic and more boyish adventure yarn cannot be imagined, nor one having less to do with conditions on Earth — but the lesson he took from it was to treat women chivalrously and with honor, to be objects of love more akin to worship than to the sordid mutual exploitation or animal attraction which modernists denigrate love to be. Again, I know a man who, as a boy, so loved *Star Wars*, that he decided to live his life as should a Jedi Knight, putting right and truth above all things, even if he lacked the mind-powers and buzzing glow-swords. Chivalry and righteousness are not unimportant things. They are not the most important things, of course, but they are more important than life, and ergo worth dying for.

So what do simple tales of adventure and romance, such as those penned by Edgar Rice Burroughs, and deeper tales that provoke the conscience, such as those penned by Charles Dickens, have in common? What is the diversion?

I suggest that if we look at the very greatest of literature we will see the answer. *The Odyssey* of Homer has enough monsters and derring-do to satisfy even the most demanding of childish tastes, but it is a poem that even millennia of study have not exhausted. The war in heaven occupying the middle books of Milton's *Paradise Lost*, or the battle scenes in Tolstoy's *War And Peace* also do not exhaust the examination of those works and the profound points the authors address. The same is true for the love story between Odysseus and Penelope, Adam and Eve, Natasha and Pierre. Nor is the pity felt for Oliver Twist or Little Nell and their troubles any less than is felt for Odysseus or Andrei or Adam, because the act of waking the conscience to support, say, compassion for the poor, is not different than, except that it is smaller in scope, waking the conscience to the issues of loss and love and war and peace and justifying the ways of God to man.

If we divide books into the lowbrow, the middlebrow, and the highbrow, running from shallow and popular books concerned with parochial things, to sober books concerned with deeper things, to books that earn eternal fame and plumb the deepest, we will see that a common current runs through all the branches of the great river called literature, the shallow currents as well as the deep. They all run to an ocean.

The great books are great because they are better than the good books and much better than the crappy guilty-pleasure books in the one regard of how well they treat with the great ideas of Western literature.

For those of you unfamiliar with these great ideas, Mortimer Adler was kind enough to compile them into a handy list: Angel, Animal, Aristocracy, Art, Astronomy, Beauty, Being, Cause, Chance, Change, Citizen, Constitution, Courage, Custom and Convention, Definition, Democracy, Desire, Dialectic, Duty, Education, Element, Emotion, Eternity, Evolution, Experience, Family, Fate, Form, God, Good and Evil, Government, Habit, Happiness, History, Honor, Hypothesis, Idea, Immortality, Induction, Infinity, Judgment, Justice, Knowledge, Labor, Language, Law, Liberty, Life and Death, Logic, Love, Man, Mathematics, Matter, Mechanics, Medicine, Memory and Imagination, Metaphysics, Mind, Monarchy, Nature, Necessity and Contingency, Oligarchy, One and Many, Opinion, Opposition, Philosophy, Physics, Pleasure and Pain, Poetry, Principle, Progress, Prophecy, Prudence, Punishment, Quality, Quantity, Reasoning, Relation, Religion, Revolution, Rhetoric, Same and Other, Science, Sense, Sign and Symbol, Sin, Slavery, Soul, Space, State, Temperance, Theology, Time, Truth, Tyranny and Despotism, Universal and Particular, Virtue and Vice, War and Peace, Wealth, Will, Wisdom, and World.

What makes a simple adventure yarn or love story simple is that it treats with these profound matters in a simplistic, unoriginal, and unexceptional way. John Carter dies and comes to life again on Mars and then cuts and carves his way across the face of the bloody planet of the wargod to win the hand of his true love, the princess Dejah Thoris. The book does deal with issues of life and death and love and honor. But it does so in an utterly unexceptional way — I say this as an avid fan and partisan of the book —

because it does not say anything about life and death and love and honor a schoolboy does not already know, nor does it correct any false ideas a schoolboy might have. John Carter neither pauses to wonder about the widows and orphans of the men he's killed, nor is the romance between man and Martian shown to be an act of will, a divine grace, something to sustain the couple through everything from domestic squabbles to disease and death. What Dickens or Milton has to say about death and love is deeper and therefore, at least to mature tastes, more interesting, but it is still on the same topic.

At this point we can answer an earlier question adroitly. Why are we science fiction buffs offended if the watchdogs of public taste treat us lightly? We are not, (I hope), offended because someone says *Synthetic Men Of Mars* is inferior to *The Brothers Karamazov*. In such a case we have no claim, and any feeling of offense would be mere partisan emotion or fannish loyalty. But we are, (I hope), deeply offended because someone says Tolkien's *The Lord Of The Rings* is inferior to Sartre's *No Exit* on the grounds that Tolkien's work involves fairy-tale creatures like Sauron, Gandalf and Saruman, angelic powers, (fallen and unfallen), who walked the earth, who do not really exist, whereas Sartre's masterpiece of existentialist drama concerns Garcin, Inès, and Estelle, three ghosts in hell, (all fallen), who do exist.

An honest observer will note that there is no great idea addressed by *No Exit*, or, for that matter, *The Odyssey*, which is not equal in scope to the great ideas addressed in *The Lord Of The Rings*.

The reason why to this day, (albeit, thankfully, less than had been), the watchdogs of literature scorn Professor Tolkien's work is twofold: one is the matter of setting. Tolkien's work is set in a make-believe past roughly as historically accurate as Robert Howard's Hyborian Age. It is set in Elfland, where foxes talk and so do trees, and magic is real. This is a setting that the sons of Dickens and servants of Marx, each one eager to be more relevant and more realistic than the last, consigned to the children's nursery.

But many an opera or work of epic poetry, from *Das Rheingold* to Dante's *Inferno* is set in places beyond the fields we mortals know, sometimes far beyond: the sheer unfairness of ignoring a great work for the shallow and trivial detail of its setting justly offends our sense of right and wrong. Would anyone dismiss *Moby Dick* as a famous work of American letters because the setting was a whaling ship? This would be like dismissing Joseph Conrad's *Heart Of Darkness* as a mere childish adventure tale on the grounds that it takes place in the same continent as *Tarzan Of The Apes.*

The second is more sinister: Tolkien's work is deeply anti-modernist. It is not the friend of progressive ideas at any point, but portrays life in Middle-Earth with a typically Catholic melancholy, as if history is one long ebbing tide of sorrow and loss that will only be amended at the Last Judgment.

Now the nihilists among the Watchdogs like the idea that life is melancholy, but they do not want any hint of final joy: Frodo should have gotten seasick on the last boat to Elfland out of the Gray Havens, and fallen overboard, and been eaten by angry krill. That would have satisfied their taste.

And the modernists among the watchdogs don't like any problems which are not caused by and cured by Man. Social injustices can be perhaps cured by a renovation of laws and customs, but innate existential sorrow caused by the nature of mortal life — that, they will hear no part of, unless of course there is a human solution to it, such as being kind to your neighbors, telling stories, staying in school, and other such mind-explodingly stupid trivialities. Of course I am using the examples taken from the ending, such as it is, of Phillip Pullman's *His Dark Materials*, a book which the watchdogs heaped with praises and glory utterly disproportionate to the trilogy's modest craftsmanship.

Pullman's book took place just as far beyond the fields we know as Tolkien's but Mr. Pullman expressed ideas and attitudes that were all safely politically correct and hence craven and parochial and trite. The Watchdogs were not challenged on any of their ideas about God and Man any more than the schoolboy in my example above is challenged to think deeply about love and chivalry, honor and death by reading about a clean-limbed fighting man from Virginia sword-fighting Martians.

Here the injustice is galling precisely because of the unfairness, the partisanship, of the Watchdogs. It is not the craftsmanship of the author, nor the beauty and depth of his inspiration, nor again the elevation of his theme, nor the profundity of the great ideas being addressed, nor the adroitness of his execution, nor the re-readability, power, and relevance of the art. No. One man writes a shallow book which echoes the conformist ideas of the watchdogs, and so they celebrate him; another man, using the same materials, writes a profound book whose ideas rear a shocking challenge to the comfortable untruths the Watchdogs would prefer to believe, and they are dismissive.

And puh-lease let no one intimate to me that writing an atheist book is brave but writing a Catholic book is conformist. I have been both an atheist and a Catholic, and written both kinds of books. The only time I have ever been savaged, (a situation I assume conformists would find trying on their reserves of courage), was when I wrote things along the second line, not the first. You may have your own opinion: here I speak from experience.

I do not say Mr. Pullman is a coward and Professor Tolkien is a hero. I know nothing of the men personally, and I have neither the skill nor the right to judge men's hearts. But I do say that Mr. Pullman wrote a cowardly book, and Professor Tolkien wrote a heroic one, since the first book repeated in the stale quest-trilogy formula all the pious and trite platitudes of the modern day, ('Be kind to people! Stay in school! Have lotsa great sex!'), and the second was a book that challenged all the conventional wisdom and the conventions of literature, and met, and overthrew them.

So the answer about what is the nature of the indignation when a book is slandered when it merits praise can be easily seen: when a profound book is called shallow, or vice versa, something burns in the indignant heart more than the emotion for which it might at first be mistaken.

If we are indignant because another man's taste in some trivial thing differs from our own, if, for example, he actually likes Kyle Rayner more than Hal Jordan, our indignation has no right to exist. We are just playing around.

Again, if we are indignant out of partisanship or party loyalty, like fans of a ball team who root for their hometown, that is merely parochial loyalty, and is not the same emotion. If the rival team wins, they are not enemies. No injustice has been done us.

In this case, we are indignant at the injustice. Each man who has read deeply in great literature knows well that there are great books simply not to his taste: but if he is fair-minded, he can see the real merits that attract the candid judgment of his fellow men, whose tastes are just as refined as his own. An injustice is not a lapse of judgment but an offense against it, when some lesser thing, such as party politics, is placed above the highest thing, which is right judgment. A literate man would be just as offended by a Catholic who despised Milton's work on the grounds that Milton was a Puritan as he would be by a Puritan who despised Dante's: and he would not consult his own sentiments in the matter of religion rather than his judgment about what makes great literature great.

In my case, I rightfully acknowledge Flannery O'Conner as a profound and great writer, worthy of public honors. But I hate her work. It is not to my taste.

What duty do authors owe literature? That we can now answer in a word. Authors serve the Truth. Not the truth as they see it, not their truth or my truth or your truth. They serve Truth. There are those who betray that service. This makes them traitors, but does not make them discoverers of a new truth.

What duty do authors owe society?

Lowbrow authors — and this includes the vast majority of genre writing — are supposed to entertain, that is, divert their audience from the dullness and horror of life and show them how things ought to be, more romantic, more heroic. They are escapist, and are meant to show the imagination that a world that should exist or that does, a world higher and finer than this valley of tears in which we are exiled.

Middlebrow authors, dealing with an audience slightly more mature, deal with an audience in no danger of dullness, but it may confront a danger of smallmindedness. Novels by Jane Austen and Charles Dickens have the advantage of being written with some human insight, so that we can be distracted and diverted from our own egotistical selves, and learn to see the world as if other people are real and their sorrows worthy of balm. They are not escapist but immersive, and offer escape from our own selfishness.

Middlebrow books, if well done, allow us to meet the saints and sinners we would not meet in real life, and refresh our souls to deal with our fellow man with clearer insight. It is still entertainment, as refreshing as a dip in the pool, but this does not mean a little dirt does not get washed out of our eyes and off our souls.

Highbrow authors, dealing with the most mature audience, speaking to generation after generation, deal with an audience in no great danger of lacking human understanding, but in very great danger of lacking a proper emotional response to the highest things. Intellectuals tend to lack intellectual structure, to be ignorant of philosophy, or to treat it like a game.

Books that treat the great ideas in the deepest way are both escapist and immersive, since they offer escape from our own worldview, and into a larger one.

All these authors, from least to greatest, from the most idle of idle entertainments to the most profound of life-changing works of great literature, are all created by one great secret. It is ironic that some of them do not know the secret, or would react with disquiet or disgust to hear of it.

The secret is that we are exiles here on Earth. This is not our home. We do not belong here.

If the readers and authors did not feel that way, if we did belong on Earth, and if we loved mortal life and mortal suffering, and if we desired nothing more, we would read newspapers for the news and engineering reports for discoveries of useful tools, and gossip about real people and histories of real events, and we would never, ever, ever desire something more. We would never dream of adventures on Mars or read about the lives of make-believe people in

Russia during the Napoleonic Wars or about a poet descending through the core of the Earth and climbing a mountain in the southern hemisphere to ascend the seven spheres of heaven to see Our Lady and Our Lord. We would not care about Long John Silver or Scarlet O'Hara or Ebenezer Scrooge; and the fate of Aragorn, son of Arathorn, heir to the fallen kingdom of Numenor would be meaningless.

If we were just beasts like other beasts, we would never raise our eyes from the troughs of temporary pleasure, and crane back our heads, and stare at the stars, and wonder, and imagine, and seek to feed not just our bellies but also our imaginations.

If we were happy here in our world, we would not dream of other worlds, and if we are not happy here, then this is not our home.

The role of the poet, aside from recalling with glory the deeds of our ancestors, or telling us to love what is lovely and hate what is hateful, is to keep alive that spark of haunting recollection.

This is done in two ways: one is the tragic mode, where the poet with lamentation pricks open the wounds once more of all the evils that this exile imposes on us, and makes us ill-at-ease and discontented with this world and its vanities.

The other is the comedic mode, where the poet tells us of the other world, the world as we all know it should be, the one where beauty triumphs rather than strength.

You can see why I rejoice that Gene Wolfe is now recognized as a grandmaster, I hope. If not, look at Adler's list of great ideas, and pick up a copy of Wolfe's novels or short stories and see how many of these themes he touches on.

And he is a member of that secret Catholic conspiracy. If

you find some of the melancholy of J.R.R. Tolkien in his works or the grotesquerie of Flannery O'Conner, that may be why. So I was afraid that our own smaller pack of watch-dogs of good taste guarding science fiction would snub a man whose worldview is alien to their own, and superior. But then, good artists, as I mentioned above, are subversive, and can lure an audience into a larger world before they notice it.

What duty do authors owe the Truth? Why, everything! We serve beauty. Beauty is truth.

Those who believe otherwise write crappy books.

9

STORYTELLING IS THE ABSENCE OF LYING

The worst attempt at Science Fiction addressing religious issues it has ever been my misfortune to run across is by a brilliant up-and-coming author named Ted Chiang. If you haven't read his short stories, you are doing yourself a bit of a disservice. You might want to rush right out and buy a copy of *Stories Of Your Life And Others*.

But don't tell him I sent you, dear reader, because I must now criticize his most famous story from that collection in the harshest terms. Since he is a better writer than I am, this exercise cannot be taken too seriously: a slow man is telling a fast man how to run a race.

Of course, even a slow runner can tell when a faster one has gone seriously off the track.

The satire "Hell is the Absence of God" reads like it was written by someone who never met a Christian, or read anything written by a Christian.

In this tale, those who see the light of heaven are grotesquely disfigured, (their eyes and eye sockets are removed), and lose free will, and become perfect in faith, so that they are automatically assured of entrance into paradise. The main character, mourning after the death of his wife, seeks to find a spot where an angel is leaving or entering the world, so that he can, if only for a moment, glimpse the light of heaven, so that he can lose his eyes and his free will, but be assured of meeting his wife again in heaven. All goes as planned, but God capriciously sends the man to Hell in any case. Hell is not a place of torment, but a bland area much like earth, merely separate from God, peopled by Fallen Angels whose sin was not rebellion, but free-thinking. Hence, out of all created beings, only the main character is actually suffering in Hell, since he is the only one who longs not to be there, and, thanks to his free will being destroyed, is the only one who loves God whole-heartedly. All efforts of the main character to rejoin his wife are futile. There are secondary characters whose lives are also ruined, and for no particular reason.

This story is seriously off track for what a story should be. It is, however, note-perfect as a piece of cheap agitprop.

I do not mean the tale lacks characterization or crafts-manship. As a story goes, it is taut and well-constructed; not a wasted word. But a well-done picture of St. Peter kissing the hairy black buttocks of Satan should be seen for what it is: a slander against religion, and a fairly childish one, even if the perspective and composition, colors and figures of the drawing were executed with meticulous craftsmanship.

When I say the work is dishonest, I do not mean to imply Mr. Chiang himself is anything but upright. I have no doubt that he writes as his muses move him. I am no sibyl of other authors' intentions, by any means. And poets are an elfin and tricky breed at best, and sometimes do not know themselves what the story that comes to life in their hands must mean.

But in this case, I humbly suggest that the point of Mr.

Chiang's story is not just clear, it is repeated and exaggerated. He is criticizing Christian theodicy.

And the criticism can be dishonest, no matter how well-meaning the artist who pens it, merely by being false-to-facts. If a painter draws a wart on a portrait, where the original face was smooth and fair, that is not merely an exercise of artistic license: that is a false picture.

He is not criticizing religion in general: his ire is confined to Christianity. The universe described in the tale does not depict the sorrow of endless incarnations; there is no hint of Mount Meru or Mount Olympos, nor does the great wolf Fenrir rear its all-devouring jaws; Izanagi and Izanami are not present, nor the Nine Immortals. The main characters do not recite the Koran or study the Torah: they go to prayer-meetings. If Mr. Chiang meant to make a point unrelated to Christianity, then he selected Christian props and tropes to clothe his meaning.

Perhaps he means to confine his ire to Protestantism, because priesthood is nowhere in evidence. The characters are revivalist lay-preachers, not sinister robed figures from Gothic churches.

Am I reading too much into it? I think I am not. There is no point to the story if it is not a criticism of Christianity, a topic fascinating to the dominant section of the SF audience, who are skeptics from the West, i.e. from Christendom. Criticism of other religions would be of marginal interest to the expected audience. When is the last time you heard someone blaspheming Thor?

I will say again, the story is well written. I will say again that Mr. Chiang is a gifted writer, touched with divine fire. The sorrow of a widower, or the wild rides of the angel-chasing truckers, make for memorable scenes. But the story itself is a misrepresentation, nay, a defamation.

Christians say virtue is its own reward; they also say to love God is good; they also say heaven rewards virtues not rewarded on earth, and martyrs are glorified. They propose the paradox of an omnipotent God who grants man free will. So all Ted Chiang does is propose an omnipotent God who removes a character's free will, and martyrs him, cheating him of any glory, but without rewarding him either on Earth or in heaven. Oh, the irony! The girl born crippled was able to stir men's souls back before she was touched with bliss, because, once blissful, the heavenly creature knows no suffering or empathy for suffering. More irony! (And we all know the Christians believe God never became flesh and never suffered, right? Of course right!) Virtue is its own reward, so the one virtuous man is stuck in Hell forever, and he is the only one to whom it is a torment! Irony upon irony! Yuk, yuk, yuk, and ain't the Godbotherers stoopid?

Well, as a matter of fact, no. They may be wrong or right, but the theology is not simple, and what Chiang proposes is not what the Christians say. Or the Mohammedans, or the Jews, or the Pagans, or anyone else, for that matter. Chiang is trouncing a straw man.

That was what offended me when I first read it, by the bye. Back then I was a hard-core Xtian-bashing atheist and was therefore on his side, so to speak, but the blatant propaganda of the story nonetheless offended me. (I am less offended now that I believe in God: I figure He can take care of His own reputation.)

My reaction back then was: Does he even know any Christians? Doesn't he know what they say? The story reads like it was written for an audience of utter ignoramuses, who have never read a word of Christian theology, and never cracked a history book.

The ham-handed symbolism is particularly awkward:

the light from heaven, the light of faith, blinds people. Get it? It's blind faith! Mr. Chiang shows us the blindness of blind faith by making his characters who have it blind! The light of heaven also burns any free will out of the brains of the faithful, because, in this loopy interpretation, faith is not an act of the will, but an absence of will.

The major objection honest atheists must level (and I was an honest atheist, back then, not merely a character assassin) is that religion is false; that even if true, it has no claim on our loyalty; that the reason of man, being reason, cannot be bound by dogma; and that the claims, true or false, are repellant to the dignity of free and rational beings. In all this, atheists are like Benedict in *Much Ado About Nothing*, saying marriage has no claim on our loyalty, that passions cannot be bound by oaths, that infatuation is repellant to the dignity, and marital bonds to the freedom, of man. Benedict says much that is true and much that is utterly beside the point. We all laugh when he falls in love himself, and it is not cruel laughter.

The major charge of honest atheists is that the claims of the Christian religion are false. The way to combat this is to uphold a standard, a rational standard, which divides true from false, and shows the difference between them: true is what can be proven by concrete observation or abstract reasoning. Wishes, hopes, poems, daydreams, are not true or false: they are moonbeams, pretty and unsubstantial.

What Mr. Chiang does here is undercut the atheist argument by abandoning the standard of true and false. Christians tell a ridiculous story about their Big Invisible Friend, who invisibly saved the world from an utterly imaginary danger caused by an entirely fictional Adam, granting to all and sundry an eternal life, which conveniently cannot be seen or sensed, but only exists in Make-believe-land, beyond the borders of the world, in Oz, where no one dies and no one is unhappy. If you don't believe in the Wizard, the Flying Monkeys of the Wicked Witch of the West will get you. When asked politely if they can see the Wizard, the atheists are told that no one can see the Wizard, not nobody not no how. Small wonder the atheists are skeptical.

You do not undercut this fairytale by saying that The Wizard is an evil bunny-killing tyrant and that the Wicked Witch of the West is merely a soulful and misunderstood victim of circumstance. You do not uphold a standard of truth by telling a lie. That is not what L. Frank Baum says, and not what any believer in the fairytale believes.

I am not objecting that Mr. Chiang is telling a story. Telling stories is like painting pictures: in this case he is representing not something from his imagination merely, but painting a picture about real people in whose midst we live, the Christian majority. Had he been honest, he would have explored what the world would be like if the Christian God were visible and obvious, and what the reactions might be. Had he been both honest and brave, he would have explored what the world would be like if the God of Islam were both visible and obvious, and what the reactions might be: some of his barbs might have struck closer to the mark. But even Allah is said to be compassionate and merciful, and it is not the faithful He sends to Jahannam.

Now, I suppose it might be objected that the God of the Old Testament at times seems capricious and cruel, never more so than when he inflicts, or allows to be inflicted, pain and suffering on Job. The argument could be made that the God of Job is the one here depicted, and that the faith of the faithful, which insists that they continue to believe in God despite all evidence, would be absurd in a world where God Himself was cruel and capricious. (Of course, this argument is undercut by Chiang's hypothesis. If God were visible and obvious, arguments about His nature would be matters of evidence, not matters of faith.)

But cruelty is not the point of the Book of Job; patience is. One major point of the Book of Job is that the suffering is redeemed in the end. Christians (and most other religions) believe in two worlds, this one and the next. Whatever injustices and suffering occur in this world are recompensed and healed in the next: God Himself wipes all tears away. That promised redemption is sometimes, (albeit rarely), glimpsed in this world, as when good fortune comes to the righteous and long-suffering man, like Job, who persevered during his time of agony. His joy on earth is a foreshadowing of the world to come, a representation of something greater. But good men are not rewarded for their goodness on Earth, as Job's friends so cruelly say. Why does God restore Job's fortunes at all? Job's happy ending is an act of mercy, not something springing from Job's merit as a good man. It is as strange and wonderful as the mercy with which God deals with Cain, who, instead of instantly being flung into a fiery pit or bed of snakes, is marked with a Sign to show that no man can take vengeance on him.

Job's sufferings are an extreme, of course. Were they not, the tale would contain no power, no fascination. Whenever anyone in real life suffers even one of the pangs of Job, a loss of wealth or position, a lingering disease, the death of a child, his real pain is as deep as Job's. If patience could not endure, or if faith could not comfort such pangs, it would be of no use, and religion would be a fair-weather affair, a belief to be held only when days are sunny, otherwise abandoned. Job is not a stoic; his lamentations are deep and heartfelt, and he wishes for the opportunity to put his case before God, that life has treated him unfairly. When God

Himself arrives in a whirlwind, and displays the majesty of all visible and invisible creation, Job is silent.

There is something mystical here, something more than a concern for justice for one man. Like the Beast in *Beauty And The Beast*, like anything worth loving in life, God must be loved before He can seem worthy of being loved. The faithful do not adore Him as a trade in return for worldly pleasure and success, no more than a wife loves her man because he buys her jewels to adorn her: that would be low indeed. But what man in love does not delight to adorn his bride?

Taken to an extreme, to remain faithful even when all worldly pleasure and success is gone, means...what? Does it mean that this world is vain, and that no philosopher would make his happiness depend on the transitory things of this world, wealth, health, kith and kin? Does it mean that this world is cruel, in the hands of malign fate, that nature is the accuser and enemy of man, and that our true home lies elsewhere, perhaps, yes, with the Author whose hand created all the glories of this world?

Or does it mean only that Job is a big sucker, a rube, a chump, someone deceived by priestcraft? Chiang sends his version of Job to eternal Hell, to suffer alone, an endless chump, a battered wife with an infinite and infinitely cruel husband, a victim of the Stockholm Syndrome. It rewrites the story by leaving out the only thing that makes the original make sense: the redemption. That is not a new take on the material: it is cheap shot.

I suppose there is nothing wrong with writing falsehoods for a particular audience already ideologically committed to enjoying them, knowing them to be lies, and taking pleasure from that very insolence. I suppose, for that matter, one could rewrite the Oz books so that Dorothy, rather than being befriended by the Tin Man, was raped by him, or that the Wicked Witch was the good guy. But such a depth of depravity is one to which only the sickest imaginable culture could fall, when audiences were titillated merely by the cruelty and foolishness of authors who have lost all sense of... hm? I'm sorry, what was that you said? Something about Alan Moore and Gregory Maguire?

In any case, such sick imaginings pretend to be challenges or revisions or updatings or answers to L. Frank Baum, but they are basically the artistic equivalent of lies. Well-told, well executed lies, of course, but lies nonetheless, and rotten to the very core.

A culture that cannot even take Oz honestly has very little chance of taking Heaven honestly.

On a personal note, Mr. Chiang's short story, as far as I was concerned, not merely failed of its object, but was counterproductive. One of the things that made me suffer no regret when I was called away from the cramped intellectual jail of atheism into a wider and more wonderful world, was my growing conviction that my fellow atheists were shallow men without insight into real human nature. I read Chiang's story and I thought: is this the best my side can do? Is this cheap slander the best argument we can muster against our hated enemies, the Christians? In those days I kept wondering why, since my side had the Sixteen-Inch Guns of Truth and Logic, our gunners kept shooting blanks. Why were we sneering all the time, instead of setting out the evidence?

To get a notion of the depth of the contrast I saw, find a comfy chair by the fire, read "Hell is the Absence of God" by Ted Chiang, and then, without rising from the chair except perhaps to toss another log on the fire, pick up and read "Smith of Wootton Major" by J.R.R. Tolkien, or perhaps

"Leaf by Niggle". It does not matter whether you are an Atheist or a Christian or are another faith or uncommitted: anyone reading those two authors' works in contrast will see that one has an insight into human joys and human woes, a compassion toward even human folly or pride or sloth. And the other one shows nothing, no humanity, no understanding. The heart of Chiang's work is not in the right place. Even though I thought Chiang's worldview was true and Tolkien's was false, I concluded Tolkien's insight into real life was keen-eyed, and Chiang's was superficial.

Now, you might say that Tolkien was an older man, like well-seasoned wood, who had been through war and tumult, joy and sorrow, and that Chiang is a young man, with a young man's superficial idealism. To compare the two is unfair! To which I might reply: Tolkien's worldview is old, two thousand years old, or, if you accept the conceit that the Christians are the heirs of the Jewish legacy, as old as any written history. Well-seasoned indeed! The Church and the Prophets before the Church have seen more wars and tumults, joys and sorrows, and kept an ongoing, unified, living tradition of written accounts, an accumulation of wisdom unmatched in the world. In contrast, Mr. Chiang's stories in this volume express nothing surprising to the fashionable modern consensus view, (no CIA agent comes on stage without being sinister, no religious figure without being a fundie, no Victorian without being narrow and absurd, no Big Business without being malign). I should call it postmodern: it is too young to be modern. These stories represent a trendy view not as old as I am: I remember when they became the trend. These are green and flimsy sticks from which to build a house.

Let us turn to a question more of interest to SF readers: is Mr. Chiang's story a fantasy? My own humble opinion is that it is science fiction. Science Fiction is distinct from fantasy by its speculative character. If there were such a thing as telepathy, how would a criminal elude a detective? Alfred Bester answered that in *The Demolished Man*. If there were such a thing as teleportation, how would society lock up crooks? Likewise in *The Stars My Destination*. Science fiction takes some fantastic notion, and asks how the nuts and bolts of it would work. In "Hell is the Absence of God", Mr. Chiang asks if there were a God unhidden from human perception, how would the system actually work? What happens when one man who wants to love God but cannot tries to outsmart the system? Chiang is asking the paramount science fiction question: "What if?"

Well, to be honest, Mr. Chiang's tyrant God is no more or less scientific than Mr. Bester's telepathy or teleportation. Compare it to the Star Trek episode 'Who Mourns for Adonis?' where the crew of the *Enterprise* meets Apollo. In that, the 'god' merely turns out to be a powerful and malevolent entity who attempts to beguile the innocent. So here. The story is solidly SF, despite its subject matter.

If we define any book with a supernatural figure in it as Fantasy, we are left in the awkward position of saying *Benhur* is fantasy, because lepers are cured by a miracle in one scene. The writer, General Wallace, and the expected readership, both believed such miracles can and do take place. A work does not become a fantasy merely because the reader happens not share the worldview of the writer.

Were that the case, *Chariots Of The Gods* by von Däniken, the *Histories* of Herodotus, and Machiavelli's *The Prince*, (which solemnly reports that the downfall of princes are foretold by Signs and Omens sent by Airy Spirits), would be shelved in the Science Fiction section.

10

THE GOLDEN COMPASS POINTS IN NO DIRECTION

M y respect for this author just hit bottom. Philip Pullman, author of *The Golden Compass*, answers critics who accuse him of peddling candy-coated atheism: "I am a story teller," he said. "If I wanted to send a message I would have written a sermon."

I answered a critic once: it was a foolish thing to do, and I lost honor for doing it. Books should speak for themselves or not at all. That was a case where I was completely and obviously in the right. (I was answering a critic who said Phaethon, my arch-libertarian hero from *The Golden Age*, was a Stalinist). What are we to make of a case where, as here, the author is completely and obviously in the wrong? Does he want people to mock him?

"If I wanted to send a message I would have written a sermon." It is to laugh. Poor man. Poor, poor man.

Someone name for me a book that is more obviously a bit of preaching that simply abandoned its storyline more blatantly? Even Ayn Rand's *Atlas Shrugged* actually had an ending that grew out of its beginning. John Galt's radio speech was long, but the book did not end in the middle of that speech.

The first rule of storytelling is the same rule every child learns in kindergarten, every merchant learns when generating customer good will. Abide by your contracts. Keep your promises.

There is an unspoken contract between a writer and his readers. Plots and characters and themes make promises. Prophecies in epic fantasy stories are blatant promises. When you are told that there is a prophecy that one and only one knife can kill Almighty God, and that one little boy is the one to do it, it breaks a promise to have God turn out to be a drooling cripple who dies by falling out of bed.

Character development makes a promise. If you start your series with a selfish little girl who tells lies, the climax of her character arc must be when she either gets a comeuppance for being a liar, or when she reforms and starts telling the truth. If you give her a magic instrument that only she can read called an Alethiometer, a truth measurer, it breaks a promise to have simply nothing at all come of this.

If your character's mother is a mad scientist who experiments on children, the promised character arc is to have her reform and redeem herself. There is a scene where Mrs. Coulter nurses her wounded daughter back to health, but nothing is reformed. Mom then seduces Lamech, who apparently is the real god God is supposed to be, the tyrant of heaven, and tumbles into the Abyss with him, killing him and herself. This happens offstage, without her daughter becoming aware of it.

The plot promised us that the republic of heaven would overthrow the heavenly kingdom. This magnificently blasphemous idea should have been something like Ancient Rome among the clouds, Senators draped in constellations and crowned with glory, with newly-immortal men voting on issues of heaven and hell, debating the destinies of stars and nations, weighing issues of fate and incarnation and reincarnation, meting out rewards and punishments for the quick and the dead, and ending with Jehovah hanged for a tyrant or sent to the Guillotine, while Cain and Ixion and Prometheus and Sisyphus, and all the dead drowned by the Deluge of Noah or the wars of Joshua, stand around hooting and throwing fruit. Instead the tyrant dies by falling out of bed. We were promised a Milton-level war resulting in a New Heaven and a New Earth, the deaths of gods, the overthrow of universes! That would have been cool.

Instead, we get a girl kissing her boyfriend, (and maybe being love-harpooned by him—Mr. Pullman is understandably coy about displaying statutory rape), and then she is sadly parted. (Because why? You can kill God, but you cannot figure out how to build a Stargate? You overthrow the Cosmic Order, but you cannot get Corwin of Amber to redraw the Pattern for you and rewrite the laws of nature?).

And the end result is that she goes to school.

Stay in school, kids! Hate God! That is my message!

Thanks, Pullman.

Oh, and the climax is where the main character commits euthanasia on a bunch of ghosts, intellectual beings whose torment is that they are bored. Gosh, boredom is a bad thing, I guess, but I would not want someone to pull a Dr. Kevorkian on me for it. And the ghosts are happy, not because they get reincarnated—that would smack too much of religion for our Mr. Pullman's tastes— they get recycled.

Joy of joys! Wonder of wonders! I know a lot of people who believe in recycling, but this is the first time I've come across characters willing to die for it. Too bad she did not keep the ghost of Socrates or Shakespeare around, just for historians to question, or the dead grandfather I never got the chance in life to talk to, and tell him how I loved him. Somehow, pure oblivion is supposed to be better than a disembodied life, even for Buddhists and Neoplatonists and Gnostics, whose only goal in life is to escape from material desires.

There are infinite universes in the Pullman background. Not one of them had a technology, or a magic spell, to put the ghosts to sleep until a way could be found to re-embody them? Even Gilbert Gosseyn had that technology, and he was just a man, not a god-killer.

You see, the problem with the message method of story-telling is that you have to stop the story to preach the message. The STORY here required that God be an evil Tyrant, as evil, (at least), as Sauron the Great, as cunning as Fu Manchu, as mad as Emperor Nero. The story required an all-powerful Goliath to be fought and overthrown by the bravery of a boy with a knife. The MESSAGE required that the Christian God be depicted, not merely as a tyrant, but as a false and shallow and idiotic creature: the Wizard of Oz, nothing more than a puppet-head and a loud voice controlled by a scared little carnival man behind the curtain.

So the story required that the god-killer be at least as impressive as Milton's Lucifer, who, no matter his flaws, certainly has the dramatic stature and the majesty to attempt deicide. Jack the Giant-killer is an impressive character precisely because Giants are big and impressive. But the message requires that God be not merely unimpressive, but despicable: he cannot be an honorable foe, or even a strong one.

Mr. Pullman started with a story, a *Paradise Lost* version

where Lucifer was the good guy facing impossible odds by defying an unconquerable god; but he ended with a message, where there are no odds because there is no god, merely a drooling idiot. So all plot logic flies out the window: the drooling idiot cannot be and could not be responsible for Original Sin or the Flood of Noah, or the Spanish Inquisition, or whatever crimes God should have been accused of, because he cannot do anything, any more than the puppet-head of the Wizard of Oz.

The story required that the mad scientist Lord Asriel be guilty of terrible experiments on children, but that his crimes be necessary in order to discover the secret of the Dust and undo the evils done by the Christian God, which have to be much greater than any merely human crime. But the message required that the human condition be merely materialistic, and that there could be no God, and therefore no crimes.

A good story would have shown all the innocent people from Ethiopia, Australia and China tormented in the fires of hell, merely for the whimsical violation of the Christian rule that they are sons of Adam not baptized by a messiah of whom they never could have heard. The writer would only need to show us one ghost, dead of sudden disease as a child one hour before his baptism, being crushed forever between the red-hot plates of a coffin of heated iron spikes, while crying for his mommy, in order to arouse the proper indignation. The crimes of God have to be, for such a story, cosmic crimes. Jehovah has to be shown as a being powerful enough to stop the wheel of reincarnation, which otherwise would have eventually saved all living spirits through many lives of learning and growing; and evil enough to have done this for a cruel purpose, perhaps to establish an arbitrary paradise and an arbitrary hell, perhaps merely for lust of power and love of praise. The story of that crime ends when Christianity is overthrown, and the reincarnation cycle which will one day save all people from all suffering is reinstated.

(Not to spoil the surprise ending, but this is not so far from the idea that Ursula K. Le Guin handled with such artistic adroitness in *The Other Wind*, a sequel to her "Earthsea" trilogy.)

But the message cannot be Taoist or Buddhist or even New Age Spiritualism. Mr. Pullman's message is atheist. He cannot have reincarnation be shown as a better alternative to hellfire, because he does not believe in reincarnation any more than he believes in hellfire. In order for his message to prosper, materialism has to be the order of the day. All the ghosts of the lordly dead, the honored ancestors to whom the pagan shrines are adorned, also have to be false. The ghosts in a Pullman fantasy world have to be bored, and dissolving back into matter has to be the only ecologically sound proposition. It is a boring and undramatic resolution, unconvincing to the point of idiocy, but it is the only one his message would allow.

The message did not allow Mr. Pullman even to list crimes of which the Christian God was accused. If there was a scene where this was done, I missed it. If Jehovah in the story had killed a child or kicked a bunny, I as the reader would have relished the scene of an overdue vengeance being visited on him: the Vengeance of Prometheus for the injustices of Heaven!

But there was no vengeance, no Prometheus, and no crimes. Asriel, at the first, is supposed to be a Promethean character, dabbling Where Man Was Not Meant to Go, and discovering the secrets of the universe. The secret he was supposed to discover is that the universe is run by a mad God who has to be destroyed: it is the ultimate in paranoid conspiracy thriller concepts. But only at first, because Mr. Pullman was telling a story at first. By the third book, *The Amber Spyglass*, when Mr. Pullman has forsworn storytelling to preach his message, instead of a mad God, we have a conclave of clerics who send out an assassin to kill the girl, for no reason that is ever made clear. It is not as if killing the ghosts or cleaning up the Dust actually did anything to the clerics: I do not see why they are not in the same position of power at the end of the tale as at the start. The message cannot accuse God of atrocities because the message is that there is no God. The message is not that God is evil: that would be a Satanist message.

The message is that God is Not, or that Thou Art God. That is the atheist message.

What are the characters in this book fighting for? Not for love, I take it: no couple ends up together, not even (I kid you not) the sodomite angels Baruch and Balthamos. When the Dust settles, the demons seem to be in charge of the universe, and they order all the inter-dimensional windows to be closed, except the window allowing the ghosts in the land of the dead to choose oblivion. For freedom? There is no one in chains at the beginning of the book who is freed at the end. For truth, justice, the American way? Again, there is nothing in the books to lend any drama to any of these concepts. Lyra is a liar (hence her name) but no lies are overthrown, no truth is revealed during the plot; Asriel is the Lucifer figure who ends up sacrificing himself, if not like Christ, at least like a man throwing himself on a hand-grenade, to push Metatron into the Pit of Non-Hell, where their ghosts will fall for all eternity; perhaps the American way was supposed to be their cause, as Americans prefer Republics to Monarchies, but the only political institution the "Republic of Heaven" turns out to support is the University. Huhn? Next to the basilica, the university is the quintessential Christian institution and invention. I assume we are not talking about Trinity College or Saint Mary's. Was anyone fighting for the ugly wheeled elephants? These creatures were allegedly innocent, but seemed pointless and repugnant on every level. Were they being threatened by the Church in some way? Was the Church trying to hoard the Dust in a fashion that harmed someone, somewhere? Pullman is not clear on this point, or maybe I missed it. The book does not seem to be "for" anything, merely against Christians in general and the Catholic Church in particular.

The problem is that the atheist message is boring and undramatic: life's a mechanical process and then you die. Now, as you believe one thing or another, you might take this message to be fact or fiction, but, true or false, it is always a false fiction, by which I mean an undramatic one. In fiction, we can come across a dungeon full of disembodied ghosts. In Christian fiction, the solution is to send them to their judgment, (think of the movie *Ghost* for a literal judgment, when dark shadows or bright lights come for you. A figurative last judgment might be the final scene in *The Lord Of The Rings*; Frodo's journey on the ship is symbolically a journey to heaven); in New Age or Buddhist fiction, the solution is to send them on to their next reincarnation, or to halt the wheel of reincarnation and send them to nirvana, (think of the movie *What Dreams May Come*, or even the ending to the television movie version of the *Mahabharata*).

But in atheist fiction, the only solution is to say that there are no ghosts. In atheist science fiction, the solution proposed by *Star Trek* or any number of *Scooby-doo* episodes is perfectly dramatically satisfying: any being pretending to be supernatural is a fraud, a computer you can destroy with a phaser, or Mr. McGready from the Haunted Museum wearing a rubber mask. In epic fantasy, where there actually are supernatural wonders, the ghosts cannot be frauds, so they have to be mistakes, and be aborted. Watching the dead commit suicide so that they are more dead (deader?) is boring. Where is the drama?

I suppose if you are so shallow you think an organism is the only sacred thing in the universe, gee, I guess being bodiless is an unimaginable horror to you. But no one could be that shallow, could he be?

Oh, wait. It turns out that the mysterious Dust that is needed for the life-force of the universe is nothing more or less than sexual liberation. Orgasm stuff. The only point and purpose of religion is to suppress the almighty Orgasm, and the only thing that can throw the universe out of its cosmic balance is chastity and marriage.

Maybe I read that part of the book wrong, because I was skipping pages and giggling with boredom about then. Someone clear me up on this point, please. Better yet, don't clear it up. Leave me with my illusions. I am not willing or able to believe Mr. Pullman, or anyone older than a very lonely and slightly perverted fifteen-year-old, believes something so blatantly stupid.

I would not have minded the preaching, (I was an atheist when I read these books), if the story had not been dropped. The Subtle Knife is never used for its foretold purpose. Lyra's role as the new Eve or the ex-nun's role as the new Serpent is never resolved. The battle with the Authority is never set up, and also never resolved—if Pullman meant for us to believe that killing one officer in a hierarchy would stop the whole Church from doing whatever it is doing (and what was it doing?—we are never told), then he is making an assumption the readers are given no reason to follow. World War Two did not end the moment FDR or Yamamoto died.

All this would be forgivable if Mr. Pullman were a bad writer. He is not. He is a very good writer: this means he knows better. One of the most chilling and unearthly scenes I have ever read in any book ever, one of the most striking scenes, is the one where the ex-nun scientist runs a test on the intergalactic Dark Matter and finds it has a hidden intelligence: the dark matter communicates with her. Who are you? she asks. Angels, they answer. Then they reveal what kind of angels: The exiles. The free angels. The ones driven out of paradise. The angels of the darkness. Fallen angels.

The scene was great. Imagine something like *Close Encounters Of The Third Kind*, and slowly decrypting the coded message from the distant aliens, only to discover that you are talking to something that is standing behind you in the dark and empty room where you are hunched over your computer, and that something is a demon.

Of course, the whole point and emotional power of this scene is fumbled not long after, when it is discovered that the fallen angels are the good guys, or, rather, that there are no good guys.

Nothing I have ever read, not by Heinlein and not by Ayn Rand, has been more blatant in dropping the story-telling, and devoting its pages to preaching a message. The writer was drunk on sermonizing. If this plotline was a motorist, it would have been arrested for driving while intoxicated, if it had not perished in the horrible drunk accident where it went headlong over the cliff of the author's preachy message, tumbled down the rocky hillside, crashed, and burned.

I am not criticizing the message. When I was an atheist, I read those books, I was on his side, and I was in his camp: and yet the third book bored me, because it made a mind-bogglingly simple error in plot.

I am not criticizing his skill as a writer. His first book *The Golden Compass* is something that deserves its rewards, and he has a right to be proud of it.

I am not claiming that there is not some deep meaning to the atheist message I am too shallow to see. I will merely take it for granted that the partisans defending this book can see the Emperor's fine new clothes and I cannot because they are Enlightened and I am Benighted. Let us merely grant this point to get it out of the way.

My big problem with Pullman is the two related writing errors of (1) plot points introduced only when convenient and not before (2) no follow-through; plot points set up but then simply forgotten.

I am claiming the PLOT SUCKS.

Lest I use a technical terminology you non-writers cannot follow, allow me to explain. In professional writing, we professionals say the PLOT SUCKS when the actions of the characters do not flow from causes previously established in the narrative, or when the reactions of the events that follow do not reflect any consequences. In the first case, something comes out of nowhere; and in the second case, nothing comes of it.

In telling a tale, a narrator is trying to cast a spell, to deceive the reader, (with the reader's cooperation, of course), into the illusion that the events being portrayed are unfolding before his eyes. The basic ingredient of the magician's cauldron is, of course, verisimilitude. The events need not be real, or even realistic. They can be larger than life or smaller than life or true to life. They do not need to follow the logic of real life cause-and-effect. But they must follow the story-logic of make-believe. The author can say what happens: but he cannot say, like a child playing a game, that it only happens because of his say-so. The puppeteer cannot stick his naked hand down in front of the small curtain or box that forms his theater lest he ruin the show. If the events or plot elements appear out of nowhere and vanish with no consequence trailing after them, it is too much unlike life. The event seem to be inauthentic, inorganic, unnatural, and each thing that happens does not seem to be happening because of what the story requires, but merely because of what the author wants. If your plot has events and elements that don't fit into the rest of the plot, if the plot is arbitrary, the spell is broken, artistic integrity flies out the window, and the reader is betrayed.

There are two ways in which a plot can suck.

The first is called the Gunrack Rule or Chekhov's Gun Rule. If you establish in Act One that there is a gun hanging on the wall, by Act Three it absolutely must go off. If it's not going to be fired, it shouldn't have been hanging there in the first place. Guns that hang on walls and never go off are a distraction to the reader, a useless element, a protuberance.

This second rule is a complement to the first: If you need to have your character fire the gun in the Third Act, you cannot simply have a god lowered from the stage machinery and hand the gun to him. This is called Deus Ex Machina. While normally this term is used to mean the writer uses an arbitrary mechanism to have the plot end well, the word is still apt in cases, such as here, where the writer uses an arbitrary mechanism to have the plot creak and lurch like

Frankenstein's monster stiffly from one disconnected event to the next.

My complaint is that, not one nor two, but each and every plot element I can recall to mind either was an Unfired Gun or was a Deus Ex Machina.

Some might claim that there are no universal rules to writing. Not everyone needs to obey Chekhov! Such famous literary luminaries as Zachariah Snarfblorcht or the famous Ugo von Pfphlzu routinely violate these rules!

The only problem with relying on the example of these famous artists, of course, is that I have never heard of them, and the names sound made-up to me. Maybe I am a philistine and these rarefied artistes are too profound for my pedestrian tastes. That may be. On the other hand, maybe there are some writers who can violate the rules of writing and do it well. My claim is that Mr. Pullman is violating the rules of writing and doing it badly.

Now, dear reader, if that is my complaint, it does no good to tell me that an arbitrarily unhappy ending that splits Will and Lyra is mature and deep and shows that life does not have easy answers and blah blah blah.

My complaint is that the reason that forces the separation is not previously established, and has every earmark of being thrown in by the author without forethought or foreshadowing. My complaint is not that the arbitrarily unhappy ending is unhappy; my complaint is that it is arbitrary.

To prove that the ending was arbitrary, let us look at the scene where it is announced that anyone living in another world for ten years gets sick and dies. Change that one sentence. Now tell me what, before that point in the manuscript for three books, what else would also have to change to make the manuscript self-consistent? I cannot think of a single plot-point, paragraph, or line.

Pullman could have easily established the unhappy ending in his background in the same way the Tolkien established the downfall of the Three Rings of the Elves once the One Ring was destroyed. Tolkien establishes his mood in scene one, when rustic hobbits at the pub talk about the elves passing through their land to the Gray Havens, there to board ships that go to some hither shore, never to return. This mood is followed through, and the plot point stated explicitly, in the scene where Galadriel is tempted by the One Ring. It is established that the end of the One Ring spells the end of the Elven magic; and that Galadriel and her people must fade and pass away to the West if the Ring is destroyed. The melancholy ending in Tolkien is established from Chapter One, where the passing of the elves to the sea is mentioned. Had Tolkien rewritten the scene where Sam sees Frodo off on the last ship out of Middle Earth so that Frodo simply decided to stay, and keep his elf-friends with him, and the elves suddenly returned to their ancient numbers and powers, and all the glory of the old days suddenly and for no reason sprang into being, that would have been a happy ending, but an arbitrary and stupid one, for it would have violated what was already established.

The melancholy ending in Pullman is exactly this kind of arbitrary and stupid one: the author merely says that no one can emigrate to other worlds, and we are expected to believe it. Well, I do not believe it. It violates what was already established, in mood if not in plot logic. Why is the gate between Lyra's world and Will's impossible to maintain, but the gate to the underworld is possible to maintain? What is there about the Subtle Knife that makes it impos-

sible to find some safe way to use it? As best I can recall, the
Dust Demons promised to destroy the Specters that were
the side effect of Knife-use. Why not simply have a Dust
Demon stand by each time Lyra and Will went to see each
other? Is this not a reward in keeping with those whose
action has overthrown the tyranny of heaven? Who else in
the plot died because of interdimensional travel sickness?
Why are the Dust creatures immune to it? How do we know
the demons were not simply lying about this point?

My complaint is not that the ending is unhappy.
HAMLET ends unhappily, and yet the author there does not
suddenly announce that the cup quaffed by the Queen
contains poison only after she drinks it. The author there
establishes in a previous scene which blade and which cup
will be poisoned, and who is doing the poisoning and why.

I am not talking about plot twists. A plot twist requires
more clever set up, not less; more attention to detail.

In *HAMLET*, when the Queen drinks a cup of poison
meant for the Prince, that is a plot-twist. It is unexpected, yet
not unbelievable, that the Queen might pick up the cup
waiting for Hamlet and carouse to his fortune. Indeed, even
in Act One the evils that follow the Danes from their wassail
are foreshadowed. But since in the previous scene the audience was told that Claudio would place a poisoned pearl in
the chalice of the prince, it is a surprise, it is a plot twist, but
it is not arbitrary, it is not Deus Ex Machina, for Laertes to
announce that the Queen's been poisoned after she drinks.

So, the argument cannot be maintained that Pullman is
indulging in a plot-twist or an unexpected turn of events in
his narrative. A writer needs to have a plot to have a plot-
twist. One needs to see a road to see an unexpected turn
in it.

Imagine the same scene in *HAMLET* if Pullman had

written it. Hamlet, using a mystic pearl, places the poison in the cup to kill Claudio. We are all told Hamlet will die by drinking the cup. Then Claudio dies choking on a chicken bone at lunch. Then the Queen dies when Horatio shows her the magical Mirror of Death. This mirror appears in no previous scene, nor is it explained why it exists. Then Ophelia summons up the Ghost from Act One and kills it, while she makes a speech denouncing the evils of religion. Ophelia and Hamlet are parted, as it is revealed in the last act that a curse will befall them if they do not part ways.

Think I am kidding? I am not even being subtle. The pearl is the knife. Claudio is Evil God. The chicken bone is him falling out of bed. Horatio is Mrs. Coulter. The Death Mirror is this sudden, unexplained, stupid abyss that winged angels cannot fly out of. Ophelia is Lyra, and the Ghost is the ghost.

Unlike *Hamlet*, not only is there no climax to *The Amber Spyglass*, there is no plot, merely a disconnected series of events. In the case of the death of Metatron, which, (in a properly constructed book, would have been the climax), I could not for the life of me figure out how killing off one bad guy, even if he was the Caesar of Heaven, would halt or even hinder the Roman Empire of Heaven.

If there was one evil being done by the Empire of Heaven, such as a war or an oppression that only that one Seraphic ruler had ordered but which the Praetorians, Patricians and soldiers, (or, if you like, Cherubim, Principalities, and Angels), had no interest in pursuing, then offing the one ruler would stop that oppression: but Mr. Pullman makes it clear that the evils of Jehovah are systemic. Killing Jove and Metatron could not uproot the Evil Catholic Church on earth, or even hinder the operations of her officers.

You see, in a well-crafted book, the evil empire of heaven

would have been doing something, up to something. In a well-crafted book there would be, in other words, a plot. There would be a goal to which the good guys are moving, and a means they select to achieve; a yardstick of success and failure. There would be a goal to which the bad guys are moving, and a means to achieve it.

Let me use a clear example. I pick this example because it is clear, and it is good craftsmanship, not because it is great writing. In *Star Wars*, the McGuffin was the blueprints to the armored battle-station Death Star. The good guys wanted to use the plans to blow up the Death Star, the bad guys wanted to recover the plans. Unlike Pullman, George Lucas establishes before even Act One, in the introduction word-crawl, this plot point. Space Princess has the blueprints. Dark Helmet in Act One captures Space Princess. To recover the plans, Dark Helmet uses drugs and torture on Space Princess to get her to talk. That is a plot, because the bad guys want something, and they are using a certain means to get it.

Plot Twist one: Good Guys rescue Space Princess. This would seem to thwart the plot of the Bad Guys, because now they cannot discover the plans from her; but, aha! Dark Helmet let Space Princess escape, so that Bad Guys could secretly follow Space Princess back to Rebel Base just in time for Big Fight Scene. Good Guys now try to use captured plans to blow up Death Star; Death Star now tries to use megadeath beam-weapon to blow up rebel base, but gas giant is in the way. If Good Guys blow up Death Star first, they win; if Bad Guys blow up rebel base first, they win.

See? THAT is a plot. Each party has something he is trying to accomplish, and he is opposed by a contrary party whose actions are mutually exclusive, and therefore antagonistic to, the first party.

Now, let us look at Pullman's opus. The McGuffin here, the "plans to the Death Star" was the Subtle Knife, the god-killing weapon. But there are no bad guys on stage when the knife is introduced. The conflict with Evil Tyrant God is not in Act One; it is not even clear until late in book two, or maybe book three. The Evil Church sends out an assassin to kill Lyra, but it is not clear what this will accomplish for them. I frankly don't remember what happens to that assassin—did Will get him with the knife? Get lost in a sewer and die? The scene did not make enough of an impact to lodge in my memory. As for the leaders in heaven of the Evil Church, one of them dies by falling out of bed, and the other one is seduced and pushed into a Bottomless Pit by a side character. The hero and heroine, as far as I know, never even hear the news that anything has happened to the bad guys.

The good guys have no goal. The bad guys have no goal. There is motion, and speeches, but no plot. Nothing is done by the end. What makes the Church in the final volume unable to send out a dozen more evil assassins to mug the girl? What advantage or disadvantage did it do the Evil Church to have the wheeled elephant things on another world innocent or fallen, if these words have any meaning in this context?

The arbitrary plot points in Pullman are countless. When Mrs. Coulter announces that she has the power to seduce Metatron, on the grounds that all angels are consumed with lusts of the flesh, this plot point is introduced when and only when needed. It is not part of the background of the rest of the story. It could be removed without damage to the rest of the story. It does not crop up again. It is not explained, even though it would have been easy for the author to do so.

This plot point also seems arbitrary because there is no sense that the author thought through the implications. To use a simple example, if you found out young women on this planet wore men's hats with wide brims whenever they walked out-of-doors, and then found out they were afraid that the angels in heaven would see them and carry them off, then the dress code of this planet would have a logical relation to the plot point. Or if women were not allowed to walk abroad without an armed priest or something. Or if the world had many stories of Nephilim and Demigods, men who were the offspring of the Sons of God and the Daughters of Eve. Or if Lyra's older sister had been carried off by a lustful angel. Or something. If the details were correct, it would seem like a real planet.

The Pit into which Mrs. Coulter pushes the archangel likewise is arbitrary. It is not the pit that was foretold to us since chapter one as the Dread Pit of No-Escape. This is arbitrary writing, as if a character in Act Three picked up a vase, announced it was a gun, and shot the antagonist with a mortar round issuing from the vase mouth.

Let us remind ourselves of other arbitrary plot points.

Will. The plot promises us the boy will kill God with a magic knife: he doesn't. He does not kill God at all; God dies by falling out of bed, through no action set in motion by the main character or any character. Will uses the Knife to open the breathing envelope around God to help Him, but the air accidentally dissolves Him in a heavy-handed attempt at irony. The Subtle Knife does not kill God, or even God's regent Metatron.

Asriel. The plot promises the evil Kingdom of Heaven will be overthrown and replaced with Republic, a place where humans get a say in how the universe is run. It isn't. As far as I can tell, two officers of the Evil Kingdom die, God and Metatron. Nothing in the book indicates that Archangel Michael will not don the crown of heaven and continue the war. The war has no point and no victory conditions.

Lyra. The girl is supposed to be the new Eve. Apparently this is a sterile Eve, because no new race is born of her. Being the "New Eve" of the entire universe is evidently the same thing as being a freshman co-ed in college. Ho-hum.

Mary. The ex-nun was supposed to be the new serpent. She simply is not. There is nothing and no one she talks to that is persuaded to depart from submission to the evil God. The wheeled creatures were not Church victims. No one is in chains to be set free.

There is no new Eden, no victory, no change, no nothing.

The Evil Church. It is merely arbitrarily said to be evil, but nothing in the plot shows it to be evil. It sends out an assassin to kill a child, but this is done apparently for no reason, and it is not a worse thing than what Asriel does in killing children to open a gate to a new world.

The Evil God. As far as I can tell the Evil Church does not even know that the Evil God exists. He does not give them Dust-power or create evil miracles when they are starting their evil inquisitions, because there are no evil miracles and no evil inquisitions on stage. Killing Evil God would not put Evil Church out of business, or even require a half-day holiday to change the branding.

Mrs. Coulter. Starts out evil, decides to rescue her child, and then sacrifice herself to slay Metatron. None of these motives are established, and nothing comes of them. Certainly Lyra never finds out what happened to her Mom. I don't remember if she even knew it was her Mom. Had Metatron died by choking on a fishbone, or some other death as arbitrary and stupid as the one that felled his boss, not a single word in the book that led up to that event and not a single word in any scene that comes after would need to be changed. No references are made to it: the act exists in a vacuum; nothing is accomplished.

This list could go on and on. Indeed, I am hard pressed to think of a single event or plot point that is not introduced arbitrarily and then swept off stage without meaning and without consequences. There was no reason given as to why Lyra was the "Chosen One" who could read the Golden Compass, no explanation of who made the artifact or why. Nothing comes from any prophecies about her, which means that the art of reading the Dust for clues about the future (Lyra's only skill in the book) means nothing.

If all the prophecies are fake, what is the point of having your main character girl be a prophetess?

Nothing comes of Will's wound to his hand. Nothing comes of Will's missing father. Nothing comes of Lord Asriel's experiments: he breaks through to a new world, but so what? All that means is that he released another specter into the environment. Lord Asriel gathers a titanic army, but so what? Mrs. Coulter offs the head general on the other side. We all know that the killing of Yamamoto would have stopped World War II, right? Oh, wait a minute....

Does the homosexual angel who was banished from heaven ever get back again and revisit his sodomite lover? Aside from whether you think this plot element is Politically Progressive or jarringly tasteless for a children's book, the fact of the matter is that the plot never returns to this character, and we never find out. Just one more point where the plot suffers from attention deficit disorder.

Let me emphasize the most pointless plot point on this whole pointless list.

Lyra kills the ghosts. This is a particularly egregious

example, and the flaw would have been particularly easy to fix. All you have to do is set it up and follow through. Nothing in her character or in the plot before this scene makes her, or the reader, or anyone, have any stake in the outcome, emotional or otherwise, in this scene. It makes sense on no level, either as metaphor or as literature. Why would the ghosts prefer oblivion to a disembodied existence? If their new life is not oblivion, then either they are going to some sort of reincarnation, to a self-hood-destroying union with the Cosmic All, or to a Last Judgment: in this last case the Evil Church is correct about life after death. In the other two cases, the Hindu or the Buddhist is correct, neither of which has any representatives in the plot. For an atheist book to be preaching an oriental religion is baffling to say the least. Nothing comes of it. Nothing that was wrong is set right because the ghosts are dead.

Compare it to a parallel situation in *The Farthest Shore* by Ursula K. Le Guin. In that book, the unwise wizard Cob attempts to extend his life by necromancy. But his necromancy upsets the equilibrium of the spirit world, and of the world of men. Crops are failing. Magic spells are fading. The Wise are forgetting the names of things. The dragons are dying. All that is good and fair is draining out of the scheme of the world. The door between the world and the after-world is breached. The living world is becoming slowly to be like the death world.

The Archmage of Roke, Sparrowhawk finds and confronts Cob, who, by then, is neither alive nor dead. Cob has forgotten his own True Name. Now Sparrowhawk must walk through the land of the dead to undo the fracture Cob made in the wall between life and death. This is accomplished, but at a tremendous cost: the magic of Spar-

rowhawk, greatest of magicians, is gone. But the magic of
the world is saved. It is the yearning of the magician Cob for
endless life, for Yin without Yang, for Day without Night,
that causes the catastrophe.

I must emphasize yet again that I am not talking about
the ideas in *The Amber Spyglass*, I am talking about the plot.
In *The Farthest Shore* the fact that some imbalance is
draining the magic from the world is established in Act One.
The reason for the evil is revealed to be something understandable: a necromancer wanted to interfere with the
natural balance between life and death in order to win more
life for himself. The consequences of the terrible act, and
the sacrifices needed to affect a cure, are carried through
with admirable plot logic. That Sparrowhawk loses his
magic is melancholy, and even unexpected, but it is not
arbitrary.

The scene with Lyra killing, (or whatever), the ghosts is
almost identical in concept, except that Pullman does everything clumsily that Le Guin does with effortless grace.
There is this stuff called Dust, which is apparently demon-
stuff. Or maybe it is sexual energy. Or maybe it is self-aware-
ness. Or maybe it is the wisdom that rejects religion. Or
maybe it created the universe. Or.... If the author had any
idea of what this stuff is, he did not make it clear to this
reader, at least. The Dust produces Angels, who are all-
powerful beings ruling the universe. Except that they are
weak, hollow-boned creatures that a crippled thirteen-year-
old can defeat in a wrestling match: Will cracks their bones
with his wounded hands when they get in his way. The Evil
Church somehow, back in the past, imprisoned a bunch of
ghosts in a boring afterworld. Why? Unlike Cob, no reason
is given, at least, none I can recall. (I am not willing to go

back and reread these books to find the passage where the reason is given, if it exists.)

The boredom makes the ghosts yearn for oblivion. Why? Just because. Lyra shows up, and, for no reason, uses the Subtle Knife to open a gateway into oblivion for them, and the joyful ghosts all annihilate themselves, so that their soul-atoms can be carried off and be recycled. Why? No reason. Does anything come of this? No.

Maybe I am wrong on this point: after all, the harpies were tormenting the ghosts with memories of their sins and crimes. If you actually think people like Stalin and Hitler and Mao, (or, if you are Dante, people like Brutus, Cassius, or Judas), deserve no worse penalty than merely a verbal recitation of their list of crimes, (a pretty doubtful "if"), then why not use the Knife on the harpies and simply kill the harpies, instead of killing the ghosts? Why not open a gateway into some other environment, a place with nice things to look at, rather than into oblivion?

If you have to sacrifice someone to maintain the spiritual ecology of the universe, why sacrifice the ghosts? Why not sacrifice a cow? Why destroy the memories of your sacred ancestors? You tell me the universe is constructed so that the life-energy or the thought-substance of the ghosts, the Dust they accumulated, has to be returned to the source? That sounds to me like the book is saying the universe needs to eat the thought-substance, the intelligence, of the ghosts in order to remain a healthy universe. If so, this universe is a worse evil god than Evil God, for it kills its children like Saturn, it kills your children like Moloch, but is merely a blind and dumb machine. Evil God sounds positively charming compared to that.

Are those ghosts annihilated, reincarnated, unified with the Cosmos, or brought to a Last Judgment? A casual reader cannot tell. The reason why a casual reader cannot tell is because none of these four options would make the slightest bit of difference to anything following after this event, nor make the slightest bit of difference to anything that led up to this event.

To add insult to injury, it would have been easy, so easy, effortless, for any editor to tell Pullman to put in a scene in Act One where the land was ailing and the crops were failing, because the ghosts were not being recycled as part of the spiritual ecology of the world. Babies were being born without their daemons. The magic is poisoned because Cob, or the Evil Church, meddled with the natural order of things. When the natural order is restored, the wrong things go right. How hard is that? How hard is that to put in a book? If anything like this was in there, I missed it.

Of the controversy surrounding whether or not Will and Lyra are lovers at the end of the book or just good friends, the author, (at least in the edition published in North America), has left this ambiguous, and I have no opinion and frankly do not care a tinker's damn, because both options are bad writing.

Option one: if Lyra and Will are lovers, not only is this grotesque, considering their age, but it is pointless. It is pointless because nothing comes from it and nothing leads to it. It is both a violation of the Gunrack Rule and of the rule against Gods from the Stage Machinery.

Nothing comes of it. Lyra is supposed to be the new Eve, but she must be a sterile Eve, because there is no New Cain, Able, Seth, or any new mankind. The idea that all the world changes merely because two teens do the Wild Thang is stupid and offensive. Love may conquer all, but, seriously, it is not that important in the grand scheme of things.

And the matter of fact is that the world is not changed at

the end of the story. All the angels in heaven are still around, and the Evil Church is still running things. The only change is that Lyra now wants to go to school, and she makes a dumb speech about being nice and kind to all living things, a speech that could not come out of the mouth of the character as previously established, and which nothing in the plot could have put in her mouth. Oh, and she lost the power to read the Golden Compass, which is okay, because we find out that the powers manipulating the compass and sending her messages through it are fallen angels, creatures who we know nothing about, not even their names.

Nothing leads up to it. If one act of pre-teen coitus is that important in the grand scheme of things, the author has to establish its importance in the first act.

Let us contrast this, not with *Hamlet*, but with the movie *Krull*. In *Krull*, in the first act, it is established that the princess is prophesied to give birth to a son who will rule the stars. This is the motive for The Beast to kidnap the princess, and the reason why The Beast does not simply kill her. It drives the plot. In Pullman, there is nothing said in Act One that establishes Lyra losing her virginity will shatter the thrones of heaven and change the world.

Option two: Lyra and Will are just good friends. Well, gee, it is nice when two pre-teenagers are friends, and even puppy love is nice, but I don't know any real life girl who is still moping, years later, after going to school, growing up, getting a man and a family of her own, for some guy she met at age thirteen. Every year she goes to the same beach and sits and looks mournfully out at the sunset. Boo-freaking-hoo. I am not saying it does not happen; I am just saying I don't know anyone like that, and if Lyra is like that, the author did not introduce me to her in such a fashion as to create in my imagination the impression that she was that way.

It is trivial, almost offensively so. After all this blood and thunder, the death of her parents, the downfall of archangels, we get, what, again, exactly, as the pay-off?

Not only does nothing lead up to this ending, the lead-up is contrary to it. We are told that daemons cease to change shape when children become adults, and adulthood is defined as being touched by the hand of a lover. The word lover, under option two, refers to an unconsummated love. We are told that it is Lyra's innocence that gives her the power to read the alethiometer. So, under option two, Lyra's innocence is lost and her adulthood gained, not because she goes from being a maiden to a wife, (which is the normal meaning traditionally attached to those words), but because she goes from being a self-centered little girl to being a girl with a puppy-love teen crush on a guy that is never consummated. This makes no sense on any level. Why would young love make anyone less innocent? The message here is that falling in love is a corruptive rather than an ennobling process: this is a strange message indeed, coming from a book where the cosmic substance underlying all reality, the Dust, is the source and side-effect of sexual passion, and the Evil Church is evil because—and only because—it preaches chastity. Or perhaps the Dust represents wisdom and the Church represents willful ignorance, in which case, having innocence be the source of magic makes even less sense. Wisdom would be the enemy of magic in that background; wise men would be the only ones not able to do magic.

This book should have been an atheist book. I mean a properly, openly, honestly, hardcore really atheist book. In an atheist book, the point would be that life consists of life on Earth, and that daydreams about life after death or

Flying Spaghetti Monsters ruling the world are pernicious. In such a book, the churchgoing characters would be shown being corrupted by the act of having their faith blind their reason. The churchmen would be shown robbing and deceiving the gullible faithful. The short term and long term effects of the evil being done by the ideas and by the practice of the Evil Church would be onstage. It is not that hard to do. The short and long term evils caused by collectivist thinking are admirably and unmistakably put on pitiless display in the philosophical novel *Atlas Shrugged* by Ayn Rand. Love that book or hate it, no one can say that Ayn Rand does not show in the plot what she conceives the wrongheadedness of collectivism to be, or does not show what she conceives to be the bad consequences that flow from collectivizing the economy. Her plot supports her ideas: she has the United States railroad industry, and indeed the whole economy, fall apart step by step in front of the reader's eyes.

In Pullman's book, nothing of the kind is done. I cannot tell what Pullman thinks is so great about atheism or thinks is so wrong about believing in God, because nothing happens in the plot to support the ideas. Nothing falls apart. Nothing is going wrong at the beginning of the book and nothing is put right at the end; or, rather, the thing going wrong at the beginning of the book, street urchins being kidnapped for Nazi experiments, turns out to be the work of Lord Asriel and his wife, who stop the experiments for no particular reason.

I say again: This book should have been an atheist book. An atheist book says not only that God is a delusion, an atheist book also says men need to take control of their own lives and their own destinies. That is NOT the message in this book, despite a nod in that direction, too little, and too late. The message in this book is that the promise of the Republic in Heaven is FALSE: You will never get to vote on how the worlds and constellations are run. You don't get a vote. You will NEVER solve the problem of separation from your loved ones. You are NOT in charge.

In order for this to be an atheist book, some character, major or minor, would need to be shown not in charge of his life, oppressed by the Church, snared by a web of falsehoods trapping him, and then, when the net is cut, he proves able to do for himself, and make all the decisions he needs to make as well as, nay, better than, what the false Gods made for him. Nothing like that happens in the... whole... boring... silly... badly-written... book.

Here is my last question to all defenders and apologists for Mr. Pullman's rollickingly bad third novel in his started-well-but-crashed-and-burned trilogy.

Why, oh, why in a book about the virtues of not listening to authority and not taking anything on faith, did everyone in the book, and I mean everyone, believe whatever a Dusty pocketwatch told them to do?

Not a single character ever asked for independent confirmation of the pronouncements of the oracle of the Golden Compass.

The alethiometer, you see, was sensitive to 'The Dust' which was the self-reflective nature of matter when it starts to become self-aware. The oldest and most powerful of the self-aware vortices of Dust, is, oddly enough, God Almighty, who is portrayed as a senile husk. So, if the Dust is all-wise, why is the God who arose from the Dust all-stupid? If, on the other hand, the Dust is a natural but unintelligent spirit force, why should anyone listen to it or follow its advice? If, on the gripping hand, the Dust is a self-aware being, or stream of beings, how do we know it did not go senile at about the same time God Almighty did, or earlier?

Oh, I get it, I get it. Yes, I know, the alethiometer is actually just a symbol or a metaphor for the Power of Reason, or the Power of Matter, or the Power of Believing in Yourself or whatever power it is that Mr. Pullman thinks is the touchstone to determine true from false. His faith in the power of whatever-it-is is touching. We skeptics are more skeptical. We skeptics reason that reason, like all things possessed of qualities and properties, has utilities it can perform and those it cannot. No one constructs a syllogism to deduce whether a woman is beautiful, for example. No one can reason in the absence of evidence, for another example.

We skeptics would have had someone give the old pocketwatch-of-materialism a few simple James Randi style tests to make sure it was working. Matter suffers entropy, you know. Sad if Lyra found out in some later scene that a slipped disk or a loose cog made the symbol arm overshoot by twelve degrees each time the dust-o-meter was measuring the truth of things. Hate to get all my positive and negative signs reversed, you know, and have it turn out the God was Good and the Fallen Angels were lying about all that stuff.

An afterword on counterarguments:

The article above first appeared, (as the time of this writing), seven years ago. It generated a degree of controversy that frankly surprised me. Some people, including some people whose opinions I respect, (but also including some orcish-tongued babbling dunderheads), take the book very seriously, and wished to challenge my statements about it.

Sadly, nearly all challenges were based on a misreading of what I said.

I did not think anyone would object to the idea that Pullman was preaching a message instead of telling a story. Indeed, more than half the counterarguments I got in reply said that I must be benighted because I did not get the profound message Pullman was preaching. What looked to me like bad storytelling was in truth, (so I was told), Mr. Pullman's subtle way of saying real life is hard and nothing works out with the neatness of a storybook. Funny how all the events in his storybook work out so neatly to make that point!

The counterarguments were saying, in effect, that storytelling had to go by the wayside for a "new type" of storytelling. What was this "new type" of storytelling? *Preaching a message rather than telling a story.*

Funny how none of his defenders noticed they had just contradicted Mr. Pullman's public statement.

Other counterarguments were better constructed. I had not recalled the events in the third book *The Amber Spyglass* correctly. My faulty memory had automatically filled in motives where there were none and plot points where there were none. People have been kind enough to describe to me scenes in the book I've forgotten, and to make clear certain messages the author put in that I had ignored.

Upon revisiting the issue, and thinking back over the books, I found that *The Amber Spyglass* was much worse than I remembered, much more chaotically written, much more sentimental and pointless and ugly, and much more... well... *stupid.*

A hard word, I know, but there is no other that will do.

The scenes I had forgotten I had forgotten for good reason: memory works by association, which is why it is easier to remember a sonnet than a string of meaningless alphanumeric symbols of the same length as a sonnet. Scenes that meant nothing and did nothing are easy to forget.

The messages, aside from the blatant anti-god message, (which I liked when I first read it; I was an atheist myself back then), I had tried to ignore because they got in the way of enjoying the story. And the messages were easy to ignore, because they were so bland, and so insipid and so unimaginative. But now I realize there is no story, only the messages.

And what messages! The worldview involved is so sickeningly-sweet, so cloying and pious, yet so innocuous, that only a bleeding heart could love it. It is sentimentality in the very worst sense of the word.

We Christians tend to forget the banal and boring nature of real evil. Not every devil can be a sharp dresser like a Nazi, or a magnetic writer like a Nietzsche. Some of them are just drab.

What were the messages iN *The Amber Spyglass*? By my count, they were: (1) Question Authority, (2) Sex is a good thing, (3) Be nice to people in small ways, (4) Tell stories, (5) Stay in school, (6) Hate God. Of these, only the last one is likely to spark any controversy worth thinking about.

How did the author choose to put across these messages? Answer: he did not. He simply did not. Let us count the ways:

(1) Question authority? The author did not have an authority that forbade anyone from questioning anything on stage, that later turned out to be a good question with an answer that improved anyone's life or solved any problem. Asriel is in trouble for investigating the Dust, but the book never quite makes clear what the Dust is anyway, and Asriel does not improve his own life or anyone else's by finding

anything out about the Dust. As I recall, he dies by falling into a pit after his ex-wife pushes an archangel into it. The only thing that came of Asriel's investigation into the Dust was that he murdered a child to open a gate into another world. Once he got there, nothing in particular happened. For a good example of this message, told correctly, see *The Machine Stops* by E.M. Foster or see *The Lottery* by Shirley Jackson.

(2) Make love, not war! I have to assume Mr. Pullman is not preaching in favor of married sex with one woman to whom one is faithful for life. That is a Christian message, and we Christians are Grendel, right? So it must be illicit sex he is on about. This is only a guess, since his trilogy is just as unclear on this as on everything. I suppose the author just thinks we will take on faith the idea that sex outside of marriage is the source and summit of human aspirations. Is he preaching against Puritans? Well, Catholics don't like Puritans either, so take a number and stand in line.

In any case, no one in the book has a sexual encounter improve, (or even change), his life. Are Lyra and Will underage lovers at the end of the book, or just good friends? The author coyly does not say. But neither option makes sense. If they are lovers, the sexual awakening did not do anything for them. It did not improve their lives: they are condemned to eternal separation. Lyra is not the Beatrice for Will's Dante. She is not even the Queen Gwen for his Lancelot. The coupling, (if it took place), did not mean anything and nothing comes of it, not even a baby. If they are just good friends, then the message is contradicted. For a good example of this message, told correctly, see *Atlas Shrugged* or *The Fountainhead*, or read a poem by Byron, Keats, or one of the Romantics.

Again, a reader tells me it is not sex per se that is good,

but the maturity that sex represents. Under this interpretation, the Evil Church was trying to keep everyone from maturing, and Mary the Lapsed Nun was the tempter trying to get Lyra to grow up. The only problem with this interpretation is that it makes sheer nonsense of an already muddled plot. Growth as a physical process of maturing is natural and inevitable, not something a protagonist can seek out or an antagonist can try to prevent, not in any story outside of Peter Pan, at least. You don't have to talk a child into suffering puberty. Growth as a spiritual process is never mentioned, and, in any case, makes no difference to the plot: it is not as if Senile God had lived, or Metatron, or Mrs. Coulter, then our young Lyra would have been propelled one inch toward or away from spiritual growth or moral or mental maturity: if anything, it is the innocence of Lyra as the Noble Savage, (an oddly Victorian value, that), that has magical properties.

(3) No one in the book is nice to anyone in any small ways. Lyra is a liar. Will is a murderer. I cannot recall a single line, not even a word, spoken in kindness to any other character. I guess they like their spiritual pets. The only act of large-scale kindness in the book is on the part of Mrs. Coulter, who turns apostate to the Evil Church in order to nurse her ungrateful daughter back to life, and who also falls into a pit during an archangelicide. For a good example of this message, told correctly, see "Leaf by Niggle", or *The Great Divorce*, or even *The Mahabharata*.

(4) Telling stories! Not much to see here either. Lyra tells some stories to the harpies in hell, so maybe something was supposed to happen here. But hell is emptied out and all those spirits die or something, so I am not sure what the point is. For a good example of this message, told correctly, see *Bridge To Terabithia*, which is a potent and ringing

endorsement of the power of the imagination to overcome grief and loss.

(5) Stay in school! Since the main character is never in a position where book-learning did her a bit of good, and since I assume all the printing presses on her world are controlled by the imprimatur of the Evil Church, this would seem to run counter to that whole Question Authority theme, unless your teachers are not authorities in their subjects. (But in that case, why stay in school?) For a good example of this message, told correctly, see just about any coming-of-age story you can think of, including, shockingly enough, *Starship Troopers*—young Mister Rico, unlike Lyra, actually gets whipped into shape in boot camp, (no pun intended), and he comes out a better man in the end, due and only due to his education.

(6) Hating God. For a good example of this message, told correctly, see *Atlas Shrugged* or read the first three books of Milton's *Paradise Lost*, whose antagonist, Lucifer, has a much stronger and clearer reason, a non-wimpy reason, for denying and defying God than anything any mushy-headed Pullmanite character can mouth. (We Christians do blasphemy better than you atheists ever will.) Or, if you prefer, read *Gather, Darkness* by Fritz Leiber for a description of what a real hard-assed theocracy bent on cowing the people through enforced ignorance would be like.

Is Mr. Pullman preaching against organized institutional religion? Well, Protestants don't like organized religion either, especially American Protestants. So take a number and stand in line.

Atheists have many perfectly sound arguments they can make against organized institutional religion, and Protestants have also. (We Catholics also have arguments we can make against disorganized religion.) To avoid those arguments and talk instead in a mushy-headed way about the beautiful oneness with the universe that comes when you commit euthanasia on the weak and helpless is simply vile.

One reader I know said that the description of the slobbery and wretched creature that once was God Almighty in this book reminded him of Gollum. Instead of killing the thing out of pity, as in *Old Yeller*, and instead of smiting the dying god out of righteous indignation, for hate's sake, as in *Moby Dick*, and instead of sparing the thing out of pity and not killing him at all, as indeed, Gandalf counsels Frodo to do for Gollum, our author hits upon the perfect plot device to squeeze every iota of non-drama and non-meaning out of what could have been an interesting scene. Will kills God by mistake while trying to help Him. So there is neither pity nor justice in the death: it is just a dumb mistake, a flourish of contempt by the author for his characters, and, I must assume, his audience.

As with what later happens with the ghosts Lyra kills, God sighs and looks pleased.

Why the sigh and the smile? Just one more pro-death moment brought to you by the culture wars! I can understand a rational and manly atheism that looks at the abyss of death and does not flinch, reconciled to an evil that no one can avoid. I can understand a religion that promises some farther shore beyond the abyss.

What I cannot understand is a sentimental and mystical atheism that looks at the abyss of death and calls it good or desirable.

Many non-Christians, (and some Christians), recoil from the doctrine of Eternal Damnation as an utter abrogation of justice. They ask why any finite crime could be punished with infinite pains? The question is a good one, and deserves a better answer than I can provide in this space:

but I will say that divine wisdom may have concluded that a painless oblivion is more unfair, since apparently many more people desire it, yearning for a black nothingness in which to quench their guilt and their hatred toward life, than I could have imagined.

So the final message is a pro-death one. Here, I cannot advise you to seek out a better, because it is a type of literature I deliberately avoid, as I wish, now, in hindsight, I had avoided *The Amber Spyglass*.

11

FAITH IN THE FICTIONAL WAR
BETWEEN SCIENCE FICTION AND FAITH

I s science fiction innately and naturally inclined to be hostile to religion?

After all, in *Foundation*, the church of the Galactic Spirit turns out to be a hoax, likewise the messiahship of Muad'Dib in *Dune*, likewise the Church of Foster in *Stranger In A Strange Land*, likewise the evil church of evil in *Gather, Darkness* or *The Rise Of Endymion*, likewise the church of the rebels in *Sixth Column*. On the other hand, Christians as a whole are pretty hostile to false prophets and heretics, and Americans, like all good Protestant nations, are pretty hostile to organized Churches. Roman Catholics, on the other hand, would like our church to get organized, and we will get around to that real soon. So are these portrayals of false religions innate to science fiction, or are they merely the dramatic inventions of stories that are not necessarily condemning religion as much as condemning falseness?

I would say this question breaks into three questions: (1) is there anything innately hostile in SF to religion portrayed as a man-made institution? (2) Is there anything innately hostile in SF to religion portrayed as supernaturally made institution? (3) Is there anything innately hostile in SF to supernaturalism in general?

All of these are difficult and subtle questions, and I am in the middle of writing a Christian Science Fiction book right now, where Mary Baker Eddy teams up with Nikola Tesla to repel an invasion of the lepers of Mars with the help of a mind-reading lion, called *Aslan Is A Slan*, so I can deal with these difficult and subtle questions in only the most shallow and trivial way.

Let us start with a definition: science fiction is the mythology of the scientific age.

Like all myths, the mythology called Science Fiction must treat with metaphysical questions and questions of the human condition. Being scientific myth, it must cast those questions in terms of a naturalistic idea that scientific progress will open either the Box of Pandora or the Cave of Wonders of Aladdin, or both, such that if the story does not concern some aspect of a change in society or life brought about by a speculated advance in technology, it is not really science fiction.

This would seem to rule out religion as part of the worldview science fiction uses by definition. If you travel into the future using the time machine of H.G. Wells, you are in a science fiction tale; if you travel into the future escorted by the ghost of Christmas Yet to Come, you are in a fantasy. If you turn invisible like Frodo by means of a magic ring, it is fantasy; if by means of chemicals like Griffin the Invisible Man or by cosmic rays like Sue Storm the Invisible Girl, that is science fiction. Your magicians can do every-thing in science fiction they do in a fantasy, provided only you call your magic 'parapsychology' or 'psionics' on the grounds that psionics is a natural if unknown phenomenon, whereas magic is a supernatural and unknowable phenomenon (or, technically speaking, a noumenon).

To craft an SF/F book, we use all the same tools and tricks as a mainstream writer, with one difference. The one thing we do that writers of Westerns, Romances, Detective novels or Pirate Stories do not do is world-building. They use a setting the audience already knows: we invent a new one, even if the invention is no more than the tired repetition of a consensus background many other authors has used, such as the generic 'space opera space empire' background adopted by *Star Wars*.

So the question becomes whether religion can be part of that background? This breaks into two questions: the natural portrayal of religion, and the supernatural.

Dune, like all SF that portrays a fantastic or futuristic society in some detail, must portray a fantastic or futuristic religion as well, since religion is one of the great constants of human nature: but the nature of science fiction is inherently interested in the variables in human society, not the constants. So in a period of history where most of the readers are Christian, those of us who want to hear sailors' stories and travelers' tales from fictional travel into other worlds and future eons do not want to hear about our own religion.

We want weird tales. (I suppose if the demographic has atheists outnumber Christians, the atheists who are as imaginative as science fiction readers boast themselves to be will want to hear about Christian worlds, merely because then that to them will have the haunting aura of strangeness.) In sum, fantasy is the weirdness of the Odyssey; science fiction is the weirdness of Einstein.

Compare Heinlein's *The Moon Is A Harsh Mistress*, where the marriage customs, for example, of the Loonies are as odd and uncouth as the marriage customs of Eskimos, early Mormons or Turks, with the marriage of the Gray Lensman to the Red Lensman in *Galactic Patrol* by E.E. Smith: the marriage customs portrayed in Heinlein's book are mind-bogglingly unrealistic, but it is very fine science fiction, because it is a speculation that a change in the environment creates a change in social custom. On the other hand, the marriage in Smith's book is so realistic it is not science fiction at all.

Likewise, the conceit in *Foundation* that the Scientists of Terminus could simply sit down one day and invent a religion of the Great Galactic Spirit, and use their advanced science to perform tricks to befuddle the yokels of worlds, (whose fathers and grandfathers, come to think of it, remembered that selfsame science, and presumably had books or tapes of such things), and that anyone would find such a synthetic religion feasible or believable is itself not believable.

This theme is a favorite of Sciffy writers, and occurs again in *Gather, Darkness* by Fritz Leiber, and *Sixth Column* by Heinlein. Nonetheless, it is perfectly cromulent science fiction, since it is a speculation about a social change caused by a change in technology. (In this case, the tech change must be the invention of the Idiot Cap which makes whole populations really gullible in a fashion only atheists are gullible enough to think could ever happen in real life.)

Compare this with the way religion is treated in *Galactic Patrol*, where the Earthmen seem to have some sort of nondenominational Protestantism, and, again, since nothing is different from the world of the reader, the make-believe world does not dwell on, nor even mention by name, the church that the Civilization of the Lens follows.

That is on the one hand. If the writer wants to argue that

the natural needs of drama of science fiction make it easy to portray all cults as deceptive, and all space churches as monstrous, he'll get no argument from me.

Science fiction is naturally inclined to dramatize and glamorize skepticism. It is easy to write about frauds like those of the ancient shrine of the Serapeum, with its speaking tubes and hollow statues. Using modern technology to fool the yokels is a natural thought to anyone impressed with Hollywood illusions or the cunning of stage magic. So the story in *Gather, Darkness* proposes a world of illiterate dupes ruled by a hierarchy of Hollywoodized technocrats. On the other hand, the merely technical difficulties of writing about fraudulent atheist conspiracies or institutions deceptively hiding the evidence of miracles and resurrections might deter the authors into less difficult projects.

No SF writer to my knowledge has written one of these "mega-conspiracies that fool the entire world" books starring an atheist conspiracy armed with high-tech tricks, even though the technique of airbrushing unpersons out of old photographs was invented by a real-life and still-in-business mega-conspiracy, namely, the international communist movement.

It is easy to pick on evil institutional churches in SF for the same reason it is easy to pick on evil institutional businesses, or evil institutional governments. Who wants to read about a benevolent Galactic Empire? We want to hear about Jack the Giant Killer. No one wants to hear about Giant the Jack Killer. To portray a galactic-wide institution, secular or spiritual, as Jack facing a foe worthy of the name of a giant would require rare skill.

On the other hand, the other hand of the argument is purely definitional. Is *Star Wars* science fiction or science fantasy? In the same way that it is abundantly clear that the

DC comicverse takes place in a Judeo-Christian background, with orthodox devils and angels coming onstage in
the pages of *Swamp Thing* or *The Specter*, it is abundantly
clear that *Star Wars* takes place in a vaguely Taoist-flavored
New-Age-y universe ruled by a mystical 'Force.' But Taoism
is a religion. The materialistic premise that all supernatural
beliefs are merely man-made myths and lies and self-deception cannot be true in the galaxy long long ago and far far
away. The Force is not portrayed as parapsychology. It is not
studied by mind-scientists and stopped by mind-shield
generators: it is practiced by an order of Samurai-Templar
style knights with distinctly monkish overtones, and
stopped by moral evil called The Dark Side.

So, if we wish, we could simply define any story which
took place in a universe that had a supernatural aspect to it
as officially out of bounds and 'not true science fiction.' This
would call for some nicety of judgment, since the miracles
performed by, say, Paul Muad'Dib or Michael Valentine
Smith might be parapsychology as natural as the mind
reading powers of a Slan or a Psychohistorian, or they might
be a manifestation of the divine as supernatural as the reincarnation of Gandalf the White. This would also eliminate
as science fiction books like *Starmaker* by Olaf Stapledon,
which, while criminally unknown and unread in these days,
has had as much influence defining the genre as anything
by H.G. Wells. Nonetheless, God Almighty comes onstage as
a character in the last act of *Starmaker*, and, as befits the
weirdness of a science fiction story, He is a cruel or
Darwinian god, a weird god not at all in keeping with the
expectations or experience of the audience.

Now, I cannot use that definition, since I defined science
fiction as the mythology of a scientific age, so I cannot rule
mythology as out of bounds for the definition of science

fiction. Indeed, I would venture to say that every genre of science fiction except maybe for military SF deals more often with mythical or religious themes than with mundane or worldly ones. When is the last time you read an SF story about the danger of a Negative Balance of Imports or Deficit Spending?

Think of any supernatural miracle or magic, and I bet some reader could name a science fiction book that treats with it. Is the resurrection of Spock so different from the resurrection of Alcestis or Aesculapius? For that matter, Gene Autry is brought back from the dead in a resurrection machine in the serial *Phantom Empire*, and so is Klaatu in *The Day The Earth Stood Still*, and so is everyone who ever lived in *Riverworld* by Farmer.

Tiresias or St. John may have visions of the future, but then again, so does Paul Muad'Dib, or, for that matter, so does Lion-O of the ThunderCats. Professor Pinero in Heinlein's first published story "Lifeline" knows the day and hour of any man's death, as does the prediction machine in "Alpha Ralpha Boulevard" by Cordwainer Smith as does the time traveler in "Try and Change the Past!" by Fritz Leiber.

Other miracles such as bi-location and levitation show up in science fiction as often as a Star Trek transporter malfunction or an experiment with cavorite.

The transcendence promised by religions both Eastern and Western happens in SF so often that there is a name for it: the Singularity, Transhumanism, even though the book that is one of the earliest portrayals of post-human evolution was purely "parapsychological" (i.e. purely mystical) in nature: *Childhood's End* by Arthur C. Clarke, which seemingly took its inspiration from *Last And First Men* by Olaf Stapledon.

So, the hostility of SF to supernaturalism, if it exists,

exists only in a nominal way. All the supernatural events and themes of mythology are endlessly repeated in Science Fiction, but merely given a different machinery and a different name. A saint healing the blind by means of prayer would not be regarded as a legitimate science fictional speculation in an SF book, but an optic-nerve-regeneration hocuspocusulator invented on the spot by Dr. McCoy at Sector General would be regarded as legitimate, even if it was mere handwavium-powered baloneytronics.

Certainly the things that are the topics and themes of myth appear far, far more frequently in SF than in mainstream literature: I can name seven 'Chosen Ones' right off the top of my head (and without sneaking a peak at the TV Tropes webpage) from SF/F movies and books, (Buffy, Harry Potter, Chandler Jarrell, Aenea, Paul Muad'Dib, Neo, Liu Kang), whereas I defy anyone to name a single Chosen One from a Western, a War Story, a Soap Opera or a Detective Story.

As far as I can tell, the only difference between science fiction and fairytales from Elfland, is that the sciencefictioneers have to leave unsaid who chooses the Chosen One, or they call it parapsychology rather than magic or miracle.

So, my answers would be: (1) Is there anything innately hostile in SF to religion portrayed as a human institution? Yes, a little, and for the same reason that there is an innate hostility to human institutions of business and government as crops up in any story where the Big Guy is the Bad Guy.

(2) Is there anything innately hostile in SF to religion portrayed as supernatural? No; the matter tends to be ignored by SF and for the same reason that the supernatural foundations of the Church Militant does not come up in Westerns or in Samurai stories. Readers of weird tales want stories about

weird things, not about the things we know from the fields we know. Only a very rare writer—only G.K. Chesterton, in fact —can portray ordinary things as if they are weird, and bring out the fantasy and wonder from our own backyard garden.

(3) Is there anything innately hostile in SF to supernatu-ralism in general? Yes, definitely. Science fiction writers are fond of saying that any sufficiently advanced technology is indistinguishable from magic, but we make this distinction every time we call one book science fiction and another one fantasy.

Yarns with "science-flavored" magic in them, such as the parapsychologists, prognosticators, or telepaths crowding the worlds of *Starship Troopers* or *Dune* or *Foundation* or *Childhood's End* or *Slan* or *Star Trek*, technically speaking, are fantasy, because the author has presumed a supernatural background, not a change brought about by technology or the scientific method.

But we science fiction types, despite our love of technol-ogy, do not speak technically, and we consider magic to be fair game even in so-called Hard SF like the books listed above, provided someone somewhere in the book clears his throat and drops the hint that the magic powers were discovered by psychiatrists rather than by witches, or that they developed by Darwinian evolution or eugenics rather than were granted by hidden powers of heaven or hell or Elfland.

For that matter, an author like Frank Herbert can call his magic-users 'Witches' and get away with being shelved as science fiction, and Sheri S. Tepper can call her mind-readers 'Demons' and get away with being shelved as Science Fiction, just as long as someone in the book drops the hint that their magic is caused by genetics rather than consorting with spirits, because 'genetics' sounds nice and scientifrriffic, whereas 'spirits' smacks of spiritualism.

Science fiction in fact is so seeped with religious ideas and ideals, themes and myths and mysticism, that we should pause in astonishment to consider why anyone is even talking about an alleged hostility. One might as well ponder whether science fiction is hostile to fiction.

The clue is not in the question but in the questioner. Some gullible folk in the last century were persuaded by a book called something like *The War Between Science And Religion*, (I am not willing to look title and author up), and it made the case that Protestants were the Sons of Light and Catholics were the Children of Darkness, and therefore the Catholic Church and her most remorseless Inquisition drove all scientists to England, where they invented everything ever. These evil Inquisitors no doubt included Nicolaus Copernicus, Gregor Mendel, Georges Lemaître, Albertus Magnus, Roger Bacon, Pierre Gassendi, Roger Joseph Boscovich, Marin Mersenne, Francesco Maria Grimaldi, Nicole Oresme, Jean Buridan, Robert Grosseteste, Christopher Clavius, Nicolas Steno, Athanasius Kircher, Giovanni Battista Riccioli, William of Ockham, and their familiars among the laity Galileo Galilei, Rene Descartes, Louis Pasteur, Blaise Pascal, André-Marie Ampère, Charles-Augustin de Coulomb, Pierre de Fermat, Antoine Laurent Lavoisier, Alessandro Volta, Augustin-Louis Cauchy, Pierre Duhem, Jean-Baptiste Dumas, not to mention Pope Sylvester II .

NOTE TO THE HISTORICALLY ILLITERATE:

If you do not recognize more than half the names on the list

given above, you are not allowed to have an opinion on any ques-
tion regarding the history of science, so shut up and sit down.

My guess is that the attempt by the International Roman
Catholic Church and our albino monk Opus Dei assassin
squads of antiscientific antiscientists to suppress science
would be more effective if the Roman Catholic Church
would only stop founding schools, universities, and
producing top-notch physicists whose work is the foundation of the heliocentric theory, genetic theory, the Big Bang
theory, and so on.

Meanwhile, the pro-scientific scientists of the League of
Science are busily promoting real science with real scientific
advancements, such as the 'materialistic dialectic' theory of
Karl Marx who discovered the scientific basis of history; the
theory that everyone who criticizes Freud, who discovered
the science of not having to produce predictions or results,
suffers from Oedipal Complexes; and the theory of Lysenko
that grain inherits characteristics from the environment by
means of class struggle in dialectic opposition to other
grain-seeds.

For those of you unfamiliar with the name, Lysenko was
the Soviet Master Scientist under Stalin. "Scientific dissent
from Lysenko's theories of environmentally acquired inheri-
tance was formally outlawed in 1948, and for the next several
years opponents were purged from held positions, and
many imprisoned."

And let me not fail to mention the scientists at East
Anglia University who hoaxed their data concerning anthropogenic global warming in a scientific attempt to scientifically fool the unwashed masses into accepting the
inconvenient truths of scientifically sciencified science.

I believe the same scientists who discovered that the Piltdown Man was the missing link confirmed these findings which were then peer-reviewed by the magnificent Rachel Carson Institute for the Abolition of Bird-Egg-Destroying Chemicals, that bastion of scientifical integrity.

Naturally, the chief of the League of Science, (all of whom have vowed to destroy the evil science-hating anti-scientists of the Roman Catholic Church), is Ilya Ivanovich Ivanov. He was involved in a controversial attempt to create a human-ape hybrid for the Soviet military. Unfortunately, Ivanov attempted to organize the insemination of human females with chimpanzee sperm in Guinea, but the French Government interfered, no doubt under orders from the Vatican.

That is real science for you! SCIENCE! It can do ANYTHING! It is AWESOME!

NOTE TO THE HUMOR IMPAIRED:

Ilya Ivanov and his man-ape experiments are real. I am not actually writing a book about Christian Scientists and Mad Scientists and Mind-Reading Lions fighting Men from Mars, even though that is a Way Cool idea. There is no Anti-science cabal of Catholic Jesuits and Inquisitors out to kill scientists, and there is no League of Science who use their rocket packs and rayguns to hunt down and burn up Inquisitors and Jesuits even though that would also be Way Cool if it happened. Rachel Carson is actually a scientific fraud, as is Freud, as is Marx, as is Lysenko, as is anthropogenic global warming.

NOTE TO THE SCIENCE IMPAIRED:

Real science is about physical things you can measure, observe, and then repeat the observation. Physical things, like ballistics, astronomy, chemistry, and so on. Speculations about Id and Superego and scare-stories about Ozone Layer depletion are no more scientific than speculations about Morlocks and scare-stories about Frankenstein's Monster. They are stories with a scientifical decor to them. The number of people who have seen an Id and the number of people who have seen an Eloi is exactly the same: zero.

All kidding aside, the sad fact is that secularization of the scientific community has arguably decreased the rate of the advance of science. Universities founded by or run by the Church study real knowledge and produce real science, because they believe God is Truth, and the cosmos was made by Him to be studied and understood. Institutions funded by the government study government-approved science, which, if not correct, is politically correct. They understand where their grant money comes from.

So where did the idea of a War between Science and Faith arise?

With apologies to my fundamentalist brethren in Christ, all that happened is that one small group in schism with the Roman Catholic Church, militant fundamentalist Christians who reject the authority of the Magisterium to interpret and teach scripture, has decided on a literal interpretation of Genesis, and insist on a six-day timeline of creation that does not fit geological, astronomical, or biological evidence.

Meanwhile, another small group in schism with the Roman Catholic Church, militant fundamentalist atheists who reject the authority of science to say what is and what is not science, has decided on a mystical, Shavian, Hegelian or

Marxist misinterpretation of Darwin's Origin of Species, and insist that scientific learning gives them the right to decree that abortion, eugenics, euthanasia, and the sterilization or genocide of those they deem unfit is licit, whereas the condemnation of fornication, abomination, or polygamy is illicit.

(These Utopians do not consider themselves cultists nor heretics, but their beliefs are mystical and religious in character, even if not in name, and copy Christian eschatological models.)

These two groups, neither of whom represents mainstream Christianity or mainstream scientific thinking, have decided that there is a war going on between science and Christianity. It is an article of faith with them, and no evidence to the contrary, scientific or historical, can persuade them otherwise.

The solution I propose is that both groups return to the Church, say confession, get shrived, make peace. I cannot imagine a less popular solution, but neither can I imagine any other that will work.

Most science fiction readers can tell the difference between science and fiction. The war between science and religion is fiction, and apparently an entertaining fiction indeed, as many who believe in it continue to do so.

12

THE BIG THREE OF SCIENCE FICTION

A s a bit of a relief to my readers who are no doubt weary of hearing my Jeremiads and screeds against the evils both political and philosophical which corrupt the modern world, let us turn from the disappointments of today to yesterday's golden dreams of tomorrow, and talk about the three major science fiction writers of Campbell's Golden Age.

The Big Three are Robert Heinlein, Isaac Asimov, and—wait for it—A.E. van Vogt.

Perhaps you have read books by the first two and never heard of the third. That is sad but not surprising. Perhaps, being a lover of triads, you thought the third Big Name of the Golden Age should be Arthur C. Clarke or Ray Bradbury.

Admired as these authors were and are, no one in the day considered them one of the Big Three. Van Vogt was, for a time, bigger than Asimov and Heinlein in popularity. I have seen articles, including the notoriously unreliable Wikipedia, list one or the other of Clarke and Bradbury as the third of the triad. It is partly to dispel this disturbing tendency toward historical revisionism that I write this article.

For neither of these were Campbell authors, and, indeed, I would argue that Arthur C. Clarke is from an older tradition of science fiction than Heinlein and Asimov, and is an heir to H.G. Wells, whereas Bradbury was a man before his time, and fathered a younger tradition. He was "New Wave" a precursor to character-driven SF, years before the New Wave was new. So even if Clarke and Bradbury are cherished men of the Golden Age, they were not of Campbell's Golden Age. Neither Clarke nor Bradbury wrote in the genre Campbell established.

I cannot speak with any authority about the economic conditions of the time, but I do know that a man could make a living wage in the 1930s and 1940s just by short story sales if he could sell regularly even to the lower scale magazines, the pulps.

And if he sold a story to the high scale magazines, the slicks, one story could pay his rent and grocery bills for a year. Magazines were the primary source of cheap popular entertainment, more ubiquitous than talkies and more portable than radio. They had a power over the popular imagination unimaginable these days.

Likewise, I cannot say anything about the condition of the genre from my own memory, since this was some twenty years or more before my time, but reading omnivorously as I did of everything in the genre that existed in my youth, any reader could come away with a fairly accurate impression of the state of the genre before and after John W. Campbell, Jr. during his tenure on *Astounding Science Fiction* later called *Analog Science Fiction and Fact*.

Indeed, the change of the name itself would give anyone a clue about that change. Aside from a few reprints of literate yet readable speculations from England, the works of H.G. Wells and Olaf Stapledon, and excruciatingly, (if not prophetically), accurate technological romances badly translated from the French by Jules Verne, science fiction magazines of the day were mostly boy's adventure stories set in space, tales actually about mad scientists, yarns of lost races, invasions from the Earth's core, and various forms of Apocalypse. It was an age of Space Opera, of the Galactic Patrol of E.E. "Doc" Smith and of the Legion of Time of Jack Williamson. It was the time of C.L. Moore and Leigh Brackett and "World-Wrecker" Hamilton, (a nickname oft I envy). It was the time of wonder and astonishment and weird tales, and the magazines devoted to such beloved juvenilia had names like *WONDER* and *ASTONISHMENT* and *WEIRD TALES*.

Campbell established a new type of story, less about weirdness and wonder and more about what we now call "Hard" Science Fiction, which consists of two elements. Both elements had been present in the prior lineage of the genre: first, a social or philosophical commentary about man's place in the universe, as we might see in H.G. Wells; and, second, a fascination with the nuts and bolts of legitimate speculation into the near future of technical advance, as we might see in Jules Verne.

Before Campbell, these two had not been combined. Campbell's genius was to wed them: Hard SF is social or philosophical commentary about the changes to man's place in the universe brought about by near future technical advances.

The social commentary we see in the dismal tales of H.G. Wells is utopian and negative. Do not be surprised if I call them dismal, but reread them for yourself, and decide whether any of them has a happy outlook or happy ending.

Nor be surprised if I say Utopianism is negative, because it is little more than revulsion toward the unhappy circumstances of the present day, combined with dreams, sometimes noble but more often naïve and ridiculous, about how progress will improve the human condition.

Reading Mr. Wells' socialist sentiments these days, now that socialism has murdered, in the Twentieth Century, some 262,000,000 people, (enough that if the corpses were laid head to toe, the line of death would circle the earth ten times), is indeed a disquieting experience. It is akin to reading a letter penned by a fourteen-year-old girl, filled with charming, goofy, unrealistic and faintly disquieting hopes, about some get-rich-quick scheme or idealistic cult she meant to join, whose handsome leader she was to wed, boasting how it would aid her impoverished mother and win her fame; but you are reading this letter while sitting in some autumnal dusk on her neglected gravestone where have been buried, years and years after the letter in your hand was written, the few parts of her body recovered from the kitchen behind the cult's brothel, such as a severed arm bruised with manacles and covered with needle tracks and gnaw marks. And no wedding ring was on the finger. To that is what reading the deluded predictions of socialist utopia from before the age of world wars is akin.

Campbell embodied the American spirit of optimism just as Wells embodied the European spirit of pessimism. The social philosophy, even among the Big Three and the other writers in his stable, had a certain common element. It is difficult to define for a modern reader, since the ideas were an extension of the scientific optimism and classical liberalism of the time.

The modern Radical would see them as conservative, since they placed faith in the free market, individual initiative and ingenuity, and the various values and standards common to civilized men which modern Radicals have set about to undermine and destroy. But the modern Conservative would see a Radical bent to such tales, since they placed faith in the malleability of human nature, had faith in the progress and improvement of man, and the omnipotence of big governments carrying out big programs. These stories dismiss tradition as mere pigheadedness. These stories show a touching childlike faith in Theory, and, for conservatives, (in the brilliant words of William Briggs), "Love of Theory is the Root of All Evil."

I suggest that the modern prism of seeing all things as either Radical or Conservative is misleading here, especially since we live in an age when the so-called Conservatives seek radical changes to our dying socialist systems and the so-called Radical are reactionary conformists seeking above all things to keep in place programs and policies dating from the days before the invention of the jet engine or the color television.

These stories were Hard SF. They were Campbelline, and come from a time and reflect an optimism which only conservatives foretelling radical changes could reflect.

Now, I have made two outrageous claims here: first, that the Big Three had even a slightly conservative outlook on anything. That certainly does not seem to be the case, since the Big Three were a Jewish Liberal, a Rock-Ribbed Libertarian, and a Scientologist.

The second outrageous claim is that Hard SF is not Hard SF.

Let me defend the second outrageous claim, if it can be defended, first.

Usually when the Linnaeus society, bored with long afternoons of debating the taxonomy of various species of beetle, wants to get drunk and discuss the definitions and boundary lines of the various genres and subgenres of science fiction and fantasy, the common consensus is that "Hard SF" is any story whose core revolves around some real science, usually astronomy and that "Soft SF" is any story whose core revolves around the humanities or some less rigorous discipline.

The short story "Neutron Star" by Larry Niven is a perfect example of Hard SF, since the tale cannot be understood, nor even told, without an understanding of the tidal effects of gravitating bodies. The novel *Languages Of Pao* by Jack Vance is a perfect example of Soft SF, since the tale cannot be understood, nor even told, without an understanding of the Sapir–Whorf hypothesis that language influences psychology.

I suggest that the Linnaeus society is wrongly gathering too many stories into the Hard SF category, because it is only looking at the one element of world-building.

I have to digress to explain that comment: In addition to the elements common to all genres, such as plot, theme, characters, and setting, science fiction and fantasy have one element no other genre, (except possibly horror), has or can have: world-building.

The science fiction story not only takes place in a futuristic or extraterrestrial setting, it takes place with the understanding that the rules of what can and cannot happen are different from the rules here and now on Earth, here in the fields we know. Indeed, many a Twilight Zone or near-future fiction is science fiction even though the setting is neither futuristic nor extraterrestrial, simply because there is something in the here and now, something in an otherwise ordinary setting, which breaks the rules we know, such as the mysterious children from *Roswell*, or their parents from the People Stories of Zenna Henderson, or Professor Pinero's machine which predicts how long a man will live.

Whether a story is "Hard SF" or "Soft SF" according to the common Linnaean taxonomy only tells you about the world-building element. I submit to you, my readers, that this is insufficient, since taxonomy should also tell something of the descent of the organism, or, in this case, the grouping of certain tales and novels into sub-genres should also tell you something of the other elements of the story, including the plot, character, and theme.

If you like, we can call this sub-genre "Campbellian Hard SF" with the understanding that when SF stories moved into novels and other media in the 1950's and later, the other families of "Hard SF" all descended from this original ancestor. I suggest here that Campbellian Hard SF had a common type of plot, characterization, and theme, in addition to the hardness of its world-building, which gave it its defining quality.

Let us stroll, or, rather, sprint down memory lane, by mentioning three or four of the famous tales of the Big Three that made them famous. If you are not familiar with these stories, you young whippersnapper, go get some anthology of stories back in the days when the moonrocket, instead of being a nostalgic memory of the old, was a pipe dream of the young.

A.E. VAN VOGT

The first story that started the Golden Age was "The Black Destroyer" by A.E. van Vogt. The story concerns an interstellar expedition landing on a ruined and seemingly empty world, and bringing aboard their ship what they deem to be a beast, but which in fact is the highly intelligent and morally degenerate savage last survivor of the once-great civilization whose towers are rotting around them. The monster is not able to contain its fundamentally emotional nature, nor to adapt to the new situation, despite the super-human control it possesses over energies and elements in its environment. Korita, the historian, is able to recognize the psychological limitations of the monster based on a Spenglarian view of cycles of history, and this enables the humans to prevail.

The tale contained in embryo the elements of the typical Van Vogt tale: superhuman powers, in this case housed in the ruthless and monstrous form of the Coeurl, the interest in psychology and parapsychology, the scope of action, and the breathless pacing which was Van Vogt's trademark, including sudden scene shifts and scenes from the monster's point of view.

Slan followed after several stories of superhuman monsters similar to "The Black Destroyer" but in this case Van Vogt rose to the challenge, (which Campbell offered to more than one in his stable), of writing a story about a superhuman being that a human audience could read.

Cleverly, Van Vogt did this by making the star of his tale a child superhuman, who in his youth is not yet beyond human comprehension. Like a Tarzan raised by apes, Jommy Cross is a Slan, a superhuman, raised by men. To make the boy an orphan not likely to be returned to his parents, Van Vogt invented a world where the humans have committed genocide on the superior beings, and hate them and hunt them down. Unusually for a science fiction story, *Slan* recounts not merely Jommy Cross's escape from his deadly foes, but unfolds the mystery which surrounds the origin and secret history of the Slans, making it a rare story indeed: a detective story about the life and death and destiny of two and three whole intelligent races. What makes the resolution doubly rare is that the problem is solved, not conquered. That is, intellect rather than courage ends the book. Instead of a set piece fight scene as one would expect in a space opera, we have instead an almost mystical revelation of man's place in the scheme of evolution and cosmic progress.

Any man living in December of 1940 could see the echoes of the evolutionary supremacy theories behind the European War and compare the superior beings of the Slans, whose moral fineness is as high as their intelligence is broad, with the loutish brutes of Germany and Italy and Russia swimming through their bloodstained headlines of the time. Also, the average SF fan regarded himself as a bit of a visionary or embryonic superhuman, for being able to imagine a future the dullards and conformists of the greater world could not, and likened his imaginary persecution of his imaginary superiority to that of the Slans. It was a book that lodged in the heart of the spirit of the times in the fandom of the times.

The World Of Null-A was Van Vogt's next serialized novel, and, I regret to say, marks the peak of his career. Few, or none, of his later books achieved the level of ingenuity, story-telling skill, nor popularity as this. Once again, the tale is about a superhuman being, and once again the challenge is how to make such a character sympathetic to the human readers, which in this case is done by making the superhuman an amnesiac.

The tale concerns one Gilbert Gosseyn, a widower who presents himself in the City of the Machine for the great Games which establish any man's role in the political and business leadership of the world. The Games in this case are not gladiatorial combats, but psychological assessments of a

non-Aristotelian philosophy of neurolinguistics called
General Semantics. The conceit of the story is that the
psychological knowledge of the future has advanced to such
a degree that psychosis, neurosis, and their resulting criminal and selfish behaviors can be trained out of the human
nervous system. Gosseyn discovers during a routine security
scan of his nervous system by a highly advanced thinking
machine, (ironically called simply a 'lie detector'), that he is
not who he thinks he is; when agents of a gang that have
corrupted the game start gunning for him, he finds he is not
what he thinks he is. To solve the mystery of himself is the
central plot of the book, if not the Riddle of the Sphinx.

I will add mention of the Weapon Shops stories,
including the novel *The Weapon Makers*. The conceit of
these tales is that men, for better or worse, get the type of
government they deserve, which means that immoral men
cannot be preserved from selling themselves into a tyranny.
The only moral way—since man cannot be forced to be free
—to preserve their liberty is to ensure that men have the
opportunity to buy weapons for self-defense so that no
government might ever take that final step of giving man a
government worse than he deserves, but then has no power
to change.

For such a reason and this limited reason only the
Weapon Shops, defended by all the instruments of unthink-
ably futuristic science, stand ready to sell energy firearms to
the common man. The stories themselves are tales of time
paradox and retribution against corrupt corporations and
institutions of the interplanetary Isher Empire. The dangers
of private firearm ownership are magically waved away,
since the guns sold by the Weapon Shops are somehow
programmed not to fire except in legitimate self-defense.
Nonetheless, the phrase "The Right to Buy Weapons is the

Right to be Free", which was utterly unremarkable when the stories were written in the 1940s, in these far darker, (and far more foolish), modern days offends many an authoritarian ear, or sounds like the lilt of golden trumpets to those who recall liberty.

ISAAC ASIMOV

Asimov's most famous three inventions were not his novels, which were clever, but his short stories.

"Nightfall" may be one of the most famous short stories of science fiction, so I feel no remorse in exposing its surprise ending. It was intended as a philosophical rebuke to the sentiment of Emerson that if the stars only rose once in a thousand years, men would glorify God in awe. Campbell drily suggested that instead they would go mad, and Asimov invented a plausible reason for nightfall to happen so rarely: namely, that the dwellers in a multiple star system, surrounded by suns on every side, would only experience night once every thousand years when all the suns were in conjunction.

The tale is is cleverly-constructed as a detective story, (dropping and resolving clues is Asimov's strong point), when three scientists, (as forgettable as they are lacking in personality—characterization is not Asimov's strong point), attempt to discover why there are ruins in the geologic strata, spaced evenly once per millennium, or why all men are afraid of the dark, a condition that never naturally arises on this world. Having never developed any artificial lights, when night falls, the population goes insane, and burns their cities and their civilization to create a few hours of light.

His positronic robot stories are all set up as detective

stories, the solution of which is based on some unexpected application of the "Three Laws of Robotics." The fame of these stories is difficult to understand except when viewed against the background of their time. Until then, robots were always Frankenstein's monsters, as in "Rossum's Universal Robots", or something of the sort which rose up and destroyed its creator; or else they were the Tin Wood-man, a human in all but his construction materials, as in "Helen O'Loy" by Lester del Rey or "Jay Score" by Eric Frank Russell. The philosophical conceit behind the Asimov robot stories was simple but brilliant: Asimov assumed that robots were neither monsters nor men of iron, but instead were tools, intelligent tools, but tools nonetheless, who could not and did not act other than as designed.

The final set of science fiction stories on which his fame rests are his "Foundation" stories, later gathered into a chronological anthology to pass as novels. It was Gibbons's *Decline And Fall Of The Roman Empire* set in space. The grandeur of the setting and the conceit was sufficient to carry the meandering series through one trilogy and perhaps another: the idea was that humans have free will only as individuals, whereas in statistically large enough groups, countless worlds upon worlds, their actions are predictable in much the same way that the Gas Laws predict the behavior of gas particles in the aggregate, never as indi-viduals. To forestall the decline and fall of the Galactic Empire, or to shorten the period of its Dark Ages, Hari Seldon, armed with the predictive science of history which he alone invents, sets in motion a few small events, such as the establishment of an encyclopedia foundation, in exactly the area and under the circumstances needed to see to the preservation of science and the rise of the Second Empire.

We never discover if the author had the Carolingian

Empire of the Franks in mind, or perhaps the Holy Roman Empire of central Germany, or the Tsar of the Russias, or the British Empire as his model for the Second Empire, because the series falls short of its promised culmination by some centuries.

ROBERT HEINLEIN

Robert Heinlein is a special case, because, unlike the others of the Big Three, he actually became bigger after he left Campbell's circle and was no longer one of the Three. His fame mainly rests with his charming and well-written juveniles, the last of which, *Starship Troopers*, made the rather unexceptional argument that nations who cannot produce soldiers willing to die in the common defense perish of terminal selfishness.

Unfortunately, this was written during a generation, the Baby Boomers, suffering from a terminal case of selfishness, and many of their more unsightly ilk threw temper tantrums at this display of plain common sense on Heinlein's part, and so they called him bad names. (Not being very imaginative, the only bad names Baby Boomers can think of are "Racist" and "Sexist" and "Fascist", and then in the late 1970s, when sodomy became fashionable, they called him a "Homophobe" a noise-word which they invented whose meaning evaporates on close inspection.)

His larger claim to fame was *Stranger In A Strange Land*, which is a paean to terminal selfishness, yea, even unto claiming divinity for one's own awesome self, (one presumes for folks who own no looking glasses). This satire mocked monogamy and monotheism, and so many a Baby Boomer was mollified and amused.

His best work was oddly his least controversial, *The*

Moon Is A Harsh Mistress, which retold the America Revolution of 1776 set in space, and stars perhaps his only truly loveable character, a computer named Mike.

The only controversial element of the tale was the praise of polyandrous polygamy, which no doubt sounded much more realistic and turned fewer stomachs to a generation of readers who lived in a fairly decent moral atmosphere, in a green land where the human wreckage of the sexual revolution waited undreamed and unimagined in their future: the skull-pyramids of abortions, the countless bastard children and fatherless children and husbandless mothers and teenaged mothers, and a worldview so lacking in hope that the majority of the population self-medicates itself into numbness to stave off despair. Yes, no doubt the speculation seemed more realistic in those gullible days, among the most gullible generation of all time, that a life of orgy was good for raising kids.

But it is his short stories and serialized novels which won him fame to the readers of *Astounding* and *Analog*, and here it was his Future History stories that captured the imagination of the readership.

These stories established a consensus of what the near future was supposed to look like. Private enterprise, in the spirit of the Wright Brothers or Sikorsky, would develop rocketry. Pioneers would first explore, then colonize Luna, Mars, Venus, and the moons of Jupiter. The difficulties and dangers would be met and overcome by much perseverance, much hard work, much engineering know-how, and a little luck. There would be setbacks due to the forces of unreason, and in Heinlein's world this meant the 'Crazy Years' or the rise of religious theocratic fascism by the year 2012. Advances in medicine would produce longevity, progress in liberty would abolish all traditional moral norms except a touchy personal honor and a gentlemanly largesse to guests, and General Semantics, (an idea he borrows from Van Vogt), would lead to the maturity of man, and a Covenant forbidding only acts of fraud and aggression. Then Man would be fully mature, faster than light drive would be invented, and a new frontier would open among the stars. Man would pioneer forever.

The three key stories in his Future History are "Requiem", which concerns a man too old for space travel hiring one last rocket to the Moon, which, as it turns out, his genius opened for colonization, but the strain of take-off and landing kills him, and so he is buried in the airless dust of his beloved Luna; "Green Hills of Earth" which concerns the astonishing personal bravery of an aging and blind poet, who, during an emergency, mans his post in a radiation-flooded engine room to ensure the safety of his shipmates, and he dies singing of an Earth he will never see again; and "Logic of Empire", a remarkably unsympathetic examination of the economics behind indentured servitude and other cruel practices needed for colonization. These stories are key because they emphasize the sacrifices needed for the interplanetary future to be made real.

In those days, before the Welfare State drained both the money and the talent needed for such a venture, and Nihilism bred the pioneer spirit out of men, and then the manhood, the colonization of space was a perfectly reasonable dream.

Contemplate the works of these Big Three in this short summation. I submit to your candid judgment that there is more in common in these stories than merely the world-building conception of "Hard SF."

Indeed, most of these stories are not very "Hard" at all. The Van Vogt stories are replete with unscientific gobbledygook as mindreading guns, time travel, teleportation, and the transfer of human memory from clone to clone. Asimov's planet without a night as well as his Galactic Empire whose history can be predicted by statistics do not bear very close investigation, and even the theory of intelligent robots whose brains can only think what they are told to think evaporates upon sober reflection.

Contemplate, despite the disparity of setting and authors, the unity of characters, theme and philosophy. This was Campbell's philosophy. It was the worldview, or, rather, since it was not defined and articulated, the mood he and his writers put across.

First, the prime philosophical assumption in all these tales was that mankind is malleable, and therefore that technical changes, and, more importantly, advances in psychology and anthropology, could lead to glorious breakthroughs in the human condition, an evolution upward. The malleability of man is the whole point of Asimov's nihilistic 'Nightfall', and the need for moral codes to bend like the Lesbian Rule to the cold needs of the circumstances is the point of Heinlein's cynical "Logic of Empire". The inability to adapt was on display in Van Vogt's "The Black Destroyer", and the ultimate triumph of malleability, which is the adaption to the next highest plane of existence above man, as far as man is above apes, the region of the superman, is the prime theme of Van Vogt's *Slan* and *The World Of Null-A*.

As a side-note, it must be observed that Van Vogt held memory to be identity—that a man was only what he consciously and subconsciously recalled himself to be, and that this forms the main point of *The World Of Null-A* and its sequel *The Pawns Of Null-A*, (also called *Players Of Null-A*). But if identity is memory, and memory can be molded, so too can Man.

Second, the characters are remarkably similar men. All these protagonists triumph, when they triumph, through their intellect and their correctly set moral compass. They are not action heroes like the Gray Lensman or Northwest Smith, nor are they mere passive observers like the Time Traveler of H.G. Wells, or the forgotten viewpoint characters who observed the Martian invasion or the death of Dr. Moreau. They are men who solve problems, from how to stop a tunnel leak on the Moon to how to stop the downfall of a Galactic Empire to how to solve the riddle of life and identity and immortality.

The point of Asimov Robot stories, for example, which may be hard for a modern reader to understand, was that robots were neither Frankenstein monsters nor humans made of metal. They were tools which, when they malfunctioned, could be fixed. All these stories are about fixing problems, which a Frankenstein monster story cannot be. In the background of all the Robot Stories and all the Foundation stories is the ideal of man as problem solver.

Finally, the theme was an optimistic one, which said that men were moral creatures who were, or could become, large enough in their time to conquer the stars.

Asimov, who was a Liberal, had no understanding of what morality was or what it was for, so it never appears in his stories, but he clearly thought it was man's duty to think clearly and to abide by what his reason taught him. Only the cleverness of science would save the Galactic Empire from eternal darkness.

In Heinlein, morality was always voluntary and always based on a firm sense of personal honor and duty: Honor that keeps a blind poet at his duty station even unto death.

Heinlein's sexual neuroses, thankfully absent from his juveniles and Future History stories might seem to be at odds with this sense of honor, but the libertarian conceit in his philosophy pretended that such vices could be indulged without harm if done by sufficiently mature and virtuous men. Given this false-to-facts conceit, it becomes at least self-consistent for a man to preach that personal independence both required patriotic defense of self and home and laws and race, and permitted any vice or self-indulgence as the self-sovereign individual or self-apotheosized god might please himself to do.

A.E. van Vogt, the least well remembered of the three, rejected, and rightly so, the shallow philosophical concepts of the European intellectuals as to what would constitute the superman, the next evolutionary step beyond man. The Europeans assumed the next stage of morality was to shed all moral scruples, and to become as cold and hard as a machine.

Do not be deceived, O reader, by such external and extraneous frippery as the mind reading tendrils of Jommy Cross, or the teleportation of Gilbert Gosseyn, or the immortality of Walter S. DeLany, founder of the Weapon Shops. These supermen were superior, precisely because the moral conscience and altruism of the supermen was superior. The superpowered Coeurl and the Rull and other monsters from his early stories were inferior because of their inflexibility, their moral retardation. For Van Vogt, the larger brain of the Martians of H.G. Wells, or the cold remorselessness of the superman imagined by Nietzsche were of no account if not also wedded to a greater moral sense.

The philosophy of all three, and indeed of Campbell himself, as we can see in the types of stories he wrote and bought, agreed on its prime axiom: Man is the measure of all things, and if he measures himself against the infinite hostility of the infinite cosmos, he must grow in his soul and reason, and be large enough to encompass that cosmos.

This was not Arthur C. Clarke's view. His was more similar to H.G. Wells's view, namely, that man would eventually evolve into something glorious in its own way but ultimately inhuman. His was certainly not Ray Bradbury's view, which was not so impressed with vast vistas and boastful futures, and more interested in the joys of home and hearth and the mysteries of the woods beyond the backyard, and the deeper mysteries of the human heart.

In the Hard SF view Campbell spread, we men are Homo Instrumenta, the Tool-Using Man, the Problem-Solving Man. Behind us is the ape-man and before us is the interstellar man, the cosmic man.

This is perhaps the inevitable outgrowth of the Enlightenment philosophy which informs the American character. These are typical or even archetypical American stories, as much as anything by Mark Twain or Ambrose Bierce.

The cynicism met in the stories is similar to the unromantic view of man, ambitious, easily tempted man, which underpins so much of the American character. It is why we mistrust Big Business and Big Government and credentialed yammerheads without a lick of common sense.

But the optimism, the belief that a clever man with a clever system can solve things, fix things, correct things, also underpins so much of the American character. That is why we trust the brain trusts and experts from City Hall and concerned activists from the college campuses to organize and solve public matters, and why we trust free enterprise.

If any man can explain why Americans mistrust Big Business and trust Free Enterprise, trust academicians and mistrust yammerheads, trust City Hall and mistrust Big Government, that man can explain the American character.

And that man, furthermore, will understand that Hard SF is not just any story that puts technology at its heart. The heart of Hard SF is this cynical optimism, the paradox of men whose feet are firmly planted on the ground, and yet whose hands reach for the stars.

13

THE FOURTH OF THE BIG THREE

During the Golden Age of Science Fiction, the Big Three Names were the three authors with the greatest prestige in the John W. Campbell, Jr. stable of authors: Isaac Asimov, Robert Heinlein, and one now is unfairly unrecognized, A.E. van Vogt. His obscurity may be due in part to a malign attempt by Damon Knight to undermine his career.

These days, the term "The Big Three" is still sometimes used, but the third name is given as Ray Bradbury or Arthur C. Clarke. Why this should be is also unclear, since no one linked the names at the time, but, again, it may be due to Damon Knight, who for all I know is also responsible for the hole in the ozone layer.

Arthur C. Clarke is a fairly convincing stand-in for a Campbell-style writer, and indeed he sold his first story to Campbell, ("Loophole", which appeared in *Astounding* in 1946), so this may be why he is often photo-shopped into the position A.E. van Vogt was airbrushed out of. But I would argue that there was a theme, or even a philosophy, to Campbellian fiction, and that Clarke represents an older, and perhaps more literate, style of science fiction harkening back to H.G. Wells and Olaf Stapledon.

I submit to your candid judgment that Arthur C. Clarke has a particular sense of a broader vision, and yet it is a darker vision, of man and his ultimate fate in the universe which is in keeping with H.G. Wells and alien to Campbell.

Asimov, Heinlein, Van Vogt and other regular contributors to *Astounding* betrayed a heady optimism typical of America at that period. The tales regularly involved heroes who solved their problems by reason, by the power of science, and they were, in effect, something like the hero in detective stories who always gets his man before the end.

Even stories that seem quite grim about their view of the littleness of man in the universe—Isaac Asimov's "Nightfall" springs to mind as an example—are based on an optimistic idea. "Nightfall" assumes that men of a world where the sunset came only once every thousand years would go mad at the sight of stars. This at first seems a pessimistic view of man, that we are like the ninnies in Lovecraft stories, who go insane upon learning the truths of the universe, rather than being fascinated. But in fact the idea is a typically modern one, full of the optimism and hence the folly of modernity. The idea here is that men are plastic and pliant in our souls, and that evolution can adapt us eventually to any environment, or propel us eventually to superhuman heights.

Science Fiction differs from all other genres. Membership in another genre is based on elements that appear in all stories. To be a detective story means to have the mystery plot. To be a pirate story means to have a pirate character. To be a Western means to have a frontier setting. To be a horror story or a romance means to have a theme or mood of fear or love. All stories, (except modern mainstream ones), have plot, character, setting, theme, mood. But Science Fiction has one thing more. It has world building. To be Science Fiction the natural laws of the story-world, which include the science and technology, must differ from the laws of the real world we know, and the expectations of the reader must be flexible enough to adapt to the new rules.

This flexibility is why imagination is paramount in the Science Fiction field, and, for hard or realistic Science Fiction, it is a disciplined imagination.

Readers are simply cheated if the story-world has laws and technologies and therefore expectations of what is possible or not altar and warp and change according to the storyteller's convenience. Readers are simply cheated if the story does not explore any logical yet unexpected side-effect of the hypothetical situation.

(If the supernatural laws differ, and include witches and magicians, dragons and elves, or anything redolent of the period before modernity, this is Fantasy, which is a sister empire to science fiction, overlapping in some places, and which these days bids fair to replace her, but the two are nonetheless distinct.)

I would go so far as to say that Science Fiction is the essential and archetypal literature of the modern age, because it is the only literature which confronts and incorporates the central idea that separates modernity from all past philosophies and worldviews: namely, change and evolution. Science Fiction is more popular during eras when technological change is faster or more profound.

To be sure, men of the Enlightenment, and Renaissance, and Middle Ages, and the Ancient world were aware of technological changes in history: But these occurred at a slow enough rate and small enough scale that it was not the central pillar of their worldview. The essential note of their worldview was one of stability and centrality. Even after the

Roman Empire was long fallen, the European mind continued to use the Empire as the basis of reference and comparison and as the source of legal legitimacy—up through the Napoleonic Era, which was the era of revolutions, and arguably the beginning of the modern world.

So I submit that Science Fiction, no matter what it seems to be about, is always about progress, and even when it is a cautionary tale, is a caution about progress gone wrong.

I would also suggest—for the point is too broad to be argued here—that Jules Verne wrote the type of fiction that Campbell would later expand upon, the hard and technophilic SF set either in a today or a nearby tomorrow of a world not much changed. Asimov, Van Vogt and Heinlein tended to set their stories no farther in the future than the launch of the Wright Brothers was in the past, or the American Revolution. When tales were set in the farther future, as *Slan* or *Foundation*, the cultures were immediately recognizable: *Slan* is set in a totalitarian fascist-state, complete with secret police, and *Foundation* is set in a Roman Empire, complete with Emperor and Senate.

In each case, the fundamental benevolence of the fate in store for man is on display in the imaginings of these and other Golden Age authors. Before the Gold Age, the pulp field was famous for stories of apocalypse and scientific Götterdämmerung. One can grow weary counting the planets destroyed by Edmond "World-Wrecker" Hamilton or E.E. "Doc" Smith. But the Age of Campbell was different.

The Future History of Heinlein ended in an era called the Maturity of Man, when, thanks to advances in General Semantics and psychology, insanity and therefore war and therefore the need for government is left behind on Earth and the stars are ours; the *Foundation* stories of Asimov

promised a Second Empire ruled by a benevolent technological elite, mind-reading psycho-historians who had
mathematical control over the future, and could obviate
wars before they began; the Slans of Van Vogt, and the Null-
A men likewise were creatures more wise, more sane, more
benevolent than man, and were secretly or openly ruling
them for the good of mankind and their own.

Please note the recurring theme. Politically speaking, no
matter where a Campbell author falls on the spectrum, he
regards the human condition, the political nature of man,
the questions of war and government, as a problem that can
be solved.

There is no Greek Tragedy for the Big Three, no
Twilight of the Gods which Odin foretells and cannot forestall. But then again, the Campbell authors rarely fixed their
eyes on the farther horizons, or told us what would happen
after the golden age of nudist telepaths on new world the
near future promised.

On the other hand, Arthur C. Clarke and H.G. Wells are
haunted by a sense of the true magnitude of time, and while
some of their stories, (*A Fall Of Moondust* or *The Isle Of Dr.
Moreau*), are near-future tales, these authors are most
famous for those which go to the end of mankind and
beyond.

H.G. Wells, when he has his Martians invade Horsell
Common, is putting on display not a truly alien creature of
truly alien psychology, such as Tweel from "A Martian
Odyssey" by Standley W Weinbaum. Wells is instead
showing the dark Darwinian future of man, a creature as
feeble compared to modern man as modern man was to, (at
least Wells' Victorian conception of), a Cave Man or Noble
Savage, but as developed in those organs of his superiority,
his brain and his hands. The Martian is the Wellsian

conception of the Man of the Remote Future as sculpted, not by some fatherly supernatural Creator but by the remorseless and bloody chisel-blade of blind Mother Nature.

Likewise, in *The Time Machine*, we see the effects of the passage of deep time on the evolution of man, because eight hundred millennia of civilized life has bred out of the possessing classes intelligence, self-preservation, and overt masculinity, and reduced them to Eloi, mere livestock for the cannibal troglodyte Morlocks, whose breeding was the opposite.

Three novels of Arthur C. Clarke show his vision of the remote or ultimate destiny of man, and they are just as cold and eerie as the vision of H.G. Wells.

In *Against The Fall Of Night* we see the city of billion-year-old Diaspar, inhabited by immortals, alone on an otherwise barren Earth, a veritable city of despair, when one lone lad, Alvin, chafes against the sterile perfection of the deathless utopia, and seeks the hidden past where once man roamed the stars. All that is left of those days is a legend of a vast and alien power that refused the other worlds to man, and drove man out of heaven and back to a barren Earth. The tale ends on a note of hope, when the siege of eternity is broken, and man once more turns his eyes outward.

In *2001: A Space Odyssey*, we see man evolved by the direct intervention of transcendentally superhuman beings from space, who wait for him to achieve spaceflight, and select one astronaut for evolution into something as far above us as we are above our ape-man ancestors. The man dies and the Star-Child, incomprehensible to us, is born.

But the clearest expression of this theme of deep time is *Childhood's End*. This tale is unique among invasion stories, because the aliens are benevolent. On the very brink of the launch of the first spacegoing ships by the Russians and the Americans, the aliens conquer mankind out of a condescending need to impose order on us, to preserve us from atomic self-destruction, and to deny us the stars.

In one of the most striking images of all Science Fiction, one copied more than once, vast disk-shaped ships hang weightlessly over the cities of man, announcing the end of human dominion over the Earth. War and crime, hunger, and even cruelty to animals are instantly done away with. There is no war, no resistance, because the Overlords are superior in technology in a fashion that is simply irresistible.

Two centuries pass, and mankind, no longer their own masters, withers under the benevolent peace, losing religion, losing will to live, turning its eyes inward away from the stars forever beyond reach, puttering away the years before the extinction of man.

For the children of men are being born with psychic powers, and an evolutionary change as dramatic as the end of the Neanderthals is coming to pass: and this is the true reason for the visit of the Overlords. With something of an apology, the Overlords kidnap all the psionic children, and explain that the invasion was meant not just to stop mankind from destroying itself by scientific investigation of the power of the atom, but to stop mankind from destroying much more by scientific investigation of the paranormal.

A man stows away on one of the alien vessels, and is the only human to visit the homeworld of the Overlords, NGS 549672 in the Constellation Carina. Here he finds the Overlords—who turn out to be the horned and winged demons from Christian mythology—are no more than the thralls of a being immensely superior to themselves, an Overmind which exists as a purely psychic entity or collection of entities. Returning home after eighty years, it is discovered that the children of the human race are no longer human, but are dull-eyed members of a vast telepathic group-mind, that they are no longer men but Man, Man-as-One, or, rather Superman-as-One.

Freed of its need for planetary, or even physical existence, and equally beyond the comprehension of human or Overlord, the mass-mind destroys the Earth and joins in an inexpressible cosmic union with the Overmind.

The last star vessel departs the now-empty solar system, and the alien Overlords regret that, for reasons unknown and inexplicable to them, while they can help nursemaid other races into transcendence, they will never join it themselves.

On this note of sorrow, the book, and mankind, ends.

Now, I suppose an utterly bloodless intellectual with no great love for mankind or any of the things that make us human might regard the theme of transcending into posthuman inhumanity as a noble or hopeful one, but that is not the message of the book. The alien-influenced children of men turn into something described as being repellent in their nonhumanity: the posthumans have no more expression on their faces than idiots, and the romp through the wilderness, naked as prelapsarian man, in some dance-pattern covering the continent, and too complex even for the aliens to comprehend. This is *The Midwich Cuckoos* where the cuckoos are triumphant.

The book is meant to depict a disquieting sensation, similar to looking at the ruins of Nineveh and Tyre, and seeing the current glory of London, or looking at the bones of dinosaurs, and seeing the men and horses on the modern street: this too shall pass.

The glory of man is to pass away, and the superhuman children of man are superior without being benevolent, or companionable, or friendly. They are not even godlike: no Zeus of the new race visits any Semele, even in disguise. There is no more amity or concern between the species than between man and ape.

I suggest that this is a thoroughly H.G. Wellsian view of man and his place in the universe. To fly off as disembodied minds in the train of a cosmic Overmind is a fate as disquieting as that of the Eloi or Morlocks, but if these creatures were at the same time as superior as the vast, cool, unsympathetic intellects of Mars.

I note also that the writing style has the same lyrical stiffness and history-book quality as H.G. Wells. While I can recall characters from Heinlein and A.E van Vogt, Lazarus Long or Gilbert Gosseyn, whose adventures were written in either a florid pulp style or a slangy journalistic style, rapid of pace, *Childhood's End* is written more like *The War Of The Worlds*. None of the main characters make any impression on the imagination, the prose is dignified and austere, more like Edward Gibbon than like World-Wrecker Hamilton; and the plot is that of a great historical event unfolding, not like that of a murder mystery in space or an interplanetary adventure or even a puzzle-solving story about a malfunctioning robot.

Partly by upbringing and partly by inclination, I tend to appreciate and savor the Big Three authors a bit more than this Fourth of the Big Three. I do not think he fits in their ranks. The American optimism, the belief in progress, the sheer orneriness of the Campbellian hero has a greater appeal to me than the Wellsian man, overwhelmed by events, evolved into Star-Child or absorbed into Overminds as a passive observer of vast unstoppable cosmic events.

Is there a rational basis for this discontent with Arthur C. Clarke's worlds? It is a judgment call, and reasonable men can differ on matters of judgment, on the weight given one thing or the other, but it is not an arbitrary judgment. Let me list the particulars in order:

First, the idea of benevolent nursemaids descending from heaven to pry the atom bomb and the spaceship from our chubby little fists is obnoxious on several levels. It is condescending, it is puerile, it is cowardly, and it is typically European. Our ancestors came to the New World to get away from slavish little men who delight in the desire for rule by the benevolent elite. The TV show "V" was more realistic. The benevolence of the elitist aliens turned out to be a trick. They came to eat us.

The Overlords in this book are never shown suffering any temptation or weakness. There are no factions among them, no argument between tradition and innovation, or between formality and expediency. The Overlords are as bland and unrealistic as any Communist's daydream of a world government that fades out of existence voluntarily at the end of its term.

Second, the idea that men would submit without fighting to the last man, without any show of brutality on the part of the aliens, is unrealistic. As I recall, all armed resistance, open of covert, to the Overlords evaporates after one stern warning. While there are plenty of men, maybe most, willing to be slaves, one need only look toward the Middle East or the Midwest to find men, who, for good causes or bad ones, are willing to fight against impossible odds, even with zero chance of success.

Third, the idea that natives just die off in the presence of superior cultures, while it has happened in history, is an exception rather than a rule: there are many cultures which kept slaves, and many slaves that flourished. (Indeed, the Janissaries ended up ruling in Egypt.) Here, the race of man is not being kept as slaves, not being sent to labor, they are merely being prevented from harming each other. Why would, for example, the Indians of South America, already conquered and crushed by the Spanish, feel any more overwhelmed and inferior now that some outerspacemen have halted the Russians and Americans from global war?

Fourth, the scene where bullfighting is outlawed by the aliens, who stick everyone in the Spanish arena in the buttocks with illusionary pain when the bull is gored, is one of those pet peeves of an author or a pet cause which strains the suspension of disbelief.

Consider: Creatures entirely alien in biology and psychology and outlook who have less in common with us than we have with digger wasps or starfish, spent the unthinkable energies needed to cross the fifty light years from the constellation Argo Navis for the purpose of stopping war and crime and—wait for it!—to impose vegetarianism on us.

Hmm. If in one of my stories, I ever have a ship land from Argo Navis, and the vast vessel is shaped like a giant crucifix adorned with stained glass windows, and out marches the Archbishop of Alpha Carinae with a miter on his insectoid head, to announce that contraception is against the order of nature and must be outlawed, do you think there is even one reader, even one, who is so unwary as to not realize that the writer is Catholic, and that I am using my story time as an excuse to preach some particular pet peeve of mine? So, here, when the benevolent space-dictator outlaws cruelty to animals, a hot- button topic of particular interest to the English intellectual class of the

1930s to 1950s, there is that creaking strain at the traces of suspension of disbelief.

Instead of imposing the dogma of SPCA or PETA on us, the story could have said that the Octopus Beings of Spica would demand that we arrange for all our mothers to die in childbirth as theirs do, or the Spider Beings of Arcturus insist that we eat our mates during copulation. Whether this is more realistic or less I leave for xenobiologists to debate, but in terms of what a reader can swallow in a story, the conceit that advanced beings care about fuzzy animals rings hollow.

It rings doubly hollow, especially since these same advanced beings later in the book allow all Earthly life to be destroyed at the hands of beings more advanced yet. All the bulls saved from the Spaniards are obliterated when the core of the planet blows.

Fifth, the idea that religion would simply fade away and disappear is stupid. If anything, the stress and pressure of being confronted by alien overlords would encourage religion. Someone would start worshipping them, if nothing else.

The book handles this by saying a time-viewing television is set up in the basement of an Oxford building, and scientists are allowed to look at some historical events and not others. There is only one religion which rests for its validity on a specific historical event—the book coyly does not name that religion by name. The book assumes that once the spacemen show a picture allegedly from the past that no one died at Calvary and rose again, gee willikers, all the Zen Buddhists would turn in their saffron robes.

I myself know plenty of Jews who don't believe Moses ever parted the Red Sea, and plenty of Witches who don't either. I don't see how a photo produced by an alien monster that no burning bush ever blazed on Oreb without being consumed would convince, or even interest them.

The fact that the pictures come from the horned and winged gargoyles of Christian religious art, of course, would increase their credibility, at least with me. And we all know Christianity is a biological theory about the origin of species AND NOTHING ELSE, so that when the central premise was shown to be historically inaccurate, the pseudo-science known as faith would simply fade away. Just the same way Mormonism vanished overnight once genetic science proved the American Indians were not the lost ten tribes of Israel.

Parenthood apparently disappears as rapidly, since there is no scene where the humans fight the aliens who come to take away their children who have psionic powers, or even voice vehement objections. Professor X, call your office.

Sixth, the whole idea of psionic evolution into a spiritual form of being as the next step of evolution is a lazy cheat. Bob Heinlein's idea of the next form of man, (as portrayed in his short story "Gulf"), as a being of greater intellect, or A.E. van Vogt's conception of a Slan as a hominid of a finer-grained and more densely packed and powerful nervous system, not to mention Way Cool Mind Powers, are both more solid and real. These ideas are not just a vague pink cloud labeled "The Superman" with nothing in it.

I say it is lazy because it is like the supremacy of the Overmind: just something that is established by auctorial fiat, not given any sense of proportion or solidity. It does not even have the solidity of showing what it looks like when someone opposes it.

In other words, a lazy conceit is one that cannot be imagined when set against a background not prepared care-fully by the author to receive it. If the Overlords of Carina, for example, were shown conquering the Middle East, and prevented the Islamic Fascists from nuking the Jews, how would they prevent them from butchering the Jews with machetes? Inflict illusion-pain? Pain does not stop suicide bombers. Stun them all? For how long; and what if the mad bombers continue their evil once the stun wears off? What then? Crucify them by the thousands like the remorseless Romans did?

For that matter, landing during the Cold War, how did the Overlords prevent Stalin from starving the Ukrainians, without any act of brutality against Stalin?

I am not saying there are not answers which could be deduced from the book to these questions. I am saying that, as an artist, there is something oddly flat and artificial about a benevolent invasion by powerful aliens who, because the author has prepared the ground and weeded away any remotely human seeming or realistic characters, neither the power is shown nor the benevolence put to a test.

The lack of any such scene makes the Overlords seem benevolent even though they are conquerors, and this illusion is preserved only by the lazy sleight of hand of not having any resistance to conquest on stage, or any brutality.

In the novel *Methuselah's Children* and again in *Time Enough For Love*, Lazarus Long, the curmudgeon who was Heinlein's 'peak' character, that is, his most Heinlein-like character, confronts aliens of supreme and godlike power. His reaction is to get a handweapon and go kill them.

Whether this is good or bad or simply gobstoppingly stupid I leave for the reader to decide, but the point is that there is no character like Lazarus Long seen anywhere on Earth at the time of the Overlords, and when someone smuggles himself aboard one of their vessels, it is not Long carrying a suitcase nuke.

The author did not bother to imagine what the Over-lords would actually act like in a situation involving some stress or moral pressure. Would the beings so advanced that they stop bullfights put Lazarus Long on trial, or would they just kill him like a bug? It would have given the aliens a specific personality, which the author here was careful to avoid.

This lack of detail is deliberate. The only way to portray something as incomprehensible is to leave it blank. If the next step of human evolution which the children of man embrace had been something other than psionic and disembodied, it would have failed to awe.

Gazing upon the fate of man in this yarn is like gazing upon a vast arctic sea frozen mile after endless mile to the far horizon beneath the eerie light of the aurora borealis. It is awe-inspiring but infinitely cold. The stars are not meant for man, and the future is inhospitable and deadly.

This leads to the final point. What was Arthur C. Clarke trying to accomplish in this book? I suggest that he was trying to tell a myth rather than a story, and that he succeeded brilliantly.

A myth is a tale of a certain narrative shape which rests for its beauty on the proportion of ideas. A myth is the most abstract, most universal and most easily told and retold of human literary inventions. Here the story is about what it says it is about: the end of the childhood of man and his evolution into unimaginable maturity, the posthuman beings of pure spirit, them to whom the stars truly belong. The universe is too vast and cool and deadly for beings of mere flesh and blood like us.

The myth is as simple and sad and dramatic as the death of the octopus to give birth to her young, or the sacrifice of the spider to her own hatched eggs: simple, horrible, awesome, and with a promise of the great mystery of the universe acting to crack the Earth like such an egg, a cast off shell the higher beings we shall birth, but never understand, shall crack.

Let me end with an idea at once shocking and obvious. Myths are about religious notions. The notion here was that science, or the purely materialistic and naturalistic world-view, the cold and dull and empty world without God, could somehow find in its remorseless grind of blind evolution something as interesting and dramatic as damnation and salvation.

The whole book is an ersatz sort of religious myth, as cold and pitiless as the Ragnarok of the Norseman, and as inescapable. There is perhaps some strange hope in the disembodied ghosts who are the heirs of mankind, but they mean nothing to their parents, and have no human properties, no, not even names. They are a type of Tarzan who never thanks the apes who raised them, a Romulus and Remus who put up no statues to the wolf that nursed them.

Which leads to a final question of why? Why does the Overmind use the Overlords of Carina, but cannot discover a way to evolve them up to his level? They are the Moses of this book, who can lead others to a promised land but not enter themselves. As in myth, this is given by auctorial fiat, without explanation. The younger brother, Man, is preferred over the Elder, the Overlords, like Jacob over Esau, or, more likely, like the ratlike mammals who conquered the world after the downfall of the dinosaurs. Again, as in a myth, this is just given by auctorial fiat.

Only upon reflection, long after the book is put down, does one realize what shabby gods these godlike beings are.

The children of men are allegedly very advanced, but why have they forgotten how to speak to their parents. Even if such speech would be baby-talk to them, the cooing and simple words of a mother to her child, it would have shown love.

And likewise, the Overmind cannot uplift its own servants, even though its resources and wisdom are transcendental. The problem is just insoluble? Or is it that the Overmind simply does not love its serfs?

You see the problem of seeking for ersatz religious sentiment among the arctic splendor and inhumanity of the blind cruelty of a universe without God. You might find some very awesome and even godlike beings, such as the Arisians of the Lensmen, or the Martians of H.G. Wells, or the Martians of Robert Heinlein, beings with powers and abilities far beyond those of mortal men, creatures as impressive as some mighty Prince of Hell with a legion of devils clad in adamantium at his command.

But a child's idea of a superior being is the same as Nietzsche's: A creature beyond good and evil. That means, in other words, a creature greater in power, but indifferent, callous, reticent, remote. The idea of love will not even be brought up, not even to be dismissed, even though this is the first idea a mature man contemplates when he thinks of superior beings who are truly superior.

The book succeeds and succeeds brilliantly on every level but this one. The core idea of seeking for religious transcendence in the dead cosmos of materialism is an incoherent idea, a self-refuting idea. The mythical image produced is one of beings of immense power and retarded capacity for love, like some super-villain caricature of an evil scientist, or the hollow grandeur of the Satan of Milton.

As far as philosophical depth is concerned, the book might as well have been called *Childhood's Idea Of Superiority*.

14

CHILDHOOD'S END AND GNOSTICISM

L et me follow up my previous essay by arguing that
Childhood's End by Arthur C. Clarke has a Gnostic attitude toward God, and I mean one God in particular. Gnostics are not heretics of Buddhism, Zen, Taoism, Shinto or
Hinduism, after all, but of Christianity.

That the good guys in *Childhood's End* look like cartoon
devils has already been mentioned in the previous essay.
Gnostics love the idea that good guys are bad guys, and bad
are good: one Gnostic sect, for example, are Cainites, who
think Cain was right to kill Abel. That the good devils lead
mankind out of their false world into the Pleroma, where we
are all gods, has already been mentioned, albeit in Clarke's
book, the godhead is called "The Galactic Overmind"— as if
that change in terminology would fool anyone. The earth is
not remade into a new world, as St. John of Patmos holds,
but is destroyed by hidden fire, the arson of an abandoned
prison, as Valentinus holds.

Gnostics take as their prime dogma the idea that the
world as we know it is a deception, and that God is the
Deceiver, that matter is evil, the human body a trap. In a

science fiction setting, God cannot come onstage as a supernatural being and be shown to be a liar, since science fiction properly so called stays within the bounds of the natural setting. (Any supernatural events, telepathy or reincarnation, are explained away as being psionic or superhightech in an SF background, phenomena as subject to natural laws as biology or ballistics, not noumenal reality.) In a supernatural setting you can kill God, and throw Him into Tartarus. In a natural setting you can destroy His lies, but there is no Him.

Hence, in a natural setting the religion of the Magisterium can be shown to be false, and their evil attempts to destroy our daemons of free will by incision can be condemned. If an alethiometer is not ready to hand, maybe an alien gizmo provided by space devils will do instead.

Here is the crucial passage:

> The instrument he handed over on permanent loan to the World History Foundation was nothing more than a television receiver... linked somehow to a far more complex machine, operating on principles no one could imagine, aboard the Karellen's ship. One had merely to adjust the controls, and a window into the past was opened up. Almost the whole of human history for the past five thousand years became accessible in an instant. Earlier than that, the machine would not go, and there were some baffling blanks all down the ages. They might have had some natural cause, or they might be due to deliberate censorship by the Overlords.
>
> Though it had always been obvious to any rational mind that all the world's religious writings could not be true, the shock was nevertheless profound. Here was a revelation that no one could doubt or deny: here, seen by some unknown magic of Overlord science, were the true beginnings of all the world's

great faiths. Most of them were noble and inspiring—but that was not enough. Within a few days, all mankind's multitudinous messiahs had lost their divinity. Beneath the fierce and passionless light of truth, faiths that had sustained millions for twice a thousand years vanished like the morning dew. All the good and all the evil they had wrought were swept suddenly into the past, and could touch the minds of men no more.

Humanity had lost its ancient gods: now it was old enough to have no need for new ones.

The smugness and dishonesty of the passage is breathtaking, not to mention the naive optimism, (if you are an atheist), or blockheaded arrogance, (if you are a theist).

Let us pause for a moment to admire four of the more amusing shortfalls, shall we?

First, there is only one religion under attack here, and it is misleading to pretend any religion but one is in the crosshairs. Like far too many an atheist's writings, this passage is not atheist, merely anti-Christian. There is only one religion that has a messiah who claims divinity. It is twice a thousand years old, which just so happens to be the age mentioned in the passage.

Note that it is the religious writings of "the world" that "any rational mind" can see cannot all simultaneously be true. Obviously the author means the sacred ideas and dogmas, and is using the word "writings" as a synecdoche. Why the emphasis on writings, that is to say, on Bible(s)? There is only one God whose word has been written into officially recognized sacred books: and that is the God of Abraham. The Buddhists have no central authority, no Magisterium, to decide which books are in and out of an official canon. I am not saying pagans do not have holy books: I am saying it is a metaphor particular to the religions of Abraham to refer to holy doctrines by referring to holy books, because we emphasize our books as testament. Clarke is not referring to the Kojiki nor to the Shahnameh nor to the Mahabharata.

Second, there is only one, (or two, depending on whether you think Christianity is a religion in its own right, or merely a heresy of the Jews), religion whose holy book makes disprovable historical claims about observable events in history.

Turning the Wayback Machine onto the image of the Prophet (peace be on him) would show a man seated on a mountain and writing the Koran, and this would prove or disprove nothing, unless you think the divine inspiration he claimed dictated to him was something the Wayback Machine could see. Can the instrument pick up thought-waves sent by Archangel Gabriel? Turning the Wayback Machine to the events in the Bhagavad Ghita, we see the supreme hero Arjuna in his chariot, listening to the teachings of his charioteer, Krishna. Turning the Wayback Machine to the Awakened One, the Buddha, would show a man seated in a deer park, teaching his disciples. Turning the Wayback Machine to Confucius or Lao Tzu would also show you a man writing a book.

Hmmm. What is the one religion which is centered, not solely on a teaching, but on an event, not on a man writing a book, but on a man hanging on a tree on Golgotha at Passover, emerging from a Tomb of the Holy Sepulcher at the Feast of Firstfruits, ascending from Mount Olivet the Sabbath before the Feast of Weeks, all this not in a mythic otherworld, but at a specific spot you can find on a map, and at a specific date you can find on a calendar? Bueller? Anyone? Bueller?

And you do not need the Wayback Machine to look atop Mount Olympus or Mount Meru, and yet, somehow, the absence of visible gods on those peaks has not caused Hindus to dismiss their many-armed pantheons, nor neopagans to cease offering wine to Diana the Moon Goddess.

What about Shinto, the beautiful ceremonial and spiritual practices native to Japan? Is there even a single practitioner of that ancient religion whose faith would be not merely shaken, but annihilated as suddenly as dew in dawnlight, if he could not find, (at exactly 620 BC in Nara Province in Honshu), Amaterasu hiding in a celestial cave while Uzume performed a lewd dance outside?

What about people who believe in astrology? We all know that the planets are not ancient Babylonian gods whose passing overhead presages the destinies of a new born babe, and showers him with unseen, occult influences. Did that belief also evaporate like dew at dawn when the single alien telly in the basement of the Smithsonian shows a picture of the Moon, and proves it is made of rock?

Third, who are the inhabitants of whatever world Mr. Clarke dwells in? Vulcans? Houyhnhnms? No doubt it is one where the more iron-willed skeptics are instantly and suddenly and totally convinced by unbuttressed empirical testimony from a single unverified source, and people who have no capacity for philosophical reasoning, doubts, hesitations, or suspicions.

It is with a sensation of unutterable disbelief that I read a passage saying one or two days of looking at a picture on a screen provided by the "magic" produced by creatures who look like devils, (whose mission, remember, is to facilitate the extinction of mankind), would be believed without reservation or complaint by everyone from Moscow to Bombay to Lhasa to Rome to Mecca. In the world I live in, people are stubborn and cantankerous. Some have faith that will not be swayed and some of us are nuts.

How is this for a thought experiment: you show a group of True Believers the events surrounding the fall of the Twin Towers on 9/11 on your alien Wayback Machine. Explain that the gizmo has odd gaps in its record, either due to Overlord censorship or a natural limitation of the unknown science. The True Believers see no evidence of George Bush dynamiting the towers, and the Wayback Machine shows them that steel does indeed melt when doused with aviation fuel and placed in the middle of a firestorm. How many True Believers would you convince?

Or you show a group of True Believers a perfectly human man trampling crops in a large circle using technology no more complex than a rope and a plywood board. How many True Believers stop believing crop circles are messages from UFO people? (Let us pretend, for the sake of argument, that the Devil-shaped Overlords keep a straight face and do not snicker through their nostrils when they testify that none of their beer-soused UFO joyriders did it.) This thought experiment is one which actually has been performed in real life, for a True Believer in Crop Circles did indeed start making Crop Circles of his own in secret, convinced his fellow believers would detect the counterfeit. He became a skeptic when they did not.

You show the True Believers the Venona Cables, proving beyond doubt that Senator McCarthy was right, and that the people he accused of being Soviet spies, were, in fact, spies in the pay of the Soviets. How many True Believers start believing that McCarthy was an honorable man and stop believing that he was a Witchhunter?

You show the True Believers Sandy Berger stuffing down his trousers documents from the National Archives, (documents proving Vince Foster was "femecuted" by the Clinton Political Machine's Honey-Ninjas, known only as the Deadly Viper Assassination Squad), as he smuggles them out, waddling like a penguin and giggling. How many Democrats instantly and without argument overthrow their entire superstructure of rationalizations and emotional fixations, sober up, and vote for Sarah Palin next election? All of them, without a single exception? Riiiight.

You show a True Believer whose dearly beloved son died as a martyr for his beliefs, who refused to recant when so commanded by Communists or Islamists: and her mother's tears and never-ending heart-wound can only find balm with the thought that her loved child, her perfect little baby, died for a reason, and now carries the palm leaf in heaven.

Or suppose it is a Mohammedan mother, whose beloved child committed filthy suicide spraying a busload of innocent schoolgirls with a nail bomb, killing others for their beliefs, which she, with blankminded Orwellian disregard for truth and logic, also calls martyrdom. With vile contempt for the teachings of the Koran and natural reason, (The Prophet damns suicide in no uncertain terms, and murder), she tells herself her son is in the paradise of Mahound, coupling with seventy-two ever-virgin houri, treating these virgins with a love more earthy and, (ahem), priapic than the love offered by Catholics to the ever-virgin Mary, Queen of Angels and Star of the Sea.

Will either of these True Believers simply glance at the Wayback Machine, watching the 90 minute film showing Jesus or Isa at Cana making water into wine by means of stage-magician slight-of-hand, (he had a bucket of fine wine tucked in his sleeve), and shrug and say, "Gee, my dumbass kid died for nothing. That's a bummer. Well, he is carrion meat now! No use crying over spilled milk! Time to move

on! Maybe I will take up aerobics to get my mind off it!"—
does that sound like any sane person? Does anyone outside
of a book written by a partisan act that way?

You show the Pope, Billy Graham, Jerry Falwell, G.K.
Chesterton, Evelyn Waugh, and Mother Teresa of Calcutta
the "magic" television produced by aliens who look like
cartoon devils, not to mention The Bible Answer Man Hank
Hanegraaff. You also show the flick to Sadhu Sundar Singh,
who converted from Sikhism after he saw a vision of the
risen Christ.

For the purpose of this thought experiment, we are
assuming here that the Overlords came when these men
were still alive, or we can assume the Ethicals of the Riverworld have resurrected them.

Just for fun, you also show the images of the bones of
Jesus to Elmer Gantry from Sinclair Lewis, the Grand
Inquisitor from Dostoyevsky, Tartuffe from Molière, and the
one-eyed Bible salesman from the movie *O Brother Where
Art Thou?* Do the crooks stop practicing their hypocrisy on
the gullible?

And, why not, to Tiny Tim from Dickens' *A CHRISTMAS
CAROL*? Does the crippled boy give up his hope?

*"And how did little Tim behave?" asked Mrs Cratchit. "As good
as gold," said Bob, "and better. Somehow he gets thoughtful
sitting by himself so much, and thinks the strangest things you
ever heard. He told me, coming home, that he hoped the people
saw him in the church, because he was a cripple, and it might
be pleasant to them to remember upon Christmas Day, who
made lame beggars walk, and blind men see." Bob's voice was
shaking when he told them this, and trembled more when he
said that Tiny Tim was growing strong and hearty.*

Ah, but then Tiny Tim watches a ninety-minute television presentation provided by horned devils whose mission is to destroy mankind and rob humanity of its children.

"And how did little Tim behave?" asked Mrs Cratchit. "As a rational creature," said Bob. "He recognizes that his bent legs and failing health are merely a malfunction of the machine of his body. He told me, coming home, that science proves that, when he dies, his body will contain as many atoms before as well as after, and ergo there is no need to suffer an emotional reaction—since emotions are produced by the brain as a gall produces bile, by a mechanical process—merely because he is condemned to die in slow and lingering pain, or, as he put it, to suffer bio-procedure cessation." Bob's voice was cool and unsympathetic, and he glanced at the malfunctioning biological unit known as Tim almost as narrowly as a man with a microscope might scrutinize the transient creatures that swarm and multiply in a drop of water.

"Also, my master Scrooge came by, dancing and singing, and with an enormous Turkey. But I told him that the space devils who are here to destroy us have proved scientifically that his visitation by Christmas Ghosts was a dream caused by an undigested bit of beef, a blot of mustard, a crumb of cheese, a fragment of underdone potato. He accepted my explanation, as the only rational theory, and joined the Overlord work gang who are dismantling St. Paul's Cathedral with tractor beams. Do you think we should sell Tiny Tim's organs to transplant clinics once he had ceased function? Is it not rational to put recyclable biological tissue into the ground?"

You also show the film clip to Prince Hamlet, who swears by the Holy Rood that he beheld the unquiet ghost of his father, foully murdered and crying for vengeance, his eyes weeping tears and wounds weeping blood. Do people who say they saw a ghost with their own eyes suddenly stop believing? All of them, as suddenly as dew evaporating?

For the purpose of this thought experiment, we are assuming we can find real people with the personality characteristics described by these fictional people. You show the Wayback Machine to Christians both honest and dishonest, to saints and Pharisees, to high and low, snake-handlers and theologians, literate and illiterate, Cardinals in Rome and persecuted peasants in Korea, lukewarm churchgoers, missionaries of lifelong dedication, Doubting Thomases, and red-hot revivalists who claim they see the Holy Spirit every day.

Now, ignore whether you are a theist or atheist. Let us not argue about whether the subject matter of religion is innately believable or not. Pay attention to your view of human beings. How do they act?

How many of these people, from the Archbishop of Canterbury to Nehemiah Scudder, do you think would be convinced in a matter of one or two days to hang up their miters, give up their ministries, foreswear their hope of an afterworld, ignore their inner spiritual life, forget the miracles they have seen and prayers they have had answered, and go out and get an honest job, or become Environmentalists or GLBT Activists or hard-drinking socialist commentators for Vanity Fair, instead—merely on the strength of one machine showing one image one afternoon of the bones of Jesus being dragged away by dogs or medical students one Saturday midnight in Palestine in AD 33 ½ ?

To a man they would change their minds like dewdrops vanishing at dawn. Are you kidding me? I know of people who think the moon landings were faked.

(Heck, I know of people who think the atomic destruction of New York was not caused by an outraged Doctor Manhattan or a teleporting giant space-squid, but by some sinister scheme concocted by Ozymandias! We all know and love Ozymandias! I've studied body-building using the Veidt Method! I don't care what the alien vision machine shows!)

Clarke's conceit that religion would simply vanish is a ridiculous idea, handled with ham-handed clumsiness that breaks suspension of disbelief. I am reminded of similar scenes in books by Olaf Stapledon, where he casually asserts that, in the future, everyone will fall out of bed one day, be jarred awake, and become Socialist Fabians without any more debate, quarrel, suspicions, war or rude questions. Their truth is so obvious to True Believers. Their truth says that if only you had a Subtle Knife you could kill Almighty God by scratching open his oxygen tent, and watching the healthy spring wind simply blow Him into powder.

No, this scene is just a masturbatory fantasy by an atheist, wishing he had the power to eliminate God, and chuckling to himself about how easy it would be. Back when I was an atheist, I was not so naïve. Religion answers basic and deeply-rooted human emotional and psychological and intellectual needs. At that time, I thought the answer was false, but I did not think it was trivial, a matter of mere lightly held opinion. I thought it was a lie, but I thought it was a cunning lie, a bear trap impossible to disarm, and only to be approached with courage and caution. I thought religion would always be among us, and never pass away, any more than racism or warfare would ever pass away. I now believe religion will always be among us and never pass away, any more than true love or times of peace will ever pass away.

Finally, the condescension is odious and contemptible.

Every rational man knows and has always known that

not all religious writings can be true, does he? Well, what do you make of those who hold that one of them is a true report of a messiah who claimed to be God, and the others are inventions of men, who claimed only that they were inspired or wise or insightful? What do you make of the Deist or Universalist who holds the one is true, but all contain some reflection or adumbration of the Light? What do you make of Henotheism and Polytheism, whose followers hold only that their gods are true, not that their neighbor's gods are false? Indeed, what do you make of those mystics who say that all sacred writings of any source are all metaphorical and poetical, not meant to be taken literally, but an attempt to find human words for something no human words can embrace?

Any man who so says any of these self-consistent things is not just wrong but irrational? What, merely because you disagree with him?

So the men on the world ruled by Overlords have no need of Gods because they are too old? But what is the evidence that religion is not a development of intellectual effort away from a more primitive state, rather than the opposite? The Christians claim to be a development and fulfillment of Judaism, and the Mohammedans claim a similar thing. Buddhism is built upon and developed from Hinduism in the same way Aristotelianism is developed from Platonism, or Taoism developed as a reaction to Confucianism. In real life, every regime that has attempted to eliminate religion for something more modern, (The Revolutionaries of France, the bloody gangsters of Russia, China, and Indochina), always ushered in a rapid decivilization, a new barbarism. It is almost as if—heretical thought alert—atheism is a regression to a more primitive state, not an improvement. Hmmm.

I would have had more respect for the story if the Overlords had turned on the Wayback Machine, and discovered that the events described in the folk tales of the Ainu of Japan, or, better yet, the Aztecs were literally true, and every other religion merely self-deception. The Overlords then reveal that they are Hierodules of the Aztec Gods Mictlante-cuhtli and Mictlancihuatl, who have announced the End of the Fifth Age and the opening of Mictlan, the Land of the Dead, and commanded all mankind to rebuild the great pyramids and march the countless thousands of slaves captured in flower wars into the steaming obsidian knives! The great Galactic Overmind, instead of being a cheap knock-off of Christian notions of the Communion of Saints, would be the dread and dreaded OMETEOTL "God of the Near and Close," "He Who Is at the Center," the hermaphroditic demon-god of Omeyocan, the highest of the Aztecs' thirteen heavens! That would have been worthy of H.P. Lovecraft. That would have taken some balls for a writer to pull that off!

Instead we get the same old boring Gnostic crap. It is always the Judeo-Christian tradition they plagiarize for ideas. No one bothers to blaspheme the Aztec Gods.

I mean, if you are going to pretend the UFO people are going to land and conquer us, why assume that our racial childhood ends with us being made the Princes of the King-dom, as Christianity has it, rather than assume that, our racial childhood ends with us as the fattened-up turkey invited to dinner on whatever Thanksgiving Day the Martians or Morlocks celebrate? (So the Overlords came To Serve Man? You fools! It's a cookbook! A COOKBOOK!!)

Let us be fair and look on the other hand. I admit that having the Space Aztecs land is a lot more like an H.P. Love-craft story than an Arthur C. Clarke story; it is not the tale

Clarke wants to tell, and maybe it's a dumb idea. Fine. The story "To Serve Man" has been done. Fine.

More importantly, if Clarke had written any other book aside from *Childhood's End* it would not have been an answer to the question posed by the Space Trilogy of C.S. Lewis.

Let me emphasize that there is a dialog going on among the great books of speculative fiction. H.G. Wells posed the speculative question in *The War Of The Worlds*, "What if Darwin is right, and evolution brought forth on an older planet a race as superior to us as we are to Tasmanians? What if that race treated England as the English have treated the Tasmanians, with genocide? Is there anything in Darwinism to save us? Are we not fit for this planet—have not our ancestors died for it?"

C.S. Lewis answers this in *Out Of The Silent Planet* with a question of his own from a Christian rather than a Darwinian coign of vantage: "What if the Creator brought forth other races, including a race that is not fallen? Would we even recognize what prelapsarian life was like? What if the things mythical on our world are reality on other worlds? What if we tried to treat those superior beings as ruthlessly as the English have treated the Tasmanians? Is there anything the angels would do to save them from us, and more importantly save us from us? What if the magnitude of space is a good and proper quarantine for a race as quarrelsome and wicked as Homo Sapiens? What if it is good for us not to venture into space?"

Arthur C. Clarke answers C.S. Lewis with speculation of his own: "What if science can take the place of religion? What if evolution, the striving ever upward, can replace these primitive superstitions, and offer a transcendence that is real? What if it is not only good, but necessary, for us to venture into space? What if that venture is the source of our salvation, the very thing that will overcome our quarrel-someness and wickedness? Why must C.S. Lewis and H.G. Wells assume the meeting between man and alien will be warlike? Why assume the creatures of space are devils? Well, even if they look like devils, what if the meeting were... wondrous!"

By itself, the condescension betrayed by the paragraph with the Wayback Machine looks like atheism, but combined with the other spiritual and magical ideas in the book such as poltergeists, telepathy, precognition, and such as the transcendence of mankind into the galactic Over-mind, aka the Pleroma, *Childhood's End* takes on a Gnostic mood and theme.

I say *Childhood's End* is Gnostic, a Christian heresy, because I do not see the attitude or mind-set of any other religion represented. Why is that? I speculate there are two reasons:

First, Arthur C. Clarke, whether he likes it or not, whether he admits it or not, is culturally from a Christian background, and, whether he questions them or not, shares the assumptions and axioms of that background.

His readers, by and large, are likewise. They might not enjoy the story or understand it if its mental background were too different from our shared cultural assumptions. (Albeit, later on in the history of science fiction, we do see authors trying to incorporate the cultural assumptions of Oriental religions into their fiction, at times with great success. No, I do not mean Zelazny's *Lord Of Light*, which has more to do with the American Revolution than it has to do with the clash of Buddhism and Hinduism in the wars of King Ashoka. I mean *A Wizard Of Earthsea* and *The Left Hand Of Darkness*, which are Taoist in mood and theme, and

Neverness by David Zindell, which incorporates elements of Tibetanism.)

Second, Arthur C. Clarke's answer to C.S. Lewis would not have been an answer unless it shared the framework of the question. I do not mean the Christian framework, I mean the general topic of human destiny, the role of evolution and transcendence.

Clarke could not help but give a Gnostic answer to the Christian challenge because, within the framework of Western assumptions about man and life and afterlife, there is no other answer. There is nothing new under the sun, (so says Solomon in Ecclesiastes). Logic allows only for minor variations on certain themes and ideas in human thinking. So if you ask a question about man's relation with God and the ultimate destiny of the race, there are really only three answers Western philosophy will give: (1) There is no God, and the ultimate destiny of the race is extinction, (the answer of H.G. Wells and of every pessimist who ever trod the planet); (2) There is a God, and the ultimate destiny of the race is salvation or damnation as the grace of God shall provide, (the answer of C.S. Lewis and of every Christian who ever ate bread); (3) Man shall be God, and the ultimate destiny of the race is transcendence or extinction, salvation or damnation, as the power of Man shall provide, (the answer of Arthur C. Clarke and of every Gnostic since the Second Century).

By sticking with the Christian assumptions about ultimate destiny, but rejecting the Christian answer, Arthur C. Clarke has no choice but to pen a naturalistic and science-fictional version of an old Gnostic myth. In the Western mind, if heaven is not in heaven, then heaven is on Earth. In the Western mind, if you cannot find the long lost Golden Age of Eden by crossing the Jordan of baptism, then you must find it by building the Tower of Babel. The Assumption of the Slans at the finale of *Childhood's End* would not make the reader's breath catch with wonder if Communion with the Overmind were not an image of Eden, a cure for the pain of the world as promised by the Holy Grail.

These are Western assumptions. I submit that an answer from a student of Confucius or Lao Tzu would be different. Confucius would be more concerned with good government and right action than with questions of ultimate destiny, and a Taoist might remark that the Way of Heaven is not to be broken, not even that breaking we do when we analyze something, and is not a road that leads to a destination. Certainly a Buddhist, who believes the world is an eternal torture-wheel of pain, would not share the assumption that life is a story with a beginning, middle and an end, and so he would merely smile at the question of what Fate or Dharma has in store at the end of the world. Likewise, for the Hindu, after the age of Kali Yuga, destruction, comes the age of Brahma, renewal. The finale of an Oriental version of *Childhood's End* would have had the Overlords reducing mankind back into primitive Cro-Magnon ape-men, and brought in the Monolith from *2001: A Space Odyssey* to reset the process.

It is not merely Oriental assumptions about eschatology that are not addressed in this book, but also Occidental pagan ones. The mood and theme, had *Childhood's End* been written to the taste of a Norse pagan, would differ.

In the shocking ending of the wondrous book *The Worm Ouroboros*, Mr. E.R. Eddison, who perfectly captures the Norse spirit, has the gods reward the heroic virtues of his grand and warlike heroes, not with a paradise of endless life and endless peace, but with a Valhalla of endless life and endless war. If Arthur C. Clarke had been writing for a

Viking audience, the finale of his book would have been that the Children of Men, the Supermen, would be drawn up into heaven as *Einherjar*, and the Overmind would have been the One-Eyed One, the Hanged God, the Lord of Ravens. Accompanied by the horrifying and beautiful singing of the Valkyries, the spirit beings of the supermen, having put away all of the fears and scruples of the under-men, the Nithlings, would have stormed away across the heavens, while trumpets roared, streaming like warrior angels toward the doomed home stars of the Kzinti and the Klingon and the brutal Eddorian, conquering and to conquer, setting whole galaxies afire, to fight the wars of the star-gods forever!

Now, THAT would have been a way cool ending. But it would not have answered C. S. Lewis, it would not have been within our shared cultural framework of thinking.

Clarke is clearly not a Gnostic. For one thing, he scorns religion, orthodox and heretical alike. But his famous book *Childhood's End* clearly is Gnostic, for the same reason Robert Heinlein's famous book *Stranger In A Strange Land* is clearly Gnostic. Both heed and repeat the lie of Satan, that old serpent, that red dragon who deceiveth the whole world; and his lie is that by eating of the forbidden fruit we shall become as Gods, or, as Michael Valentine or Valentinus Smith would say, "Thou Art God".

Western humanist transcendentalism always reflects a Gnostic theme, because there is no other rebuttal to Christian thought available to any man who accepts non-Oriental and non-pagan assumptions about destiny, eschatology and transcendence; there is no other, aside from Gnosticism. Either you glorify Man with the Gnostic and call God a liar, or you glorify God with the Christian and call Man to repent.

15

SAVING SCIENCE FICTION FROM STRONG FEMALE CHARACTERS

1 Foes in the Culture War

Anyone reading reviews or discussions of science fiction has no doubt come across the oddity that most discussions of female characters in science fiction center around whether the female character is strong or not.

As far as recollection serves, not a single discussion touches on whether the female character is feminine or not.

These discussions have an ulterior motive. Either by the deliberate intent of the reviewer, or by the deliberate intention of the mentors, trendsetters, gurus, and thought-police to whom the unwitting reviewer has innocently entrusted the formation of his opinions, the reviewer who discusses the strength of female characters is fighting his solitary duel or small sortie in the limited battlefield of science fiction literature in the large and longstanding campaign of the Culture Wars.

He is on the side, by the way, fighting *against* culture.

Hence, he fights in favor of barbarism, hence against beauty in art and progress in science, and, hence the intersection of these two topics, which means against science fiction.

Different reviewers no doubt mean slightly different things when they speak of the strength of a female character: but the general meaning is that the strong female character is masculine.

Masculine in general means direct in speech, confident in action, coolheaded in combat, lethal in war, honorable in tourney or melee, cunning in wit, unerring in deduction, glib in speech, and confident and bold in all things.

Hence, a strong masculine character in a story is one who can pilot a jet plane in a thunderstorm while wrestling a Soviet-trained python in the cockpit. He can appease a mob, lead a rebellion, give orders, follow orders, seduce a countess, fight with a longsword, build a campfire, repair a car engine, write a constitution, comfort the grieving, (usually with a brisk slap in the face and a curt command to snap out of it), receive confession, sway a jury, suture a wound, and escape from a sinking submarine with a knife clutched in his teeth. In a science fiction story, a strong masculine character can also pilot a starship; in a fantasy story, he can resurrect the dead. See the cover of any lurid men's magazine to see a concise summary of the essential characteristics.

Of the classical virtues, fortitude and justice are essential to masculinity, as is magnanimity: a real man neither complains nor says "I told you so."

Much more rarely do reviewers speak of strong female characters as having the virtues particular to women.

Feminine in general means being more delicate in speech, either when delivering a coy insult or when buoying up drooping spirits. Femininity requires not the sudden and angry bravery of war and combat, but the slow and loving and patient bravery of rearing children and dealing with childish menfolk: female fortitude is a tenacity that does not yield even after repeated disappointments and defeats. And, believe you me, dear reader, a woman in love has a very clear-eyed view of the faults and flaws of her man, and if her love is true, she does not yield to despair or give up on him. The female spirit is wise rather than cunning, deep in understanding rather than adroit in deductive logic, gentle and supportive rather than boastful and self-aggrandizing. The strong feminine character is solid in faith in all things.

Hence, a strong feminine character in a story is one who can overcome the prejudice against her family's humble origins to win the heart of the proud Mr Darcy. She can appease an angry mother-in-law, reconcile a feud, arrange cooperation without seeming to take or give orders and without anyone feeling left out or overruled, lure a Lothario to his destruction, unman a Benedict with her wit, build a family, repair a broken heart, restore loyalty, comfort the grieving, (usually with a sympathetic ear and a soft promise of better days ahead), receive confession, sway a jury, suture a wound, and escape from an arranged marriage to find true love. In a science fiction story, a strong feminine character can also halt a planetary war; in a fantasy story, she can resurrect the dead, and then marry him. See the cover of any woman's trashy romance novel to see a concise summary of the essential characteristics.

Note that men in fantasy stories tend to revive the dead by going to the underworld like Orpheus or Aragorn, and wrestling Cerberus like Hercules. They get revived like Gandalf the White, by being sent back by angelic higher powers. Women tend to pull Tam Lin off his horse as he is being led to hell. They get revived by love's first kiss, which is more powerful than angels.

Of classical virtues, temperance and prudence are essential to femininity, especially that temperance of the sexual appetite called chastity, and that prudence not to excite the sexual appetite outside courtship nor to invite flattery, which is called modesty. A real heroine does not manipulate good men by their affections, nor copulate out of wedlock.

This leads us to two immediate and controversial questions. First, is there a difference between masculine and feminine strengths and virtues? Second, should there be a difference?

To speak of masculine and feminine is not the normal way of speaking of things. Modern political correctness requires one to speak incessantly and indefinitely of whatever is the topic without ever naming the topic, because certain words and ideas are taboo, the source of black magic. The theory of black magic is that if a word has a connotation the social engineers do not like, by avoiding the word, thought and psychology can be sculpted or habituated to a more perfect form. It is the theory that calling black-skinned men not born in Africa and who may or may not be Americans by the term 'African American' rather than by the term 'Black' will somehow abolish race hatred. It is the theory that linguistic mannerisms and queer verbal tics can save mankind from our sinful nature, rather than, say, the Enlightenment of Buddha or the Blood of Christ.

Likewise, to speak of the sexes is thoughtcrime. We are to speak only of 'gender' which is a word that properly only refers to parts of speech, or, among anthropologists, social roles rather than spiritual and biological realities. Hence there is no word in the vocabulary of Political Correctness to speak of masculine or feminine things. The theory here is that by eliminating verbal reference to reality the offensive reality will softly and suddenly vanish away like a Boojum.

Hence, the Politically Correct theory is, first, that there are no differences between masculine and feminine strengths and virtues, and, second, that even if there were, it would not be pleasing to the amateur social engineers to acknowledge that fact; and indeed, it may be an offense against women to do so, and unwitting treason to the cause of radical egalitarianism.

The theory is borrowed without change from Marxism, except that instead of capitalist Jews being the evil and sadistic oppressors, the husbands and fathers and sons are the evil; and the women are the saintly and utterly innocent victims instead of the proletarians. The theory here is that that every pretense of any difference, however slight or obvious, between the sexes will be used by the ruthless oppressors as a ruthless excuse to exploit the weak and helpless women. Hence the theory of women as weak is built into the very bones of feminism.

By this theory, anyone admiring femininity in women or masculinity in men can be presumed to be motivated by savage and unforgivable yet unadmitted racism, but as if the female sex were another race, not the opposite and complimentary sex of the same race. This type of make-believe racism is called 'sexism', of which few stupider words exist in the modern lexicon. (One would think 'sexism' would be rule by copulation, an inventive form of government yet to be tried.)

As a rule of thumb, it is safe to assume that Political Correctness is not merely false but is as lunatic as a man who hops energetically on his cracking skull, both legs kicking wildly aloft, screaming that his hat is a pogo-stick. The Political Correctoids seem to regard it as all the more admirable the more defiantly their words defy reality. Like the White Queen in Alice, they seem to admire not merely believing lies, but believing impossibly false and utterly outrageous lies.

But in this case, we should hasten to admit that the Politically Correct lies, like most good lies, contains a grain of truth to them. Masculine nature tends to be adversarial and domineering where the feminine tends to be yielding and conciliatory. Left to ourselves in a Hobbesian state of fallen nature, sexual alliances between men and women tend toward situations of mutual exploitation where the women get the worst of it; without the institution of marriage, the mating dance becomes a sexual melee, and the more callous masculine nature of the sex who cannot get pregnant and hence is less dependent on his mate, has freer latitude to use and abuse the other sex, not to mention being more violent in the passions and more prone to violence considerably.

The institution of polygamy is an attempt devised by men to check the excesses of this free-for-all by enforcing standards of chastity, but this institution is blatantly unfair to women, rendering them little more than slave chattel.

Monogamous matrimony as practiced in the West, that is, in Christendom, is an attempt devised by heaven to check the excesses of polygamy, by rendering the bride and bridegroom equal in chastity and voluntary in vow. Even so, women were not afforded the equal rights to vote and own property until quite recently, even in the West. Hence, we must admit that there is a real problem of feminine inequality that Political Correctness attempts to solve. We can merely reject with jovial contempt their means of solving it: one does not rectify deeply rooted historic injustices by means of euphemisms and nonsense-words.

Let us therefore at the outset acknowledge that the majority of strengths and virtues are the same in both sexes.

It is not more admirable or less to lie or steal or cheat in a man than in a woman. We here are concerned with those few areas where the strengths and virtues differ, which are the areas that Political Correctness pretends do not exist.

I propose that women can commit the same vices as men, but they do not commit them in the same way; and likewise practice the same virtues, but not in the same way.

For example, when men in a locker room, or on a battlefield, use the name of the Lord in vain, and no one hears them but their team mates or brothers in arms, the vulgarity may have the positive effect of stirring up emotions ranging from team spirit to desperate anger which aids the will to win. It is the same vice as if a woman swears, but the rough nature of the masculine task mitigates some of the roughness of their tongue. A man who is crude can also inspire fear because he fears neither God nor men.

Contrariwise, when women in the kitchen or the nursery use the name of the Lord in vain, and the children they are nursing and teaching hear them, the vulgarity has the negative effect of deadening the emotions of the youngsters and making them vulgar and indifferent to vulgarity. Youngsters indifferent to vulgarity with very few exceptions cannot have a reverent or respectful attitude toward man or God. This absence of respect infiltrates to every compartment of their lives; they are mean to the poor, callous to women, negligent of duties, contemptuous of authority, and so on. The point of vulgarity is to desecrate the image of man in the eyes of man: filthy language is meant to make us seem like filthy yahoos to each other. It is the same vice as if a man swears, but the delicate nature of maternal and educational tasks, not to mention the greater need for consensus-building in the circle of women, gives this vice a darker and longer-lasting stain.

Also a woman who is crude inspires contempt, because she has contempt for God and man. The difference is that a woman who loses her native delicacy and modesty does not become an object of fear and respect, but an object of contempt and loathing, because the aura of sanctity women naturally inspire in men is tossed away.

For another example, when men complain to their team mates about some petty irksomeness in their job, it shames them by making them look weak-minded and whiny. Women, it must be noted, complain more than men. There is nothing sinister in this: if women did not complain, the things of which they complain would not be corrected. The feminine way to correct the problem is to get someone else in the group to volunteer out of kindness. It is not duty oriented. The masculine way to correct the problem is to endure it, fix it yourself on your own time, or command an underling to correct it if and only if that falls within the scope of his duty, or demean yourself by asking a superior out of noblesse oblige to fix it for you, whereupon you will owe him. It is not kindness-oriented.

Now, it must also be clear that men have free will, and can train themselves either to fulfill their nature or oppose their nature. Merely because we have a natural inclination toward something tells us nothing about whether we ought to do or avoid that impulse. I have an impulse to be kind to children with big eyes, which I think I should indulge, and I have an impulse to stab my rivals through eye and into the brain pan with my sword cane, which is an impulse I think I should suppress, not the least because my blade is dull and I am past the age when one can face the gallows with dignity. So in looking at the formal causes of masculinity and femininity, I make no remark as yet recommending whether we ought to train our young men and women to adhere to these roles or to oppose them. We can go against nature if there is a greater good to be served. Likewise, we can all learn to walk on our hands rather than learn to walk on our feet. The question there is whether the good outweighs the cost.

The quickest way to examine the good of male and female roles in romance ,(hence in romances of adventure), is to look at their origins, that is, at the causes which encourage those roles.

Biologically, females can bear children and nurse them. While it is a very popular idea these days that nature only creates physical and biological reality, but leaves psychological, mental and spiritual reality to the arbitrary and absolute power of the individual willpower, this is a popular error. Mind and body are two aspects of the same reality.

It would be wasteful and absurd for nature to give women the sexual organs needed to bear children without giving women the sexual nature of women needed to use those organs properly or raise those children properly. That women would be more concerned with the tasks related to childrearing than men is neither absurd nor unfair, but reasonable and natural.

Like it or not, nature has oriented female thinking to make them generally better at teaching a child how to volunteer to do a task, so that he will naturally and willingly do his tasks once he is grown; whereas men are generally better at commanding and punishing, so that the task gets done whether the child is willing or unwilling.

The female concentrates on the doer; the male on the deed.

Whether or not nature is being cruel and arbitrary with this specialization of roles is a debate for another day.

But the purpose of the specialization is also difficult to deny: children need both a father-figure to mete out justice and fight for the family against the world, winning bread and slaying foes, and need a mother-figure to quench the thirst for mercy and nurture the family within the home. The mindset needed for these tasks is different, hence the approach is different. Men fight and women nurse the wounded, and then tongue-lash any malingering men into going back into the fight. Their role is support rather than front line duty.

This has a second ramification, also difficult to deny: the qualities that attract women to men are influenced by the specialized roles nature intends, and likewise the qualities that attract men to women. Since the roles differ, the qualities differ. Women generally must govern a consensus between family members within the home between homes in the neighborhood, and arrange the harmony of all the souls involved. By the nature of her task, a bride must be more concerned with the soul and psychology of her bridegroom than he is with hers. Being friendly and kindly is not what she primarily seeks, but instead confidence and leadership. His role will require him to protect her during the vulnerable seasons in the marriage, and this requires that mysterious quality called good character.

Men generally must accomplish missions in a team or warband, either to kill the enemy in wartime, or in peacetime to overcome and outperform the competition in the marketplace, which ironically calls for many parallel considerations of courage and discipline. These tasks require a sense of honor and a certain unfortunate touchiness of pride, a sense of teamwork and orientation toward the goal. We men do not care how you feel about your job, just so long as it gets done on time and under budget, and we don't want to hear any complaint. We don't want to hear complaint because that betrays a weakness of emotion, a lack of honor, which harms the team spirit and morale. Spiritual and psychological reality is a secondary concern. By the nature of his task, the bridegroom must be more concerned with the bride's ability to perform the goals of marriage than with her emotional nature or mood. A central goal is child-rearing: this requires a fit physique and a willingness to submit to masculine sexual desire. Another goal is friendship. Hence, a man's attraction tends to be rather shallow. Nature inclines him to emphasize that she is physically fit, healthy and young, and willing to undergo the travail of childbirth, chaste and friendly and amiable.

Hence during courtship, nature places a paradoxical burden on the maiden. She has to discover, not how her suitor acts during the fun and sunny days of courtship, but how he deals with adversity. Character is that trait which a man displays under distress, during wintery days when things are going wrong.

Character is a hidden trait. Many a young man undertakes foolish risks and stupid dares, leaping from rooftops or riding bikes on railroad trestles, not from any self-destructive impulse, but because of a burning need to discover what his own character is. Is he a coward or not? He cannot know this unless he sees himself under stress, in an emergency. Hence some young men concoct artificial emergencies by taking up dares or doing daring stunts or doing deeds of derring-do.

During courtship, nature inclines the woman to seek out the character of the man. If she were to act in the direct and masculine fashion of satisfying the physical sexual urge with the first potential mate who was no more than physically attractive, that is to say, if she were to dive bomb the target of her lust like a man, she would have no opportunity to test his character. He, in return, winning cheaply what he craves, would not and could not prize it, and he will ignore or betray her as soon as his physical appetite is sated, for experience will have told him he can lift another skirt as effortlessly.

But if she lures her candidate in by her amorous coy flirtation, teasing, blowing hot and cold, pretending indifference then surprising him with sudden signs of affection, if, in other words, she torments him with her allure, then she can see whether he has the fortitude and depth of passion needed to continue the rite of passage to the end. Courtship is trial by ordeal.

Naturally, if she can see him during a brave deed like wrestling that Soviet-trained python in the cockpit of a smoldering jet plane in a thunderstorm aforementioned, this will satisfy her as to his bravery. But it will not tell her if he is true and faithful to her, rather than attracted on a shallow level to her looks, or her wealth or position. She needs to know if he will be true in better or worse, rich or poor, sickness and health, because she does not want to be abandoned if she falls sick and loses her hair or her eyesight or her fortune. The only way to test that hidden trait is to see how he overcomes obstacles interfering in the courtship, including obstacles she herself puts in the way. The reason why girls do not phone up boys for dates is that if the guy is not interested enough in you to pick up the phone, he is not in love with you enough to wrestle that damned Soviet-trained python for you.

The paradox here is that even if the woman were a mind-reader, even if she were totally honest with her courting candidate, she cannot discover from him what she wants and needs to know, because he does not know it himself. He himself does not know how much in love he is with her, because infatuation camouflages itself as true love every time. He does not know the steadfastness of his own character until it is put to the test.

This is also why the mating dance cannot be reduced to a merely logical contract between two persons negotiating at arm's length. They are not negotiating for the exchange of goods and services. Indeed, treating sex like a service is the mere opposite of true love, and hence is rejected with disgust wherever it appears by honest men, as gold-digging if not as harlotry, and honest women hate cads and ladykillers. They are not negotiating a contract, which is an exchange of goods, but proposing a covenant, which is the exchange of souls and lives. Each lover gives his whole self, body and soul, to the beloved, and marriage is the sacrament to seal that surrender of self.

A certain degree of ritualized formality has been painstakingly developed over the years to channel and cushion and guide the mating dance and matrimony and so on.

On the man's side, the courtship does not entail a paradox. His mission is to pursue the girl to whom he is attracted, overcoming her indifference, and perhaps her angry family if she is a Montague or a Shark and he a Capulet or a Jet, and winning her heart with courtesy, sincerity, wit, savoir-faire, and physical or mental muscle or both.

His mission is not to give into despair, and, when she walks out on him, to walk after her.

His mission is not to let his own pride spoil the relationship. Of course, heartbreak is certain here, because the formula requires you men to continue to nosedive at the target even after her ack-ack guns have shot you down. The other part of the masculine formula is to abandon her as a candidate if she is unchaste. If she cannot be trusted with sexual self-control before the marriage, there is no reason to suspect that she can be trusted after, when the temptation is all the greater.

Now, if that is the essence of the male-female mating dance, as you can see, nature places a much greater burden on the woman. All he needs to do is be brave and persistent. She needs to be wise and insightful, and make an accurate judgment about his character. She needs to understand his real emotions and motives and moods.

At this point we can return to the main question above and consider how this influences fiction, including science fiction.

A poet portraying the mating dance in fiction by the nature of the art must portray only the essential elements. This is why Romeo and Juliet do not have a long courtship: we have one balcony scene and a secret wedding soon thereafter.

If the essential element of the female side of courtship is discovering the man's true character, then a book like *Pride And Prejudice*, which is concerned with the misjudgment and the correction of misjudgment about a suitor's character is the central theme, is the quintessential feminine book. Women, if they are feminine women, will be fascinated by a book such as this, as it will allow them in their imagination to play through the steps they themselves, if they are not to live as nuns, will go through, or which they went through as maidens.

Even if she were not at first more interested in love stories and the play of romance than little boys, a little girl should be encouraged by the cold logic of the circumstance in which she finds herself to pay close attention to that one life-decision upon which so much of her happiness and success depends.

Girls who do not like love stories are well advised to learn to like them, because such stories deal with the essential and paramount realities on which much or most of that girl's happiness in life will hinge.

Likewise, if the basic nature of the male side of courtship is overcoming obstacles between the suitor and the bride, then a book like *A Princess Of Mars* is the quintessential masculine book. John Carter is so deeply in love with Dejah Thoris that even death cannot hinder him, nor the wide uncrossed interrupt of interplanetary space, and he fights his way past men and monsters and Martians, red and green and yellow and black, all the way from the South Pole to the North in search of her, even though she is promised to another man.

These elements might strike a modern reader as offensive to the equality of women, particularly if the modern reader has been unwary enough to absorb modern ideas without examining them. This objection has always struck me as slightly comical. It is not the equality of the sexes that is at question in a story like *A Princess Of Mars*. If memory serves, nearly every heroine of the several Barsoom books of Edgar Rice Burroughs and his many imitators is a princess. In other words, in such simple adventure stories the woman usually outranks the man. She is royalty and he is a nobody, a stranger, or an earthman. He is in love not with an equal but with a superior, hence winning her heart is a more difficult victory, hence more satisfying a drama.

Likewise, on the distaff side of the equation, I note that in the particular example I selected of an exemplary woman's romance, *Pride And Prejudice*, it is Elizabeth Bennet who is lower in status than the proud and handsome Mr Darcy. Equality is not a part of the mating dance: the drama of such girlish tales comes from the humble girl, the

Cinderella, winning the high and aloof prince, and likewise the drama of boyish tales comes from the humble boy winning the heart of the princess.

In that most famous homage to sciffy serial adventure, namely *Star Wars*, please notice that it was a princess who needed rescuing. While the space farmboy Luke is low class enough to be a proper suitor, when he becomes imbued with magic powers as a psionic Warlock-Samurai, he is no longer low enough in rank to be a satisfying suitor, and the lovable space rogue Solo the Smuggler is selected instead. And Luke is not the brother of the space princess until the third movie, a plot twist needed to eliminate any possible romantic interest.

But perhaps it is not the inequality of rank between space princess and space rogue that concerns us here. The objection is that the space hero does the rescuing, his is the initiative and the action, and he gets to fly the spaceship through the palace wall, whereas the space princess is given no role but to languish in prison, perhaps wearing chains or perhaps wearing a silky harem outfit, and await rescue. The inequality is between the active versus the passive role.

I submit that this is not inequality, any more than Fred leading and Ginger following during a stirring waltz is inequality. It is complementary. Those who object that men should not lead in the dance, whatever they say, are not friends of women; they just want to stop the joy of the dance.

Please consider the nature of the art present even in the humblest pulp story. Stories by their nature are meant to be a culmination and sublimation and example of some idea, preferably a true idea, coming from the human condition.

The human condition, for better or worse, puts men in the position that the natural strategy for a suitor to pursue to find true love and win the girl is as outlined above: it is analogous to defying a world, sword in hand, and fighting an entire globe for her. It certainly feels that way.

There are no real alternatives to the strategy of persistent defiance of obstacles. The strategy of picking up an attractive stranger of loose morals, or hiring her for a fee for sexual favors, is so repugnant to prudence if not to human nature itself as to induce vomiting. This is what is portrayed as the norm these days, but that fact by itself betrays that we live in psychotically sick days these days.

The strategy of alluring a sexually aggressive woman by coy and amorous teasing and batting the eyelashes, so that she throws the man over her shoulder like a female Tarzan and carries him off to a floral bower for dangerously passionate ravishment makes the man weak and comical, a joke akin to Bugs Bunny wearing a dress.

There is a reason why Superman rescuing Lois Lane remains a charming and beloved center of their myth even after more than half a century, whereas no one remembers or cares to remember any scenes of Wonder Woman rescuing Steve Trevor. The stark fact is that a healthy woman admires and should admire strength in her man, including when such strength sweeps her up in his arms. She should be delighted even if she is offended when Tarzan throws her over his shoulder, or her bridegroom carries her across the threshold. A man should not admire physical strength in women, because this is not a characteristic that differentiates the sexes for him.

The sexes are opposite, and culture should exaggerate the complimentary opposition by artifice in order to increase our joy in them, including artifices of dress and speech: when women dress and speak and act like men, some joy is erased from both sexes.

The best image and analogy of this male strategy of courtship in action is pursuit and combat and rescue. The simplest way in a story to have pursuit and combat and rescue is if the girl has been abducted, so that her abductor must be slain and she liberated. The man then is both her servant and her savior: this combination of service and salvation exactly pictures the heart of the lover.

It is extraordinarily rare that a man in real life has chased the abductor of a fair maiden, slain him with a sword, and untied her from the railroad tracks or sawmill log, to win her grateful kiss and hand in marriage. I doubt if it has ever happened in the history of the world that a young damsel met the man she later married when he rescued her from a shipwreck or a house fire. But this image, corny and hackneyed as it is, of rescuing a damsel in distress is the central image of the male strategy of courtship, the central sexual image in all male dreams.

In real life we might outperform a rival for the affections of our true love, but it would be more satisfying to stab him to death with a sword, and the victory in love feels like the victory in a duel. Rarely if ever has the object of our affection been tied to a tree in a clinging white dress to be sacrificed to a dragon, but every bridegroom rescues his bride from the dragon called loneliness. It feels like a rescue. The purpose of a story is to capture such feelings in a concrete image.

This kind of adventure story scenario also affords the story a chance to display the other elements which give the particularly masculine virtues a chance to shine, including airplane crashes, tornadoes, and escapes from dungeons, or, in the case of a fantasy story, grasping with your teeth the vulture who stooped to peck out your eyes while you were being crucified, and breaking its neck with your incisors.

Perhaps there are young girls these days who daydream about doing such a feat as strangling a vulture with your teeth, but it would seem unusual.

A woman perhaps will be offended at being portrayed as a prize; but none should be offended at being prized.

A main objection to the damsel in distress scenario is that by the logic of the plot, she does not have much to do, aside from perhaps knifing a too-familiar dungeon guard. If Andromeda by herself slips the chains and strangles the sea monster, there is nothing for Perseus to do, nor has he done anything for which she might reward him with her hand in marriage, for his character has not been put to the test.

I should also hasten to mention that while many people complain about the portrayal of weak heroines in boy's adventure stories, the complaints are narrower than it might first seem.

Four examples will suffice: Notice that while Dale Arden of *Flash Gordon* has nothing to do aside from being captured and forced into a slinky harem outfit and menaced by the lust of Ming the Merciless, Wilma Deering of *Buck Rogers* is a soldier fighting in an endless and hopeless resistance against the Air Warlords of the invading Han. While Dorothy Vaneman has nothing to do in *Skylark Of Space* aside from being space-napped by that most magnificent of space opera villains, Marc C. 'Blackie' DuQuesne, the Red Lensman Clarissa MacDougall is an officer in the medical corps, fearless in war and in the operating theater, (where she must perform a quadruple amputation on her wounded beloved without flinching), and has at least one scene blasting Boskonian space-pirates, crashing a spaceship through the palace walls to rescue a damsel in distress of her own, ironically enough, an Amazon. In other words, weak and fainting female characters do indeed crop up, but they are not as prevalent even in the boy's adventure fiction as the complaints would lead one to believe.

Another point to be made here is that annoying girly characters who do nothing but scream and need rescuing do exist in science fiction, but that they were more prevalent in the 1960s, the era of the Playboy Bunny, than in the 1940s, the era of Rosie the Riveter.

The modern women's liberation movement got started in the same era when the sexual revolution was imposing on women a demeaning role from which she needed to be liberated, the dumb blonde sex bombshell role of the postwar years. During the 1940s, the Serial Queen from the Cliffhangers were action heroines, Daughters of Zorro or Jungle Girls more often seen with dirk or sixgun in hand, and sometimes whip, than she was seen clinging to cliffs, menaced by killer apes or being lowered slowly into the fiery abyss, (albeit, of course, she was seen there as well).

My theory is that in the postwar years, the returning servicemen, having survived the hell of war and emerged from the purgatory of the Great Depression, yearned for and created the most pleasant environment imaginable to the human race: the well-tended suburb, complete with elm trees, white picket fences, automobiles with tailfins, televisions with rabbit ears, schoolhouses, (and shoes), for their children, washing machines, and, in yearning for domestic bliss, asked for an exaggerated form of domestic femininity from their women, complete with high heels, aprons and pearl necklaces. They had certainly earned it; and the women graciously granted their wish, and behaved in a more feminine fashion than their mothers.

The dark side of that grant was that the relaxation and celebration of the fat years of peacetime also encouraged the red light districts of American life to begin to sneak into main-street. It was the era of Marilyn Monroe and of Playboy Clubs, where femininity first began to be treated as a soulless commodity.

In those days the feminists, instead of reacting with Puritanical horror against the dehumanizing sexualization of their sisters, saw the pornographers and sex peddlers as allies against domestic life, which the feminists, inexplicably, saw as the greater threat.

The cigarette companies encouraged women to smoke as a sign of liberation with the slogan *"you've come a long way, baby"*. And the feminists made a common cause with the Madison Avenue types who thought it was cute to call them babies. Figure that one out.

However, in my own admittedly unscientific review of science fiction, I noticed that the useless female characters whose only role is to look pretty and scream at danger, the Playboy Bunny style girls, date from the 1960s, in works by Keith Laumer or Robert Heinlein. Female characters who act more like Roman Matrons or Pioneer Wives, dames with dignity but tough as nails, ready to pick up sword or raygun, or stab a salacious dungeon guard with a dirk, mostly date from during and before the war, as in works by Edgar Rice Burroughs, A Merrit, Jack Williamson, or C. L. Moore.

Admittedly there are some, more than a few, heroines in boys' adventure stories given little or nothing to do. My argument is first that the complaints are exaggerated, and second that introducing masculine traits to female characters does not make them strong, merely unrealistic to the point of dishonesty.

The unspoken idea being foisted across on the unsuspecting reader, who might have thought he was reading a book review rather than a political tract, is that to be feminine means to be weak and despicable, hence the only way to be strong and admirable is to be masculine. These reviewers, almost without exception, take for granted that it is an offense to female readers, and perhaps an offense to the grand and glorious revolutionary social cause of feminism, to present to the audience a female character who does not inspire admiration and emulation. They also take for granted that the only people women readers can admire or would emulate is a woman who acts with manly virtue, masculine power, male strength.

In other words, when reviewers urge writers to put strong female characters into their works, they are asking the writers, in effect, to add Amazons, women with stereotypically masculine behavior patterns, values and attitudes. The only difficulty with the idea is that Amazons are as mythical as gynosphinxes.

I return once again to my example of Miss Bennet from *Pride And Prejudice*. I defy anyone to dismiss as weak a character who, in the climactic scene where Lady Catherine de Bourgh commands her not to marry Mr Darcy, and Miss Bennett, unmoved and unimpressed despite the high rank and vast influence of the earl's widow, flatly refuses. If I may quote: "I am resolved to act in that manner, which will, in my own opinion, constitute my happiness, without reference to you, or to any person so wholly unconnected with me."

Is this a weak character? I think not. She handles the confrontation in a fashion exemplary of feminine courage, particularly since, after the marriage, Elizabeth's firmness of character allows harmony to be restored within the group, and the conflict reconciled, once Lady Catherine is one of her in-laws.

Strong men do not want reconciliation but victory. An action hero in that situation would have simply stabbed the fussy matron with a snickersnee, eloped with his fiancée, and fled to the coast to sign on with privateers, with her disguised as the cabin boy. Then he would have wrestled a sea-serpent.

Femininity is not weakness. In many ways, perhaps in most ways, female strength is greater than male strength, since our strength is based on a fragile sort of selfish pride that comes from triumphs, whereas feminine strength is based on selfless faith, in her beloved man or her beloved God, which defeat and the adversity of the world merely strengthens all the more. Male strength is like a fire among Autumn leaves, which burns brightly but quickly, then is gone. Female strength is like a sacred fire among coals, which comes again to life when it seems to be out.

Is there a danger that the repeated urging to introduce female characters that manifest masculine rather than feminine virtues will damage science fiction? Ah, but that is a question for my next essay. Space does not permit I answer here.

2. The Joy of Sex

In this space we have been examining and excoriating the attempt of many reviewers and activists in science fiction to increase the number of "strong" female characters in science fiction yarns. I put the word strong in scare quotes because it is my contention, given above conflates two distinct ideas. Good authors can make strong female characters who are strong with the virtues particular to women, feminine strength. Lazy authors make strong female characters by making them masculine.

Now there are several arguments that can be raised against this position: the first is that virtue is the same in men and women, so that what I am calling feminine strength in reality is the same as masculine strength, and ergo the distinction on which the argument is based fails. This argument has the strong point that temperance, justice, fortitude and prudence are the same in both sexes. The counterargument, which I think is sufficient as far as this point goes, is that the particular character of male and female virtues comes not from the virtues, but from the difference in priority, emphasis, approach, and skill sets involved in expressing those virtues.

The argument is experiential rather than logical: if you have not noticed that men, and for good reason, tend to be proud of their physical prowess, tend to be direct and adversarial, and tend to look at the world in terms of winners and losers, then I can do no more than to bring it to your attention. My witness is experience, which anyone can the call to the witness stand as well as me.

If you have no experience of real life, aside from what you see on the modern television or read in modern books, I might remind you that these jolly pastimes are not meant to reflect reality, but are instead meant to reflect a vision of the world, a narrative, with which I am taking issue. Your witnesses, modern television and modern books, are corrupt, and have impeached themselves.

Second, it can be argued that while indeed men do act in a more masculine fashion than women, they do not have a good reason for this: that the typically masculine and feminine roles are the product of historical accident or perhaps cruelty and social injustice. By this argument, the fact that they have always existed hence is an argument for their overthrow, because injustice has always existed, so any alternative is worth trying. The counterargument is that femininity is based on female biology, and that psychology, despite the fact that it can be trained to defy biology, ought not to be, as this leads to inefficiencies, injustices, and a general lack of joy.

Here again I point to experience as my witness: compare the divorce rate, the suicide rate, the crime rate, the rate of drug abuse, or any other honest indicator of social happiness between a modern urban setting, where the modern and Politically Correct ideals have had full sway for more than half a century, with a postwar rural setting where the traditional ideals once had full sway. Neither one is utopia, but the number of bastard children belonging to drug running gangs beaten to death by his mother's live-in lover is far smaller in rural Pennsylvania of 1953 than urban Detroit of 2013.

Third, it can be argued that while there are natural efficiencies involved with women being feminine and men being masculine, it does not produce the greater joy of which I speak. This argument goes that females do not want to be feminine, but to be free, and the restrictions of femininity are both artificial and limiting; men do not want to be masculine, or to be leaders, or to be strong; they would rather whine like girls without being criticized for whining like girls. They certainly do not want to be policemen or soldiers or firemen, or to do any task requiring physical courage and clarity of thought and boldness of action.

This argument cannot be answered, because it is two arbitrary assertions: first, that femininity implies inferiority, because it tends toward a support and nurturing role rather than a showy leadership role; second, that pleasure in life after weighing the pros and cons is seen as a matter of experience to favor liberated women who talk and act like men. The liberated woman can smoke cigars and grab waiters on the buttocks and sleep around and get drunk and join a pirate crew and raise the Jolly Roger and start slitting throats, or stand for public office, which is much the same thing.

The counter argument here is that if feminism consists of this doctrine, then it consists of eliminating the particular qualities that emphasize the feminine nature of women. Feminism abolishes femininity.

Now, logically, since there is no such thing as an asexual human being, even from a fertilized egg in the womb, eliminating the feminine can only be done by getting men to act more feminine and getting women to act more masculine. It does not liberate women from an artificial set of expectations and leave them at liberty to live as asexual beings with no social roles. All it does is ask them to live partly in the masculine role, and partly to improvise, and then not to know what to expect from anyone else in the system.

The implication then is that, if these roles are based on natural tendencies built into our psychology because they are built into our biology, then men will naturally be more masculine than women and women more feminine than men, even if social artifices hide or distract or make the manifestation of these traits different than those manifested in the past.

If women act like men, they will be, by and large, (with some few exceptions like Anne Bonny), not as good at male-behavior patterns as males, (like Blackbeard and Calico Jack Rackham and Sir Francis Drake).

Now, a rebuttal to this counter argument is that the categories of masculine and feminine are completely artificial, a social product of a sinister conspiracy of the Patriarchy. (I assume this refers to the government of the alien catlike species inhabiting a world circling 61 Ursae Majoris; and I assume and that this is meant as a serious argument, not merely tomfoolery and nonsense like the conspiracy theory behind Marxism, which proposes that investment bankers, not patriarchs, are the conspirators.)

Here again, I can only point to experience. I am a newspaperman and an attorney. I have seen real life in a way that few other people, perhaps policemen and certainly priests who hear confessions, have seen it, unfiltered by an entertainment industry or media complex devoted to an agenda.

But don't take my word for it. It is possible that my personal experience is atypical. Let us look nationwide: fifty percent of marriages end in divorce, and ninety percent of divorces are initiated by women.

My conclusion is that you dear ladies are unhappy about something.

Many ladies. Very unhappy.

Ready for another statistic? Couples who practice the Catholic method of Natural Family Planning have a divorce rate of about five percent, markedly lower than the fifty percent divorce rate of couples who utilize contraception. Correlation is not causation, so you may draw your own conclusion about what this statistic means, if anything.

The conclusion I draw is that old fashioned religious Moms who listen to St Paul's oft misunderstood injunction that they submit to their husbands, and Dads who heed St Paul's oft misunderstood injunction that Dad be the head of the family the way Christ is the head of the Church, that is, by total self-sacrifice, are happier with each other than two liberal-minded and free and equal and rather selfish partners who made an alliance to service their mutual friendship and pleasure and call it a marriage. A marriage between a submissive woman and a self-sacrificing man may be many things — it sounds a bit kinky to me — but it certainly cannot be selfish. But this conclusion I offer here only as a personal aside, an opinion, not part of the argument.

Let us look closer to home. Look at science fiction stories and movies. What has the attempt to produce strong female characters produced?

On the one hand, I would be the first to say that the Miyazaki characters Nausicaä and Kushana, the heroine and the villainess respectively of *Nausicaä of the Valley of the Wind* are the exemplars of perfectly strong and perfectly feminine women. Being in leadership roles does not strike me as unfeminine, not when we are dealing with princesses and war leaders. Nonetheless, the particular masculine characteristic of touchy pride, the desire to slit throats, machismo, vulgarity, roguishness, and the other one-dimensional stereotype writers who don't know any real men use when trying to make their females more masculine are utterly absent from Miyazaki's characters.

Again, throughout the film, (and manga), Nausicaä shows more concern for the suffering of enemies, including horrid insect monsters and radioactive biotech god-soldiers, than a man would. Her attitude toward war is hardly the same as that of a Lancelot or Achilles.

One example: when the princess Nausicaä commands her men to don their gas masks and they do not obey, she does not shoot one of them in the leg. Instead she takes off her own gas mask, provoking their concern for her, hence loyalty, hence they then listen to her. This is feminine in approach.

By that I do not mean illogical or cunning or whatever negative implications feminists and other people who simply hate women apply to *feminine* when they hear that word.

I am a romantic; to me, who loves women in their every

aspect, the word is complimentary and highly so. I am also a Catholic. I say fifty prayers a day to Our Lady and only five a day to Our Lord, so do not tell me there is something illogical or cunning or negative about feminine leadership. The Queen of the Angels disagrees.

I am calling such behavior feminine because I hold that femininity is more concerned with the doer than with the deed. The masculine approach is to be businesslike and curt, and not concerned with one's emotions, only with one's performance. This approach is useful both on the battlefield and in the marketplace. It is results-oriented. It is concerned with duty, outward actions, not with inner motives.

Typical masculine thinking: I do not care why you salute just as long as you do salute. You are not saluting the man, you are saluting the uniform. It is impersonal.

The masculine approach is the way to get your squad mates to do their duty, be it a battle or a barn-raising, despite any laziness, fear or pain, and run toward the trumpets and clamor of battle rather than away. The masculine approach is not concerned with sentiments or nuances of emotion, because if the battle is lost or the barn not raised by harvest time, the sentiment do not matter.

The feminine approach, since females are biologically more suited to bearing and nursing children than males, and since the female is given the infinitely important task of domesticating the male barbarian of her husband as well as taming and training the children, must be more concerned with the doer than the deed; this is because the woman must train the children to volunteer to do the right thing, so that as adults, when she is gone, they do the right thing. It is character-oriented. This is the more useful approach in peacetime and in cooperative rather than competitive situations. It is not concerned with duty, but with inner motives.

Does anyone seriously, honestly think that a goals-oriented approach is always superior to the personality-oriented approach? Does anyone seriously think that we can treat squadmates like children or children like squadmates?

By the way, gentlemen, this is why women talk more than men and talk about more trivial things. The act of talking is attempting to form a bond and open a channel of communication, which the woman can use to deduce information vital to her approach about your personality and moods and your character. She is trying to see behind the mask all too many of us wear as a matter of convenience. She is trying to cure us of our hidden pain.

By the way, ladies, this is why we guys don't talk about important things and never open up and share our feelings. We don't have any, not what you call feelings. We have tactics and goals. Anything outside the goal is a distraction. We do not care about how we 'feel.' Feelings pass. Pain is endured, not cured.

And, by the way men, the old canard about men being logical and women being emotional is and always was meant as a joke. If a woman points out a matter that is outside the immediate goal on which the one-track male mind is focused, he will call it irrelevant. That is because women are generally better at thinking in multiple parallel tasks at once, and are less goal-oriented and more personality-oriented. However, during the high-stress type of tasks to which men, especially young men, tend to gravitate, having a one-track mind is a benefit: it is a mind stripped down for action.

However, the way to deal with this canard is not to pretend it does not exist, or to tell men that women are logical after all. They are, but they are not logical in the same way. Women tend to think strategically and men to think tactically. A strategic thinker also thinks of arranging the peace terms after the battle is won or lost.

So much for an example of a strong female character done well: strong female characters done badly are almost numberless. Consider Xena Warrior Princess, or more to the point, Red Sonja, the she-barbarian who invented the chain-mail bikini.

Anyone examining the cleavage of Red Sonja can clearly see why boys like Red Sonja, especially lonely boys. I do not see that any honest feminist would think that this is an example of a strong female character as opposed to a buxom female character.

Agreed, Red Sonja does not need rescuing, and she is not going to scream like Fay Wray. But she is a Playboy Bunny, just one who wears a sneer and carries a honking big sword.

Compare this to, say, the toothsome Scarlett Johansson as the Black Widow in the *Avengers* movie or Milla Jovovich as Alice in *Resident Evil*, or Kate Beckinsale as Selene in *Underworld*. Ladies, If you think these leather-clad ninja-bunnies with guns represent strength rather than exploitation, then you have been rooked, cheated, bilked, and tricked. These are not more realistic and stronger images of women being set out before the public eye than the images from 1950s space adventure fiction magazines. They are merely newer. Such images are eye candy, if not fetish fuel.

My conclusion is that there is not an iota of real difference between the way women in the past were treated in SF stories and women now.

The fake difference is that some women are masculinized in order to satisfy a fundamentally illogical doctrine of Political Correctness.

In the next part, I will attempt to explain why Science Fiction needs to be saved from this scourge of absurdity.

3. Women Good at being Men

Let us address the basic question:

> *Why cannot both men and women be free, and leaders, and strong? Why cannot as many members of either sex as wish perform tasks requiring boldness of action, and clarity of thought and physical courage?*

This is a typical way such questions are usually phrased, but note the assumptions on which it is based. It assumes that to be feminine is to be inferior to a man rather than to be complementary to a man.

It assumes the feminine role is the unfree role. If the word free means free from male companionship and leadership, it is sufficient to answer that this is a barren freedom.

As for leadership, women cannot be kings for the same reason men cannot be queens. Women in leadership roles do not lead in the same fashion as men do. They still lead, (as we have seen in leaders from Queen Boadicea to Queen Elizabeth or Margaret Thatcher), but the tone and approach is different.

As for strength, physical courage is something boys are good at and proud of and naturally inclined to do. Even those effete intellectual men such as myself who do not cook outdoors and bow hunt grizzly bears nor know how to fix a car engine still nonetheless approach life through a metaphor of conflict, war, duels, and tournaments. The reason why I behave honorably in a philosophical discussion is that I think of it as a duel to the death, but where the Code of Honor are the rules of logic from which gentlemen do not deviate.

As for boldness, the virtue of courage is the same in both sexes, it is merely that males tends to take the foe by the throat with their teeth, and females to befriend the foe. To call one better than the other is like saying lances are better than shields. Lances are better for the right hand in the same way boldness in attack is characteristic of manliness. Shields are better for the left hand in the same way boldness in defense, usually called fortitude, is characteristic of femininity.

As for clarity of thought, the virtue of prudence is the same in both sexes, it is merely that it is masculine to be narrow-minded and concentrate on the work, women to see a wider view and concentrate on the workers, which is usually called wisdom. Women are as clear-thinking as men, but they are generally better at multitasking and juggling priorities rather than being obsessively single-minded.

The question above perhaps assumes social units do not exist, and that the decision is individual rather than communal. Women who are narrow-minded rather than wise, or who attack problems with boldness rather than with fortitude, are playing to something they are generally not good at, and women often don't really enjoy it when they win using those tactics: maybe some women like being domineering, but all too often they are called bitchy rather than called strongwilled. For better or worse, it is simply more feminine to talk someone into volunteering to do something than to browbeat and overawe and scare him into doing it, which is the male technique.

Last time my boss yelled at me it scared the bejezus out of me, and I straightened up and flew right after that, but I did not take it personally, and would not take it personally, because there was honor involved but no emotion involved. Contrariwise, female bosses I have had took everything personally and dished out everything personally, and there was no honor involved. One of them fired me once without ever telling me what, if anything, I had done wrong. She did not want the confrontation, I assume, because the confrontation would have been, (in her mind), personal. The other time a female boss fired me, she felt sorry for me, which made it worse. I would have greatly preferred the matter be handled in an impersonal and professional fashion. I did not want her to have concern for my feelings. Had we been in a social or domestic situation where feminine nature is queen, her sympathy would have been useful and welcome.

(Just for the record, I have been fired more often by men than by women, so please do not take these examples as anything but examples. I draw from them not because they are typical or atypical, but just because I have them in my experience, as it were, convenient to hand.)

My conclusion from those and other examples is that women, by and large, do not have a neutral emotional setting like men do. Perhaps societies less friendly and more hierarchical, like the British or the Japanese, can produce a woman who can be cool and neutral while retaining both her dignity and the dignity of her underlings. I don't know.

This raises the next question:

Granting for the sake of argument that they are real, at what point do these differences in male and female roles justify a disbelief of the depiction of women in masculine roles? I mean, stories are make-believe anyway, so why not have a female Saint George, a female Achilles, a female Ishmael the harpoonist?

Even in the most male-dominated periods of history, we still had women saints like Joan of Arc or the Virgin Mary, queens like Semiramis, and military maidens like Camilla and Britomart were portrayed in literature and epic. The tradition of warrior women is as old as legends of Amazons. No one here is suggesting absolute disbelief in stories about warrior women.

But the general answer as to when masculine female characters become unbelievable depends on how the problem of females in male roles is handled in the story. It depends on where the dividing line falls.

Let us note in passing that even to discuss this question rouses the ire of the Politically Correct, for it is an article of faith with them that there IS no problem, and ergo there IS no dividing line. Making a female into a believable Achilles figure is not a problem, because, (so says the article of faith), to believe that women are not now and have not always been super warriors is a sign of bigotry and ungoodthink. To them, it is akin to a Southern Planter discussing how to make a character who is a Negro slave, yet who somehow is wise and brave seem realistic in literature, and how to overcome the natural and obvious fact that no such slaves, or few, exist. Let us note this in passing, and return to this question below.

As to where the line between suspension of disbelief and absolute disbelief should fall, that question is a matter of personal judgment. I cannot speak for other men.

For myself, the line falls at physical combat. When Hawkeye is punching and kicking Black Widow in the otherwise excellent *Avengers* movie, my suspenders of disbelief, (as I call them), both snapped, and suddenly it looked like muscular 5'10" Jeremy Renner kicking the snot out of wispy 5'3" Scarlett Johansson. It is like a fight between a thirteen year-old boy and a thirty year-old man. (I am sure fights between adults and children can take place, but they are not even-steven fights and should not be portrayed as such).

If Supergirl is from Planet Krypton, fine, she can punch goons through solid brick walls, no problem. Ditto for Starfire of the Teen Titans. If Buffy the Vampire Slayer is possessed by all the strength of the ghosts of all the Slayers back to the First Slayer, fine, she has superduper strength and it is magic. Fine. That is all fine with me.

But when the heroine is Hit Girl or Batgirl or some leggy blonde selected for her cup size rather than fighting ability, such portrayals of wispy little she-adventuresses able to tackle boatloads of thugs built like linebackers not only as absurdly unrealistic, they have the sinister tendency to make it socially acceptable for boys to hit girls.

Such portrayals do not make the women good role models. If anything, they are misleading role models, because all those leather-clad vampire huntresses are built like Barbie dolls. Remember how feminists complain that such dolls give little girls an unrealistic body image? Well, the pursuit of strong female characters has captured the worst of both worlds. Now all the comic book images of superspies and superbabes and superheroines are both built like Barbie and have the fighting skill of Chuck Norris and Jackie Chan.

Read the first chapter of my book *Orphans Of Chaos*. The scene where Amelia Windrose, who is tall for a girl, and athletic, and, before puberty, was able to out-run her brothers in track and field events, encounters a day when she finds out that the boys now have muscles powered by testosterone, which she simply does not have and simply cannot match. Her younger brother can now out race and outwrestle her, and as she is pinned down under the strength of his hands, she realizes with a shock that she will not be able to train hard enough to beat him again, not now, not next year, not ever. Her muscles will stay at the same level as that of a thirteen year-old boy from now until forever.

Before you condemn me as a misogynist, let me say that it is reality that is misogynist, not me. That scene is the only thing in the book I did not make up. It was based on real life.

Not one, but two girls of my close acquaintance both had this happen to them.

They had been convinced, and everyone had told them, and all the movies and television shows had shown them, that girls could fight boys and be victorious. One girl was shocked when a male friend of hers, just horsing around, pinned her down with one hand. She had always thought she'd be able to fend off an attacker. Not without an equalizer, she wouldn't. The other friend was equally shocked when the boy she was with was walking down the beach with her, and he picked her up, (I do not know whether bride style or Tarzan style), and ran full speed down the beach with her. She realized with a shock that she could not have picked him up no matter what, not even in an emergency, not even if he was helping. These were not even linebackers built like Conan or men on the leading edge of physical strength for men, they were ordinary boys of ordinary strength.

I have once or twice in shows seen a fight scene where a boy punches a girl and knocks her out immediately, but have never seen a scene where the boy beats the girl slowly into unconsciousness after a ten-round or twelve-round match. It is never, ever portrayed that way. After a male and female exchange a series of blows, the woman is always sure to win because she is the underdog, and to have the man win at that point is not dramatic. I have never seen a scene where a woman fighting a man gets scared and starts crying and gives up, even though, without the madness of male hormones, that emotion of fear and surrender is much, much more common in women than in men. Look at the police statistics if you do not believe me. (I used to cover the crime beat in my county. There was not a single murderess during the three years I had that job, although I met more than one murderer.)

So my point is that our disbelief should be suspended just so long and exactly so long as it is clear this is make-believe.

But the agenda of Political Correctness is trying to make this make-believe seem real.

Women will go insane and go into despair if asked to compete at a male task on male terms with male rules. Do not get me wrong, there are top-flight female athletes who can outperform men who are below average. But top-flight female athletes in nearly all fields perform about as well as top-flight high school boys, but not as well as top-flight college boys, who are at their statistical peak of physical performance.

Putting women in a situation where they are sure to fail but are not allowed to admit that they are overmatched and not allowed to quit is the best possible way to induce despair. How can the woman be sure, even if she does win over some male athlete at some male sport, that the standards were not lowered to accommodate her?

The other thing that was the turning point in my

personal opinion on this matter, (believe it or not, back in the days of darkness, I was an ardent egalitarian and fan of women's lib just like everyone else), was another thing shocking to me, but which is apparently fairly common. The most physically attractive woman I have ever met, I met in college, during the premier of a film she was in. This was the starlet Virginia Madsen, and we were both 24 years old when we met. I waltzed a dance or two with her, and taking her out on the balcony, asked her what she admired in a man? What kind of man did she want in life? She answered that she wanted Caveman, a Tarzan, a man who would sweep her off her feet, pick her up, and, (she nodded toward a tall tree in the distance), carry her off to that tree at a run. In other words, she wanted physical strength, confidence, courage, directness, leadership. Manliness.

I have since heard the same thing from many other women, but usually in whispers, as if someone told them it was a shameful and weak thing to be feminine.

Someone told them that little boys should want to grow up and be Tarzan, who wrestles lions, but little girls should not grow up to want to be Jane, the one who civilizes the ape-man who wrestles lions. Instead little girls should want to grow up to wrestle lions. But I know of no little girl who picks up Barbie dolls and bend the feet to make a shape she can hold like a gun to shoot attacking pirates and ninjas and dinosaurs. So the standard of trying to warp little girls to be jealous of little boys, and telling them that they can be better than little boys at the very things nature and upbringing conspire to make little boys better at. It is unnatural and unnecessary and its drives the women who grow up trying to live up to this warped standard bat-guano crazy.

It drives them to hate being wives and mothers. It makes even such unthinkable atrocities as killing your own child in the womb seem normal, even seem like a right that no one can deny.

And then the crowning irony is that when a woman writer, (for the feminists care about the sex of the writer rather than the sex of the muses—who are female, for those of you keeping track, and can visit writers of either sex), manages to portray a female character who is strong and well-rounded and the heroine of the plot, one of the main drivers on whose decisions and reactions the plot hangs— then the world calls that character a 'Mary Sue' and the character and her author are mocked.

This is something I neither understand nor condone. As far as I can tell, all characters, male and female, (with the possible exception of the stars of tragedies ending in a pool of blood), are Mary Sues, that is, wish-fulfillment characters. And even the tragic heroes would fulfill my wishes, if they died in the noble fashion, poetry on lip and firmness in eye, as a stoic should die.

So what is behind this mockery? Is it just a cruel back-lash from the Patriarchy, (by which I mean the government of cat-people of 61 Ursae Majoris), trying to stifle the self-esteem of the feminists who want to read about feminine heroines?

I am sure there are readers with discriminating patrician tastes who want to read stories with well-rounded and real-istic characters, drawn with warts and all, granting some memorable insight into the melancholy grandeur of the human condition. I also read such stories, but only when I have run out of *Galactic Patrol* novels, or Barsoom books, or *Justice League* comics. I have no problem with wish-fulfill-ment characters like the Gray Lensman, who is good at everything; or John Carter, who can outfence and outfight everyone on two worlds and comes back to life when killed, except on another planet; or Superman, who can outfight and outfly everyone and comes back to life when killed, except blue.

What people find annoying is not wish-fulfillment characters. What they find annoying is wish-fulfillment characters who fulfill unseemly wishes.

The wish is to do without Prince Charming. The wish is to be as good as a man at men's work in a man's world. Ironically, the characters are from a Disney movie where all the main characters are female and everything that happens, happens because some female makes it happen. (The females are fairies, but so what? Women are magical in real life anyway, as far as I am concerned). The Prince does little more than dance one waltz with the maiden fair, get his butt kicked by orcs, and end up in chains while the evil fairy queen mocks him. Not only is he rescued by women, they are women no bigger than my pinky finger.

But his is the task to face the poisonous thorns and slay the dragon, who is filled with all the powers of Hell.

That anyone would see this, this small role occupying only a few minutes of screen time, as an insult to women, or as a threat, or as an imposition, is madness. So what is the wish being fulfilled, where the Sleeping Beauty needs no rescue and needs a man only about as much as a fish needs a bicycle?

It is not a wish for female equality. This is one fairy tale where every female character is either royalty or is supernatural.

It is a wish for sexlessness. It is a wish to do away with everything feminine, and to be better at Prince Charming's task than the Prince. Ultimately, it is a wish to do away with human nature itself.

But human nature cannot be done away with. Consider

that epitome of liberated strong femalehood, Buffy the Vampire Slayer, who has spawned as many homages and imitations in her day as John Carter did in his. He created a genre of his own, called the Planetary Romance. She created a genre of her own, sometimes called Urban Fantasy, but which should really be called Monster Romance.

It should be called Monster Romance because the main story arc for Buffy was about her love life. First she was sweet on Angel, but that did not work out, then Riley, and then Spike. Despite that she was a kick-ass wire-fu super-heroine with a smile full of quips and a hand full of stakes, the main point of the drama was, as in most stories of this kind, her love life.

And Anita Blake? And countless others? Where is the main conflict? Where is the reader's interest? Where is the drama? It is all about Jean-Claude or Spike or whomever the semihuman male lead is. It is all about the romance.

Most if not all of these urban leather clad ninja-babes and modern swordswomen feed a need in the audience. The males, by and large, just like seeing cute girls dressed as Catwoman. The females, by and large, like the romantic drama. There is no drama if the boy and the girl kiss on the first page and get married on the second. The drama exists if something prevents the marriage. These days, there are no real taboos to marrying whomever you would like, and the guy can even start out married to someone else, because divorce is no fault. Modernity allows no dramatic and realistic obstacle to romance.

The solution is to employ dramatic, unrealistic obstacles, such as by having your male lead be a nonhuman from the Night World. In urban fantasy, the vampire or the werewolf can fulfill this role neatly. Also, the half-monster can be masculine in a fashion no soft modern man is likely to be:

werewolves can be badass as Conan, and vampires as seductive and dangerous as Lord Byron. (Who no doubt was a vampire anyway.) And since the heroine is the Chosen One, and destined to kill monsters like him, she is placed in a situation where she must overcome both his fallen nature, and the powers of hell, and her own best judgment, and defy the Council of the Illuminati, to win his heart and restore his soul.

Which is a perfectly satisfying book because this is exactly what finding and domesticating a man feels like or should feel like to a woman.

And, of course, in the modern age, where the despair of women is at a historical all-time high, and the divorce rate is high and the suicide rate is high, romance feels like a back alley brawl with a supernatural monster. These books are a picture of the despair of women in the sexual free-for-all that exists in a Post-Christian, feminist world, a world where a woman is defended by no one but herself.

A leather-clad street fighter with a sword and a chainsaw, covered in blood, is what life feels like to the female readership, who need an image of strength and security to admire. No wonder such books are popular.

4. Thought Policewomen

To recap: by the nature of male and female biology, a certain stereotypical psychology and set of virtues, priorities and values was necessary and desirable to differentiate the sexes and increase their joy in each other.

The virtues of men are called masculinity; the virtues of women are called femininity. The argument given there was that females can be strong and should be portrayed in stories as strong in the way that is particular to women, but not in the way that is particular to men. What writers should not do, so the previous essay argued, is merely give female characters manly characteristics and call that 'strong'.

So far, in none of these essays, have I mentioned what the objection is to the effort to making these masculinized glamour-model Amazons into main characters.

I have said I have no objection to Supergirl, who is Kryptonian, and stronger than any mortal, and no objection to Wonder Woman, who is, er, an Amazon. Not only do I have no objection to Batgirl either when played by Yvonne Craig or when drawn by Bruce Timm and voiced by Tara Strong, I actually have an unsightly crush on her.

I have no objection to Mary Sue style wish-fulfillment characters who are good at everything and loved by all men. I do not see them as different from James Bond style wish-fulfillment characters who are good at everything and loved by all women.

I have no objection to an angst-ridden yet buxom leather-clad vixen in high heeled boots fighting her werewolf ex-lover not in high heeled boots with her silver switch-blade on the back of her flaming Harley-Davidson motorcycle in the moonlight on a storm-drenched burning train-trestle collapsing beneath the roaring unmanned freight train carrying jet fuel and nitroglycerine bearing down on her. Will she be able to stab the handsome brute in time to swan-dive to safety into the raging piranha-filled and ice-choked river far below, and still find forgiveness and love, before the inevitable explosive break-up of the Transcontinental Railway and her relationship with her brutally handsome demon-lover?

Who am I to criticize any of this? I mean, good grief, I watched *Resident Evil: Retribution* and almost enjoyed it. (I actually have rather plebeian tastes. Albeit I suppose a real plebeian would not know the word "plebeian". He would use the phrase "the hoi polloi" instead.)

So what is my objection?

My objection is to falseness, insincerity, propaganda, bad drama, bad art, and treason against the muses. My objection is to using art for propaganda purposes. My objection is to Politically Correct piety. My objection is to the Thought Police.

My objection is to the spirit of totalitarianism.

For about ten years now, I have been writing and posting essays and articles on my electronic journal, and in all that time, I have been subjected to the Leftist mob tactics of mass hatred once and once only. It was the time I mocked the Sci-Fi Channel, (now SyFy), for kowtowing to Political Correctness. My motive for objecting was perfectly clear to everyone: I would like to write without censorship, formal or informal, based on political considerations. Formal censorship is state enforced; informal is enforced by organized mob-tactics, minority pressure groups, yelling, screaming, boycotts, hysteria and general bullying.

Because I would like to write without informal censorship interfering with my livelihood, I objected to the Sci-Fi Channel, or anyone in my field, surrendering to the minority pressure groups screaming and yelling and mob-tactics and bullying. So I mocked the Sci-Fi Channel for encouraging the bullies by bowing the knee to them.

And in return the mob tried to bully me, of all people. As if I give a tinker's damn for the opinions of these yowling halfwits. (There was exactly one person of the seven hundred or so who wrote in to me who seemed sincerely offended, and to him I apologized. To the remaining six hundred and ninety-nine or so, I offered defiance in public, and in private prayed for their fool souls, hoping despite all appearances they were not damned fools.)

This taught me a lesson, but not the one the mob organizers wanted to teach. It taught me what they were afraid of. Not of me: no one can be afraid of a fat and balding near-sighted science fiction writer with a dull swordcane.

Nor were they offended by hearing sodomy called a sexual perversion, which I have done frequently before and since, never eliciting a single angry comment in reply, nor attracting the slightest notice.

Since my legions of drug-maddened terror troops are all stranded on Salusa Secondus, the third planet of Gamma Piscium, 138 light-years away, surely the mobsters of Political Correctness are not afraid of any physical force I can bring to bear. Neither am I in a position to deny any man any economic opportunities, nor am I influential enough to provoke public opinion or create any controversy. I doubt I could even do as much myself against them as they have done to me, such as hack a Wikipedia page or send around an open letter and expect it to be published and reprinted.

To explain what they are afraid of, I am afraid I have to explain something of the pathology of Leftism.

They actually think they are fooling us.

No, stop laughing. I will give you a moment to catch your breath again.

They think we think they care about gays and lesbians and blacks and women and Jews, and that their motive is compassion for all these poor oppressed groups....

Please stop laughing. I will give you another moment.

Now they know what their real motives are: to give themselves a sense of greatness which they do not deserve by thinking that they fought for civil rights that they actually oppose, out of compassion which they do not have for victims of utterly imaginary hardships and oppressions.

Am I being unfair? Remind me of the last time a group of feminists rioted outside of a Saudi Embassy.

They want what they have not earned. I do not mean monetary earnings. Their socialism, the craving for the unearned in the economic sphere, is not the main thrust of their psychopathology, it is a side-effect. I mean spiritual earnings. They want self-esteem without the effort of doing anything worthy of esteem. They yearn for the palm of martyrdom without actually suffering the pain of being a martyr in the same way they want the crown of right-eousness without actually being right.

My theory is that the schoolgirlish overreaction prompted by my comment had nothing to do with the particular topic of gay characters in Sci-Fi shows. My theory is that the unadmitted reason for the degree of hostility in that one case was that I happened accidentally to tell the truth about them.

They are censors. The Politically Correct are Thought Policemen.

They do not think it is evil if a man commits crimes; for them, evil is a matter of thinking the wrong thoughts. Hence, Bill Clinton can abuse women without limit, but if he mouths the correct thought in reference to abortion, the feminists love him. Hence, Mrs. Cheney can be loving and compassionate toward her gay sister, but if she disapproves of gay marriage, she is the same as a Nazi lusting to extermi-nate the Jews.

'Censors' is perhaps not the right word. In ancient Rome, the office of the Censor, in addition to counting the numbers of the tribes and orders for voting, was to bring public shame upon behavior unbecoming to Roman dignity.

Later, the office was to bring shame upon books thought heretical or immoral or deleterious to the public order, or redact, or forbid them.

What they are is anticensors: the Politically Correct try to bring shame onto books thought orthodox or moral or insufficiently deleterious to the public order. If a book does not promote sexual perversion in a sufficiently flattering and fulsome way, our anticensors hold it up to public shame.

Now, these self-anointed Thought Police would have no appeal if they admitted their true motivations, even to themselves. They need rationalizations, they need excuses, they need a mask.

The mask is compassion for the downtrodden.

Now, if you look through all human history, you will not find a single instance where the Leftists have actually helped the downtrodden, but many instances of the Left enthusiastically trampling the downtrodden, and grinding the faces of the poor into the dirt. That is the mental image which causes the Leftists their semi-sexual leg-tingles of sadistic lust: they want to see the human face trampled forever beneath their bootheel.

The examples of Cuba, China, Soviet Russia, and Nazi Germany should be sufficient warning of what the true motives are behind movements like Occupy Wall Street, or what the moblike anger of the Ku Klux Klan, which formed the military arm of the Democrat Party after their defeat in the South, can do when its grip on the levers of power goes unchecked.

A reasonable objection to make at this point is that the Fabian-style socialists do not want violence. Clement Attlee managed to bring postwar Britain to adopt all the same economic and social policies as Mussolini's fascist

Italy, after all, without firing a shot, without making any arrests.

An even more reasonable objection is that nearly all Leftists think of themselves and talk of themselves and tell narratives about themselves where they are kind and compassionate and softhearted and filled with pity and brimming with the milk of human kindness, and so violence is the farthest thing from their mind.

Then they explain why Che Guevara is a hero, why George Washington is not so much a hero, why Castro's Cuba has free health care, and why the guillotine was necessary because the aristocrats and the Jews are enemies of the people, and you cannot make an omelet without murdering 259,000,000 million people in wars, pogroms, and government-orchestrated famines.

So they might not approve of killing the victims of Communism by the millions, but they strongly, strongly object to you criticizing Communism.

After all, Castro and Che and Mao and Stalin murdered more people than Attila the Hun, but Senator McCarthy terrified self-important Hollywood people by following legitimate evidence indicating that the State Department was infiltrated by Soviet Agents, and, after the fall of the Soviet Union, it was discovered that each and every person McCarthy accused was guilty of exactly that which he accused them.... So, this means McCarthy was such a bad person, you cannot criticize Che or Castro or Stalin. Ronald Reagan was the real terrorist, and may have been a madman.

In other words, not all Leftists are violent, but Leftists are blind to violence on their side, because whatever their side does is not judged by moral standards.

Hence in the Politically Correct cult worldview, violence

is permitted when it serves the cause, but not necessary. Violence is merely icing on the cake, an extra, something in which to indulge when and if opportunities permit, such as among barbaric Russians who passively will endure it, but easily eschewed when opportunity does not permit, such as among civilized Englishmen who might well take up arms if provoked, as Englishmen, judging by their history, are wont to do.

Violence is not the point of Political Correctness.

The central point of Political Correctness is *faith.*

It is a religious faith, similar to Christianity and growing out of her, but opposed to its host organism and seeking forever to destroy her.

Leftists will trace their roots back to Marx or to the left hand seats of the French Assembly during and before the time of the French Revolution, but the transformative and utopian spirit reaches back to Cromwell and the Puritans. The Puritans in their early days were the arrogant intellectual elite precisely like our current ones, and it was bishops, not beer, to which they objected.

The Puritans gave birth to the Unitarians who gave birth to the Progressives who gave birth to the modern Left, which takes little or no inspiration from the French Revolution. The religious and crusading impulse of the Puritans, the hatred of Christmas, of worldly wealth, of Jews, of Catholics, all of those things remain.

What the Puritans wanted was totalitarianism. The Catholic Church wanted the secular power separate from the spiritual power, and always has, and always will, and the Church always grants her children freedom to make their own judgment in any thing where God has not spoken. The Puritans want no freedom at all, no latitude. Teetotalism and Prohibition and living without private property and that sort of rigorousness have never been a Catholic thing meant for the Catholic laity. Just ask the Irish.

The Church has always allowed and encouraged those called to a special spiritual adventure to live without worldly pleasures or worldly goods, but never demanded each and every one of us dress in broadcloth like the Puritans year round, rather than just for Lent. The Church demands modesty from her daughters, but not the head-to-toe veil of the Islamic Fascists or the austere unisex drabs of the Maoists.

The Puritan plan was to have the King of England be the Pope, to combine the secular and spiritual power, and when that failed, to establish a utopia in the New World. The Church says there is no paradise before Doomsday. The Church says Man cannot save himself without the grace of Christ. The Puritans say some men are born elect, and cannot be damned, and others are born depraved, and cannot be saved. So to create utopia, all that is required is to give all spiritual and temporal power to the Elect, the elite, the enlightened. Does that sound familiar?

I am emphasizing the spiritual roots of Political Correctness to support the argument that PC is fundamentally a religious movement, a faith tradition, a cult, and not a political movement except in a trivial sense.

Like all faiths, the cult has certain articles of faith. Like all heresies, this cult takes the main propositions of the traditional historic Christian faith for granted, and these are its only source of strength and only source of appeal. The concern for the poor, the widow, the downtrodden, the belief of the brotherhood hence the equality of all men, all this comes from Christian thought: there are no corresponding doctrines to these among the Stoics or Aristotelians or Neoplatonists, and the opposite is preached by those who follow Confucius or those who believe in Karma and in the caste system.

Like all heresies, this cult rejects vehemently other propositions of the Christian faith, and anathematizes them not just as bad opinions, but as an evil to be vilified in absolute terms.

Unlike other heresies, the cult rejects God and the supernatural altogether, and presents itself as if it is not a heresy, not a cult, not a religion, and not based on faith.

It claims to be based on iron-clad scientific reasoning of the latest and most intellectually sound and objective sort.

Please stop laughing or I will never finish.

One of the articles of faith of this religion is that it is not a religion and that their conclusions are the product of clear and logical thinking, or perhaps the product of pellucid clarity of pure motives and high-minded compassion, and that to disagree with the articles of faith is a sign, not of lack of faith, but a lack of intelligence, education, or compassion.

They think they are smarter than us.

These undereducated boobs who cannot follow a syllogism of three steps, who do not speak a word of Greek or Latin, who do not know the difference between Arianism and Aryanism, who have never read *The Origin Of Species* or *Das Kapital* or *The Republic* and who do not even know the intellectual parentage of all their ideas, these vaunting cretins whose arguments consist of nothing but tiresome talking points recited by rote and flaccid *ad hominem*, whose opinions are based on fashion, they, of all people, think they are smarter than the rest of the world.

Yes, you can go ahead and laugh at that one. I'll wait.

It is merely a fact that no Politically Correct policy has ever had the outcome planned. These are not stopped clocks who are correct twice a day: the PC cultists always,

always, always, side with whatever is the most evil, illogical, destructive, nihilistic, perverted, and foolish measure in any debate or decision of policy. PC ruins everything it touches.

Instead of providing an endless list of PC schemes, ideas and policies that have failed, since they all fail, I will issue a general challenge to any reader who wishes to dispute the obvious to list the PC success stories. List one. A single example will overturn the universal affirmative. Knock yourself out.

You will find that the candidates on the list are one of two things:

First, the cultists will claim credit for something they opposed, such as the Civil Rights Movement, which was a Republican movement, spearheaded by a Christian minister named King, aided by Nixon, voted into effect by a Republican majority, to overcome Democrats who stood in schoolhouse doors or turned firehoses on peaceful protestors or lynched blacks. Meanwhile the NRA was arming blacks with handguns, Saturday Night Specials, that the Democrats tried, often with success, to remove.

Second, once the true depth of the evil is undeniable, the cultists will deny something that they once supported, such as Stalin's Soviet Union, (of which Lincoln Steffens said "I have seen the future—and it works"), was really actually honest Injun a truly true example of the true faith after all. It was not REALLY socialist. They did not really try hard enough. They did not spill enough blood. We need to try again and try harder.

These two factors acting in concert create what I call the Unreality Principle. The Unreality Principle is the principle that whatever is truth is called not true and whatever is not true is called true. It does not matter what the topic is. The point is to break the mind of its ability to focus on rational thought.

This conditioning of the brain to flinch away from reason and embrace unreason is done by making the unreality principle the paramount moral and ethical principle in the cult. It is the principle that trumps all others.

So the first article of faith of Political Correctness, the one from which it takes its name, is that to think or speak what is factually correct, that is, whatever is really real, is morally wrong if it harms the party or the cause.

Moral righteousness consists of thinking and speaking falsehoods and nonsense-words that are factually incorrect but politically correct, that is, by slogans, jeering, noise, commotion, jingles, hullaballoo, alarums, and cacophony which aid the party or the cause.

And it is only moderately meritorious to speak small falsehoods, (such as blaming the failure of the Soviet Union on the need of the idealistic revolutionaries to arm themselves against the vicious attacks from the capitalist West), but truly meritorious, because it is a true sign of deep faith that resists all fact and ignores all logic, to tell truly huge, outrageous, utterly unbelievable lies, (such as saying all opposition to Obama is racist, or saying the National Socialist German Worker's Party was not Socialist, or saying Capitalism produces poverty, or saying the only truth is that there is no truth, or saying that one man's freedom fighter is another man's terrorist).

Those who take up the pen to argue against this endless drip of nonsense are often baffled by the fact that the PC cultist, when discussing any other matter aside from one of his articles of faith, is capable of humanity, wit, logic, and seems like a normal human being. But once on one of the subjects where this mental disease has taken hold, the cultist will and must say things no one is stupid enough to believe but which no one is dishonest enough to lie about: lies on the level of saying his head is a pumpkin, things a child would not believe.

These cultists are not monsters. Why, then, do they say things that anyone can see are utter evil, utter nonsense, utter folly?

What makes kindly gray-haired old grandmas who act like humans at all other times suddenly curse the United States for opposing the spread of International Communism to South America, and unable to believe that the Communist assassin Lee Harvey Oswald shot Kennedy, but instead think a Right-wing conspiracy or an evil redneck city in Texas is to blame?

One might as well ask why Eve and Adam, our first parents, favored of Heaven so highly, and blessed with endless life and lordship over the gardens of paradise, thought that disobedience to God would get them some greater good, such as equality with God, a good that God whether through cruelty or unfairness wished to deny them.

The cultists will tell you their motive. Their motive is kindness. They want to help.

The cultists are shocked by the unhappiness and unfairness of human life on earth.

But that is not what makes them cultists. Christians are also shocked by the unhappiness and unfairness of human life on earth, and they explain that shock by reference to the Fall of Man, and seek the solution of the world's pain in a supernatural power from beyond the world, seeing all men's devising must fail.

What makes otherwise rational men into PC-cultists is

that they do not believe in the Fall of Man; they believe in the Interrupted Perfection of Man.

They believe perfection of paradise is within arm's reach, perhaps less than 25 years away, but that the achievement of this eschaton is thwarted by the folly and inertia of the uneducated masses, and by the sinister conspiracy of the malign vested interests favored by the current world-system.

This conclusion is not as bizarre as first seems. The Politically Correct cultists see that reason and decency and honesty have not solved that unfairness nor alleviated that unhappiness. Therefore, (so their reasoning goes), reason and decency and honesty, also called factual correctness, are worthless.

Reason and decency and honesty seem to the cultists to deny to them some greater good that reality has always denied them. It is the same logic Eve used when reaching for the apple. They want to be gods, or, what is the next best thing, the fathers of the New Man who is destined to occupy the shining towers of Utopia.

Ergo, the cultist concludes that if factual correctness and loyalty to truth has always failed throughout all history to produce perfect utopia, then political correctness and loyalty to falsehood and outrageous lies must serve in its place.

This thought is like an addictive drug, a drug that gives pleasure only the first time it is used, and thereafter only produces pain if it is withdrawn. After the first euphoric days of the Movement, the cultist quickly finds he cannot get what he wants.

He does not conclude from this that utopia is a self-contradictory and appallingly stupid and Escheresquely impossible idea. He merely feels frustration.

Then he finds a scapegoat for his frustration, usually

some harmless bystander, perhaps a Jew, perhaps an Investment Banker, perhaps the Pope, perhaps his father, and blames him.

This scapegoating does not necessarily involve a conspiracy theory of history, but it must have the mood and savor of a conspiracy theory: it must assume action in concert of many groups widely dispersed through time and space, whether that group is called Capitalists or the Patriarchy or The Establishment or The Man or what have you.

If the cultist is frustrated, and if the frustration cannot be admitted honestly to be because of the foolishness of his goals, then the frustration of his goals must be blamed on an opponent, an oppressor, a conspiracy, a group of wrong-thinking people who have some base and vile motive for maintaining all the injustice and unfairness of the world. The wrong-thinking people are sadists, who thwart the utopia because and only because they want people to be unhappy. The wrong-thinking people are witches on whom all bad harvests are to be blamed.

With the freedom from facts and logic which is the core of Cultist thinking comes a number of defense mechanisms too numerous to list here. I will mention only two.

The first mechanism is placing ideology over logic. Because logic is not a priority, the cult does not demand uniformity of belief even on the core doctrine. The cult has a number of propositions or special interests it serves, and loyalty to any one of them makes you a cult member, so you get the benefit of unearned sensations of moral superiority and self-congratulation on your kindness, even while other members of the cult are carrying on to do the opposite of whatever you support.

Your loyalty is still to them, and you attack anyone who attacks them. That is the bargain.

This is why some PC Cultists can even admit that communism is mad, bad and evil, but they also must think McCarthy and Reagan are even worse. Some cultists can think that Islamic terrorists are bad, but the price is that they have to think that criticism or mockery of Islam is even worse. That is why Gay activists and Islamic terrorists can agree to attack their mutual foe, Christendom, despite their mutual hatred for each other.

The second mechanism is placing ideology over honesty. Whenever the lies become too obvious, the cult denies itself, changes its name, and the shadow takes another form and grows again. It cannot call itself Liberalism once it becomes too obvious that the cult yearns with semi-sexual lust for totalitarianism, and seeks totalitarian control over all media, all communication, all thought. It cannot call itself Progressive once it is clear that the progress is toward the edge of a cliff. They cannot even call themselves Left once it is clear they have no relation to the left-seated liberal delegates in the French assembly. They cannot call themselves socialist once everyone sees what socialism does to the economy, to human honesty, to self-reliance, to manhood, to humanity. They cannot call themselves communists once it is clear they have no intention of sharing all property in common, but instead bestow villas and mansions to the elite party members as their share but slums or Siberians gulags to underlings as their share. This is why the cult keeps changing its name.

There is no center to the cult. There is no Pope in charge of this antichurch of antihuman belief. It is a loose collection of gibberish whose elements have nothing in common with each other except for the psychological effect on the cultists. They get to feel good about themselves as morally superior while thinking they are saving the earth while doing everything imaginable to sink more and more deeply into moral depravity, infanticide, euthanasia, sexual perversion, theft, half-lies and whole lies, revolutions, riots, violence, wars.

The cult offers complete freedom from morality and reason while also offering to them the palms and laurels and coronets granted to the saints and saviors and beauty queens.

Everything is permitted to cultists because the cult enemy, the witches or wrong-thinking people, have no rights and merit no respect, no, not even the respect due an honorable opponent, or due a man honestly mistaken.

It goes without saying that if utopia were possible, anything done to achieve utopia would be permissible; and likewise any opposition to utopia would be an evil so monstrous as to be beyond explanation. That is why the cultists are not just appalled by opposition to their feather-brained and bloodthirsty schemes, their desire to loot and lie and give the guillotine work to do, they are honestly baffled by it.

The same reason that utopia, by being so valuable permits any sacrifice needed to build it, and makes all opposition into devils and madmen, so too does an emergency permit large sacrifices allegedly for the duration and silences all opposition as being impermissible given the limited time and the severity of the emergency.

This is why the cultists are always shouting at the top of their lungs.

This is why the best health care system in history, with little or nothing wrong with it, which, perhaps, to be made even better, could have used a few minor tweaks, is described as a crisis demanding immediate action.

A crisis is like a miniature utopia, in that the severity

allows foolish actions, like passing a law without reading it first. And any objection to solving the crisis can be denounced as being prompted by an evil desire to prolong or deepen the crisis, a wrongheadedness and willful blindness to the looming severity of the coming disaster.

The end of the world is always immanent for the Cult. The stakes are always all or nothing, world salvation or world damnation. Nothing can be discussed calmly.

Nothing can be discussed calmly for the same reason there is no loyal opposition nor honorable rivals: everything opposed to the cult must be described as absolutely bad and evil in all ways.

(Even science fiction writers, like yours truly, who speak against the cult cannot simply be making an innocent mistake, they must be both uneducated and untalented in the writing of science fiction. Correct political opinion seems also to grant all talents and all graces.)

The only way to escape being accused of being a wrong-thinking person is to denounce other wrong-thinking persons with the vehemence and correct formula of speech to show that one believes the cultists. The formulae change from decade to decade and year to year—Colored to Black to Afroamerican to African American to whatever—so that no one can be a cultist without paying close attention to the cult and its fashions.

And, like the Gnostics before them, the cult has an inner and an outer circle. The inner circle are the ones who half-believe their own lies, and the outer circle are the ones who the inner circle deceives and misleads.

And this is one of the best defenses of the cult: the outer circle members like the sensation of belonging to a group, and like the flattery of speeches and stories and movies telling them, over and over, that they are smarter than average, more compassionate than average, and that the witches and wrong-thinking persons are to blame for all the crop failures and everything else wrong with their lives.

Did you get fired from your job? When all things are controlled by the state, no more unjust firings will happen. Did your boyfriend break up with you? Once feminism is taught to one and all, an era of mutual understanding and equality will grow, where men will no longer be unfair to women. Do you have a longing for something hard to name? This is because the witches are keeping you from your true heritage.

The Jews are to blame for the Fatherland losing the Great War. The White Man is to blame for my poverty. He makes more than me. He is handsomer than me. He is happy and I am not. Vote for me, and I will stop the witches from cursing the climate and creating a hole in the ozone layer. By November, the Utopia should be up and working. But I need more power over your lives because I am an elite expert and wiser and more compassionate than you, and I will stop the wrong-thinking people, who are all-powerful witches.

And on and on and on. It is a formula that explains all failures and promises all success and shifts blame to the wrong-thinking people, and the beauty of the cult is that facts never, ever get in the way.

That is the strategic overview of the Cult belief of Political Correctness.

What has this to do with science fiction?

Nothing. The Cult is totalitarian. It does not want to control merely your beliefs about God and angels or your beliefs about race relations or your beliefs about the proper forms of law and government or your beliefs about questions of capital and labor or your beliefs about relations between the sexes or your beliefs about the relations between man and his environment or your beliefs about your diet and your smoking habits. They want to control your beliefs on purely scientific questions, such as the role of human activity in relation to global temperatures over the next century, or the average intelligence quotients of various racial groups.

They want to control EVERYTHING. The totality. Your whole mind and whole heart and whole soul, during your every waking moment.

And they want you to believe – this is also a central tenant of their dogma – that they do not want you to believe anything, that their beliefs are nothing but the independent conclusions of disinterested scientific thinkers who just so happen to agree in perfect lockstep on these matters.

The central dogma of the Cult of Political Correctness is that there is no cult, and no dogma. The dogmatists are the other people, the wrong-thinking people, the witches whose malign magic powers somehow cause utopia not to be born.

So the Cult is interested in science fiction only because science fiction exists and the Cult demands total control over every aspect of human life down to the last nuance, (while denying that it makes that demand).

Ah, but is it not true that science fiction back in the unenlightened days before our messiahs of female equality Hugh Hefner and Bill Clinton treated women as secondary characters, and female authors were hunted down by Senator McCarthy and his Sardaukar Terror Troops?

5. Women as Proles

Political Correctness is not a political program but a cultic worldview with no particular center and no particular goal, bound together only by a general discontent at the sufferings of the world, and the belief that a rebellion destroying the legitimacy of all prior institutions and the erection of a totalitarian utopia will solve everything.

Has this anything to do with science fiction? I submit that it does not, or rather, it has about the same relation that commercial advertisements have to the magazines in which they appear: The cult wants to put leftwing messages into stories to influence the minds of the reading public and make their leftwing worldview seem like the norm, the default view, so that everything natural and decent and traditional and rational seems unbearably wicked and disgusting.

The cult operates by a very simple formula defined by Marx: find something that does something good, and blame it for not being perfect, identify a victim group, preferably one actually being benefited by the good, identify their benefactors as witches, that is, as the wrong-thinking people. Then, make windy claims that the imaginary victim group will have its imaginary problems obliterated once the witches are burned and the witchhunters get all the property, material or spiritual, once belonging to the witches, and then everything will be copacetic.

Of course, all this is total bullshit, and even most of the cultists, those in the outer ring, know it, so it is better to imply it without saying it.

In the case of Marx, the good thing was the industrial free market. He made up a bad sounding word to describe it, calling it capitalism. Ironically, the free market is such a good thing that the insult term came to be a term of endearment, and many of the wrong-thinking witches now use the term proudly, and call themselves capitalists, and call the freedom to own property and trade without permission from the state 'capitalism'.

The victim group was the factory hands and farm workers. Of course the free market benefited them so enormously that there is no parallel in history. Poverty in the West was once the same as it was in the undeveloped world, a matter of near starvation. Now a man below the poverty line in America is more likely to be overweight and own a cell phone and a used car than he is likely to starve to death. Marx called these men the proletarians, a Roman word referring to those who served the Empire only by producing children.

Marx made the stupid and unsupported argument that the proletarians were a class or category of persons, who, by virtue of the fact that Marx used one word to refer to them all, therefore had a unity of interests.

There is of course no unity of interests. Ask a sailor on a whaling ship put out of business by a field hand working on an oil rig, whose boss has found a way to bring petroleum oil to market more cheaply than whale oil. Ask the blacksmith's apprentice who no longer can find work shoeing horses because of the efficiency of the factory hand working in the automobile plant.

Marx identified the men who made this explosion of wealth and long life possible as the deadly enemies of the poor as the bourgeoisie, a word from the Middle Ages referring to those who occupied Burgs, or walled towns, and primarily engaged in trade. They were also asserted to have a unity of interests, equally as foolishly. Ask Mr. Macy about Mr. Gimbel.

The interests of the bourgeoisie and of the proletarians were asserted to be locked into a Darwinian competition to the death with no quarter and no peace possible or desirable. The proles were supposed to hurt the bourgeoisie as much as possible in any way possible, and hurt them more and more until each and every one of them died.

And, of course, this theory was enthusiastically adopted by the middle class intellectuals and students and the newly minted millionaires who were the prime beneficiaries of industrial capitalism, and they sought, with the eagerness of a young bridegroom on his wedding night, to have the proletarians kill them in a worldwide bloodbath. Or, rather, they wanted to pretend to be proletarians so that they could engage in the worldwide bloodbath. It is not clear which. Sadists are often masochists and vice-versa.

Now, there are of course in reality real problems caused by industrial capitalism. Anything in reality has a cost. That is the nature of reality. All Marx did was reverse cause and effect and blame the free market for all the problems it was solving, because the solution was not perfect.

In the case of Feminism, the victim group was women, all women, and the oppressor group was men, all men. The fact that male babies need and want and love female mothers to raise them and the fact that male fathers need female wives to make more male babies never enters into this enrapturing vision of the eternal war between the sexes. The feminists are not as clear as the socialists about the need for a worldwide bloodbath, but they are even angrier about it.

Most women I know, who are, to be frank, Christians of a rather traditional strength of mind, do not buy into this feminist agitprop, but most of the men I know, who are Wiccans and Atheists, do. This indicates once again that a certain degree of deranged masochism is present, perhaps prompted by nebulous feelings of guilt and a need for propitiation by sacrifice, or just a weary desire not to shoulder the burdens of manhood.

Now, there are of course in reality real problems caused by specialization into sexes or organization of society into sexually differentiated roles. Anything in reality has a cost. The suffragettes of our grandmothers' time, or, if you are younger than me, great-grandmothers' time, had a real problem that was open to solution by legislative change, namely, to afford each member of the fairer sex the right to vote and to own property in her own name.

The feminists in our time have also reversed cause and effect, and blame on the existence of sexual roles problems which either are caused by the lack of such roles, or problems that do not exist at all.

By any measure, feminism has won an absolute triumph and swept the field of all opposition. The women have more freedom, if by that we mean the lack of legal or cultural restriction or restraint, than ever did any of their mothers for all of time.

So why are they in despair? Why are women killing themselves in record numbers, killing their babies in the womb in record numbers, getting divorced from their spouses in record numbers?

Now, I have taken all this time to describe at length— tedious length, so I know that no one has read this far except for my one fan (Hi, Nate!)—how the Cult works, so that I can briefly—briefly for me, which means an orotund and endless pontificating for an ordinary mortal—say how the Cult works in reference to science fiction.

Let me use an example from my own writing, not because it is the best example, but because I happen to have it to hand:

I wrote a book where the expedition to the nearby dwarf

star V886 Centauri had an all-male crew. I did this because I wanted to have one character born aboard the ship without a clear explanation as to how exactly she was born; it was part of the mystery.

One of the cultists pretended to review the book. Pretended, because checking a book for cult-loyalty is not a review. Telling the readers whether the book performs the meaningless ritual gestures and genuflections of political correctness does not tell the readers whether they will like the book or no, which is what a review is. The cultist was shocked into gibbering Nyarlathotepian insanity by the fact that I was capable of imagining a ship with no female crew aboard. After all, such a thing has never happened before in all of history, nor has it been imagined, nor is there any excuse for such a thing. The fact that the mysterious child born aboard ship was female, and is the savior of mankind and the galaxy, the first superhuman, et cetera and ad nauseam, did not restore your humble author to the good graces of the Grand Inquisitor, but condemned me as a misogynistic sexist.

So why are the ladies in despair? Why do they commit suicide in record numbers?

Is it because of me, John C Wright, internationally recognized science fiction author, failed attorney, retired newspaperman, savant and scholar with my fat belly and outrageous beard and nearsighted eyes, my glorious bald spot, my dull swordcane?

Did I suppress you, my dear ladies?

You see, the moment the question is asked, it sounds ridiculous. No one man can be blamed. The Cult belief does not permit that. It only deals with collectives: all men as a whole must share this guilt.

The logic goes as follows: we all, except for the males

who have joined the screaming witchhunters, caused the crop failures. The crop failures do not show up because of natural causes. It must be because of the witches, the wrongthinking people. I am one of the wrongthinking people. Ergo, QED.

In order to be a witchhunter, you have to make a ritual propitiation.

As far as science fiction goes, the theory here is that all the unfairness and unhappiness of history is cause by some sort of undefined and dim half-subconscious miasma or influence of thought, an attitude of which even we are half-unaware, which is fed by seeing stories where the women characters are in the stereotypical weak female roles of being feminine.

Sorry. My sarcasm gland became inflamed. The theory is that stories cause or at least influence the subconscious mind with a set of expectations, so that if little boys read stories where Superman saves Lois Lane from a radioactive moon robot or something, the little boys will grow up to be rapists, therefore little boys should read stories where women are Amazons fully able to rescue themselves from radioactive moon robots without male help.

I am not clear on the details of how the theory goes. The practice is that you can be accused of sexism for any reason or no reason, and once you are accused, there is no defense and no verdict other than guilty. There is no example in the history of the world of a sexist reforming and becoming a properly orthodox lover of feminism. The only way to escape accusation is to be a witchhunter yourself, and accuse others.

Now, since stories, like industrial capitalism, do exist in reality, they do have drawbacks, as does everything in reality. Boys adventure stories since the days of *Treasure Island* tend to be an all-boy's affair. Earlier stories had more heroines in them, such as *The Faerie Queene*, because romance was a part of Romance. The tale goes that the boys of Stephenson asked him to write a tale with no women in it because, (being little boys), they did not want to hear about love and romance.

Science fiction sprang out of the tradition of *Treasure Island* and the like, since Jules Verne did not want to add any romantic subplots to his tales of technological wonder. I am sure H.G. Wells has some female characters somewhere, but I cannot bring any of them to mind aside from Weena the Eloi from *The Time Machine*.

So, as far as I can tell, the complaint about Science Fiction having at one time being an all-boys club where women were scarcely ever seen is a perfectly reasonable complaint. There were and are stories where the only female characters are fodder for abduction or some worse fate.

I leave it to the reader to count the number of women shown as helpless in 1940s-1950s popular magazines versus the number in the average slasher flick or torture porn sequel.

And there have always been stories with two-dimensional characters, cardboard and unconvincing, and women in those stories have been portrayed in unconvincing ways.

If the kind reader recalls, there is an inner and an outer circle to the cult. The inner is the liars and the outer is the suckers. The suckers are sincere but ignorant. They don't know what the cult wants or what is wrong with it, but they have been warned not to listen to any criticism of the cult, because the wrong-thinking people are so horrible.

The suckers are completely honest when they ask for stronger female characters either in SF or in mainstream fiction. They look at cheesy, cardboardy, unconvincing female characters, at the lazy use of stereotypes, or plain old bad writing, and they demand better.

Good for them, say I. Nothing wrong with their demand. I applaud it. I myself do not care to read stories where all the female characters are victims with nothing to do, who have no role in the plot. That is not my idea of feminism or of femininity. That is just bad writing. Away with it.

My argument here is that they are asking for realistic female characters and calling it strength, or they are asking for female characters in starring roles, whose decisions are central to the plot, and calling it strength, because they don't know any other word for this quality.

Marx analyzed all human behavior as a contest of strength between oppressor and oppressed, and a certain hefty percentage of modern feminism adopted that analysis as the analysis of the man-woman dynamic, and so the only thing that matters to them is strength: the strength to do without men, to achieve without men, to overcome men, to despise men, to walk away from men. To be not dependent. Independence. There is no nobler goal, is there?

But the analysis overlooks the same thing in both cases. Marx overlooked that a situation of mutual benefit can be found when labor is free to seek employment and investors free to seek return on investment. The investors seeking profit will buy stock in ventures that hire laborers seeking to sell their labor for a wage. Marx characterizes this mutually beneficial relationship as a master-slave relationship, a one-way zero-sum game where the investors gain and gain and the laborers lose and lose. Likewise, modern feminism, or this branch of it, characterizes the male-female relationship as a master-slave relationship, a one-way zero-sum game where the males gain and gain and the females lose and lose.

And surely there is sufficient evil done by the greed of investors or the lusts of men to lend more than a little credence to either view.

The argument looks reasonable to anyone kept in a pitch of perfect anger and envy and resentment and hate and contempt against the other partner in the mutually beneficial relationship.

So the cult, to maintain the falsehood of the analysis, simply has to tell half the truth, paying attention only to cases where one partner betrays the other; or else has to tell outright lies.

Likewise the cult, in order to maintain the atmosphere of hysteria needed for the pitch of resentment to be maintained, has to devalue the use of reason. This is the reason why the cultists adopt what I call the unreality principle, the principle that make-believe is real and reality is optional. It is to halt the possibility of rational discourse. It allows them to tell outrageous lies without the slightest twinge of shame. This in turn is the reason why the cultists never argue: they only accuse. There is no groundwork to argue in a purely subjective world, because there is no evidence to consult, no objective rules of logic. Whatever seems to be a persuasive argument can be rejected unread based on the accusation that the person giving the argument, no matter who he is and what his argument is, is a wrong-thinking person, the source of all evil, a witch.

So likewise, the perfectly reasonable desire for better writing with more realistic female characters turns into a weird ritualistic demand to strengthen females in society by means of creating inspiring role models in Spaceman Spiff novels.

This would be fine except that the inspiring role model means and only means a female who repeats the bromides of Political Correctness.

Am I wrong? I would be delighted to hear about contrary examples. But here is what it looks like to me, given my limited experience. I have heard C.S. Lewis and J.R.R. Tolkien denounced, even though Queen Lucy, even as a little girl, had enough strength of character to stick to the truth and keep the faith despite the jeers and disbelief of her older siblings, in the first volume of *The Chronicles Of Narnia*, and despite that no one else, in the second volume, saw the Lion she saw. Is Galadriel of Lothlórien a weak character? In addition to being a queen, and immortal, and wise and far-seeing and morally upright, she has greater strength of character than the warrior-prince Boromir, *and* she has magic powers. So how is this weak?

I will repeat my examples from *A Princess Of Mars* of Burroughs and *Galactic Patrol* of E.E. Smith, books that are hardly on the Shakespeare level of great literature, but also books from before the Women's Liberation movement. Princesses get kidnapped with the clockwork regularity of potboiler writing on Barsoom, but not a single one of these dames faints, or screams, or complains, or shows anything but ironclad resolve worthy of a mother of a Spartan. I have already mentioned girls knifing guards who are too familiar and space-dames blasting away at drug-runners with their white-hot ray guns. Weak? In what sense?

Now, again, it may be my limited experience, but the only female characters I hear being complimented as strong by the Left are the ones in traditionally male roles, such as military officers, vampire hunters, and vigilantes.

I keep thinking there must be some common ground of characters that anyone can admire. Nausicaä of the Valley of the Wind, or Saint Joan of Arc, are ones I would assume would seem perfectly 'strong' to anyone seeking a strong female lead to admire.

Now, I do not mean to sound cynical, so I will ask rather than speak my opinion. Is there any strong woman character which meets with the approval of the Politically Correct who also happens, as the characters in Lewis and Tolkien, to reflect a Christian worldview, or, as happens in Burroughs or E.E. Smith, to reflect what one might call the traditional heroic worldview, a worldview reminiscent of the Stoic and military virtues of the ancient Romans and Greeks?

I have heard some Leftists praise the female characters of Robert Heinlein, who, with one exception, I myself find to be somewhat demeaning to women. (The one exception is Cynthia Randall in 'The Unpleasant Profession of Jonathan Hoag', perhaps the only honest portrayal of a woman throughout Heinlein's whole oeuvre.) Other Leftists, as I do, despise Heinlein's portrayal of women.

My cynical question is this: when they ask for 'strong' female characters, are they actually honestly asking for strong female characters, Deborah from the Bible, Antigone from myth, Britomart from poetry, or are they only asking for Leftist female characters, that is, for poster children for Leftist causes?

If so, what they are asking for is Political Correctness, which means substituting true narratives about the real glories and sorrows of the human condition for a false narrative, an advertisement for Leftwing political causes, which tell lies about the glories of man, bemoans with crocodile tears only the sorrows of their particular mascots and special causes, and makes false promises about the cure for the world's pain.

If so, they are giving up art for an ad.

Myself, I want to see women writers not because they are women, but because I would like to have the genius of the distaff half the human race writing new and brilliant science fiction stories for us to enjoy.

In sum, as far as I can tell, the complaint that Science Fiction lacks strong female characters is akin to the complaint that Science Fiction is meant for juvenile audiences. That has not been true during my lifetime. I have not seen even the slightest trace of the all-boy club mentality ever, neither in any writer nor in any editor nor in any reader.

I have seen plenty of people like me, who are annoyed with the cheerless preachy monotony of Political Correctness and would like the dullards to stop ruining good stories with their sucker punches and pauses for their political advertisements, but, hey, the PC types answer any criticism of PC by calling the complainer a sexist, or saying he is paranoid, or saying that PC does not exist. Any lie will do, just so long as it is an accusation.

To tell the truth about what they are doing, which is informal censorship, that is, thought policework, is the one thing they fear.

As I said before, the PC-niks think they are fooling us into thinking they are honest and compassionate people, and we know they are not, and they know they are not, but they do not know we know, so when one of us mentions, for the umpteenth time, that the Emperor has No Clothes, they react with exaggerated fear and fury. This is because they are afraid of anyone, no matter how humble or obscure, who punctures their little daydream of make-believe, their land of colored cloud where they are the effortless saints and the cost-free saviors of the world.

But the complaint about the way too many female characters are treated in SF, especially earlier SF, is either reasonable or is an understandable exaggeration of a reasonable complaint. No one wants nor likes boring or silly characters, or characters who rest on lazy stereotypes.

What is not reasonable is PC, for which the reasonable complaints ought not to be confused, any more than a sheep should be confused for a wolf in sheep's clothing.

Let there be no mistake about what I am objecting to. I am objecting to the idea that a woman has to give up being womanly in order to be a real man. I do not regard feminine nature to be the same as weakness or folly. I do not regard, as some feminists seem to regard, *masculinity* as synonymous with *strong*.

Myself, I would like to see strong characters of either sex doing things in stories. The very concept of heroism, of humans taking control of the forces around them and doing good, is fundamentally antithetical to the dull dispirited flaccid despair which is the natural moral atmosphere of nihilism and moral relativism, which just so happen to form the moral standard promoted by Political Correctness.

So in other words, even the female characters I here in this essay dismiss as being lame and PC, if they are truly heroines, actually undermine, whether knowingly or not, the PC worldview.

In other words, even these attempts by the PC to subvert the dominant paradigm, if they use the concepts of heroism, and show how virtues triumph and vices destroy themselves, they subvert the attempt at subversion.

So, go, Girl Power!

6. Strength in Women, Women in Drama

I gave this essay the provocative title "*Saving Science Fiction from Strong Female Characters*", but in it propose a rather unprovocative idea: namely, that woman can be both strong and feminine, and that one does not need to make them overtly masculine to make them admirable and edifying characters.

Indeed, I propose the idea that confusing strength with masculinity is in truth not a feminist ideal, but a misogynistic idea. He is no friend of woman who says women must act masculine to be equal to men, because that merely makes the word 'feminine' equal 'inferior'. Masculine and feminine are a complementary relationship, not a master-slave relationship. Is Ginger Rogers inferior to Fred Astaire when they waltz, even if he leads? She does all the same steps he does, and she does them backward, and, most impressive of all, Ginger can make goofy Fred look like a dashing figure of elegant romance.

I propose further that a brief, utterly unscientific survey of pre-1950s science fiction showed a healthy number of perfectly strong female characters even in the most boyish of boy's literature, for example, Jirel of Joiry or the Red Lensman Clarissa MacDougal or Dejah Thoris, (who, in the text, is both a scientist and a maiden who talks and acts like a Spartan were his wounds in his back? -style matron).

The same unscientific survey shows a rise of weaker female characters in the form of Playboy-bunny-styled bits of fluff in the 1960s and 1970s. I believe I was the only respondent to this survey, so the answers showed one hundred percent of respondents quizzed being in agreement.

I suggest it to be no coincidence that this was when Feminism was at its height, for it was a time when, thanks in part to modern labor saving appliances, housewives were no longer mistresses of a separate but equal sphere, a domestic realm where they were queen; but neither were they welcome in the workforce, which was mostly a man's world. It was a time when the returning servicemen, having survived the Four Horsemen of World War Two and the Great Depression, the Dustbowl and the Polio Epidemic, asked their women to be more feminine and domestic, and the women granted the prayer. It was also a time when the erosion of standards of decency made open immodesty in dress and behavior acceptable to the mainstream. It was the time of June Cleaver and Marilyn Monroe. It was the time of the dumb blonde, utterly unlike the sharp-witted and sharp-tongue blondes from the decade prior, Mae West or Jean Harlow. It was a time when feminism was most nearly justified in its claims.

Nonetheless it was a time when, in Science Fiction, even the writers who thought they were rebelling against the mainstream—Bob Heinlein springs to mind as an example—went along with the 1960's ideas of domestic women or Bunny women.

I would have no problem whatever with the feminist demand for more strong female characters in Science Fiction, and only a technical problem concerning the demand for strong female characters in Fantasy, if the demand were honest. (The technical problem is the difference in upper body strength between swordsmen and swordswomen). If the goalposts move, the demand is not honest, and the motive for the demand is not what it seems.

What would a strong female actually be like? I mean, if the demand were honest?

Here is an example from the pen of Robert E. Howard:

The woman on the horse reined in her weary steed. It stood with its legs wide-braced, its head drooping, as if it found even the weight of the gold-tasseled, red-leather bridle too heavy. The woman drew a booted foot out of the silver stirrup and swung down from the gilt-worked saddle. She made the reins fast to the fork of a sapling, and turned about, hands on her hips, to survey her surroundings.

They were not inviting. Giant trees hemmed in the small pool where her horse had just drunk. Clumps of undergrowth limited the vision that quested under the somber twilight of the lofty arches formed by intertwining branches. The woman shivered with a twitch of her magnificent shoulders, and then cursed.

She was tall, full-bosomed and large-limbed, with compact shoulders. Her whole figure reflected an unusual strength, without detracting from the femininity of her appearance. She was all woman, in spite of her bearing and her garments. The latter were incongruous, in view of her present environs. Instead of a skirt she wore short, wide-legged silk breeches, which ceased a hand's breadth short of her knees, and were upheld by a wide silken sash worn as a girdle. Flaring-topped boots of soft leather came almost to her knees, and a low-necked, wide-collared, wide-sleeved silk shirt completed her costume. On one shapely hip she wore a straight double-edged sword, and on the other a long dirk. Her unruly golden hair, cut square at her shoulders, was confined by a band of crimson satin.

...this was Valeria of the Red Brotherhood, whose deeds are celebrated in song and ballad wherever seafarers gather.

Now, from my admittedly plebian and pulpish taste in fiction, this is seems more like a fantasy meant for boys with a pirate-girl fetish than a description of the historical Anne Bonnie.

Be that as it may, Valeria is, by the express testimony of the text, both unusually strong yet feminine, and all woman, in spite of wearing breeches. Did I mention her hips were shapely, and her shoulders were magnificent? I suggest such characters were found periodically among the SF/F of the pulp era.

In other words, Valeria is the kind of strong women that boys like. Not actually strong, but a girl in revealing clothing with a sword in her hand, who requires a rough and manly man to tame her wild heart.

In other words, this allegedly strong character is still open to the accusation of being a weak character on the grounds that she still plays a feminine role in the story.

I submit that any female character can be accused of being a weak character, precisely because the goalposts move, that is, precisely because the demand for 'strength' in female characters is dishonest.

Nausicaä from Miyazaki's *Nausicaä Of The Valley Of The Wind* is a perfectly strong character who is brave, active, the center of the action, the main driver of the plot, nobody's fool, considerably higher in stature than a mere prize or reward for the hero to win. She is my exemplar of a strong female character who is not artificially masculine. She is a princess, and she issues commands and is obeyed in a perfectly queenly fashion, she owns a rocket powered jet glider called a cloud climber or a mehve, (depending on your translation), and she fires rocket-powered bullets, and is active, intelligent, athletic, and so on. But this is not the true genius of the character. The genius of the character is shown in a short scene in the beginning where, when her finger is bitten by a tiny wild animal no bigger than a kitten, instead of reacting with fear or annoyance, Nausicaä radiates a serenity that calms the creature, who, in remorse, begins where it just drew blood to lick the finger with its little pink tongue. This compassion and spiritual kinship with all living things, including the titanic and insectoid monsters of the all-destroying Toxic Jungle, is a spiritual strength in her that grows and grows in power as the story rolls toward what seems a tragic climax. In the final scene, it is not weapons, not even an ultimate weapon of destruction, that saves the day and changes the destiny of empires and kingdoms, but her self-sacrificing compassion on what to us at first would seem a hideous larva. But only at first. By the story's end, we see through her eyes.

I myself have never heard Nausicaä accused of being a weak character, but please note that the very thing which makes Buffy the Vampire Slayer allegedly a strong character, her physical strength and snarky attitude, are precisely the strength and the attitude missing from Nausicaä.

I once heard Mr. Joss Whedon in an interview discussing the origin of the character idea. He was weary of seeing scenes in monster movies where the blonde cheerleader Valley Girl wanders into a dark alley, is confronted by a vampire, and can do nothing. For reasons I cannot speculate, Mr. Whedon. Whedon did not think of making a Valley Girl carry a pistol whereby to defend herself, (even an undead monster can be chopped off at the knees if your handgun has sufficient stopping power), but instead thought it would be a cute reversal of traditional roles if the cheerleader could take out a stake and drive it through the vampire's heart. That way she is not the helpless victim. That way she does not need a man.

Then Mr. Whedon writes a simply excellent show, truly one of my favorites—let no man dare to say I am not a fanboy of that show—but I notice with the slightest lift of an eyebrow that the main dramatic tension in the show is the romance, the girl's love interest, Angel and Riley Finn and Spike. The traditional role is not reversed after all, is it?

Buffy must be saluted. She is the inspiration for an entire genre of fiction, the urban fantasy. Few characters can make that claim: Sherlock Holmes for detective stories, Juan Rico the starship trooper for Military SF, Harry Potter for the magical schoolkid genre, Frodo and his Fellowship of the Ring for the epic quest genre. And perhaps a few others. But considering that Buffy is the very epitome, or so I assume, of strength in a strong female character, a feminist icon akin to Xena the Warrior Princess, why is her main dramatic point her love story? Could it be because she is a female character, and that there is something in the female genius which naturally inclines itself to love?

By way of contrast, I would list Katniss Everdeen from the movie *The Hunger Games* as a relatively weak character —and here I am only talking about the movie, which I saw, and not the book, which I did not read. Aside from her extraordinary act of self-sacrifice at the beginning of the film, for the rest of the film she is basically helpless, and shows very little initiative. Whether the character develops in the sequels, that I do not know, and about that I make no comment. She is, however, physically and morally brave, which is not a trait to be scoffed at for anyone living in a nation of physical and moral cowards.

Something unclear in the movie is how any girl survives the first ten minutes of combat with relatively athletic young men of roughly the same age: the difference in aggression and fighting strength in an average sixteen-year old boy and an average sixteen-year old girl is immense. That is why the Romans did not stage gladiator fights between male and female slaves, or, if they did, we have no record of it. That is why boxing is not a unisex sport.

Katniss Everdeen is what I would call weak because she cannot articulate the cause for which she fights. She is not fighting for truth, justice, and the American Way, nor is she leading—yet—the rebellion; she is trying to stay alive. Oddly, had she been the only girl in a roster of boys, volunteering to take the place of her younger brother, the plot would have made more sense, because then it would have been a Jack-and-the-Giant story, with Katniss as Jack.

Weaker still is the character of Valeria mentioned above. She is the stuff of boyish daydreams, not a fully developed character at all. While established to be a ruthless, rough and hardy pirate queen, the equal of any man when it comes to climbing rigging, storming a city wall, or cutting down sea dogs in a sea fight, her role in the story is entirely feminine. Her main role in the story is for romantic interest and sex appeal. She is there to be menaced by the lusts of men, including Conan, to make dumb suggestions Conan wryly shoots down, and to be afraid of things that don't scare Conan, because, as a barbarian, he is such a badass. For all that, she is not a weak character, not a milksop or lily-livered, and is strong and hearty and bold as any soldier. It is just that, next to Conan, any soldier would seem like a girl.

Podkayne of Mars from *Podkayne Of Mars* is a spunky and lovable teenager who dreams of being a space pilot. As the plot goes on, however, she takes no steps at all, not one, toward achieving this dream. Instead she gets abducted, saved by her brother, and then blown up by a bomb when going back into the villain's lair for the cat or some other annoying fluffy critter. In the first draft, she died the death, and in the second, at the editor's insisting, she was merely mostly dead. This teaches her psychotic supergenius younger brother to learn to love and be loved, or some such nonsense. And the moral of the story, placed in the mouth of the Uncle, tacked awkwardly onto the end of the book is that Podkayne's Mom should have stayed home and raised her correctly.

Podkayne is a perfectly fine science fiction character. She does as much, or as little, as the Time Traveler from *The Time Machine* by Wells, or Professor Aronnax from *Twenty Thousand Leagues Under The Sea*. More to the point, she does as much, or as little, as Matt Dodson in *Space Cadet* or Bill Lermer from *Farmer In The Sky*, who are mostly observers rather than initiators of the action. But the fact that the space girl is blown up and never becomes either a space cadet like Matt nor a farmer owning his own land like Lermer should leave any feminist cold. Is the purpose in life of girls to be blowed up by bombs as an object lesson to psychotic younger brothers so they can learn to love and be loved?

Jill Boardman in *Stranger In A Strange Bed*, buxom space nurse, becomes the lover and disciple of Michael Valentine Smith, the studly Man from Mars, and happily joins his harem of several lovers... and becomes a stripper. Yes, she takes off her clothing to excite the lusts of men for modest pay. They can stare at her boobs, which she bounces for their enjoyment. Such is the 1960's version of women's liberation. You've come a long way, baby.

The novel portrays this gross degradation as a dignified profession, whereas preaching the Gospel is portrayed as charlatanry less honest than selling used cars. Yet, had you asked, I am certain Mr. Heinlein would have described himself as an ardent supporter of women's liberation.

Compared to this junk, Valeria the Pirate Queen with the shapely hips is practically as nuanced and three-dimensional a character as Lady Macbeth. But could someone claim, with perfect justice, that Jill is a strong character? She is certainly witty, as brave as a Marine, and she kidnaps the Man from Mars out from the clutches of the tyrannous world-state. Could someone else claim she was a weak character? Yes, and with equal justice, if not more so. She is a lonely schoolboy's idea of a strong and independent woman, that is, a woman with all the virtues but chastity and modesty, independent enough to use contraception, and strong enough to violate the rules of chastity, presumably, in his daydreams, with the lonely schoolboy.

I should add the third example of Friday from her eponymous book, but there is too much about that book and that character I find personally distasteful. Let me just say that she combines the worst characteristics of physical strength—she can beat up a Marine guard—Playboy bunny looks, an odd desire both to marry and have a family, and to sleep around like a minx in heat.

If you have not read *Friday*, you can always watch *Dark Angel* by James Cameron. The main character, Max, is a personal favorite of mine. Let no one believe I dismiss or dislike the show. But I do note that she is a Friday-style woman: sexy and adorable, and she goes into heat, so that she can both beat up Marine guards with her biogenetically enhanced superhuman strength, and sleep around. You've come a long way, baby. The writers there perform the opposite trick as Robert E. Howard. To make the girl Max the manly character, James Cameron puts the male lead in a wheelchair, so that he has no possibility of being either the main romantic interest nor being the Riley Finn or Steve Trevor character.

(By a Riley Finn, I mean simply that a writer who makes his alleged strong female character physically strong, strong in masculine ways, the writer has no use for a male romantic lead, unless he is a superhuman, such as Conan or Angel. Riley Finn was despised by the fans for much the same reason that Steve Trevor is forgotten.)

No writer can write a man who swoons over the strength of a superheroine or vampire-huntress, admires her knowledge of French wines and Japanese karate, and find himself swept off his feet by her, carried back to her magnificent castle, married in a splendid but secret ceremony, ravished to within an inch of his life, and make it seem other than a satire. No writer has this power because that is not the way human nature works.

How does nature work? Women like men who are virile, vigorous and potent. They like men who are confident, decisive, courageous, and assertive. They want a man who fights. They like strong men. Look at the cover of a trashy romance novel if you don't believe me.

More truth is held in the pages of trashy romance novels than in all the worthless books penned by college professors.

Men like women who are nubile, fertile and fecund. They want a girl worth fighting for. They want beauty in body but loyalty in spirit. They want a woman who has faith in him and who keeps faith with him.

Why does nature saddle us with these, (to a feminist), uncouth and inconvenient urges where different things attract the different sexes to each other?

It is one of the dubious joys of the modern age that otherwise sober men must take the time to explain the obvious, over and over again, to those ideologically committed to denying the obvious.

It is obvious that men and women are different both in fine and in gross.

(I read with some skeptical bitterness that when neurologists first started publicly admitting that there were neurochemical differences in brain structure between males and females, Gloria Steinem said that social conditioning could overcome these innate genetic predilections. I understand that the Left also says that homosexual attraction is caused by innate genetic predilections, but that to use any form of social conditioning to overcome such predilections is illegal in California. Consistency is not the strong suit of the Left.)

Because of these differences between the sexes, the characteristics of sexual attraction in men and women must be opposite and complementary in order for it to be sexual attraction.

Do I need to repeat that in shorter words for the intellectuals to grasp it?

Girls want strong men because strength in men, brute muscle power and leadership ability, is a primary sexual distinguishing characteristic related to the sexual process. Boys want faithful women because fidelity in women is a primary sexual distinguishing characteristic related to domestic life and the demands of domestic life.

But a writer writing an adventure story or a drama that wants to challenge or ignore the basic difference between what men and women find attractive in each other faces a paradox. How is he to make it dramatic?

Now, keep in mind that men and women can admire each other for non-sexual reasons. I am a great admirer of Margaret Thatcher, for example, or Mother Theresa, who are both world-magnitude leaders, one of political and the other of spiritual authority. Any tinge of sexual attraction toward these women from me would be grotesque.

But in a story, especially in an adventure story, the needs of drama want to introduce an element of romance even if the writers at first do not want one there. Romance is as dramatic as death, or more so. It is nearly impossible to keep out of storytelling, despite brave efforts by H.G. Wells and Jules Verne. Brave but futile.

Note that every later retelling or movie version of any of their tales always introduces a love interest. The movie version of *First Men In The Moon* introduced a female stowaway, played by sweater girl Martha Hyer. The movie version of *Journey To The Center Of The Earth* has the junoesque Arlene Dahl, likewise. The movie version of *Clipper Of The Clouds*, which was named for its sequel, *Master Of The World* has the adorable Mary Webster, likewise.

Examples could be multiplied endlessly. I think only *Twenty Thousand Leagues Under The Sea* by Disney did not intrude an apocryphal female love interest. Hence my conclusion is that if there is no love interest at first, the pressure of the needs of drama always urges one be introduced later, in any sequel or retelling.

If I may use an example from a cartoon, just to dispel anyone's idea that I have refined tastes in the matter: I am a great fan of Disney's *Kim Possible*. I love that show. Every element is perfect. Teen superheroine Kim Possible is the daughter of a rocket scientist and a brain surgeon. On her website she boasts that she can do anything, and so instead of getting the babysitting or yard working jobs she supposed, foreign governments and major corporations hire her to solve crimes, stop revolutions, and track down supervillains. The show's supervisors told the writers that, as a Disney show, they needs must put in a cute pet sidekick like the raccoon of Pocahontas or the flounder of Ariel, and the writers subverted the paradigm by introducing a naked mole rat. Who is also a super genius. Kim Possible's comic relief sidekick and Sancho Panza is named Ron Stoppable.

Unfortunately, the needs of drama interfered with this perfect balance of elements in the last season, when some nitwit decided that Kim Possible should fall in love, not with the handsome and competent Will Du, agent of Global Justice, nor with Josh Mankey, the boy on whom she has a legitimate crush, but with Ron, her sidekick. (Who, by the way, was in love with and loved by the alluring and exotic high school ninja-girl and exchange student, Yori).

It is unsettling and stupid, as stupid as deciding that the alluring and snarktastic supervillainess Shego would go for her freaky blue supervillain boss Dr. Drakken rather than for the rich and handsome and stump-stupid but devotedly romantic Sr. Senior, Jr.

It nearly ruined the show to pair the heroine with the comic relief, because the needs of drama require that the romantic male lead save the girl to win the girl, something the comic relief cannot do. Otherwise no one can tell why the girl likes the guy. He must appear virile and vigorous and potent, remember? But the fans complained, not without some justice, in the last episode of the last season when Ron saves the day and saves a suddenly helpless Kim Possible when in every previous episode she was able to do everything whereas he was the ineffectual sidekick whose comedic antics involved running in circles with his pants on fire, screaming.

But the writers almost had no choice. Romance is innately dramatic because the whole life and future happiness of the characters hangs in the balance, and it is something everyone in the audience over the age of seven can understand and sympathize with. The romantic lead has to be a superior guy. If he is of lower social rank than the girl, or less wealthy, he has to be higher in some other quality that she needs more, even if it is only pluck or impudent daring, (cf. Jasmine falling for Aladdin).

This means that superheroes can fall in love with normal muggle women, as when Kal-El of Krypton falls for Lois Lane, but that Supergirl cannot fall in love with Dick Malverine but needs a superhero to be her beau, like Querl Dox or Dick Grayson. And Wonder Woman should definitely dump Steve Trevor for Bruce Wayne.

(If you asked who Dick Malverine is, he is the utterly forgettable male equivalent of Lois Lane or Lana Lang who was always trying to prove that Linda Lee was Supergirl. The dynamic of the plot tension there should have been the same, but since the sexes were switched, it did not work. In real life, there is some drama to a woman trying to find out a man's secret, especially if she has marital designs on him. It does not work the other way around, the drama is lost, and the guy looks weak and foolish.)

Does that seem unfair? The story logic requires that if a superheroine falls for a guy, he has to be virile and potent in relation to her, in some way her superior, so that she has something she thinks is sexy to admire and adore; and likewise she, even if she is physically stronger and shows directness and leadership and cooks outdoors and has great clumps of underarm hair and in every way is masculine and manly, she has to be shown as devoted, because fidelity is what sexually attracts men to women.

The old cliché of rescuing a damsel in distress is based on the idea that a woman rescued from danger by a man will be devoted to him, because ingratitude in such life or death situations is unthinkable, particularly for an admirable female lead.

Again, the logic of Political Correctness requires that

men and women not be complementary because the
concept of complementary strengths and weakness is not a
concept that Political Correctness can admit, lest it be
destroyed. The concept of complementary virtues undermines the concept of envy, and Political Correctness is
nothing but politicized fury based on politicized envy. We
can define Political Correctness as the attempt to express
fury and envy via radical changes to legal and social institutions.

Hence, the Politically Correct writer attempting to make
the female 'strong' cannot make her strong in the particular
feminine way of, for example, Nausicaä, because that would
be the same as admitting that there is a particular nature of
male and female, which are different and complementary,
which, as I said above, undermines the envy-fury on which
Political Correctness is based.

So the logic of Political Correctness directly defies the
logic of drama. The more you have of one, the less you have
of the other.

The more Political Correctness you have, the less
Science Fiction you have, because Politically Correct science
is Junk Science.

Political Correctness requires the women not to be of
complementary strength to men, that is, not strong in a
feminine way, because that would legitimize femininity.
Remember, feminism is the foe of femininity, hence of love
and romance.

Instead, Political Correctness requires the female to be
as strong as a man, as good as a man, in the very areas men
are good at and want to be good at. It is a deliberately unnatural pose. The women characters have to be portrayed as
the types of character female readers, by and large, do not
want to be like nor to read about, and the female characters

have to do things women by and large do not attempt because they don't create a big thrill in the feminine heart, or create many bragging rights. The male characters are basically extraneous.

Can it be done? Sure. Writers are endlessly inventive, and we get to set the situation and the plot and, in science fiction, we get to set the laws of nature, too. So the basic physical limitations of the female physique in real life need not hinder us in science fiction situations, because your heroine can be from Krypton, or armed with a phaser weapon, or have cat-girl genes spliced into her DNA, or be an Amazon. Second, the writer gets to set the period and the genre. No one can claim that Hermione Granger is in any way a second-class citizen of Hogwarts, because, like a detective in a detective novel, physical strength and fighting prowess are not the main point of a magical school-chums novel.

Third, if your superheroine is stronger than any normal man, and does not need Prince Charming to settle the hash of the evil dragon, but can wield the sword herself, you can either leave out your male love interest, or you can, Anita Blake style, make him superhuman also. This, of course, is a sly cheat, because it puts the girl back in the position of being allured to a dangerous male figure who is more powerful than she, so your vampire huntress falling for a fallen angel, (or whatever), is in the same dainty shoes as the spitfire Irish lass kidnapped by the ruthless but devilishly handsome pirate Black Jamie, (or whoever), which we all see in the Bodice Ripper racks at the paperback bookstore.

Paranormal Romance, in other words, is an example of the logic of drama subverting, (or perhaps superverting), the logic of Political Correctness. It allows the writer to eat her cake and have it too: she can make her warrior-princess or vampire huntress as tough and strong in any way she likes, as tough as Scarlet O'Hara vowing as God is her witness never to go hungry again, and then also bring in a supernatural version of Rhett Butler, and she can retell the story of Beauty and the Beast while retelling *Gone With The Wind*, and make her man a human being. (Since young men are often ill-reared these days, this is not as far from real life as it once was.)

Another solution is to make the warrior woman into a sex babe, so that if she is not feminine and attractive in demeanor and words, her luscious body betrays her, especially if she is wearing a halter top and spray-on leather pants. This approach turns the strong female character into a figure of sexual fetish, and it titillates the boy audience while apparently satisfying the female audience looking for an action heroine who does not need a man to kill her vampires for her.

The problem with such characters is that the logic of Political Correctness has been subverted by the needs of drama at the expense of all realism. You end up with scenes like I mentioned in a previous essay, with a hulking huge Hawkeye of the Avengers kicking wispy little sexdoll Black Widow in the face, and both boys and girls get used to the idea that boys kicking girls in the face is normal, and, just as bad, both boys and girls get used to the idea that the only way for a girl to be attractive is to dress like the Catwoman. That is fine if you have a perfect hourglass figure like a 1950s cheesecake model, but otherwise it basically robs women of an entire arsenal of feminine wiles to use on the menfolk, and silences an entire social vocabulary of unspoken signs of feminine dignity.

You also end up with warrior women who should be

armed and armored like Joan of Arc dressed in microbikinis that would embarrass a stripper.

And any feminist worth her salt should be able to accuse, with much justice, the fetishistic ninja-babe super-heroine archetype as being a weak female character. Such characters are nothing more than action models, eye candy, male fantasy figures.

And all of these characters can be accused of being weak, for the reasons I said at considerable length above. And if the character has no weaknesses, she can be accused of being a Mary Sue.

Why is this? Because, at first, the cry for strong female characters is perfectly reasonable and perfectly welcome.

To use another example which betrays my low taste, in the second season or so of *Naruto*, our feisty pink-haired girl-ninja Sakura is left with nothing to do. She simply cannot fight as well as the boys, and the writers had her not do anything, despite that she was the third member of Team Love Triangle. (So called because Naruto the brash main character in love with her, and Sasuke with whom she is in love. For the life of me, I cannot figure out why she is crushing on Sasuke. He is merely dark and handsome with a troubled past, tormented by inner demons, a dashing rebel who plays by his own rules. Go figure.) But the feisty pink-haired girl-ninja was useless until the writers wised up and powered her up in the next season, giving her not only magic healing powers, but magic super strength, which make a nice outward sign of her inner exasperation, so she could create an earthquake with her magic ninja punch.

It gave her something to do in the plot, unlike Dorothy Prudent and Carla Göteborg, the characters added to the film versions of *Master Of The World* and *Journey To The Center Of The Earth*, which intruded a romantic subplot where none was needed nor wanted, and the female characters there had nothing to do. They initiated no action and solved no problems.

If that is what those who cry for stronger female characters want, more power to them, and I add my voice to theirs.

Penelope of Ithaca and Clytemnestra of Mycenae and Helen of Troy are not insignificant characters with nothing to do, nor is Deborah in the Book of Judges. Nor is Ximena from El Cid. Neither is Guinevere of Camelot, even if she never fights a joust while disguised as a boy. Neither is Olivia from *Twelfth Night*, even if she does fight a duel while disguised as a boy. Neither is Bradamante of *Orlando Furioso* or Britomart of *The Faerie Queene* even if she fights jousts and duels while not disguised at all. There are plenty of examples from ancient and classical sources to follow. I cheer on such efforts.

But look again. If I am cheering on such efforts, why am I getting hate mail from Political Correctors, along with anyone else who says what I say?

Because Penelope and Clytemnestra and Helen and Deborah and Guinevere are all romantic figures. Ximena is perhaps the most romantic of all, a woman of noble birth who loves and loses all because she loves the Cid, but loves honor more.

While many a feminist still admires them, I have heard the Martial Maids dismissed because they are depicted as outliers, that is, extraordinary because a woman is performing feats of arms which would be ordinary if done by a man. I do not know if this is a mainstream criticism or not, but it strikes me as telling.

The call for strong female characters is like the call for more environmental purity and cleanliness. In the 1950s, (ironically, the same period, thanks to the growth of mass media, when women were being treated in a less dignified way than their mothers), there was pollution in the air and in the streams that formed a danger to public health. Some reasonable laws were made to curb the problem, and the problem was solved except in areas of the country administered by Democrats, and then unreasonable laws were made, and then slightly insane laws, and now we live under totally nutastic barking-mad at the moon bat-guano crazy laws, which have declared human exhalation and cow farts to be pollutants.

It was reasonable at first. The demand was satisfied. There are now plenty of female characters in books and films these days, many of them quite well written.

And then the demands became unreasonable, then became slightly insane, and are rapidly becoming barking mad. Why is this?

Because the demands are not honestly made. They are made for the sake of making a demand, not made for the sake of satisfying a demand.

Any female character can be accused of being weak. ANY ONE. The trick is to have your female characters be good characters, having central roles in the plot, and reasonable character arcs, and as many vices and virtues as the logic of drama and your inner burning vision demand.

Ignore whether she is strong or weak. It is like worrying about whether your male character is winsome, devoted and loves babies. He needs a reasonable amount of devotion to be a hero, but it cannot be his main point, because in real life girls look for strength in men first, leadership, trustworthiness, that sort of thing. Even shallow women look for outward signs of competence and strength, like fancy cars and smoothness of wit.

Likewise, strength in female characters is not what

makes them dramatic and memorable, but fidelity and compassion do.

What makes Scarlett O'Hara one of the most easily recognized heroines of all time, despite the obvious selfishness and shallowness of the character? It is her fidelity, no, not to a man, (she weds idly and yearns for Ashley), but to Tara, the land. Her faith in the land allows her to survive the War and the Reconstruction.

Scarlett, despite being selfish and shallow, shines with these other virtues. Commitment. Fidelity. Faithfulness. Maintaining hope when hope is gone. Having the strength to carry on.

That is something women do better than men. We males tend to break when our brittle pride is shattered. Women handle disappointment and defeat better. (Consider what a disappointment most men are, I am sure there is a logic to that, too.)

So ignore the demands for strong female characters. You cannot satisfy them.

You can satisfy your readers, though, by making your heroine interesting. Nay, make her fascinating.

Make your heroine as fascinating as Miyazaki's Nausicaä, or Homer's; or Dante's Beatrice, or as fascinating as Deborah, Clytemnestra, Helen, Penelope, Camilla, Britomart, Bradamante, and you will have readers for centuries to come, or millennia, still discussing her; or make her as interesting as Katniss or Hermione or Scarlett O'Hara, and you will be a bestseller and have your books made into movies.

A closing note on hate mail. I said I would return to this point.

Why in the world would anyone in his right mind pen a poisonous letter on this topic? I am not trying to Save Science Fiction from Strong Female Characters. The idea is ridiculous, so ridiculous that I honestly thought nobody, not even a humorless Political Correction Officer would take it seriously. The title is meant as an obvious joke.

It is as if I were to say we should stop having Basque Characters, or Albigensians, or Left-handed Wesleyans. No matter what I or anyone said about the type of characters I or anyone preferred, *if the demand were honest*, no one would give a tinker's damn about it one way or another.

No one would give a tinker's damn because readers who wanted character of a certain type would seek out writers who wrote characters of that type, and readers who wanted something else would seek out writers writing something else.

But the demand is not honest. It is not even close. The demand is that female characters of which some tone-deaf artistically and spiritually dead sexual neurotics disapprove be swept off the bookshelves and into the memory hole. The demand is political, that is, it is a call for a uniform change in the power relations of the society. The demand is that society change its tastes, change its values, and do so collectively, as a unit, permitting no dissent.

The demand is not on we writers, my dear readers, but on you readers.

The demand made by these subhuman genetically defective control freaks is that YOU the readers, stop liking the books and stories you like, books with females realistic or unrealistic as you prefer, and start liking the books and stories which these genetically defective control freaks demand you should like, in the name of the glorious cause of whatever the glorious cause is this week.

The demand is that you be ashamed of liking popular books and stories, that you be ashamed of nature, ashamed of romance, ashamed of love stories, ashamed of superhero stories, and so on, *ad nauseam*.

You see, you and I and every sane human is willing to live and let live, and if you want to read trashy bodice rippers and I want to read about space princesses while our neighbor wants to read stories about he-men wrestling ponds of flesh-eating weasels, to each his own. If I write the story I want to write, and even put the odd space princess in it, either the story on its own artistic merits or entertainment value, if any, finds a fit audience or not, as the sovereign will of the readership demands, without imposing on or being imposed upon by others who write and read stories of another kind.

You must understand that you, O my masters, are the sovereigns here. What the readers read is what the writers write and the booksellers sell.

The rebels and the subversives of the Glorious Cause of Political Correctness are not about overthrowing the sovereign power of the state, or not just about that. It is also about overthrowing the sovereign power of the culture, O my masters.

They want to overthrow *YOU*.

They have only one weapon, which is the unearned moral superiority they pretend to have, and the unearned guilt which they throw onto you.

The serpent cannot force the apple down Eve's fair throat. All he can do is make her feel ashamed for being so naive as to obey the commands of right reason. The snake tells her she is stupid for thinking that right reason was right.

Likewise, here, the harpies shriek that you are stupid for wanting to read a story where Rhett carries a struggling

Scarlett up to the nuptial bedroom, rather than Scarlett carrying Rhett.

Unearned moral superiority for them. Unearned guilt for you. That is their only weapon. Merely pointing it out, naming it by its right name, is enough to disarm it.

Science fiction does not need to be saved from strong female characters. It needs to be saved from Political Correctness, which makes a demand that all stories be uniform, and all serve the Glorious Cause, and become propaganda told for the purpose of social engineering, not stories told to glorify the beauties and horrors of life.

It is, in fact, a demand that stories not be stories at all.

It is a demand that we wreck our culture, ruin our lives, and damn our souls. Stories are just the smallest part of it, and science fiction stories are smaller than that. Stories save souls, and give strength to sanity, for tales, even the simplest, even the shallowest, can refresh our faith in truth, in beauty, and in virtue. In stories, the muses bring us wine from heaven.

Political Correctness serves politics, that is, the power struggle between factions seeking to govern our laws and customs. Art serves truth. Do you wonder at the venom of the struggle? Political Correction Officers attempt to mock and destroy even the concept of truth. Political Correctness is the foe of all truth, all beauty, all virtue. Their ambition is immense, nay, awe-inspiring: They want to drown the universe in excrement.

The sole weapon of the Political Correction Officers is to make the innocent feel guilty by making a reasonable demand followed by an unreasonable demand, a demand you can never satisfy.

We must save the world, and, more importantly, science fiction from that.

From the Pen of Tom Simon:

The whole point of Political Correctness is that it's impossible to be politically correct: someone always has a free pass to attack you for something. Just as the whole point of Sustainability is that nothing is ever really sustainable, so someone can always attack you for insufficient dedication to Mother Gaia. Modern Leftism is not about doing what is right; it is about believing that everybody else is wrong, and always having a stick handy to beat anyone you want to beat.

16

RESTLESS HEART OF DARKNESS

I had an insight recently, one of those Archimedes-sloshes-the-bath moments where a great mass of otherwise disorganized observations and rules of thumb suddenly fell into a pattern as neat as a periodic table. It is no doubt something many thinkers have seen and discussed erenow, but this was the first time I saw it, and to me it was as new as a young man's first infatuation, as new as spring.

The insight occurred during three discussions with fellow writers for whom I have enormous respect, but whose ideas I condemn as misleading, deceptive, even poisonous. (If you wonder how one can respect a man whose ideas you loathe, imagine being a mother whose child grows up to be a drug addict, or a sexual pervert, or demon-possessed. The greater her love for the child, the deeper her hatred of the addiction, perversion, or possession enslaving him.)

At the risk of giving away the surprise ending, (which, honestly, I suppose is not a surprise to anyone but me), I realized why it is that the current mainstream modern thought, despite its illogical and pointless nature, is so persistent, nay, so desperate.

I realized why these Moderns never admit they are wrong no matter how obvious the error, nor can they compromise, nor hold a rational discussion, nor a polite one, nor can they restrain themselves. They can neither win nor surrender.

I realized why their hearts were so restless. It is obvious once one sees it.

No doubt I should explain first why this was such a puzzle to me.

The Nameless Darkness

There is a certain darkness slowly absorbing ever more of the intellectual life of the West which seeks, for various reasons, to remove the common morality of mankind from our souls, to deaden normal and natural emotions and passions, to break up the family, to abolish honest and human sentiments, patriotism and gratitude among them, to abolish a belief in objective truth, to abolish love of beauty, to abolish all passion for virtue, to kill God, and, in sum, to abolish everything that makes us truly human.

By mainstream modern thought, I mean that unnamed general tendency which, in politics, is totalitarian; in economics, socialist; in morals, libertine, decadent and perverted. In art, this nameless drift of modern thought adores ugliness and distortion; and favors aborticide and euthanasia and holds human choice to be absolutely sacrosanct, but not human life; in epistemology, the drift of modern thought is mystical.

Modern thought oddly claims to be scientific and to rely

on the certainty of empiricism, but in fact takes everything on authority, and on anonymous authority at that.

Anonymous means no modern man would dream of discovering the qualifications of the members of the U.N. panel on climate change, nor has modern man any impulse to question the findings of bribed bureaucrats or political appointees drawing conclusions about the relative dangers of DDT. The modern man is ironically proud of skepticism, but has no ability to question the authority of experts utterly nameless, utterly faceless, utterly immune from question or contradiction. The Middle Ages, taking on faith some dogma decided at the Council of Ephesus, would know the name of the defenders of the faith, and the heretics had their names affixed to their beliefs; and the dogmas were all carefully written down, not merely a drift of opinion.

In ontology, the modern drift is subjectivist; in language, moderns are nominalists and magicians, believing words have the power to mold thought and perhaps change reality; in metaphysics, moderns are materialists.

Obviously these various principles contradict each other, (one cannot be a materialist and a nominalist, for example), but modern thought takes no account one way or the other about logic.

Obviously again, no one person could consistently believe these various principles, or live up to, (or down to), the vices these principles demand. Ergo the partisans of this nameless modern drift are hypocrites because their world-view makes hypocrisy inevitable; they accuse others of being hypocrites since accusation is their sole weapon and sole defense.

Being without a sense of the objective nature of reality, they are without a belief in objective morals. Being without a belief in objective morals, they lack honor, and, lacking honor, they lack courage, lack decency, lack courtesy.

Hence, their one, sole and only means of discussing their principles in debate is to accuse whomever dares question them of any and every thing they think evil: they call normal people stupid and evil and heartless, bigoted and racist and fascist and thisist and thatist.

The content of the accusation does not matter, only the relief of being able to accuse, and accuse, and accuse.

Their only consistent principle—a principle never admitted, of course, but obvious in their every manifesto—is the Unreality Principle, which holds that it is better and braver to believe in make-believe than in genuine reality. The more unreal the belief, the less based on fact, the more open the self-contradiction, the greater the power of will and nobility of spirit needed to believe it, and hence the greatest applause from the modern mind is reserved to those of their number that believe the most unreal and unrealistic things. And yet, with typical unselfaware modern irony, they call themselves the reality-based community.

In sum, their philosophy consists of the single principle that no philosophy is valid. Their ethics consist of a single precept that making ethical judgments is 'judgmental' that is, ethically wrong. Their economic theory, socialism, consists of an arrogant denial that the laws of economics apply to economic phenomena. Their theory of psychology says that men do not have free will, because cause and effect is absolute; their theory of metaphysics is that subatomic particles do have free will, because cause and effect is statistical, approximate, uncertain, incomplete, and illusory. And on and on. All their thought is one self-refuting statement after another.

Philosophically, theologically and morally, the modern

mindset is an end-state. Once a man has utterly rejected reason, he cannot reason himself to another conclusion. Once he has rejected morality, he has no sense of honor to compel him to live up to a philosophy more demanding than narrow selfishness.

Again, once he has rejected the authority of tradition, so that his one precept is to ignore all precepts of his teachers, he has no motive and no way to pass along to the next generation this selfsame precept, for he then is himself a teacher teaching them to ignore all teachers. And so on.

It must eventually destroy itself. It will contracept and abort its children out of existence, if nothing else.

Naming The Nameless

This movement goes by many names, all of them misleading. Any name that ceases to mislead is dropped, and another misleading name adopted, so no name is permanent. Liberal they call themselves, albeit they diminish liberty, and Progressive they call themselves, but they retard or reverse progress. Political Correctness is the least misleading of the names, and hence the one least likely to be used or admitted. They call themselves Freethinkers, but they think like slaves.

Technically, they are a variant of a heresy called Gnosticism, that is, a deviation or corruption of Christian thought which holds that superior secret knowledge, not faith, is sufficient for salvation. They retain enough of Christian thought, such as compassion for the poor, or a belief in equality in the eyes of God, to appeal to the hearts of the gullible (for even the most gullible is not moved by merely an appeal to self-centeredness) but they reject the sovereignty of God, or even the existence of God, and most reject the significance of any spiritual dimension to reality, or reject the existence of the spirit. The parallels to Gnosticism are many, but the most obvious is the principle of rebellion against every aspect of the world-system. To the ancient Gnostic, this meant rebellion against the Demiurge or world-creator; to the modern Gnostic it means rebellion against the establishment, the social order, the civilization, all rules and all customs. There is some promise of a Pleroma in ancient Gnosticism to justify the destruction of the current world; likewise, there is some vague hint of a promise of a utopia, or at least an improvement, to justify the destruction brought by protests, riots, convulsions and radical transformations of all long-standing law and custom.

What they actually are is blind souls lost in a fog of hazy ideas and soggy sentimentality and howlingly angry self-righteousness with no logic and no fixed purpose, but one fixed enemy that they likewise never name. His name is Christ.

For the purpose of this essay, I will interchangeably call them 'Progressives' or 'Abolishers of Man'.

The Four Worlds

The so-called progress of the Progressives at first seems in the direction of greater liberty. In truth, it is the progress of corruption, and does not follow any particular order or pattern.

There are four stages of corruption, each one an over-reaction to the stage before, but no one man passes from one to the next to the next in a simple or predictable order. The ship of each man's soul sails whereso his restless thought blows; but we can define the ports where restless thoughts find harbor.

These are not even schools of thought, but families of schools of thought, each with countless variations. Each should be thought of as a world, a complete explanation of every basic question of life, a worldview to which a man can devote himself for a lifetime. But none are entirely satisfying, for reasons that will become clear. I describe them below in roughly the order they appeared in history.

The first stage is Worldliness. This is the legacy of the Enlightenment thinkers like Rousseau and Voltaire and Thomas Paine. The Worldly Man diminishes the importance of the Church, seeks disestablishment, and promises that all men of any denomination will be able to live together in peace provided all religious activity is a matter of private conscience rather than public organization. Why this promise was kept in the United States after their revolution but broken in France after hers is a discussion too deep to breach here. Without the guidance of the Church, the denominations fragment into ever smaller groups, and eventually lose the ability to guide public policy. Again, this did not happen until my generation in America, but it happened a generation earlier in Europe.

Capitalism and political liberty become the agreed-upon highest principles of the social order: each man is secure in his rights, especially property rights, if he respects the rights of others: thrift, industry, honesty in dealings, reliability, productivity, and so on replace the ancient virtues of faith, hope and charity in the limelight of public imagination. Most Worldly Men are deeply religious in private life; indeed, worldliness cannot long endure without a solid foundation of Christian tradition to feed and sustain it. In the last few years in America, the foundation is exhausted, and the public routinely condemns Christianity as vile, and denounces all faithful Christians as bigots. See the recent debacles concerning Chick-fil-A, Duck Dynasty, Orson Scott Card, and Mel Gibson's *The Passion Of The Christ*.

The second stage is Ideology. Man's soul cannot long endure without a superhuman purpose to which to devote himself. If Christ and His kingdom are no longer available, man invents various chimerical utopias or causes or callings to take the place of the New Jerusalem. The most famous and most successful, while at the same time the most illogical and bloodthirsty, is, of course, Marxism. However, the basic assumptions of Marxism underpin all Progressive thinking. Marx divided the world into the Elect and the Reprobate. The Reprobate are the sadistic oppressors. The Elect are the helpless victims. The Reprobate have no redeeming qualities whatsoever. The Elect have no flaws whatsoever. The two are locked in a remorseless Darwinian struggle for survival at any cost, and the battle is one in which no quarter and no mercy is possible, and no negotiation has any purpose, save to win concessions from those gullible Reprobates who do not realize the deadly and implacable nature of the struggle.

This simple, nay, this idiotic black-and-white analysis can be fitted to any cause. Feminists see males as the oppressors and women as victims. Greens see mankind as oppressors and nature as the victim. Race-baiters see Whites as oppressors and Blacks as victims.

Loyalty to the cause becomes the agreed-upon highest principle of the Ideologue. Truth and honor and honesty are jettisoned with unseemly haste and enthusiasm. Ideologues like telling lies. They love lying, and will lie even when it is counterproductive, (see the Obamacare debacle for an example). The other virtues are offspring of this one virtue: the willingness to lie for the cause, to betray one's family for the cause, to accuse the innocent for the cause, to riot for the cause, to shout down any opposition to the cause, replace the values of honesty, productivity and efficiency.

However, unlike the Worldly Man, the Ideologue is willing to sacrifice for a cause greater than himself. He can correctly despise the Worldly Man as worldly, even selfish. Despite that he is in reality less honest and less noble than the Worldly Man, the Ideologue feels more honest and more noble, because he has the zeal and fervor of a religion in his soul, despite that it is an atheist religion or antireligion. In some ways, this stage of corruption is healthier than the previous, for the criminal idiocy of the Ideologue is powered with the confidence of a true believer, whereas the common decency and common sense of the worldly man is powered only by the weak and self-condemning moral vacuum of selfishness.

The next corruption is Spiritualism, which throws off the materialistic worldliness of the Ideologue, and the weak and wavering ideals of the Worldly Men, and retreats into full-blown mysticism. The most popular forms of Spiritualism in the modern world was the blood-and-iron mysticism of the National Socialist Worker's Party of Germany, known as the Nazis; but there were other variations, such as theosophy of Madame Blavatsky, the occultism of Crowley, the ideas of Blake or Shaw, and any number of modern New Age claptrap.

This is the point at which the corruption reaches incoherence because by the ineffable nature of mysticism, no definition of Spiritualism can be drawn. At most, one can notice some familiarities between some of the properties, such as a fascination with vegetarianism or reincarnation or homosexuality or pacifism, or an insistence on the universal nature of all religions. Spiritualism is syncretism, and seeks a synthesis of all world religions, provided only that Christianity is demeaned from its world-historical significance. For better or worse, the principle of individual and secret enlightenment which runs through spiritualism prevents them from forming a unified organization, except in the single case of the Nazis, where the political program, which was Socialism, trumped other considerations. The Nazis attempted to syncretize Christianity into their rather confused program not because, (as has often been falsely said), they were friends of the Christians where Communists were not; it was because they were Spiritualists, whereas Communists were Ideologues. Spiritualists do not seek an intellectually coherent or satisfying picture of the universe.

Do not be deceived. Worldly Men seek not to destroy, but merely to privatize and de-emphasize the Church, as a danger to public peace and good order, or as an oppressor of private conscience. Far different is the Ideologue. Ideologues seek to destroy the Church by replacing it with an atheist socialist utopia, or perhaps with the goddess Reason as briefly appeared in the French Revolution.

On the other hand, like the Gnostics of old, the modern Spiritualist seeks to destroy the Church by incorporating parts of Christian teaching into an alien and antithetical philosophy. But those who worship Tashlan are no friend of Aslan, if you take my reference. Once Christ is merely one lightworker among many, along with Socrates and Buddha and Lao Tzu, Vespasian and Swedenborg and Edgar Cayce and Obama, then, by definition, he is not Christ at all.

The final corruption is Nihilism, which dismisses the delirious daydreams of the spiritualists with the same intense skepticism with which it rejects the hypocritical ideals of the Ideologues and the uninspiring pragmatism of the Worldlies. The best exemplars of nihilism are Nietzsche and Sartre.

Nihilism is the default metaphysical assumption of our current time. It says that there is no one truth applicable to all circumstances. Truth is relativistic, plastic, variable, inconstant.

Nihilism preaches that all philosophies are worthless, since they are 'narratives' that is, social myths or lies, instigated for the unseemly purpose of self-flattery, or for controlling the lower orders, or for some other hypocritical, false and unadmitted purpose; never for the love of truth. The one thing the Nihilist believes to be absolutely true is that no one seeks truth for its own sake, nor for any honest reason. He is the Cretan who says all Cretans are liars.

Unlike the Ideologue, the Nihilist does not believe that tearing down one myth will reveal a truth beneath. It will reveal a void. Into this void any man can, by his willpower, establish the laws of reality as he sees fit. The motto of Nihilism is 'Believe in Yourself' or 'Embrace Your Own Truth.' The only sin in the Nihilist system is the attempt, even if peaceful, to persuade others that an objective standard of right and wrong exists.

Because of this, Nihilism has only one enemy in the modern age. Ideology is not an enemy, because the Ideologue is true to his own truth. The Spiritualist is not an enemy, because he invents his own truth which happens to be ineffable. Nor is the Buddhist nor the Jew an enemy, because Nihilism is compatible with Buddhism at least insofar as Buddhist rejection of life as an illusion is concerned, and the Jew seeks only to live according to laws and diet particular to his own people. Only Christianity is the foe. (Logically, Islam, which is a heresy of Christianity, should also be a foe, but the Islamic glorification of self-destruction and their fanatical hatred of the West and all things Western endears them to the Nihilist.)

Nihilism has not won a complete victory yet, but its basic principles are assumed as the default in polite society.

The Promise of Nothingness

Once Nihilism wins, the only emotions left as socially acceptable in the heart of man is an insincere tolerance for the sins of others, and a vehement demand that all others not merely tolerate, but actively approve, of his sins.

Once Nihilism wins, unfortunately, all is over. All informal social organizations require some level of unselfishness, civility, mutual trust, or civilized sentiment to operate. Once these are dismissed as illusions, or destroyed as enemies of whatever cause it is fashionable to support this season, then the only social organization left is the state, whose role it is to assign to single mothers the paternity payments from whatever victim can be found to pony up the cost of childrearing.

Now, obviously again, few or none of the moderns caught in the grip of this mindset have reached the logical end-point at which reversal or repentance is impossible. This is an end state that is the result of the philosophy carried to its logical extreme, but it is a philosophy that also rejects logic. Other nations are deeper in the grip of this neo-barbarism than the United States, which is the last, best hope for mankind; but in recent years the culture seems to have redoubled its efforts to remain loyal to the nihilism of modern thought, despite that its failure rate and self-destructive nature is obvious even to the most casual observer.

What is their motive? Their motive is that they think

that human nature stands between them and some higher good which they hope to get in return. They think human nature blocks the path to utopia. The utopia will open to the posthumans, once human sentiment and thought are abolished, and once men are not men.

The thing we are alleged to get in return for abolishing human nature changes it name. Some say it is equality, some call it social justice, some say it is peace, some say Utopia, some say an endless orgy, some say it is life without guilt but with immense self esteem, some say some other falsehood.

Since the price is our soul, hence our ability to use, (or even to crave), the things for which we exchange our souls, it does not matter what these things are. They are nothing. Something you cannot use or crave, as far as you are concerned, is nothing. We are being asked to give up everything and get nothing in return.

What we are being asked to give up is only three things: first is faith in God, second is love for anything outside our precious rights which allow us to make demands on our neighbors, and third is our conscience, that sense of natural right and wrong which exists in potential in all men, and is awake in all decent men of all honest religions and all honest philosophies.

It cannot be made more obvious by an argument than by a simple statement that the surrender of the conscience, the sense of right and wrong, makes us no longer human in any real sense of the word.

We would become exactly what the Nihilists already think we are: animals of no more dignity than an ape, meat machines programmed by blind and pointless natural processes, semi-malfunctioning computers suffering from the delusion that our selfhood is real.

With the final triumph of the philosophy of nihilistic hedonism, we would become demons of pride living only on pride, sucking on the worthless and dry husk of life, taking pleasure in nothing, hating ourselves, and hating all other life whatsoever, but hating the lives of children most of all. The current fanaticism pressuring women to kill their own precious and helpless babies—their own, not even the babies belonging to a stranger!—is a precursor, a slight taste, of what nihilism promises.

But the seductive lure of Nihilism is not merely the freedom from humanity and freedom from the chains of prudence and honor and self-respect, it also promises freedom from want, (once Caesar is all powerful and you are his dependent for him to feed), and freedom from all war and all crime, (once no one loves nor wants anything, nor has any human desires, nor any point of view, nor any religion, nor any patriotism, nor any family to protect, then there is no obvious source for any conflict, neither violence nor vehement differences of opinion).

In a sense, the bargain Nihilism offers is merely a logical extension of the Worldly Man's bargain by which the sectarian conflicts between Protestant and Catholic were extinguished in the common peace of the First Amendment in the United States. Namely, the violence between religions was quenched when no denomination was allowed to touch the levers of secular power. All parties agreed not to use the power of the law against each other, but to compete for the souls of men with the truth of their words and deeds alone. Then history erupted into two World Wars, followed by a deadly Cold War, and the world shivered in the shadow of promised global thermonuclear destruction. These wars were fought over political and economic theory, the placement of boundaries of nations or spheres of influence. The

Nihilist promises that once we realize that no political system, no economic theory, no nation and no influence are worth fighting over, all fighting will cease. It is the same logic again. If men no longer believe in God, they will never fight wars over religious issues. Likewise, if men no longer believe in anything, they will never fight wars over any issue whatever, and universal peace for all time will reign.

The only thing that is forbidden is expressing disapproval about any other man or his way of life. Since man is fallen, the only thing forbidden is to recognize that man is fallen, or to seek some mystic water to wash away the stain of sin. The only thing forbidden is to seek salvation.

The Alliance

Now the great question is, if the Ideologues hate the worldliness of the Worldly Man, and if the Spiritualists hate the atheism of the Ideologues, and likewise the Worldly Man hates the injustice and greed of the Ideologue and the fuzzy-headed nonsense of the Spiritualist, why do they all agree with the default assumption of the Nihilist that truth is private and faith is in vain?

That is not what puzzled me. That is as obvious as the Sahara sun at noon at Summer solstice. Christ is critical of the Worldly Man, with his preoccupation with wealth and efficiency and his coldness to the poor. Christ condemns the Ideologue for his pride and greed and general bloodthirstiness. Christ has no dealings with the various witches and wizards which comprise the Spiritualists, who cannot accept the shocking statement that He is the Way, and the Truth, and the Life. The witches insist that all the roads eventually lead to heaven, including the road paved with good intentions.

All parties in corruption agree that the Church is the enemy. Those who are not in open rebellion against Christ are at least in a position of discomfort, for they think that to speak or act in defense of Christ, or to rebuke slanders against Him, is in bad taste, is inappropriate, cannot be taught in public schools, cannot be said on public airwaves, and merely causes discontent and commotion in the public square. Those who are Christian in name only think Christ is a private matter, not to be discussed nor defended in public. The atheists among the Ideologues and the Witches among the Spiritualists have a guilt complex about rejecting and reviling the faith of their fathers, and are sickened when they look in the mirror and see themselves destroying Western Civilization, so they revile Christ either with the bellowing anger of a mad thing, or with the smirking, sneering, anonymous cowardice like that of a graffiti artist painting swastikas on Jewish headstones, but who runs away, giggling, at the sound of a footstep.

All parties differ only in degree and approach. They all like one part of the Christian teaching, but differ on which part. The Worldly Man says Christ established not one church, but many, and He meant religion to be a matter of private conscience only. The Worldly Man likes and will keep the teaching of Imago Dei, that all men are created equal. He will not keep the teaching that life on Earth is vanity, merely preparation for life in heaven, and that wealth is vain. The Ideologue likes the teaching of common property as seen among the Apostles, and likes compassion for the poor, but he will not keep the teaching that Christ is divine; the Spiritualist will not keep the teaching that there is but one Christ.

All parties are agreed on the one point. They are for the spirit of Antichrist.

The Puzzle

As I said, it was a great puzzle to me as to why anyone should so vehemently continue with this process of corruption. Logically the only thing for a Nihilist to do, once he is convinced that nothing is real and nothing is worth enduring life to achieve, is find some pleasing method of suicide, perhaps an overdose of morphine during an orgy, and slay himself at once. If he is too uncourageous for the manly suicide of paganism, at least he can shut the hell up and leave the rest of us, the decent and sane people not obsessed with the terror of the void, to live our lives in decency and sanity. But no. The accusations never cease. The servants of the nothingness never tire. And they never shut up, and never stop shouting at us to shut up. What gives?

Ours is not the first age to adore and support totalitarianism, but ours is the first to support totalitarianism in the name of liberty. Ours is not the first Dark Age, where ancient learning was lost; but ours is the first where ancient learning was lost not due to the collapse of civilization, but deliberately, willingly, purposefully, as if to bring about collapse.

Those who oppose this darkness and seek to preserve the sinking wreck of civilization, or even, by heaven's aid, to float it again, the men of logic and reason, we are their enemies, and they hate us with an extravagant, absurd hatred and contempt. Meanwhile they are busily drilling holes in the deck in hopes of letting the water drain out.

And I suddenly realized why the soulless ones never stop drilling holes in the Titanic, no matter how clear it is that the ice-choked water means death for us all. They have nothing else.

I will not impose upon the patience of the reader by listing everything that fell into place once this key thought unlocked the pattern to me. I will mention but the three discussions that provoked the thought in me.

First Discussion: Why are we still discussing this?

The first conversation concerned that never-ending favorite topic among modern writers, how to write strong female characters.

Anyone unwise enough to be reading my essays is weary and over-weary of my opinions on this boring topic, which I have flogged to death. I will repeat them one more time here, just out of a sheer sense of impish perversity: I think female characters should be realistic and interesting if you are writing a realistic story, should be unrealistic and interesting if you are writing an unrealistic story, but in both cases should be interesting, because no one wants an uninteresting story.

By 'realistic' I mean feminine female characters; by 'unrealistic' I mean superheroine characters.

The conversation in this case was even more boring, because, as it turns out, the solution of making women characters willing and able to drink beer, kick ass, and blow up the Death Star as gallantly as a male character has fallen into disfavor as a type of tokenism.

The Progressives have been given strong female characters in every genre from detective novels to horror movies to space opera, but, to no one's surprise but their own, this is not satisfactory. Now they want realistic superheroines, who are feminine but not feminine; the superheroines must be equal to men but not different from men and at the same time different from men, ever keeping in mind that all differences are signs of inequality.

So the female character, to satisfy the demands of modern politics, cannot be a realistic heroine as Antigone, Penelope, Deborah, Vasilisa the Wise, Juliet Capulet, or Natasha Rostova; nor be an unrealistic superheroine as Buffy or Ripley or Supergirl.

The conversation then suggested that real feminist icons should be characters like Oracle, aka Batgirl, after she is paralyzed and consigned to a wheelchair. Or Buffy's Mom who dies of a heart attack.

So a cripple and a dead single mom are the new icons of true womanhood. This, from persons who alleged themselves to be supporters of womankind.

The conversation about how to put strong female characters in stories is boring because it is a conversation, beneath its mask, about how to use stories not to serve virtue, truth, and beauty, or even how to serve a well-crafted entertainment to a paying customer, but how to disguise propaganda to advance Progressive causes, that is, to advance the abolition of man.

The complaint was that making heroines too masculine suppressed the femininity of the heroines, and that THIS was now, suddenly, a sign of patriarchal oppression; whereas last season, making the heroines feminine was a sign of patriarchal oppression.

But the conversation turned an interesting corner, and asked why it was that the conversation on this topic is never-ending. I mentioned only that the conversation was never-ending because what was being asked of writers was logically absurd, due to the natural tendency of women toward femininity and the natural tendency of men toward masculinity, not to mention the natural tendency of the readers to admire and love manly men and womanly women as characters.

At this point, I was corrected, not as if I had offered an alternate opinion, but as if I had uttered an inexplicable and inexcusable mistake of certain and uncontested scientific fact, as socially awkward as believing the earth was flat. With a note of honest surprise, I was informed in a peremptory fashion that masculinity is cultural.

I do not think I laughed aloud, but I did call it nonsense.

Also, as if a flashbulb had ignited in my brain, I suddenly saw the source of the bitterness and discontent of the modern world.

The conversation on how to portray women can never come to an end as long as the modern idea of womanhood is unnatural. The feminists can never get what they want, because what they want is as impossible as a circular triangle.

By 'feminine' I mean all the characteristics of female genius feminists hate, namely, temperance, justice, prudence, fortitude, but also compassion, insight, loyalty, maidenly modesty and matronly dignity. Femininity means taking an indirect rather than a direct approach, being neither a braggart nor a whiner, being a support and sustenance, a healing and an inspiration. The female approach is to get you not only to do your chores but to want to do your chores; it is more concerned with motives than results. Femininity is a genius that turns children into adults and savage and shaggy bachelors into civilized and domesticated men. Femininity is delicate and fine. It means being damned sexy, which means being nubile, fertile, and fecund; and it means being romantic.

Feminists, at least as represented by their spokesmonsters, prefer women be aggressive, manly, boastful, foul-mouthed, ruthless, crude, cruel, whorish, shameless, sterile, selfish, and alone.

Feminists want women not only to be childless, but to kill their own helpless children in the womb with a blood-thirsty infanticidal mania difficult to understand and impossible to overestimate. Feminists feel about the unborn the way Nazis felt about Jews. They blame the unborn for everything and promise that the Final Solution of Planned Non-Parenthood will solve everything. It seems more like a brain disease than a sober philosophical or political posture.

To those who object that feminism is nothing more than the proposal that women should be equal to men, I reply that since the Married Women's Property Act of 1882 and the Nineteenth Amendment of 1915, women have been equal in the eyes of the law to men. Few or none number the feminists who speak against the misogynistic inequality of Islam, or speak against the adultery of Bill Clinton, because so-called feminists these days are merely apparatchiks of the Democrat Party. When women's rights clash with Progressive strategic or tactical goals, the modern feminist lifts no hand in defense of women's rights, utters no word.

Whatever it may have been at one time, feminism is no longer the proposal that women should be equal to men. It is now the proposal that men are evil and women are helpless victims locked in a remorseless death-struggle for supremacy, and the only hope for women to prevail is totalitarianism in government, socialism in economics, political correctness in speech and thought, and the abolition of man.

But, of course, the abolition of man means the abolition of woman as well.

There are the same four steps involved. First is the Worldly philosophy, where the attempt of the suffragette begins as the perfectly reasonable and perfectly just demand that they be granted the vote.

Second, the Worldly feminist becomes an Ideologue. Feminism becomes a paranoid neurosis once the idea takes root that any source of difference between men and women is a lurking threat to equality, or a potential excuse to rob women of their rights. All differences are abolished and unisex is the order of the day.

Third, a retreat into Mystical feminism, from paranoia to extreme gullibility, where women are told that full expressions of their womanhood include sexual liberation, including sex with strangers; and at the same time, all gallantry is sexual harassment, all men are rapists.

Finally, the paranoid neurosis and gullible neurosis falls into full blown screaming psychosis once the self-contradiction involved becomes clear, (namely, the self-contradiction of making women homogenous with men while preserving their unique feminine differences which make them women).

The only thing left to do, once women are told BOTH to act like women and never to act like women, is to revise the view of women into pure victims: hence the turn of the conversation toward cripples and victims and dead mothers. And this final stage is Nihilism, where the only thing to admire about women is nothing.

When I was told by someone who, again, I admire and to whom I mean no disrespect, that masculinity and femininity *OF COURSE!* were nothing but cultural artifacts, not based in nature, the first of three tumblers clicked into place in my mind.

Of course they do not believe in nature. Of course they think man is infinitely malleable, can be turned from anything into anything else. If man cannot be trained to be unisex, and if women cannot be trained to be happy, then man by his own efforts cannot break the curse of human nature, nor can women be free of their unfortunate, (unfortunate from the point of view of the Nihilist), desire to serve and suffer for the men in their lives, to be loving and giving, to submit to the leadership of their bridegroom.

Once one accepts the premise that all differences are inequalities, there is no such thing as two complementary sexes. If either differs from the other, then one is superior, (ergo a sadistic oppressor bent on exploitation and destruction on the second), and one is inferior, (ergo a victim whose only hope of freedom is the destruction of the first). Therefore if all differences cannot be removed by social engineering, by changing laws and customs, by peaceful education or forced injections of hormones, why, then, no peace between the sexes is possible, and all dreams of women's freedom from the horrific bondage of being a woman are dashed, and the ecstatic vision of unisex utopia fades like a mirage. Horrors!

If they did not think mankind endlessly open to endless improvements, then the endless improvements needed to cure all the ills and sorrows of the human condition are out of reach forever.

Of course they think human nature is a cultural artifact, which we can change at will. To believe anything else, if you live in an empty and godless world, is flat despair.

You have to believe that. You have nothing else.

Click. So much for the first tumbler.

I said before that the insight was based on three discussions I recently encountered, but, to be precise, one non-discussion must be added. This is one of the sets of facts that fitted itself suddenly into place with a click like a tumbler falling.

The one non-discussion must serve in the place of an endless number of non-discussions. A non-discussion is that particular act of craven intellectual treachery whereby a man flees from confronting any honest inquiry into his arguments by decreeing imperiously that no discussion is profitable or possible: the matter was settled long ago, and to dissent is a sign of mental incapacity and moral depravity and treason and blasphemy and worse.

The Sound Of Silence

I will use the example of the non-discussion on the sensitive matter of women's role in a post-gendered, Post-Christian and post-rational society. If the gentle reader recalls from our last chapter above, your gentle but innocent host was taken unawares, elbows and knees jerking in angular yet antic surprise, eyebrows aloft, to discover a respectable lady of the science fiction persuasion expressing discontent with the way strong female characters are portrayed in genre writing.

Now, to be clear, she was not saying that she was tired, because she had seen it too often, of seeing sweater girls in tight leather skirts carrying naked swords on the covers of Urban Fantasies and Buffy Ripoffs. Nor was she saying that she was tired, because she had seen it too often, of the gritty realism where a female character must be raped in order to give her a tragic back story or a motive for revenge. Any fashion becomes wearisome after a while.

What she was saying ,(if I understood correctly), was that portraying women as sword-wielding Amazons was tokenism, and was condescending, and was not true to life for most women's lives, and therefore was insulting to women, and an enemy to female equality.

What she was saying, (if I understood correctly), was that women are portrayed as rape-victims in order to portray them as weak and inferior to men, to make sure women are not uppity, are kept in their place, and kept weak. This portrayal was also an enemy to female equality.

What bemused me not a little was that both these conceptions of how to portray women in stories have their origin in the Left and only in the Left.

It was not any author loyal to conservative ideals of decency in speech and writing, decorum and honor and the defense of female honor who was clamoring for the portrayal of more grim and gritty and dark undersewer realism in genre fiction, who wanted, for example, to portray a sweet and innocent Mary Marvelesque superheroine as a rape victim in the pages of *Miracleman*; it was Alan Moore. Likewise for the portrayal of the Phantom Lady style super-heroine Sally Jupiter in *Watchmen*. It was not Gene Wolfe or Tim Powers who larded an urban fantasy with chapter-long digressions on the evils of raping children, and had both major female characters in the drama be victims of child sex abuse in the pages of *The Onion Girl*, it was Charles de Lint.

Let no one misunderstand my point in marking these examples. I mean no disrespect to these authors, whose fame and genius need no additional lauds from me. Both Alan Moore and Charles de Lint are seminal writers, and stand as colossi in our field, alongside the very few who can claim to have founded an entire subgenre of work: Urban Fantasy in the case of de Lint and Anti-superhero comics in the case of Moore.

I do however mean disrespect to the literati Left who rejoice shallowly in the perpetual degradation of our culture, who in my generation applauded these sickening desecrations of women as 'brave' and 'edgy' portrayals, and in the current generation now do an about-face and condemn that same desecration, not because the rape scenes or warrior babes are insulting to the image of women, (which they are), but because they are insulting to the image of equality, (which they are not).

The question again arises as to why the Left cannot take 'Yes' for an answer. Having succeeded beyond their wildest dreams on the issue of women's equality, why are they gnawing on their own entrails in orgasms of spite and rage and mewling hatred, and making more demands?

It is not a question of moving the goal posts, as when our grandmothers wanted the vote, our mothers wanted to enter the work force, our daughters want to kill our granddaughters in the womb. It is a question of why the goal posts move. Why, in the West, the only place on the globe and the only point in history when women are legally equal to men, is equality not enough to make women equal?

It is not a question of moving the goal posts. There are no goal posts. There is only envy and discontent. The divorce rate is way up, nine out of ten of which are initiated by wives, and the suicide rate among women is way up, and the rate of venereal disease among women is way, way up. I take these rates as signals of discontent on the grounds that the normal, sane, and prudent way of life, the way of life which displays self-control in sexual matters is for a virgin girl to marry a virgin bridegroom and cleave to him and forsake all others until death. That is a contented life. Suicide, divorce, and promiscuity are not signs of contentment and happiness and joy. They are erratic distractions or vain and desperate lunges toward false pleasures; they are signs of discontent, unhappiness, self-hatred.

The women have equality in every real sense of the

word, and it is still bitter in their mouths. Vanity of vanities, they have found equality is vanity.

Why are they unhappy?

Is it because, as they claim, masculinity is a cultural artifact? Because if masculinity is cultural, then changing our laws and customs can change masculine nature, tame it, break it. Once unsocial masculine behavior and masculine 'gender roles' are happily abolished, womankind will be free to define each happy maiden her own role in life, and be truly free. Such is the promise.

The promise is false.

The unhappiness of women is a feminine version of the unhappiness of men, and both are versions of the unhappiness of the Fall of Man. We are unhappy with life because life does not give us—and can never give us—what we truly desire. It is human nature to be dissatisfied with life, and it is the nature of the proud, (that is, it is the nature of those with high self esteem), never to blame themselves for their own failures. It is the nature of the proud to hate any superiors, real or imaginary. It is the nature of the proud to blame superiors, real or imaginary, and to see each disappointment and imperfection in life, real or imaginary, as an oppression and as an injustice, only some of which actually are injustices.

Ladies, you cannot change our nature. The best that anyone has ever done to tame the masculine spirit, and make it useful rather than antisocial, is to impose the norms, values, laws, and customs associated with chastity and charity into the male psychology. The Church once persuaded or pressured or commanded men to marry, and to love their wives, and to fight with chivalry rather than with pragmatic ruthlessness, and to treat the weak, the humble and the fallen with honor, and to let women and children get to the lifeboats first.

This society no longer teaches that. This society teaches the opposite. This society teaches self-esteem. A man with high self-esteem shoves granny aside while running for the lifeboat, and a woman with high self-esteem divorces a man and has the courts of law punish him the moment she fears he will one day bore her. Marriage is no longer a mechanism useful for domesticating the male warrior-animal. You've broken it.

You've broken it in pursuit of the promise that abolishing laws and customs will change human nature for the better, because human nature is cultural. Suckers.

The promise is false because masculinity is natural, not cultural.

If masculinity were cultural, then there should be many, or at least some, or at least one, culture where men did not fill the masculine roles.

This is not to say that the specific form of masculine fashion does not change from culture to culture or year to year. In some years, it is fashionable to shave your whiskers, and in others, to grow your whiskers, but a bearded lady is always a freak, never a fashion.

In some places, the men fight with guns, and in others with knives or poisoned-tipped spears; but in all cultures, the fighting role is masculine. Nor does this say that females do not fill fighting role in times of need or emergency, such as when the poverty of the Celtic tribes or the vastly outnumbered military of Israel forces them to expose their daughters to the rigors of war.

No, what was meant by calling masculinity 'cultural' was a hope that a new civilization, not based on any of the values or virtues, philosophy, tradition, standards, faith or morals, laws or customs of our current civilization, would somehow grow out of our own by evolution, or spring from our ashes by revolution, in which the enlightened despots of the future could condition or brain-program the sexless humanoid beings of that era, and turn them into unisex supermen, oops, I mean unisex superhumans.

In the sextopia of Ungenderland, some humanoids would have breasts and some whiskers, or both or neither, some endowed with penis or womb, or both or neither, but these matters would be merely a question of plumbing, unrelated to psychology, soul, mind, or social expectations. Babies would be raised or slain by the State, or by everybody, or by nobody, and the curse of Eve would be lifted: women would no longer desire men, no longer bear children in pain, and no longer be subject to men.

Ah, do you doubt me? You think I exaggerate? If anything, I am understating the matter.

Notice that while persons apparently educated and sane not only think masculinity is cultural ergo open to being re-engineered by society, they are unable to imagine the opposite opinion. Meanwhile, Miss Macfarlane over at Tor.com, (my publisher, I am ashamed to say), writes a manifesto calling for the end of Binary Gender in SF:

> Post-binary gender in SF is the acknowledgement that gender is more complex than the Western cultural norm of two genders (female and male): that there are more genders than two, that gender can be fluid, that gender exists in many forms.

She means 'sex' or perhaps 'sexual roles.' The word 'gender' refers to words in declined languages.

She goes on to say:

I am not interested in discussions about the existence of these
gender identities: we might as well discuss the existence of
women or men. Gender complexity exists.

Since she is not interested, I will not address that topic
here, nor read one word more of her no doubt fine and fascinating essay.

But I will address what is betrayed by this unintentional,
(and unintentionally hilarious), admission that the matter
cannot be debated.

When Worlds Collide

This is, of course, the same attitude expressed by the baffled
surprise of those who cannot imagine that masculinity or
femininity is natural rather than cultural.

The Left cannot see both sides of any issue. They
cannot, (or dare not), treat any rival viewpoints with respect,
not even the respect needed to address or refute them. This
alleviates the Left from the burden of actually meeting a
burden of proof, indeed, of actually making any argument at
all. They just ask opposing viewpoints to shut up.

The great selling point of the Left, the great promise of
Political Correctness, is that all issues are orthodox and
settled, and the great debate of the human condition, all the
mysteries of life, no longer are open to discussion. The
matter is closed. Talk must stop. Correct thinking is true;
incorrect thinking is heresy. You must shut up. You must
shut up. You must shut up.

And the burden of human reasoning, the torment of the
paradoxes of life, the need for learning, education, or
curiosity is done away with. Everything the faithful need

know can be printed on a bumper sticker, and chanted as a mantra or a mob-slogan at a rally.

It would be an insult to religion to call this a religion. Real religions take their theology seriously, and debate hair-splitting nuances of phrase over centuries to arrive at precise truth. Cults are not serious. Cults chant slogans. Leftism is a cult.

No theology can be reduced to a slogan, even if it can, (at times), be reduced to a credo or formula. The Incarnation, the idea that Jesus was both fully God and fully Man can be uttered in a sentence, or even a single word, but the theological implications of that will puzzle and awe the saints and angels forever.

What is most annoying is that the partisans of the Left deserve something better than Leftism. Feminism, at its root, is a just and noble idea: the idea of women enjoying the same civil rights as men. In its freakish corrupt form, feminism is just another excuse for the abolition of all moral norms, the abolition of humanity.

The idea of Women's Liberation can be said in two or three words, but the implications will puzzle and exasperate the feminists forever; nor will the feminists of one wave ever agree with their sisters in another. "Equality for Women" is, in fact, a theological statement, a mystery of faith, a paradox as puzzling as the paradox of the Incarnation.

A woman in America has the right to vote and to own property in her own name—but what other rights, real or not, must be protected, or invented, or bestowed, in order to achieve the utopia?

Some are more reasonable than others. The right to be chaste without social repercussion? The right to be promiscuous without social repercussion? The right to dress, talk, and act like a man? The right to urinate in a urinal? The right to force all employers to grant equal pay for equal work? The right to commit abortion? The right to marry a lesbian? The right to force the Roman Catholic Church to pay for the abortion and perform the lesbian marriage? The right to force the Roman Catholic Church to pay for the lesbian marriage while performing the abortion on the marriage altar with one bride while the other bride is urinating in a urinal?

The right to force the sperm donor to pay for the child-drearing of a lesbian couple once the couple breaks up, and no longer wishes to raise the child together?

This last is a real case. I am not making it up. I note with considerable wry irony and perhaps a pinch of schadenfreude that a culture which has tried its level best to divorce all sexual matters from nature and sanity, until we have lesbian so-called families attempting to rear a fatherless child in imitation of the Virgin Mary, nonetheless retains at least one judge who does not allow that a man can use his seed to father a child without incurring the responsibilities of fathering a child; in this case, supporting the single mom after a lesbian so-called divorce.

You see, in the case of the Sperm Donor and the Lesbians, two worlds collided.

In the first world, the world of reality, the child that grows from a man's sperm is his child, and he is responsible for it. The institution of marriage serves many purposes, but the primary purpose is to make fathers responsible for rearing the children they father.

In the second world, modern science allows sexual reproduction to take place without the sex act, hence without marriage, hence without laws and customs to prevent improvident fathering of children in situations where both parents are not present to rear them. In the second world, modern acceptance of contraception allowed the growth of the false-to-facts emotional fixation on sex as distinct from reproduction. First a small group, then a larger, than nearly the whole society developed an emotional complex utterly antithetical to reality, that is, a. neurosis. This neurosis treats the sex act as a subjective emotional and physical experience unrelated to the act of sexual reproduction; this in turn is unrelated to the pleasures and duties and social roles of childrearing; this in turn is unrelated to the pleasures and duties and social roles of marriage.

In the first world, fornication is forbidden, and women are frequently segregated from men so as to prevent even the opportunity for fornication to arise.

In the second world, the sex act has no bearing on sexual reproduction, hence no bearing on childrearing, hence no bearing on marriage.

In the second world, this sexless form of marriage becomes nothing more than a legal and social sanction to an emotional relationship, either permanent or not, as the partners wish.

If sex means the emotional and physical act of stimulating the sexual organs, then one can have 'sex' (by this odd definition) as easily with one's own sex as with the opposite sex: or, for that matter, with children, corpses, animals, or inanimate objects.

According to the fashions of the moment, this second group is still considered perverse, but the consideration is a matter of sentiment and not logic: that is, an arbitrary reason can distinguish them (for example, capacity to give consent) but no reason actually pertinent to sexual reproduction.

If you doubt me, ask a partisan of sexual liberation why

copulating with one's adult sister, (with her consent of course), or with a menstruating fourteen-year old, (with the parent's consent, of course), or with the corpse of one's wife, (with her permission granted in her last will and testament, of course), or with an ape, (assuming she gave consent in sign language to the best of her ability, of course; or her owner gives consent on her behalf), in each case where actual coupling takes place, is evil, sick and perverted, whereas sexually stimulating the private parts of a person of one's own sex, a situation where no copulation can take place, is nonetheless a cherished and romantic fulfillment of utterly natural longings which law, custom, society, public opinion, and the Roman Catholic Church must not only tolerate, but support, applaud, and approve. Ask them.

The partisans of the Sexual Revolution will not give you an argument, merely sneer, or shriek, or pretend to faint like an overexcited Victorian matron, or call you names like a schoolyard bully, hack your Wikipedia page, send hate mail, ad nauseam. They will not give reasoning, by which I mean a structured line of deduction from identified axioms to valid conclusions.

This is not to say an argument cannot be made. I heard and read such arguments commonly enough in my youth. But that was half a century ago. These days a syllogism is a thing many a college graduate has never formed, no, not once. We live in an age of gullibility, where all statements are taken on authority, but always on the authority of anonymous academics, jurists, entertainers, pundits, and bureaucrats who are never, no, not once, asked to produce a warrant of authority. We live in an age of emotion, especially the emotion of offended self-righteousness.

You may be more successful than I, and can, perhaps, find someone willing and able to construct an argument in favor of Sexual Liberation that does not logically necessitate the legalizing of everything from algolagnia to zoophilia; but he is as rare as the bearded lady. Yet I suspect you will find "I am not interested in discussions about..." to be the standard response, with few exceptions, or none.

Rome Has Spoken

There are many valid reasons why a particular topic cannot be broached in polite company.

First is that the company is met for another purpose, and that certain topics are so fraught with emotion or so complex with so many ramifications, that the social cost of holding a debate at that time and place exceeds the good of talking. This is why gentlemen do not discuss politics at dinner parties, or at work, or discuss the merits of their previous sweethearts with their wives on the honeymoon, or discuss the most effective methods of torture while addressing a grammar school class.

However, in no case is this reason universally valid to silence debate—particularly in the places and at the times when debate is allowed, encouraged, or necessary. The pages of an editorial, particularly an editorial advocating radical and permanent changes to the lives, virtues, values, and norms of society, cannot silence debate on the grounds that ladies are present, and discussing politics will spoil the dinner party.

Second is that one has no qualifications to have an opinion on the topic, or that all the facts are not in.

In no case does this reason allow you to prevent another man from talking, only you yourself, and only in areas where expertise is required, and you lack that expertise. In a democracy, or on a jury, every free man is assumed to have the basic knowledge of right and wrong, sick and hale, sane and insane, which the Abolishers wish to abolish. No one is disqualified from holding and promoting an opinion about the sickness of sexual perversion on the grounds that he has no doctorate in the area. The moral law natural to man is known to all who have achieved the age of reason.

Third is that the other party in the discussion has retreated, will not answer questions, or has nothing to say while never shutting up. I pass lightly over the question of why Abolishers, of all people on Earth, ought not use this excuse to back politely out of a conversation.

Fourth is that the matter truly is settled by an authority to whom you and your debate partner must refer all questions to be satisfied.

If I report the diameter of the Earth based on the experiments and calculations of Eratosthenes of Cyrene, or the distances to the sun and moon based on based on measurements taken by Aristarchos of Samos, and I cannot satisfy you, it is not unseemly of me to refer you to those authorities and have you take up your argument with them. If I am aware that I cannot give an argument more clear than the original I am repeating, humility, if nothing else, dictates that I direct you to wiser minds and that I step aside.

Likewise, while I am aware, in a general way, of the arguments for the Big Bang and against the Steady State theory, I could not win an argument against Fred Hoyle. My golden tongue is not so golden as that. I could do no more than refer him to Georges Lemaître, and bow out.

But note that at no point while bowing out of a conversation one is not qualified to hold is it legitimate to accuse one's opponent of disqualification. To say, "Argument from Authority is the strongest form of argument, as many eminent people will attest!" is a joke, not an argument.

Likewise, saying "Global Cooling is Settled Science! The consensus of opinion says... etc." is an informal logical error. It is another way of saying "Shut Up."

Just this morning on the news, I heard an article saying that school officials oppose a proposed law to teach the children critical thinking about science, by offering more than one point of view, on the grounds that it may provoke children into questioning matters of settled opinion, such as Darwinian Evolution or Global Warming. I am not making this up, not kidding, not exaggerating. The Abolishers are not even bothering to pretend to be honest. Their express reason for opposing teaching children how to think is that they want non-Left points of view to shut up.

Of course, this is a favorite tactic of Abolishers, which is why all the nonsense and offal they utter is asserted to be expert opinion, but any attempt to track down an authority to its source ends up being a maze paved with paper. The authorities being quoted are all anonymous. The experts, upon examination, turn out to be journalists, academics in other fields, political operatives, bureaucrats, paid hacks, and so on.

The Abolisher obsession with detailed statistics generated by allegedly scholarly studies, now that the scientific field is as utterly politicized as the journalistic, is a pathetic attempt to win arguments by false and meretricious authority. No attempt is made to establish the credentials of the authority beforehand. And, in any case, few men are patient enough to look at the actual numbers, who understand the pitfalls of statistics and know what statistics can and cannot prove.

Fifth is that the subject matter is ineffable. If I am discussing how I know my wife loves me, or why I am stirred by Beethoven's Seventh Symphony, or a mystical experience of the oneness of Creation, mere words fail, and I must fly to poetry and music, the language of heaven, or fall mute, the language of awe.

Legal and moral issues, however, are not ineffable, but are open to as much clarity and precision as any philosophical issue.

Sixth is that the point in dispute is a dogma, part of a theological system accepted on faith in its entirety, or else rejected in its entirety. Dogma is accepted, if at all, upon faith in the authority of the man or institution (or divine being) proposing the dogma.

As with other matters resting on authority, it is permissible to disqualify oneself from defending an issue which one believes only for another's sake. If a child is asked by her father for his sake to believe a certain matter, she cannot argue the point. Loyalty to her father, and her own awareness of her own inadequacy, prevents her from entertaining questions on the matter.

Now, a dogma can indeed be questioned by anyone willing to question his entire loyalty to whatever authority is asking for his consent, but then the particular matter is subsumed into a greater question. In this example, to question the daughter's dogma, the point to be discussed is the legitimacy of the authority of her father. That point is always open to question.

Except among Progressives, of course. They are devoted to the Unreality Principle.

Their system is as dogmatic as Catholicism; the difference being that we are honest about it and they are not.

When our Pope makes a statement Ex Cathedra, or invokes the doctrine of Papal Infallibility, or a General Council settles a dispute about some theological point, such as the divinity of Christ, we admit it. We admit we are sheep following a shepherd, whom we love.

When the vague consensus of anonymous opinion-makers, however, invokes the Leftwing equivalent of Liberal Infallibility, and speaks Ex Cathedra, and suddenly decrees some absurdity, such as the doctrine that gays are to be thrown under the bus for Islam, the no one who follows the authority of the vague consensus admits it. The freethinkers all pretend that they each man independently came to the same opinion as the received dogma. They are sheep pretending to be lone wolves, and they fear their alpha wolves turning on them and rending them. They fear being denounced as a bigot, (or whatever the meaningless swear word of the day is).

So the dogmatic reason for disqualifying oneself from debate is legitimate, but at this price: one must be honestly willing, then, to give whatever reason one has for placing faith in the authority whose dogma one receives. It is not the end of the debate, but the opening of a deeper one. Any Christian not ready to give a reason for the hope he has within him is disobeying Christian teaching.

But the Progressives would rather die than admit their beliefs are dogmas. They each pretend they are all fearless and independent thinkers, who have all come to the same fashionable conclusions because the matters are so clear and obvious—too, too obvious to bother discussing—that no other opinion is possible, nor needs to be explored.

In other words, they are conformists pretending to be nonconformists, they are stupid people pretending to be smart, and they are cowards pretending to be brave. One wonders whom they think they are fooling.

The final reason is illegitimate. It is a knowledge of the weakness of one's own position, and the desire to silence the opposition. Now, at best, this betrays an impatience with the thickheadedness of the opposition, or disgust with their willful blindness, or condemnation of their lies. However, a gentleman continues a conversation even with fools and liars in the hopes that onlookers will come to understand on whose side truth stands, and he abides by the rules of debate even if the other does not. There are many reasons for this, one of which is that one is entirely clear of any accusation of retreat.

It has been my unfortunate experience never to have met a legitimate reason for retreat from the combat of debate. I have never been asked by an Abolisher to hold my tongue because ladies and children were present, so that we could meet out back and continue the conversation outside the hearing of those who would not understand that we can debate a point without ill will and argue without hatred. Indeed, I have never met an abolisher who could argue without hatred. Indeed, I have never met one who pretended to argue without hatred, or who held intellectual integrity to be a value worthy of pursuit.

I have never met an honorable enemy. Nothing but caitiffs and vermin meet my sword. Perhaps I have been spoiled by long years being an atheist, when not one, but many apologists for the Christian religion expressed themselves logically, clearly, without rancor, without sneers, without hate, without heat.

At the time, I thought love of reason was the universal heritage of all men, or, at least, of all intellectuals. Since then, I have never met more hatred of reasoning anywhere more vehement than the hatred of intellectuals for reason. It is the treason of the clerks.

I truly hope you have better luck than me.

But for the moment, I think experience sufficiently

demonstrates that the Abolishers wish to abolish reason first of the human faculties of mind to be discarded on our way to afterhumanity.

To them, questioning any of their received dogmas about politics, economics, human sexuality, or any other topics including climate science is not a sign of curiosity but a sign of mental flatulence, moral depravity, and treason against the universe.

But, you may ask, if they are not willing to discuss matter, why is all academia, all jurisprudence, all entertainment, all media, and the entire leftwing blogosphere filled with nothing but talk, talk, talk?

I propose a simple answer. These words are apologetic for their doctrine, or preaching to the choir, or missionary work to the unenlightened.

Progressivism is a heresy of Christianity, that is, based on Christian ideals taken out of context but ignoring other Christian ideals; but it retains the Christian catholic nature, that is, small-c catholic, meaning universal. Progressivism is meant to be sovereign in the hearts of all men in all the whole world, and rule all nations, tribes, languages, and peoples.

The reason for all this talk combined with so much silence on so many crucial issues is because of despair. Progressives do not believe in philosophy, do not believe in metaphysics, do not believe in reasoning about matters of faith, which, to them, includes politics and economics and science, and every other matter they find so confusing but do not admit they do not understand.

The Progressives also hold, as a matter of their Pseudo-Calvinist dogma, that we Reprobates are destined to be damned from Creation, that we are trapped in a false consciousness of an ideological superstructure, or deceived

by a narrative, or poisoned by testosterone, or something —
so that it is impossible to reason with us.

The crowning dogma of their nihilistic, pro-irrationality
worldview is that we, who have reason and right reason, we
the normal and sane people, we are irrational to the point
where no debate with us is possible, and no speech.

The insight which flashed upon me was that this was
not merely cowardice, not merely the desire to avoid humili-
ating defeat in debate after debate, but was despair. They
think they are the elite, the only true humans, the Tarzan,
living among a grubby tribe of ape-things with whom no
speech is possible.

They are not willing to discuss matters because they
have no hope.

I am engaged in the difficult task of explaining an
insight it required my dull brain several decades of experience and one moment of epiphany to see.

Again, in all fairness, this is something which I assume
nearly everyone but me has seen for years; but to me it was
an intellectual adventure, as shocking as opening a hidden
door and coming across the Minotaur in the center of his
bone-littered maze. Many others no doubt have trod here
before, but still I feel the excitement of discovery, for I have
found the heart of the labyrinth.

I have been puzzled for years how it is that so many
otherwise wise and educated people can be Leftists; why so
many otherwise compassionate people simply overlook the
bloodthirsty enormities routinely perpetrated, applauded,
excused, and rationalized by the Left, from prenatal infanticide to lauding Che and Castro and other butchers of men;
why otherwise honest men approve of the Orwellian lies of
Political Correctness, which corrupts both speech and
thought; why so many otherwise good and faithful Chris-

tians routinely ignore Christian teaching and cling to the shibboleths of Political Correctness on any point where the two worldviews differ; why so many good people so routinely support, applaud, and encourage so blatantly vile an evil.

It is too obvious for the blindness to be anything but willful, and yet it does not seem to be willful, for who can will the destruction of themselves and all they hold dear? How is it possible for so many children of the most blessed, most powerful, most successful, most wealthy, most free, and most benevolent nation history has ever known to hate it? Why are the heirs of Western Civilization the enemies of Western Civilization?

The epiphany visited me in the space of a single hour, along the course of three conversations with honest men I happen to respect, despite our deep differences of opinion.

It was as if I suddenly could see clinging to the countenances of these otherwise honest and able men, the Facehugger from *Alien* which had been invisible up until that point, whose long proboscis entered their skulls though mouth and palate and shot poison into their brains. I wondered why they did not tear the Facehugger away, and breathe free.

Not to spoil the surprise ending, but the reason that exploded into my awareness like a bolt was this: they have nothing else. They leave the alien thing lodged in their brains, eating away their happiness, ruining their lives, spoiling friendships and darkening the light of heaven for the simple, tragic reason that without the alien thing, they would be lonely.

I mentioned the first discussion and one of many, many non-discussions which clicked the first two tumblers into place in the process of unlocking this moment of insight. Here is the next.

Second Discussion: I Forged My Own Life

The next clue came during a particularly elliptical conversation about the alleged demerits of Disney: there were some in the conversation who despised Disney because his films retell fairy tales without the gore and horror found in some of the Brothers Grim versions, as when the evil stepsisters in *Cinderella* do not have their eyes pecked out by songbirds, blood and vitreous humor dripping down their screaming cheeks, and because Disney tacks happy endings on tragedies, as in Disney's *The Hunchback Of Notre Dame*.

The basic point being made was this: children should be exposed to all the horrors of real life as young as possible, and kept away from any stories which give them hope. There are no miracles. There is no magic. No marriages are happy endings. You cannot fly. Curse God and die. Give up. Shut up.

As with all Abolisher ideas, it starts as a perfectly reasonable-sounding notion. In this case the notion is that telling children that to "wish upon a star" is enough to win the battles of life without hard work, self-discipline, and suffering is deceptively optimistic. The idea is that the child will grow into a more realistic view of life if the fairy tales he sees depict hard work and self-esteem as the source of victory, rather than fairy magic.

This sounds reasonable at first. Who wants to raise a child to have faith in something, like an omnipotent and benevolent God, which will disappoint him, rather than have faith in something much more true and practical, like our omnipotent and benevolent and utterly ruthless Political Leadership, which never disappoints anyone?

But the idea that Disney sugarcoats his bitter medicine is patently false. There is more evil—and it is more horrible to a child—in any Disney animated film than you will find in a Progressive and optimistic show like *Star Trek*. Any show where you have to die and get resurrected to overcome the evil is not a show that promises easy victories.

I will point at the evil Witch in *Snow White*, along with the death and resurrection of the heroine; the slaver who turns children into mules in *Pinocchio*, not to mention Monstro the whale, who engulfs the father in a symbolic death and resurrection before the boy suffers a true death and resurrection; the imprisonment of Dumbo's mother, and his humiliation as a clown, and the symbolic feather of hope which alone allows him to prevail; the death of BAMBI's mother; the humiliation of *Cinderella*, and her 'Magnificat' moment, when, as in the Canticle of the Virgin, the proud are cast down and the humble are raised; the loss and death and resurrection in Peter Pan, not to mention Captain Hook; the false accusation in *Lady And The Tramp*, and the mess created by the Siamese Cats; the curses and thorns and thunder and flames unleashed by the she-dragon in *Sleeping Beauty*, with yet another symbolic death and resurrection; and the frightening spectacle of the devilish mountain come to life in the "Night on a Bald Mountain" sequence in *Fantasia*... what is a Klingon compared to that?

Need I go on? Need I also mention the sea-witch in *The Little Mermaid*, the huntsman in *Beauty And The Beast*, (with yet another symbolic death and resurrection), the evil sorcerer in *Aladdin*, the scheming brother in *The Lion King* and the father slain before his son's eye, the sinister magistrate in *The Hunchback Of Notre Dame* whose song of lust conjures up images of hellfire....

The idea that Disney does not scare the peanut oil out of little kids' brains, and confront the wee ones with death, curses, dragons, monsters, more death, injustices, pirates, even more death, loss, loneliness, and on and on... is simply a lie unworthy of refuting.

No. Any child watching a Disney movie has the idea driven into the depths of his tender soul, and fixed there as if with nails, that evils and horrors exist, and pain, and loss, and death.

What Disney gives, as all sound fairy tales must give, is a eucatastrophe, a good and miraculous ending beyond hope, with joy as huge as woe, and the terrible, secret promise that if you wish upon a star, heaven will send salvation in some secret disguise, to resurrect you.

Allow me to quote the Apostle of Common Sense, Mr. G.K. Chesterton:

> *Fairy tales do not give the child the idea of the evil or the ugly; that is in the child already, because it is in the world already. Fairy tales do not give the child his first idea of bogey. What fairy tales give the child is his first clear idea of the possible defeat of bogey. The baby has known the dragon intimately ever since he had an imagination.*

What the fairy tale provides for him is a St. George to kill the dragon. Exactly what the fairy tale does is this: it accustoms him for a series of clear pictures to the idea that these limitless terrors had a limit, that these shapeless enemies have enemies in the knights of God, that there is something in the universe more mystical than darkness, and stronger than strong fear.

Hence what the Abolisher wishes to abolish is not the fear caused by a fairy tale, but the hope, for he finds it to be a false hope.

To the Abolisher, all hope is false hope.

All hope? No, not quite. Some Abolishers, at least, retain the Enlightenment faith in mortal man, that most warped of building beams.

The conversation dwelt for a moment upon the scene in *Sleeping Beauty* where the three fairies rescue the Prince out of the dungeon of the beautiful but evil witch, (so sue me, I always thought she was beautiful). He is told that only truth and righteousness can overcome the evil power of Maleficent, and he is given a magic sword and shield. The fairies protect him from the gargoyles and hobgoblins of the castle, and brush away all their stones and arrows, or turn them into bubbles and flowers, for his fate is not to be stopped by them.

Then, in a scene that hardly seems in keeping with the gentleness of Disney, the evil fairy in a whirlwind of fury appears before the prince, and sheds her beauty forever for hate's sake, and becomes a monster, announcing: *Now shall you deal with me, O Prince, and all the powers of Hell!*

I voiced the opinion that this climactic scene was perfectly true to life, truer than any documentary, since indeed this is exactly the way life works. No man by his own effort can free himself from the dungeon of sin, despair, and death, but by supernatural intervention by a higher power. And yet that power, not because of any ineffectiveness or indifference, cannot fight man's final battle for him, but only provide the weapons of truth and virtue, which are magic indeed, enough to slay monsters, and defy not merely some, but all the powers of Hell.

The sacraments and gifts from heaven will do their part;

man must see to it that he does his, if true love is indeed to conquer all, as all prophets have promised it shall do.

Ah, but the rebuttal to this was swiftly said: my interlocutor thought the scene was a cheat, if not a lie, because the fairies aided the prince. No man needs any help to win life's battles, or to achieve his dreams. And no help is coming.

This was said, not by a bricklayer, but by a writer, and I fear I swooned in astonishment. Many questions whirled in my pounding head, to which I, strangled with surprise as I was, could give no tongue.

I wondered where he thought his ideas came from? From himself, or from the muses, or whatever name one gives to the mystery of inspiration? Where did the traditions and tropes and tools he used in his writing come from? From himself? Or from his masters and teachers and ancestors? Where did his fame come from? From himself? Or from the kindness of his audience, the grace of good fortune, the smile of heaven?

I must have gasped out some question along these lines of some sort, because he polled all who were listening to the discussion, which was not a small number of people, and asked them who was responsible for their success, in art or in life? Themselves? And all but two raised their hand.

Everyone in the room was content to take credit for the blessings in their lives, as if it were no more than their just wage, the merited reward of their own works.

It is an inescapable truth that no man can take all credit to himself and at the same time feel any gratitude to any for his blessings. If you earned it, it is not a gift. If you earned it by yourself with no one's aid, you owe no thanks to anyone.

And this indeed was the attitude, which I take to be the modern attitude. The Abolisher triumphantly announced that he needed no good fairies, no magic, no grace, no gift from heaven to achieve all his dreams. He disdained to take a magic sword of Efland; he would forge it by himself, for himself, or do without.

I had a prophetic vision then, and saw how Siegfried, who did indeed forge his magic sword for himself, and relied on none but his own strength, came to an end. For he is fore-doomed to fall speared in the back, a coward's blow, by Hagen, a man with the heart and heritage of a dwarf. The man who lives by himself cannot escape his fate, which is to die by himself.

I hope I will not be misunderstood. I do not mock. I bow my head almost in respect akin to fear. I salute the melan-choly, doomed, and gloomy pride of this sad and great pagan with whom I spoke. I do not doubt his word, no, not by an iota, the tiniest of letters. I think he is entirely respon-sible for his life, and he accepts no aid.

And he will die, and his loved ones will die. Some of his loved ones will die in slow pain, and others in merciful swiftness. Some will die before him, so that he will weep by their graves, and there will be no consolation; and some will die after him, so that they will weep by his, and likewise find no consolation.

I bow my head, because at once, as if with a stroke of lightning, I saw that he and all his kind live in a universe that is a sepulcher.

To be sure, it is a coffin of appalling vastness, fifteen billion light-years in radius, too large for the imagination of man to comprehend even its smallest moiety, godlike in its sheer magnitude of size;: but it is a coffin nonetheless, an airtight coffin, hermetically sealed with all the stars trapped inside, and all within are the prey and sport of death and entropy. Everything dreamt and everything done inside the sepulcher will come to nothing in the end. Escape is not merely impossible, it is unimaginable.

They cannot wish upon a star because to them the sky is black. There are no stars, nor Star-Maker, nor light.

For the pagan, there is by definition no outside, no other realm, no home to which to return, no happy ending, no efland, no magic, no hope, and if you wish upon a star, you are a childish fool.

And if you pray to that sovereign Providence who fashioned the stars, when all the Sons of Light shouted aloud for joy, then you are both fool and enemy.

For the noble pagan did not spare to tell all his audience how terrible the false beliefs of the Christian were, and how strong and great the fairies and spiritual beings and princes of the middle air he worshiped were. No, I am not speaking in a metaphor: the man was an occultist.

By no means is every Liberal, Leftist, Progressive, Nihilist, Socialist or other Abolisher of Man a warlock trafficking with unseen powers in hopes of worldly gain; but they all share his goal and his spirit. Only their methods differ.

Let me explain what I mean. I propose that, with minor variations or precursors, in the modern world, there are only three true and honest philosophies which make an honest attempt to deal with the intolerable truth of the world of despair and death in which we live.

Here again is the intolerable truth: without hope of heaven, without true love, every single desire and aspiration of any kind whatsoever is in vain, for in time, long or short, all pleasure will be gone, and even the pleasure of memory will fail as memory fades.

Death comes unto all estates: princes, prelate, potentates, both rich and poor of all degree. His awful strike no man can flee. *Timor Mortis Conturbat Me.*

Even an elf as immortal as Oberon would perish when the Earth is swallowed by the sun; even a living machine, long ago having lost all trace of his human origin, who flees beyond the farthest star, will in time be overcome by entropy, degrade, and perish.

The three ways to deal with this intolerable truth are Stoicism, Hedonism, Christianity. Stoicism is true to the character of the noble pagan; Hedonism to that of the ignoble.

When I speak of pagans, I do not mean only those who serve the classical gods and spirits of wood and mountain, sky and underworld. I include their modern brethren who believe in nothing but mortal matter and mortal minds.

Those who speak in cold tones about how life is a Darwinian war of all against all, and pity and mercy have no place, but the state needs self-sacrifice and noble courage to fall in battle if the state is to survive — such men are pagans even if they are atheists, because they are Stoics. They are dignified and noble, but doomed, for in their world mankind is the most rough and tough hardcore streetfighter in the circus of life, and we will flourish until some monsters rougher and tougher overwhelm us, and we go down fighting, gaily, to the unmarked grave. Read Robert Heinlein's STARSHIP TROOPERS if you want an undisguised dose of such rhetoric.

Likewise, those who speak of life as a hunt for pleasure, the soaring fumes of wine sparkling in the sun or the profound kisses of women in the dark, and that the deep matters of the end of life or the ends of life need not concern us, for today we laugh, and scorn those who mock our fellowship and cheer — such men are pagans, even if they are atheists, for they crown themselves with floral wreathes and loll at ease like lotus-eaters. Read *Brave New World* by Aldous Huxley to see the logical outcome of such a philosophy in action.

Hedonism seeks to distract the mind with pleasures, and find fulfillment in them, as a means to turn away from the looming and silent inevitability of death. It says, let us eat and drink and be merry, for tomorrow we die.

Stoicism turns to look at the oncoming night, and, knowing there is no remedy, seeks to train the soul to die without fear or tears. The choice is to die with dignity like a man or to die shrieking and begging like a slave. The Stoic logic is cold and irrefutable: man has no power to avert death forever, nor to escape pain, but he does have the power to do his duty and to adjust his mind to reality, and live according to nature, that is, according to logic. What he cannot avert or avoid, such as death, he accepts with tranquility; what he can avert and avoid, such as falsehood or immodesty or cravenness, he rejects absolutely.

The Stoic teaches that man can only find what tranquility is open to him, within his own mind, where he is sovereign, but in absolute obedience to reason, which is to say, to the conscience. And he leaves the world to inflict pain and wounds and death upon him when so events decree, and he suffers without fear and without regret, knowing that these external things are indeed indifferent to him. He takes firm hold only of what is in his grasp, namely, his soul, and he does not reach for things beyond him, namely, his fortune and his body and his life.

The Christian is akin to the Stoic in despising the world, but surrenders more, even his own soul, into hands he trusts more than he trusts his own, and he hopes for more than merely tranquility and the hope of enduring pain with dignity. He does not resign himself to death, because his Master has overcome it, and promises to share the endless joy of that infinite victory with any who follow Him.

For the pagan, wishing on a star, or holding a feather of hope to help one to fly, or trying to overcome the rude nature of our birth so as to grow one day into a real boy, all these things, if at all, are pleasing distractions.

They are the distractions of the hedonist, the child's version of sex and drugs and rock and roll, and the suicide by morphine in the needle of a euthanasia doctor, once hope for luxurious pleasure in life is gone.

For the Christian, wishing on a star is childhood practice to train the sterner mind of young women and men to wish upon the Bethlehem Star. Holding onto hope as thin and light as a feather is practice to train for grasping angels' feathers as they bear us aloft in rapture. Seeing puppets made in the image and likeness of man grow by miracle into the higher life of man is practice for man growing into the higher life into which he is made.

Fairy tales are sometimes claimed by the pagans to be their special property, growing from their traditions. Nonsense. They are as thoroughly Christian as diatonic music, or chivalry, or the Gothic Arch, or the romance, or the Gregorian calendar, and the pagan names for months and weekdays mean only that those lesser gods are now vassals of our greater.

Greek tragedies, I grant you, belong to the pagans, and express in perfect clarity the hopelessness of a world where death leads either to nothingness, or to the endless suffering of an endless torture-wheel of reincarnation.

No doubt some alert reader will object that there are many other views of life, many other ways of addressing the tragedy of the human condition aside from these three.

What about the Eudaimonism of Aristotle, or the sober philosophy of Confucius? What about the mysticism of Lao Tzu, the sublime visions of Theosophy, the rash boldness of Nietzsche, or the Millenarianism of Marx? What about the faithful Mohammedan or the observant Jew? Surely none of these fit into those three categories.

If the categories are taken in their broad sense, these three suffice: whatever is not done for duty and not done for pleasure is done for the sake of the divine. Buddha preached a mystical form of Stoicism, but it was still an attempt to reject the attachments human nature forms to vain and transitory life in this world. Confucius sought the good in the discipline of the social order, and this was to serve human ends defined by duties and pleasures: a combination of Stoic and Hedonistic philosophy. Nietzsche was a pure hedonist, but his pleasure was in spiritual pride, and he scorned bodily pleasures. Mohammedanism is an offshoot of Christianity and Judaism is a precursor, but both place faith in God rather than in duty or pleasure. In sum, there are only three reasons for any ethical imperative: you should do this because you ought to, (and it is noble to do as one ought, no matter any pain involved); you should do this because you want to, (or you should want to, considering your long term best interest); you should do this because God wants you to.

If I wanted to be technically accurate, I would distinguish between Hedonists, who seek base and bodily pleasures only, and Epicureans, who seek the longer lasting and truer pleasures involved in a clean conscience, good fellowship, the educated life and the uplifted sentiment — but even this endless essay must have some metes.

Back to the matter:

So the second clatter of the tumbler falling into place

was hearing this sad, doomed voice of a tired old man, old
as Nestor, still talking with the zest of youth about how he
had created his own life himself, by his rules, made himself,
saved himself, and owed nothing to any.

And I seemed to see his face, still boasting vainly and
smiling an empty smile, as it might look if he were trapped
in a coffin of glass like Snow White, and sinking ever deeper
into a dark and silent ocean with no farther shore and no
bottom, drifting slowly out of sight into oblivion, void, and
darkness. If his nerve does not break, he can spend his last
hours in the airless oblong box playing with his fingers and
toes, or writing brave sonnets in his blood on the inner
surface of the cover.

Do not think for a moment I am mocking or joking. I
would honor and salute any man brave enough to face that
prospect unafraid. All my life I sought such stoic courage as
that, and indeed, deemed it the only prize in life worth
having: the Stoic fortitude to live life without craving life. Ah,
but experience is a cunning jester. The only time I ever lost
my fear of death and become a true Stoic was the hour when
the Holy Spirit came to me and baptized my soul, and I
became a Christian and left the vain and empty arrogance of
Stoicism behind forever. Throwing my Stoic philosophy to
the wind, I found the Christ returned that and more to me.

Because Christianity is the fulfillment and perfection of
human nature, and humans should not fear death, not after
death is swallowed up in Christ. Stoicism, much as I admire
it, was an early attempt to abolish human nature, by
decreeing certain fears and desires absolutely central to
human nature, such as the desire for life and fear of death,
to be illogical and unbecoming.

Let us return to the question from whose seed this oak

of vast and sprawling essay sprung. Why are the Abolishers of Man filled with hatred for all things normal to human sentiment and human pleasure, of which Disney, by his sheer charm and goodwill, surely must serve as the best example of optimism, hope, wishing upon those highest and fairest and brightest of things we call stars?

Why are the Abolishers so angry, so unhappy, so noisy, so bent on destruction and on self-destruction?

I will tell you the secret of happiness Oriental sages sought in vain for eons. It is gratitude. When you are grateful for it, a spoonful is a feast. When ungrateful, a feast is a spoonful.

The Abolishers have fled their source of strength, which is Christ. The noble ones fled to Stoicism or some form or variation of it, such as Buddhism, the hardheaded willingness to take the harsh world at it is, without complaint. The ignoble ones fled to the harem and the barroom and the opium joint, seeking to drown their awareness of life's harsh reality in the soft haze of distraction and entertainment. The ignoble pagan becomes infantile and whiny, and wants his Nanny and Nurse to do everything for him, from wipe his bottom to pat his fluffy head and feed him pablum. These cravings are shifted by a psychological maladjustment to the government in this modern time, hence, the modern Liberal movement.

Do you see? The noble pagan condemns Christian hope as if it were the false haze of distraction and diversion of the ignoble pagan. The noble pagan cannot tell the difference between the ignoble pagan's desire for the opium of paradise, and the hard command of Christ that we take up our crosses and follow Him. One moron actually called Christianity the opium of the masses.

Hence, the noble pagan thinks hope is false and despair is truth.

When one knows despair, there is no room for gratitude. Hence, no gratitude, hence, no happiness.

They can never be happy, and so their hearts are restless. Another quote from Chesterton is here needed:

> ... the pagan was (in the main) happier and happier as he approached the earth, but sadder and sadder as he approached the heavens. The gaiety of the best Paganism, as in the playfulness of Catullus or Theocritus, is, indeed, an eternal gaiety never to be forgotten by a grateful humanity. But it is all a gaiety about the facts of life, not about its origin.
>
> To the pagan the small things are as sweet as the small brooks breaking out of the mountain; but the broad things are as bitter as the sea. When the pagan looks at the very core of the cosmos he is struck cold. Behind the gods, who are merely despotic, sit the fates, who are deadly. Nay, the fates are worse than deadly; they are dead.
>
> The common bond is in the fact that ancients and moderns have both been miserable about existence, about everything, while mediaevals were happy about that at least. I freely grant that the pagans, like the moderns, were only miserable about everything—they were quite jolly about everything else. I concede that the Christians of the Middle Ages were only at peace about everything—they were at war about everything else.
>
> The mass of men have been forced to be gay about the little things, but sad about the big ones. Nevertheless (I offer my last dogma defiantly) it is not native to man to be so. Man is more himself, man is more manlike, when joy is the fundamental thing in him, and grief the superficial. Melancholy should be an innocent interlude, a tender and fugitive frame of mind; praise

should be the permanent pulsation of the soul. Pessimism is at best an emotional half-holiday; joy is the uproarious labour by which all things live. Yet, according to the apparent estate of man as seen by the pagan or the agnostic, this primary need of human nature can never be fulfilled.

Joy ought to be expansive; but for the agnostic it must be contracted, it must cling to one corner of the world. Grief ought to be a concentration; but for the agnostic its desolation is spread through an unthinkable eternity.

This is what I call being born upside down. The sceptic may truly be said to be topsy-turvy; for his feet are dancing upwards in idle ecstacies, while his brain is in the abyss. To the modern man the heavens are actually below the earth. The explanation is simple; he is standing on his head; which is a very weak pedestal to stand on. But when he has found his feet again he knows it.

Christianity satisfies suddenly and perfectly man's ancestral instinct for being the right way up; satisfies it supremely in this; that by its creed joy becomes something gigantic and sadness something special and small. The vault above us is not deaf because the universe is an idiot; the silence is not the heartless silence of an endless and aimless world. Rather the silence around us is a small and pitiful stillness like the prompt stillness in a sick-room. We are perhaps permitted tragedy as a sort of merciful comedy: because the frantic energy of divine things would knock us down like a drunken farce. We can take our own tears more lightly than we could take the tremendous levities of the angels. So we sit perhaps in a starry chamber of silence, while the laughter of the heavens is too loud for us to hear.

Joy, which was the small publicity of the pagan, is the gigantic secret of the Christian.

Perhaps, like me, you have wondered how it is that so many people, otherwise honest, can adopt without demur the Orwellian anti-language of Political Correctness; how it is that so many people, otherwise rational, can adopt without demur the paradoxes, self-contradictions and logical absurdities involved in relativistic morality, materialistic ontology, subjective epistemology, and the other nuggets of vacuous blither forming the foundations of modern thought; how it is that so many people, otherwise possessing good taste, can without demur fund and support and praise the blurry aberrations of modern art, praise ugliness, despise beauty; how it is that so many people, otherwise good and peaceful, can praise and support and excuse the hellish enormities and mass murders of figures like Che and Mao and Stalin and Castro, and make such enemies of the human race into heroes; or can view with cold eye the piles of tiny corpses heaped outside abortion mills; or can rush to the defense of Mohammedan terrorists with freakish shrieks of 'Islamophobia!' and 'Racist!' even though to be wary of Jihadists bent on your destruction is rational rather than phobic, and even though Mohammedanism is a religion, not a race; how otherwise happy, moral, reasonable and decent people can not merely excuse sexual perversion, but will be swept up in a fervor of righteous indignation even if someone points out the biological or Biblical reality of the situation; and likewise excuse lies in their leaders, and adulteries, and abuses of power, and abuses of drugs, and any number of things these otherwise ordinary people would never do themselves.

And, finally, perhaps, as have I, you have wondered why it is that these people who are otherwise civil nonetheless can neither explain their positions nor stop talking, and their talk consists of nothing, nothing, nothing aside from childish personal attacks, slanders, sneers, and accusation, accusation, accusation. Why are they so angry? Why are they so noisy? Why are they so blissfully unaware of the vice, injustice, ugliness and evil they support?

As I said in a previous essay, I had an insight into the answer, or part of the answer, to this question. It is an answer which I do not pretend is original, but which I happened never to have seen before, so it is new to me.

The insight grew out of three conversations and one non-conversation.

Two of those conversations, (and one non-conversation), I have described previously, and they convinced me that the core of postmodern, Progressive thought, or, (to be precise), thought-avoidance mechanisms, consists of the following:

1. Human nature is cultural, that is, manmade.
2. Your nature is made by you, including your natural talents, gifts and good fortune.
3. There is no point in discussing the matter.

I examined these points previously. First, if human nature is cultural, then the sorrows and limitations of human nature, including such things as the inevitability of death and the ineluctability of decay can be met and over-come by some change to the culture, some progressive improvement to our laws and customs. However, in reality, the attempts to change the culture lead to four stages of decay, from the Christian to the Worldly Man, to the Ideo-logue, to the Mystic, to the Nihilist. The conclusion of my investigation was that the belief that human nature is infinitely plastic or pliant leads to despair.

Second, if individual nature is personal, then for the sorrows and failures of life you have none to blame but yourself; and likewise for the glories and accomplishments you have no one to whom to be grateful, nor to give thanks, but yourself.

Again, if individual nature is personal, and death is inevitable, the only available philosophies to contend with this intractable fact are the Stoic or the Hedonistic, which means either the idea of living for duty or the idea of living for pleasure.

The conclusion of my investigation was that individualism logically necessitates ingratitude as the default emotional response to life. This is an airless and suffocating emotional atmosphere, one not suited to sustain human psychology.

The Stoic in this atmosphere maintains himself by pride and iron willpower; and when they fail, he is left with nothing. The Hedonist in this atmosphere maintains himself by distraction, by diversion, by the constant clamor of the stimulation of the senses, by wine and women and song, by sex and drugs and rock and roll; and when they fail, he is left with nothing.

Third, the unwillingness of the Progressives to discuss their beliefs, or unbeliefs, or whatever they are, in a rational, civil, and calm fashion, and their inability to shut up once it is clear they cannot defend, or even explain, their opinions, is not the product of the several reasons a gentleman might have for retreating politely from an unwanted discussion.

It is not the courtesy which prevents a gentleman from discussion divisive matters at family gatherings, (remember how Mr. Obama wanted the Progressives to ruin Thanksgiving and Christmas by having them proselytize his health care scheme to their ungood thoughtcriming kinfolk?); it is not an admission of one's own lack of qualifications to have an opinion in the matter, for the Progressive does not shut up when he is ignorant of the facts, he gains confidence and talks louder; it is not frustration that their enemies will not listen to reason, for reason is the enemy; nor is it because the matter is a highly technical topic reserved to experts, nor an ineffable topic reserved to mystics, nor a matter of dogma reserved to the faithful, since the topics involve matters of common knowledge and common experience known to the common man.

The unwillingness of the Progressives to discuss their beliefs is because one of their beliefs (the most outrageously false of all, and most easy to prove false) is that they are superior beings, superior by virtue of their greater intelligence, broader open-mindedness, higher education, finer sentiments, and greater compassion, surrounded by yowling and filthy yahoos. These Progressives, who have never read a word of Aristotle, much less read him in Greek, boast that they cannot discuss philosophy honestly with a psychotic yet retarded Neanderthal like me, due to my inferior nature. Well, I cannot argue with their assessment of my education, except to say ἀντικεῖσθαι δ' ὁ ἀλαζὼν φαίνεται τῷ ἀληθευτικῷ· χείρων γάρ.

And yet this propensity, which naturally leads us to anger at the hypocrisy, self-flattery, and incivility of the Progressives, instead ought to lead us to pity: for this is also an upwelling not of narcissism but of despair. It is not that they think they can reason and that we cannot; they think reason is vain, and philosophy is useless.

It is not as if they talk to each other in a rational fashion in the faculty lounge or news bullpen, and then only assume a demeanor of barking moonbat lunacy when they talk to us. They talk to each other in the same way, like loyal party members in George Orwell's *Nineteen Eighty-four*, exchanging meaningless and soothing slogans and nonsense words, lulled to sleep by the perfect agreement in the perfectly empty word-noises, unless someone jars the serenity by disagreeing on some small point. Immediately the barking moonbats close in, screeching and caterwauling, until the deviant offers servile apologies and self-flagellation. The power of speech is not entirely removed from them, as it is removed from the disloyal animals at the end of THE LAST BATTLE by C.S. Lewis; but it is removed from them on certain topics, wherever Correct Speech and Correct Goodthink vetoes individual thought.

Political Correctness is a trap, like an iron snare that closes on the leg of a wild animal. Once they have entered into the delirious realm of non-thought and non-language, only a radical change, only a miracle, can pull them back into the realm of light.

The benighted fools have surrendered the power of speech and thought out of despair. These gifts have not made them happy, have not ushered in perfection and paradise. If they are useless, why keep them?

In other words, I realized the same root stood at the bottom of their principles:

1. Human nature is cultural, that is, manmade. Because if it is not, there is no cure for any of the many intolerable evils of the human condition, and all life is but despair.
2. Your nature is made by you, including your natural talents, gifts and good fortune. Because if it is not, there is no cure for any of the many intolerable evils of my personal condition, and my life is but despair.
3. There is no point in discussing the matter. Because if there were a point in discussing the

matter, it means that the thought that human
nature is manmade is not necessarily true, and
that my good fortune was self-made is not
necessarily true. In either case, life is but despair.

Or, more briefly:

1. Despair
2. Despair
3. Despair

It may be somewhat redundant to recite the final clue
that allowed the final tumbler to click into place for me, and
unlock this dark and clear vision of what was really behind
the paradox of kindhearted evildoers, intelligent idiots, and
bewildered innocent villains, but I give it here for the sake of
completeness.

Third Discussion: We Don't Need No Stinking Heroes.

I actually forget what this topic of conversation was. I may
have been discussing heroism in science fiction books, and
what is behind the drop-off in readership in recent years. It
does not matter for my account here.

What matters is that one of the participants in the
discussion waxed philosophical, or, to be precise, waxed
psychological, in attempting to explain the otherwise
incomprehensible appeal of books with heroic heroes in
them.

Her theory, (I think it was a female science fictioneer
speaking), was that teens like heroes because the teenaged
readers are uncertain of their social position. An act of
heroism will tend to confirm the hero as being a high-status

figure, a man with many friends and admirers, perhaps even make him attractive to the opposite sex. Acting heroically feeds the hunger teens have for security in their social relationships. Where the teen has no ability to act heroically, he lives vicariously in a fantasy of heroic action by reading about heroes in books.

My theory is that I, as imaginative as I am, could not come up with a theory as insulting to my fellow human beings—yes, I consider teenagers to be human beings, despite any evidence to the contrary—not even if I pondered the matter for a thousand years, and sat in the center of the Infinite Egg of Meditation with ten thousand swamis assisting me with their mantra energy.

Do I need to say anything to emphasize how despicable this theory is? A hero is someone who is willing to fall in battle for a noble cause. That is the basic definition. It is the sum of the virtues of fortitude, prudence, justice, and self-command, because anyone lacking these qualities will either lack the brains or the heart or the stomach needed to conduct himself in an heroic yet not foolhardy fashion. The craving for heroism, in other words, is a craving for virtue, for good character, for the strength to be unselfish, and to put the greater good above one's own interests.

All that is blown away like a puff of cigarette smoke, using the Abolishers' favorite, if not their only, tool and weapon. Instead of taking the motive for heroic acts at face value, (we admire such things because they are innately admirable), the theory of the Abolishers of Man pretends there is a hidden and occult layer beneath the hero's thoughts and passions, a layer of utterly selfish appetites, which only the divine insight of the Abolisher can penetrate. And, of course, like every allegedly true and inner motive allegedly laid bare by the alleged insight of the Abolishers of Man, this motive is utterly base and self-serving, namely, a desire for the good opinion of foolish peers, or, in other words, vainglory. Every hero from Achilles onward, as it turns out, died to impress some shallow girl.

This reinforces the other aspects of the worldview we have seen. In fact, the Marxist worldview allows for no heroes, only victims and oppressors. No victim can be a hero, because that destroys the alleged moral superiority being a victim allegedly bestows.

And no oppressor can be a hero, or have even distorted versions of any virtues, lest any man feel a trifle of sympathy toward any of them. The designated oppressor class must, each and every one of them, be as utterly void of any redeeming qualities as imps from hell, or else the whole program of the Two Minute Hate is hindered.

Theirs is the worldview of a pagan, robbed of Christian hope, rooted in unshakeable despair. Life's a bitch and then you die, so eat and drink and be merry today. Today is all you have.

Indeed, the worldview is sub-pagan. The pagans at least believed in heroism, in justice, in prudence, in moderation and in fortitude. To be sure, it was common among the classical pagans to believe that heroes, once they had burned brightly in their brief moment of godlike glory, fell and fell hard into tragedy and madness and death, to become twittering shadows in the underworld, or amnesiacs trapped on an endless wheel of reincarnation, like a series of books with no meaning, no happy endings and no ending at all. The most a hero could hope for was that the poets would recall his name in generations to come, but even that would fade with time.

Our modern Post-Christians do not even have that. Most do not believe in reincarnation, or believe the only escape from the endless pain of the endless cycle of reincarnation is flight into the paradise of self-obliteration. The more optimistic believe that obliteration comes immediately at death, and there is no soul nor spiritual substance to survive the decay of the body into elements, any more than there is anywhere for any software to linger when a computer is smashed to dust, or a place for words to rest once the book is burnt to ash.

Now, the natural desire for heroes cannot be expunged from the human breast, any more than the natural desire for meaning in life, and all high dreams and noble things. But this particular worldview allows for heroism only in martyrdom and victimhood, or perhaps those who leave their lives of ease and speak up for the martyrs and victims. But even these are not admired for fighting in the physical sense, which requires physical bravery. The heroes of the Left are protestors, and when they cannot find any policemen to beat them to death, they riot in an aimless fashion, over nothing that can be described nor explained, hoping for wounds to make their lives grand.

The Christian martyr dies in the belief that death is not the end, but is the gateway to glory, including the reward from a grateful sovereign divinity for longsuffering loyalty. The Post-Christian martyr believes death is the end, and ergo he may be willing to expose himself to some discomfort in his activist efforts to tear down, ruin, or destroy some ancient institution or productive corporation for reasons that never seem to make much sense: but he can never give the full measure of his devotion which even the most commonplace soldier, fireman or police officer is prepared to give. This gives an atmosphere of cowardice and hypocrisy to all they do.

Gratitude is the only thing that makes life worth living.

The gratitude of the civilian whose liberty or life is saved from evildoers by soldiers and policemen should be spontaneous, because it is healthy. The gratitude of child to parent, student to teacher, penitent to father confessor, patient to doctor, man to his bride or wife to her bridegroom: we all, all feel the natural impulse to those who save and sustain us.

Heroes sacrifice for the common good (and even those placed not in harm's way surrender freedoms and pleasures civilians take for granted, such as where in the country, or the world, you will reside). They also give us goals, dreams, idols, someone to look up to and admire.

In the Post-Christian world, a confirmed and long-standing effort is in effect to denature all heroes and heroines, and hold them up to disrespect and disgust. First, any person not of one's own race or sex or narrow grievance group is disqualified as a hero, for it is assumed that no one can identify with nor imitate any person outside the group. You cannot be as brave as George Washington during his many heartbreaking defeats and retreats because you are not a Caucasian, Male, Heterosexual, Wooden-toothed, Slave-owning Virginian. You cannot be as temperate as the Virgin Mary because you are not a Jewess. You cannot be as prudent as Confucius because you are not a Chinaman. You cannot be as righteous in judgment as Ahasuerus or Job or Noah because you are not Persian or Chaldean or Antediluvian.

Every hero held up to admiration must be regarded with suspicion by the Post-Christian mind, because, in a world with no fixed measures of right and wrong, where vice and virtue are arbitrary value-judgments, the only purpose of holding up a hero to admiration is to deceive, swindle, or enslave the unwary. Ergo the only fair-minded thing to do when beholding an alleged hero is to sit in the seat of the scornful, and mock. You must give your idol feet of dull clay even if his feet are shining like unto fine brass as if they burned in a furnace.

Even imaginary heroes must be subjected to the destruction of deconstruction: see, for example, the brilliant, and brilliantly vile, *Watchmen* comic book of Alan Moore, which ,(despite the vacuous moral evil at its core), merited all the high praise heaped on it; or the poorly constructed and fatuously applauded *His Dark Materials* trilogy of Philip Pullman, which did not.

The process never ceases, because the despair that drives him makes the Abolisher unable to refrain from abolishing his own heroes. Admiration is too akin to gratitude; gratitude is too akin to humility; humility is antithetical to self-esteem; and humility is deadly to the project of acting as the creator and savior of the future generations of mankind which the Abolisher fondly wishes to create, once normal human sentiments, morals, thoughts, and rational faculties are abolished.

Star Wars continues to win fans precisely because it was a deliberate and wholehearted dip into the wellsprings of nostalgia. It was Buck Rogers and Flash Gordon and all the terrible, cheap, shallow, penny dreadful, pulpish goodness of totally unsophisticated popular entertainment come again. The galaxy long, long ago and far, far away was filled with heroes and villains. The public, weary of a long line of movies pleasing to Postmoderns yet alien to human nature, reacted with overabundant joy. When an older and less talented filmmaker made the prequel trilogy, he added elements pleasing to the postmoderns: heroes who were weak and flawed, villains who were sympathetic, and a denunciation of absolute standards of good and evil—and the audience, for this and many other reasons, was deeply offended.

What is this prejudice against heroism? Whence comes it? I suggest that to have a hero is like having a star in the sky to guide your bark. And the Abolishers hate the stars.

Stars are too elvish, too high, too pure, too proud, and remind man of his humblest and lowest place in the universe. Looking up at the constellations on a dark and clear night is like looking into the stained glass windows of some celestial mansion, vast beyond the imaginations of astronomers. It makes a man feel glorious in his smallness.

To look up at the giant figures in history, mighty lords renowned in battle, or wise sages whose words still ring like trumpets calling man to virtue as to battle, or modest and temperate philosophers or maidens or servants or fools who avoided vanity and vainglory, or prudent saints and martyrs whose wisdom was beyond this world, likewise makes a man both small and glorious, bright as a star himself.

That star must be quenched if the Post-Christian post-rational post-human Abolisher of Man is to be successful in his despair.

AFTERWORD

Despair is the key. It explains nearly everything that is so puzzling about the madness of modern life, the pack of self-contradictory dogmas that make up the default assumptions of the Dark Ages in which we live.

They have nothing else. No wonder they are bitter. No wonder they are irrational. No wonder they lie like dogs. No wonder they boast. No wonder they are full of envy and malice. No wonder they kill babies in the womb and fete socialist dictators and mass murderers. No wonder they love death. No wonder they admire, protect and love Islamic terrorists. No wonder they admire, protect, and love sexual perversion.

It is because they have nothing else. They live in a world of darkness, without hope, with nothing but their seven great friends to sustain them: pride, which they call self-esteem; envy, which they call social justice; wrath, which they call activism and protest; sloth, which they call enlightenment; gluttony, which they call health food and legalization of recreational drugs; greed, which they call fairness in taxation; lust, which they call sexual liberation.

The modern age is suffering from spiritual and philosophical starvation in the midst of what should be the greatest feast of mind and spirit imaginable. Someone has told them offal was food and food was poison, and so they gnaw on foul things which cannot satisfy them, which make their hungers grow. They are dying of thirst, and someone offers them seawater to drink.

Let us now and forever eschew anger and indignation at these creatures. They are blind kittens who cling and claw and scratch at the hand that come to feed and comfort. No man should be angered at a blind scratch.

Neither should we do them the honor of assuming theirs is a philosophy, political or otherwise, or a coherent worldview, or anything that can be discussed or debated. It is a dream, a delirium, a vision, a nightmare.

Surely we can answer, or at least fend off, any questions they might have concerning our vision, which is brighter and better and sane and whole and true, because more often than not, it is a frivolous reason, a matter of mere emotion, which prevents them from seeing this light. Their eyes are closed, their reason is dark. Reason is of limited use to them, who have no faith in reason.

Beauty is the key to lure them into opening their eyes. I mean not merely the physical beauty in song and architecture and storytelling where Christendom has no lack and has no peers; I mean also the beauty of virtue, of charity, of sympathy, of humanity, of heroism, of martyrdom.

Did not the sheer mind-boggling beauty of Mother Teresa of Calcutta attract more skeptics to our banners than did the sneering sarcastic ugliness of Christopher Hitchens attract to his?

They are lost in the dark. That is the truth that stabbed my soul like lightning. They wander in their jerky motions from one idle fashion and meaningless fancy to the next not because they are bored, but because they are desperate, because they are starving.

To cure them we must love them. That is what I saw.

To cure them, we must be a light to them.

We must actually live up to the difficult, nay, the impossible task of becoming saints, as humble and glorious as stars in the host of heaven.

We must first cure ourselves.

ABOUT THE AUTHOR

John C. Wright is a retired attorney, newspaperman and newspaper editor, who was only once on the lam and forced to hide from the police.

He is the author of some twenty two novels, including the critically acclaimed THE GOLDEN AGE, and COUNT TO A TRILLION. His novel SOMEWHITHER won the Dragon Award for Best Science Fiction Novel of 2016. He has also published numerous short stories and anthologies, including AWAKE IN THE NIGHT LAND and CITY BEYOND TIME, as well as nonfiction. He holds the record for the most Hugo Award nominations for a single year.

He presently works as a writer in Virginia, where he lives in fairytalelike happiness with his wife, the authoress L. Jagi Lamplighter, and their four children: Pingping, Orville, Wilbur, and Just Wright.

Wisecraft Publishing specializes in stories of wonder. It is a supporter of the Superversive Literary Movement.

You can join our newsletter, A Light in the Darkness, here:

Http://eepurl.com/cg-4oH

www.ingramcontent.com/pod-product-compliance
Lightning Source LLC
Chambersburg PA
CBHW032051090426
42744CB00005B/168